CHURCH AND CONFESSION

August Wilmar

Wilhelm Löhe

John Newman

John Keble

John Nevin

John Hobart

CHURCH AND CONFESSION

*CONSERVATIVE THEOLOGIANS
IN GERMANY, ENGLAND, AND AMERICA
1815-1866*

By
Walter H. Conser, Jr.

MERCER

ISBN 0-86554-119-1

Church and Confession:
Conservative Theologians in Germany, England, and America, 1815-1866
COPYRIGHT © 1984
MERCER UNIVERSITY PRESS
ALL RIGHTS RESERVED
PRINTED IN THE UNITED STATES OF AMERICA

LIBRARY OF CONGRESS CATALOGING IN PUBLICATION DATA
  Conser, Walter H.
    Church and confession.
    Bibliography: p. 331.
    Includes index.
    1. Theology, Doctrinal—History—19th century.
  I. Title.
  BT28.C57   1984   230'.044'09034   84-18990
  ISBN 0-86554-119-1 (alk. paper)

CONTENTS

ACKNOWLEDGMENTS

In the course of the research for this comparative and international investigation I have come into the debt of several persons and institutions. Prominent among these is the Deutscher Akademischer Austauschdeinst which provided me with a grant to carry out research in Germany. In the Federal Republic of Germany the Gesellschaft für Innere und Äussere Mission im Sinne der luth. Kirche, the custodians of the Wilhelm Löhe papers graciously allowed me complete access to the materials on Löhe. Dekan Klaus Ganzert, editor of the collected works of Löhe, gave me the benefit of his thorough knowledge of Löhe. Similarly, the Hessisches Staatsarchiv Marburg put their collection of papers by August Vilmar at my disposal. In the German Democratic Republic I wish to thank the Staatliche Archivverwaltung of the Ministry of the Interior, as well as the staff of the Staatsarchiv Schwerin for their assistance.

In England the Principal and staff of Pusey House provided me with ideal conditions for my research on the Oxford movement. I am grateful to the Governors of Pusey House for permission to quote the papers in their holdings. Likewise, at Oxford the staff at Bodleian Library was quite helpful, as was Mrs. J. E. Robinson, Librarian of Keble College. For permission to quote from the Keble papers I acknowledge the Warden and Fellows of Keble College, Oxford. Similarly, the staff at Birmingham Oratory allowed me to study the relevant portions of the Newman and Froude papers and I thank them.

My debts closer to home are no smaller. The staff of the Evangelical and Reformed Church Historical Society were unfailingly helpful. The archivists at Princeton University and Princeton Theological Seminary put the Charles Hodge papers at my disposal. The staff at the Lutheran Archives Center in Philadelphia also gave me access to the papers of Charles Philip Krauth out of their larger collection. The staff of the University of Notre Dame gave me permission to cite material from their holdings. The staff of the Southern Historical Collection at the University of North Carolina, Chapel Hill, and the director of the Archives of the Episcopal Church in Austin, Texas, allowed me to use their collections of John S. Ravenscroft papers.

Four archives and a museum have generously permitted me to reproduce the six portraits that adorn the frontispiece of this book. For the portrait of August Wilmar, I thank the Bildarchiv Foto Marburg, Marburg, West Germany; for the portrait of Wilhelm Löhe, Concordia Historical Institute, St. Louis, Missouri; for the portraits of John Newman and John Keble, the National Portrait Gallery, London; for the portrait of John Nevin, the Evangelical and Reformed Historical Society, Lancaster, Pennsylvania; and for the portrait of John Hobart, the Archives of the Episcopal Church, Austin, Texas.

Portions of chapter 5 appeared in the *Journal of Church and State* 25 (Spring 1983): 323-41. They are used by permission.

Professors Wendell Dietrich and Donald Rohr of Brown University read this manuscript at an earlier stage, and their critical suggestions have greatly improved it. Professor John Van Seters and my colleagues at the University of North Carolina at Chapel Hill provided me with a congenial setting for my work and I am in their debt. Finally, Professor William G. McLoughlin has been a model of friendship and scholarship. Beyond the improvements in this study that he recommended, my perspective on the history of American religion has gained much from him, as has my understanding of the historian's craft.

PART ONE

PROLOGUE

CHAPTER ONE

THE CULTURAL CONTEXT OF CONFESSIONALISM

In the opening decades of the nineteenth century, as in the closing decades of the twentieth, conservatives and liberals in Western Europe and North America grappled with one another over the shape of the future. The "confessional" theologians of Germany, England, and America, who form the focus of this study, developed a classically conservative social and religious vision. They were uncomfortable with the liberal-nationalist ideology growing up in their societies during the first half of the nineteenth century. Liberal social thinkers provoked particular rage with their model for society cast in terms of the morally complete person of laissez-faire individualism. Indeed, liberalism's critics on the left and right focused on the concept of the autonomous individual, freed from the bonds of geography, caste, and faith. Critics on the left disparaged the concept as an ideological fiction. For conservatives, including religious conservatives, such an autonomous individual symbolized the dissolution of the world as they knew it.

Three groups of nineteenth-century Protestant theologians—neo-Lutherans in Germany, Oxford Tractarians in England, and a disparate collection of Lutheran, Reformed, and Protestant Episcopal church leaders in America—conceived a confessional theology as their answer to this turbulent world. For these religious thinkers' theological reflections on human nature, a just society, and

even individual salvation were usually couched in the context of
practical concerns such as political and religious freedom of expression, church-state relations, tax assessments, and the administration
of missions or schools. Characteristically, these confessional church
leaders were pastors as well as theologians, accountable to the pressures of politics as well as to the canons of scriptural interpretation.
Yet their pastoral concern likewise reflected their conservative point
of view. Ordained individuals were sacramentally distinct and hier-
archically superior, in their proper sphere, to laypersons. Finally,
this paternalistic attitude characterized the confessionalists' opposition to the increasing social and geographic mobility within their
societies, and their preference for relations securely anchored and
strictly defined in time and place.

If they are to be properly understood, these confessional theologians must be seen against the background of their societies. Germany—by which I mean the states that later formed the
Hohenzollern empire—England, and America were all experienc-
ing similar though differently paced processes of social, political,
and economic change. The processes of economic industrialization
and political emancipation were transforming these three societies
during the first two-thirds of the nineteenth century. In all three
countries entrepreneurs built new factories and developed new
markets, while improved and innovative systems of canal, road, and
railway lines linked buyer and supplier. Significant population
growth occurred in each during these years, and this demographic
expansion was matched by internal territorial consolidation. Germany, for example, slowly groped towards unification, first at the
hand of Napoleon and later under Bismarck. England, which had
earlier united with Scotland and Ireland, now increased its position
of domestic leadership. Finally, the United States spanned the
North American continent, incorporating all the lands west of the
Mississippi River as territories or states within the Union.

Political emancipation represented an element more amorphous
and culturally specific than that of economic change. In Prussia between the years 1807 and 1819 civil officials initiated reform programs in agrarian, constitutional, and military affairs, undertook
reorganization of the Protestant church in 1817, and attempted extensive educational and commercial revisions. Parallel moves out-

side of Prussia abolished servitude in Nassau and Bavaria in 1808 and Hesse-Darmstadt in 1811 and often allowed peasants to make cash payments in lieu of corvée labor. All these measures attempted to loosen the bonds of tradition by abolishing guild requirements, freeing individuals from specific types of obligations, and extinguishing restrictions of trade, commerce, and property holding. Further attempts at political reform took place in Germany during the Revolution of 1848. Much of the discussion at the Frankfurt Parliament centered around the goal of creating a written constitution to establish legal norms rather than relying on autocratic whim as the basis for the state. Additionally, constitutional liberals agitated for popular representation through limited suffrage. Yet the inability of the revolutionaries of 1848 to generate sufficient popular support for their programs coupled with Friedrich Wilhelm IV's refusal of the proffered crown dashed the revolutionaries' hope of a complete enactment of their program.

Political reformers had better luck in England. With the Reform Bill of 1832 aristocratic and middle-class elements reached a *modus vivendi*, one that dampened gentry dissatisfaction while preserving the aristocratic system. The core of this reform legislation established a uniform franchise of ten pounds, abolished sixty rotten boroughs, and widened representation to include some new and underrepresented cities. The Reform Bill followed the repeal of the Test and Corporation Acts and the passage of the Catholic Emancipation Act, legislation that likewise served to broaden the political constituency in England. Here then, as in Germany, a crusade for a wider degree of political participation took place, and in this case achieved more visible and long-lasting success.

In America this desire for increased political representation was synonymous with Jacksonian democracy. The Jacksonian emphasis on a more egalitarian ethos, combined with the diminution of property requirements for voting (though both were still confined to white males), signaled a shift towards a more democratic experience in American life. Once again the extension of political participation was the hallmark of political reformers, and given the gender and racial definitions within which it operated, this reform achieved a broader degree of success than its European counterparts.

New types of associational bonds accompanied this pattern of political reform. Reflecting the greater diversity and increased competition of economic and political interests, distinct political parties became much more visible within these three societies. Instead of being feared as signs of social decay, as had been the case in the eighteenth century, political parties were slowly accepted during the nineteenth century as legitimate and functioning components within the body politic. The frequent calls for "disinterested" politics or the attacks on "party spirit" appearing in the public press and oratory demonstrated that this legitimacy was hard won. Yet by the midpoint of the nineteenth century, party politics was a reality. Along with political parties, voluntary associations assumed an increasingly important role in nineteenth-century society. These purposive alliances dedicated to moral improvement, charity dispersal, literary discussion, and a host of other goals could be found in Berlin and Boston, London and Hamburg, Dresden and New York City. Their prominence, like that of the political party, was not entirely welcomed. As one writer in a German newspaper dryly remarked,

> Thus in recent times arose the associations—associations for all possible and impossible purposes. . . . Indeed a man can be from the first seconds of his existence to the funeral bier, and even beyond, the subject of innumerable association activities.[1]

The results of these economic and political transformations were diverse, but one important element should be noted. In all three national settings, the agitation for increased political opportunity, particularly on the part of political liberals, occurred within a broader appeal for national unity. In each case these liberal-nationalists sought to free the individual from the restraints of traditional society in order to harness him again to the cause of the modern nation state. The common challenge of these liberal social thinkers was to redirect this newly freed individual's energies back

---

[1]Quoted from P. H. Noyes, *Organization and Revolution: working-class associations in the German revolution of 1848-1849* (Princeton, 1966) 125. Compare the remark by Orestes Brownson on America: "Matters have come to such a pass, that a peaceable man can hardly venture to eat or drink, to go to bed or to get up, to correct his children or kiss his wife without obtaining the permission and direction of some . . . society." Quoted in Stow Persons, *American Minds* (New York, 1958) 160.

into society. Here, of course, was the point of contention for conservatives. They saw chaos and anarchy rather than creative individuality unleashed in these economic and political alterations. As General Ludwig von der Marwitz stridently exclaimed regarding the Prussian reformer Karl vom Stein,

> [He had] begun to revolutionize the fatherland. He began the war of the propertyless against property, of industry against agriculture, of the transitory against the stable, of crass materialism against the divinely established order, of imaginary profit against justice, of the present moment against the past and future.[2]

Forces of change were also at work on western Christianity during the nineteenth century. Some of these pressures originated in secular society, others reflected internal tensions within the Christian tradition. Roman Catholic, Lutheran, and Reformed believers, for example, competed with one another in Germany; High Church, Low Church, and latitudinarian all coexisted within the same Anglican establishment; and a multitude of clashing religious institutions contended with each other within the American voluntaristic framework. Beyond that, dynamic missionary expansion, new scientific findings, and provocative linguistic studies produced a number of theological reinterpretations. Within this religious context an accent on individualism, parallel to that developing in secular liberal thought, emerged within Protestant religious thinking. Here an emphasis on the church as an ecclesiastical voluntary association made up of saved persons provided the counterpoint to the liberal conception of society as composed of autonomous individuals who chose to participate in society through their cooperative efforts in secular voluntary groups.

The exponents of this brand of religious individualism were nineteenth-century pietists (or evangelicals or revivalists as they were also called) and religious liberals (or latitudinarians or liberal-rationalists as they were called). The pietists stressed the availability of unmediated grace to the individual and viewed the church as a voluntary company of like-minded believers. They also willingly en-

---

[2]The quotation is found in Theodore Hamerow, *Restoration, Revolution, and Reaction, 1815-1871* (Princeton, 1966) 69.

tered into nondenominational benevolent societies with other Christian believers. The pietists trusted in faith rather than reason as the basis of belief and this set them apart from their latitudinarian brethren. Yet in other respects pietists and religious liberals shared much in common. Liberals, like pietists, appealed to tolerance and moral duty and tended to view the church as a voluntary society. Liberals and pietists alike downplayed creedal differences in favor of a broad-minded ecumenism. In the early nineteenth century, then, individualism was a concept elastic enough to encompass these strange partners and desirable enough to form otherwise unintended alliances against the defenders of traditional church and society.

Prominent among those forces marshaled for the restoration of tradition were the confessional theologians in Germany, England, and America. At first sight the confessional theologians exemplify Ernst Troeltsch's typology of church and sect. For these thinkers were, if nothing else, theologians of the church. They believed in the church, as Troeltsch described it, "as a universal institution, endowed with absolute authoritative truth and the sacramental miraculous power of grace and redemption." Troeltsch identified this churchly tradition with Roman Catholicism and counterposed it with that characteristic emphasis in Protestantism on religious individualism, "that inwardness of communion with God which is independent of man or of a priesthood." Mediation through personal or institutional hierarchies as well as insistence upon the sacramental nature of grace were both discarded. While it was true that Protestantism, according to Troeltsch, had developed in this individualistic direction, he also acknowledged that the churchly perspective, with its claim that the church was a divine institution, had real roots within the Protestant tradition.[3]

Furthermore, as the name I have given them indicates, these theologians emphasized the need for historic confessions of faith as interpretive aids for correct theological understanding and scriptural exegesis. They believed that unaided scriptural interpretation

---

[3]Ernst Troeltsch, *The Social Teachings of the Christian Church*, 2 vols. (New York, 1931) 2:461, 470, 478.

was too prone to personal subjectivism, too apt to misunderstand the delicately nuanced and subtly interwoven meanings of the Scriptures as a whole, too likely to fasten on a proof text wrenched out of context.

These confessional theologians did not simply recapitulate the beliefs of a previous social era, and this is nowhere better attested than in the crucial and determinative influence of nineteenth-century romanticism on each of them. Romanticism, as Rene Wellek has argued, meant an antipathy towards rationalism, particularly as a means of analysis. Likewise, romanticism contained an awareness that life was a mysterious, creative, expressive, and symbolic whole, a totality of sensual, cognitive, and affective powers that made up the individual and society. Finally, romanticism emphasized that the micro- and macrocosm were organic entities, that growth, development, and maturation provided the relevant categories of analysis and understanding for contemporary society.[4] Significantly, while conceptions of organic change contained the seeds for progressive measures, the confessional theologians demonstrated, along with others in the nineteenth century, how these dynamic conceptions could be directed to conservative ends.

This book compares the confessional theologians of Germany, England, and America. It indicates, in a fresh way, the range of positions and circumstances that the critical posture of these theologians represented. For each of the three countries the book recounts the prevailing ecclesiastical situation, discusses the leading spokesmen for the pietist and religious liberal movements, and presents the conservative confessional response. The chronological limits of this study are roughly 1815 to 1866. Such political markers do not always correspond to the reality of intellectual and religious experience, but in this case they do provide a useful framework.

Through their confessional trademark, their distinctive ecclesiological views, and their stance towards contemporary political and social issues these theologians stood apart within their respective

---

[4]See the discussion of romanticism by Rene Wellek, "The Concept of Romanticism in Literary History," reprinted in Stephen Nichols, Jr., ed., *Concepts of Criticism* (New Haven, 1963) 160-167.

societies. They criticized the naiveté of evangelicalism, they opposed the encroachments of governmental bureaucracies, and they condemned the abuses of industrial capitalism. As they did so, these confessional theologians through their words and deeds made a significant contribution to nineteenth-century Protestantism.

PART TWO

GERMANY

CHAPTER TWO

UNIONS, AWAKENINGS, AND REVOLUTION

THE PRUSSIAN UNION OF 1817

On 31 October 1817, a common celebration of communion by Lutheran and Reformed Protestants took place at Berlin in the presence of the Prussian king, Friedrich Wilhelm III, and his court. Because this joint association of Prussian Protestants occurred on the tercentenary anniversary of the posting of Luther's Ninety-five Theses, it was especially significant for those in attendance and augured, many thought, an end to age-old religious strife in Germany. Change was occurring in German religion as well as in German politics and economics. The meaning of this religious innovation was hotly debated, and as this chapter will show, the Prussian Union and then later the Revolution of 1848 precipitated a full-scale discussion by several gifted theologians of the relationship between the different sections of Christianity, the affiliation of church and state, indeed the very nature of the church itself. It was within this context of liberal alterations that the neo-Lutheran party, examined in the next chapter, emerged. Participating generally in the discussion engendered by the Prussian developments, this neo-Lutheran group, particularly in their analysis of the Revolution of 1848 and its repercussions for the *Landeskirche*, provided a coherent conservative response to the proposed innovations in religious life, and thereby took a measure of this epoch of change within German society.

Germany at the outset of the nineteenth century still lived with the legacy of its Reformation heritage. For example, under the principle of *cuius regio, euius religio*, established by the Treaty of Augsburg in 1555, the German lands were divided up into exclusive religious holdings. Pressure for change in this situation came from the German Enlightenment in the middle and late eighteenth century. Under the banner of *Aufklärung*, pleas for religious toleration were heard and some concessions granted. By the beginning of the nineteenth century, the religious map of Germany was still a complex one. To the north, Mecklenburg, Brunswick, Saxe-Weimar, and Saxony were almost entirely Protestant. Prussia's king was Protestant, but fully one-third of his subjects were Catholic; they were located primarily in Prussia's Rhineland holdings. To the south, Baden was one-third Protestant, while Württemberg, conversely, was one-third Catholic. Finally, Bavaria was nearly three-quarters Catholic. Added to this mosaic of religious geography were the smoldering disputes between Lutheran and Reformed (or Calvinist) Protestants. Disagreements over the doctrines of grace, faith, justification, and the sacraments divided these Protestant bodies and further exacerbated religious animosity in Germany. Religious contentiousness was familiar in Germany, but to the north in Prussia a new attempt at reunion was about to begin.

The union of the Lutheran and Reformed Churches in the kingdom of Prussia was officially celebrated on 31 October 1817; however, its roots extended back a full three decades into Prussian history. Friedrich Wilhelm II in 1787, for example, had expressed some interest in reorganizing the Protestant church in Prussia as a means of strengthening it. On 13 July 1798, a close adviser and high church official, Karl Heinrich Sack, memorialized the new king, Friedrich Wilhelm III, and called for sweeping liturgical revisions. In defense of these proposals Sack cited the prevailing spirit of tolerance regarding church matters. He further contended that the traditional issues responsible for the division of Lutheran and Reformed confessions no longer carried any weight. One week later Friedrich Wilhelm responded to Sack, applauding the idea of reuniting the two Protestant churches and setting up a commission to study its feasibility.[1]

Further support for church reform in Prussia came from the Prussian reform movement, and some readjustment of the Protestant church figured prominently in the vision and plans of all the major reformers. As with other parts of its program, the reform movement's interest in church renovation was ultimately subsumed within its overall vision of regenerating and strengthening the Prussian state. Thus, Karl vom Stein, Karl von Hardenberg, and Karl vom Altenstein all believed that the church as a religious institution needed to be reorganized, so as to foster the spiritual development of believers. This reform would nurture not only individuals and the state separately, but reinforce the bond between them as well. Within such a perspective, however, differences could arise. Stein, for example, saw religion as an entity financially independent from, and philosophically coequal with, the state: a sphere dedicated to the education and cultivation of the spiritual resources of citizens and state. Karl vom Altenstein, in contrast, viewed religion as part of the domain of philosophy and insisted upon subordinating all administration of religious affairs under the jurisdiction of the ministry of culture within the Prussian government. Both Stein and Altenstein were convinced that reform in the Prussian church could only be realistically initiated "from above," from the highest level of administration within the Prussian government, and their views had quite an influence upon Friedrich Wilhelm III.[2]

Other influences were likewise favorable towards a union of the Protestant confessions. The War of Liberation had once again suggested the need for a unified Germany and the possibility of common action in support of one. Religious differences no more than regional ones need stand in the way of a common effort to liberate

---

[1]See the discussion of church reform proposals in the reign of Friedrich Wilhelm II and the memorial by Karl Sack in Theodor Wangemann, *Sieben Bücher Preußicher Kirchengeschichte: eine aktenmäßige Darstellung des Kampfes um die lutherische Kirche im XIX Jahrhundert*, 3 vols. (Berlin, 1859-1861) 1:8-13.

[2]See the discussion in Herbert Hafter, *Der Freiherr vom Stein in seinem Verhältnis zu Religion und Kirche* (Basel, 1932) and Franz Schnabel, *Deutsche Geschichte im Neuenzehnten Jahrhundert*, 2d ed., 4 vols. (Freiburg, 1951) 4:310-12.

and consolidate the Fatherland. The hopes of the patriotic preachers went unfulfilled, but their efforts on behalf of a union were endorsed by both rationalist and pietist theological circles. Though the rationalists and pietists were opposed to one another in several specific doctrinal interpretations, the rationalist emphasis on a minimalist "reasonable" Christianity, tolerant and flexible in its outlook, and the pietist stress on the brotherhood of all Christians in the love of the crucified Lord functioned to diminish confessional differences, to overlook disputed points of interpretation, and to accentuate the desirability of a fusion of separated Protestant bodies.

The rationalist theologian, Julius Wegschieder, for example, in his major systematic work, *Institutiones Theologiae Christianae Dogmaticae*, which first appeared in 1815, emphasized that the church was an association of moral individuals bound together by mutual tolerance and subscription to a series of commonly held doctrinal positions. Once again, open-minded toleration was a cornerstone in the rationalist formulation, an attitude that overlooked allegedly superfluous interpretive differences in order that the powerful beacon of reason could highlight the common Christian core within all. The quest for a common front of like-minded Christians also found a sympathetic hearing in pietistic circles. Gottfried Thomasius, a revivalist leader and later university professor in Bavaria, noted the pietistic emphasis on the unity of all believers, the bond that made all Christians one in the Lord. Thus, Thomasius observed that "freely joining together all believers from the various confessions" was indeed a praiseworthy task. Together these rationalist and pietist attitudes developed a context that downplayed the significance of doctrinal division, substituting instead an emphasis on faith and moral rectitude.[3]

Within this situation the decisive factor that precipitated the formation of the Prussian Union was the personal interest of Friedrich Wilhelm III. A devout believer, in part influenced by pietism, Friedrich Wilhelm yearned to be known as a moral and righteous mon-

---

[3]On Wegschieder see Karl Barth, *Protestant Theology in the Nineteenth Century* (London, 1972) 471-81. The quotation by Gottfried Thomasius is from his book, *Das Wiedererwachen des evangelischen Lebens der lutherische Kirche Bayerns. Ein Stuck süddeutscher Kirchengeschichte, 1800-1840* (Erlangen, 1867) 143.

arch, worthy to lead a spiritually strong Christian state. He fully agreed with the Prussian reformers that a strong church was needed to further the rejuvenation of the Prussian state and society. He thus hoped to unite the Protestant confessions during his reign. While praising the value of the doctrinal statements of both Reformed and Lutheran confessions and stressing his acquaintance with them, the king remarked that all Christians "should belong to Christ alone," for in consolidating the two Protestant confessions, one arrived at a new evangelical Christianity whose sum was greater than either of its parts.[4]

Knowing of the king's interest in the union proposal, his counselors at court and in the royal cabinet used a variety of arguments to encourage him. Like the king, these royal ministers reiterated the irrelevancy of confessional differences by appealing to a heartfelt faith in the Lord. Like Sack, the king's aide, they invoked an enlightened spirit of tolerance. They waxed eloquent as did the royal adviser, R. F. Eylert, in contrasting the present age in which neighbors were separated by their confessional affiliations with a future in which all such divisions were erased. They pointed to union as a solution to the problem of mixed marriages between Lutheran and Reformed, a topic of which the king was poignantly aware. Finally, they acclaimed the anticipated effects of such an enterprise, as Eylert phrased it, "in strengthening and broadening the church . . . supporting the unfortunate" and furthering the divine mission of the Lord.[5]

Several different royal commissions had studied the possibility of such a union, each making a series of proposals and all agreeing on the feasibility of such an idea. Friedrich Wilhelm finally settled on the plan of celebrating the 31 October tercentenary with such a union, and on 27 September 1817 he announced his intentions. Calling for the combination of the historically separated Lutheran

---

[4] The king is quoted by Wangemann, *Sieben Bücher*, 1:25-26; see also Walter Wendland, *Die Religiosität und die Kirchenpolitischen Grundsätze Friedrich Wilhelms des Dritten* (Gießen, 1909) 29, 101.

[5] Eylert is quoted by Wangemann, *Sieben Bücher*, 1:26-27. Because the king was Reformed and the queen was Lutheran, they could not attend communion together.

and Reformed confessions, he proclaimed throughout the kingdom their union in "one evangelical church." "This long desired step," the king said, was "the true goal of Christianity" and "the real intention of the sixteenth-century reformers." Such a union stood in clear contrast to "the earlier unfortunate sectarian spirit with its previously insurmountable obstacles." Now however, this divisive attitude had given way to an attitude that recognized the essential unity of the two sister churches of Protestantism. Such a union of confessions, separated heretofore, the king observed, "only by external differences," neither would be one "in which the Reformed church became the Lutheran nor the Lutheran dissolved into the Reformed," but rather both would be joined into "a rejuvenated, evangelical, Christian church, established in the spirit of its holy founders." This union, to be celebrated on this special anniversary, would find its true realization "not only in simply an amalgamation of outward forms, but rather a true harmony of hearts," and it was to this goal that the concelebration of the communion service was to be dedicated.[6]

Thus, with the royal court in full attendance and over sixty prominent and influential Reformed and Lutheran ministers participating, the Prussian Union was celebrated in Berlin. One month later the king happily noted newspaper reports that told of other Prussian congregations following the Berlin example. Significantly, interest in church union was not confined to the Prussian court. In an edict of August 1817, the duke of Nassau also chose to celebrate 31 October by proclaiming a union of the Lutheran and Reformed churches within his state. Over the next six years several church unions were formed, as for example in Hanau, the Rhineland Palatinate, Waldek, and Pyromont (1818), Anhalt-Bernburg (1820), Baden and the Hessian Rhinelands (1821), and Württemberg (1823).[7]

---

[6]See the text of the cabinet order of 27 September 1817 in *Kirchenunion im 19. Jahrhundert*, ed. Gerhard Ruhbach (Gütersloh, 1967) 34-35. The decision to use the tercentenary anniversary is discussed in Erich Foerster, *Die Entstehung der Preußichen Landeskirche unter der Regierung König Friedrich Wilhelms des Dritten*, 2 vols. (Tübingen, 1905-1907) 1:267.

[7]For a description of the ceremony and its immediate reception, see Wangemann, *Sieben Bücher*, 1:48, 82. For discussion and texts of other Union pronouncements, see Ruhbach, ed., *Kirchennunion im 19. Jahrhundert*, 15ff.

Prussia's prominence among the other German states attracted special attention to its attempt at church union. However, the union proposal was but one part of a plan for reforming the Prussian church. In the eyes of the post-Jena reformers, more than a unification of confessions was needed. Thus, the church was more widely reorganized, and a new liturgy and administrative apparatus were put forward. Once again, royal commissions were set up to study the problem, and in 1816 one of these committees produced a new liturgy for use in the royal congregation. Though influenced by a simultaneous study led by the Prussian church statesmen, Karl Sack and R. F. Eylert, for comprehensively reorganizing church administration, the liturgy of 1816 found little favor except with the king. Finally in 1821, the king himself produced a new liturgy. Prompted to further study by the criticism of the 1816 liturgy, Friedrich Wilhelm had returned to the symbolic books of Protestantism and fastened upon Luther's Formulas of 1523 and 1526 as the purest classical forms of Protestant worship. The liturgy of 1821 was to be used initially by all Prussian chaplains and military units; in the following year the king introduced a similar order of worship for general use. In conjunction with the new liturgy, the king festooned the Reformed cathedral in Berlin with paintings, candlesticks, and crucifixes. Further emendations were made including a marked emphasis upon ritual formulation and prayers and a corresponding de-emphasis upon preaching.[8]

The third aspect of the reform program dealt with the administration and governance of the Prussian church and the nature of the formal relationship between the Prussian church and state. Two possible directions were open to the king and his advisors. On the one hand, they could establish a decentralized pattern of church authority vesting power in synodical bodies and thereby building the ties between church and state from the bottom up. They could then emphasize simultaneously the spiritual and practical independence of the church from the Prussian state. This alternative was in line with the ideas of Karl vom Stein and Friedrich Schleiermacher. On the other hand, the king could tie the church even more closely to

---

[8]Wangemann, *Sieben Bücher*, 1:22-24, 56-57; Schnabel, *Deutsche Geschichte*, 4:331-34.

the state, integrating all church administration and centralizing all power in the hands of government officials. This was the recommendation of Karl vom Altenstein, and by 1815, with Stein out of power, the latter pattern was adopted. Under the direction and authority of the king, vom Altenstein headed the ministry for spiritual training and instruction. Furthermore, a network of supervisory consistories, abolished in 1808, was reintroduced over the existing synods. Dismissing decentralist administrative proposals in the spirit of Stein as "constitutions of a purely republican spirit," the king ordered the consistories to closely supervise all aspects of religious life in their districts. By strengthening the hierarchical direction of authority in this manner, the king reduced the synod bodies to little more than advisory pastoral committees with no practical input into the governance of their churches.[9]

With each of these three specific reform programs the Prussian state accrued power. Whether that power was expressed through the initiation of reform as in the Union of 1817 or through the centralization of authority within the framework of the state, consolidation and control were the key features of the overall organization. In this context the entire network of church-state relations in Prussia—ranging from consistories supervising theological education, through public tax assessments for the support of religion, to the exercise of local dispensations regarding marriage and burial ceremonies—came under review. When Friedrich Wilhelm promulgated these initiatives, he did so by virtue of being *praecipuum membrum ecclesiae*. Not as a prince of the realm but as a prince of the church did the king exercise what he believed to be his unilateral right to interpret doctrine, liturgy, and church polity and to inaugurate changes as he saw fit.

If such an assertion of sacerdotal rights appeared to harken back to an earlier age of royal power, the nature of the specific reforms—above all, the Union—attested to the influence of the intervening age of the Enlightenment. For it was an indifference to doctrinal

---

[9]See the discussion in Schnabel, *Deutsche Geschichte*, 4:338; Johannes Wallman, *Kirchengeschichte Deutschlands II* (Frankfurt, 1973) 215-16; Johannes Kißling, *Der Deutschen Protestantismus*, 2 vols. (Münster, 1917-1918) 1:20-24. The king is quoted by Kißling on p. 23.

tradition, couched either in rationalist or pietist terms, that provided the context and made acceptable the meaning of such reforming efforts. Yet the Erastian overtones of the king's claim did not go unchallenged in Germany, for there, as well as in England, conservative forces developed to defend the spiritual independence of the church.

Not all response to the three-part reform program was positive. From 1817 to 1848 several voices cried out against one or another of the royal decrees. Popular resistance contended with calls for obedience and enforcement of the king's edicts. One of the earliest protests against the church-union movement came from the Lutheran pastor, Claus Harms. On 31 October 1817, Harms published his own ninety-five theses, and in the name of Luther, cursed the current predominance of rationalism in the Lutheran church, especially in the form of the church union. Among Harms's theses were the following:

> When reason lays its hand on religion, it throws the pearls out and plays instead with the shell, the hollow words.
>
> Reason runs amuck in the Lutheran church: it pulls Christ down from the altar, hurls the Word of God from the chancel, desecrates the baptismal font, mixes together all sorts of people as godparents, wipes off the address from the confessional booth, hisses at the minister and has done so for a long time. Yet we are still bound to it. Better that we were much more purely Lutheran and not so much like Carlstadt!
>
> They want to make the Lutheran church rich through a marriage, just like a poor maiden. But do not do it over Luther's dead body. He will rise up from the dead and then—Woe to you!
>
> Those who say that the separations between the Lutherans and Reformed are annulled do not speak the truth. It is an open question, who has fallen away from the beliefs of their church, the Lutherans, the Reformed, or both?[10]

The timing of this appeal was not accidental, nor was Harms alone in his desire to preserve the historical heritage and doctrinal purity of Lutheranism. Within a year, over two hundred petitions both in support of and in opposition to Harms had appeared. Yet, as if in answer to Harms's objections, two further developments in

---

[10]The theses are reproduced in *Claus Harms: ein Kirchenvater des 19. Jahrhunderts*, ed. J. Schmidt (Gütersloh, 1976) 61-71.

1821 by the Prussian government demonstrated its determination
to persist. In the ministerial order of 8 May 1821, the government
called on the consistories specifically to examine prospective ministerial candidates regarding their stand on the church union, in order that the government might be sure that vacancies were being
filled with pastors sympathetic to the new union. This edict was followed by another one two months later that called for the replacement of the names *Lutheran* and *Reformed* with *Evangelical.* Fully in
line with the king's sentiment, this measure was designed to erase
any further outward distinctions between the two Protestant
churches.[11]

In contrast to the initial widespread support of the Union, the
liturgy, or Agenda as it was called, had been criticized from the outset. The Reformed theologian and influential Berlin University
professor, Friedrich Schleiermacher, for example, though consistently advocating church union, had earlier opposed the Agenda.
In January 1817, Schleiermacher described the introduction of the
new liturgy by the king and observed, "all the world finds this liturgy poor, however no one has the heart to say a word. Nevertheless,
in such cases I believe that I am duty bound to show a clear example."[12] Late in 1824, he again lamented the state of Prussian church
affairs, and laconically suggested that he was being represented as
the "head of the entire opposition against the liturgy."[13] It was also
in 1824 that a pamphlet by one "Pacificus Sincerus" first appeared.
Entitled "Concerning the liturgical rights of the protestant sovereign," the essay discussed the scope of legitimate involvement on the
part of secular heads of state in the internal affairs of the Protestant
church in Germany. Arguing from the previous three centuries of
experience, the anonymous author claimed that the right to regu-
late, amend, or reform internal church affairs resided fundamen-

---

[11]See the discussion in Wangemann, *Sieben Bücher,* 1:82-83 and compare the
comments of Gottfried Daniel Krummacher for an example of Reformed opposition to the Union, in Schnabel, *Deutsche Geschichte,* 4:343.

[12]Schleiermacher to L. Blanc, 4 January 1817, *Aus Schleiermacher's Leben. In Briefen,* ed. L. Jonas and W. Dilthey, 4 vols. (Berlin, 1860-1863) 4:213-14.

[13]Schleiermacher to W. Gaß, 28 December 1824, ibid., 328.

tally in the church organization itself, or in its appointed representatives. Membership in the church on the part of the sovereign gave him no special prerogatives, as he was a magistrate of the realm, not a bishop of the church. Only in the royal chapel did the king have wider powers, and any other unilateral exercise of royal power was presumptuous, unhistorical, and unjustified.

It was widely believed that Schleiermacher was the anonymous "Pacificus Sincerus" and in 1826 he admitted to writing the piece. From late 1824 through 1826 more widespread public protests against the Agenda confirmed Schleiermacher as one of its leading opponents. Calling its introduction an act of "the greatest arbitrariness" Schleiermacher deplored the counterproductive effects of the Agenda for Protestant unity. "I see everywhere only a caprice which does not fit well with the times," he wrote.[14] In the summer of 1825 Schleiermacher and eleven other Berlin ministers petitioned the Berlin Consistory against the Agenda. The protest charged that the liturgical innovations of the king were closer to the Roman Catholic liturgy in their effect. Furthermore, the king had overstepped the legitimate bounds of his position in proclaiming an agenda without first thoroughly consulting the appropriate ministerial bodies. The same concerns were expressed in a grievance sent to Minister vom Altenstein in which the twelve Berlin ministers reaffirmed their support for the church union, while avowing their inability to do the same for the royal Agenda. Finally, in 1826 after he had sent a personal letter of complaint to Altenstein, Schleiermacher wrote to a friend, "I believe, generally, that the King would not hesitate for a moment to sacrifice his Agenda, if its retention would destroy the Union."[15]

Schleiermacher's belief proved incorrect. In 1825 the king issued a series of royal edicts. The first, delivered on 28 May, again called for the adoption of the Agenda, describing it as "truly biblical and conforming to the oldest agendas of the church," and citing its

---

[14]Schleiermacher to W. Gaß, Spring 1826, ibid., 342; Schleiermacher, "An den Herrn Verfasser der Schrift: der Zweispalt in der evangelischen Kirche," ibid., 444.

[15]Ibid., 450-70 for the text of the two protests; Schleiermacher to Groos, 4 August 1826, ibid., 353.

intention "to protect against the dangers and abuses of growing doubt and indifference, and to restore a lost spiritual community to all of the parishes." The same decree claimed that 5,343 out of 7,782 Protestant churches in Prussia had taken up the new liturgy, and it commended those ministers who had "realized the importance of the task and the needs of the age," and had complied with the royal wishes. Two further edicts ordered that all churches adopt either the new royal Agenda or an older anachronistic one. Every Protestant minister had to report which of these he used and by what criterion he used anything other than the monarch's. In those cases where the new Agenda was not employed, its use was required when the minister was replaced.[16]

Pressure to use the royal liturgy of 1816 increased. The government of Friedrich Wilhelm penalized those pastors who had not yet voluntarily adopted the agenda. Should a pastor who did not use the new liturgy arrive at a parish where the king's formulary was in use, the minister was forbidden to change the practice of the parish. Finally, in 1831 all pretenses of voluntary adoption were dropped. The Prussian parishes were requested one last time to utilize the royal Agenda. Then, in a royal decree, 26 August 1831, the prosecution was ordered of those ministers and parishes that had not adopted it.[17]

The possibility of having to fine and imprison ministers and their parishioners was not a step lightly taken by the king and his court officials. In many ways the royal decree of 1831 was the final response by the Prussian government to opposition that had been developing ever since 1817 to its reform programs. However, it was also a response to a specific series of events that took place in 1830. To begin with, 1830 was the tercentenary anniversary of the Augsburg Confession. In a royal proclamation of April 1830 the king indicated that he saw in the celebration of the Augsburg Confession the completion of his aspirations for church reform and especially for church union. According to the monarch, the confessional statement stood next to Scripture as a foundation for the church and a

---

[16]See Wangemann, *Sieben Bücher*, 1:65-67 for a discussion of these edicts.

[17]Ibid., 69.

bulwark against incorrect interpretation. Moreover, this forthcoming commemoration would also honor the divine benediction symbolized in the successful union of the two Protestant churches. Consequently, the king proclaimed a commemorative festival to take place on 25 June 1830, during which there would be a special worship service celebrated by representatives of the Evangelical Prussian Church.[18]

Further evidence of the Prussian government's interpretation of the meaning of the Augsburg Tercentenary was given in a small commemorative pamphlet written by the king's loyal and trusted adviser, R. F. Eylert. Eylert, whom Friedrich Wilhelm IV once unsympathetically described as a "bureaucrat of the kingdom of God," began his piece with the triumphal claim that the desire for church union evident in 1817 had been fulfilled in the introduction of the common liturgy. Furthermore, with the dissolution of confessional differences symbolized in the union, attention to specifically Lutheran or Reformed statements of faith ought to cease, as well as should catechetical instruction based on such creeds. In their place should rise a new evangelical faith, transcending the creedal disputes of the past, veering neither into a subjectivism nor a dead literalism. The preconditions for the task had been set in the king's Agenda, Eylert claimed. The Agenda "contained the major points of the Christian faith," he stated, "that which every Christian must know and about which every Christian has known: the Ten Commandments, the Apostles' Creed, the Lord's Prayer, the sacrament of baptism and of holy communion. Concerning the adoption of these articles there has never existed in the church a difference of opinion." Here, then, was the goal, a church "free from every confessional and party spirit . . . not an evangelical-Lutheran or an evangelical-Reformed but rather a Christian-evangelical church bound together in a living faith in Jesus."[19]

---

[18]Ibid., 89.

[19]The description of Eylert is quoted in Karl Kupisch, *Die deutschen Landeskirchen im 19. und 20. Jahrhundert* (Göttingen, 1966) 53. His memorial is quoted in *Sieben Bücher*, 96-103.

Eylert's desire to see a church free from confessional and "party spirit" was markedly akin to the liberals' hope for a political arena devoid of the same conscious opposition. Yet Eylert's wish had no more chance of realization than had those of the *Vormärz* liberals in the Frankfurt parliament, for the commemoration of the Augsburg Confession witnessed the development of two movements of protest and renewal within the Lutheran church. Both of these groups had their beginnings in the 1830s and both adhered to a strict confessional position and in so doing, directly opposed the Unionist aspirations of the Prussian monarchy. One of these developments was the neo-Lutheran movement, the other was the religious drive of the Silesians, the so-called Old Lutherans, to separate from the dominant Prussian church.

Led by the minister and professor of theology, Johann Scheibel, and the jurist, E. Huschke, the Lutherans of Silesia attempted to separate completely from the Prussian church rather than engage in a union that they thought clearly compromised their faith. Scheibel had abstained from participating in the Union communion in 1817, as well as in the Union synodical meetings held in Breslau in 1822. Transferred from position to position in the 1820s, Scheibel was suspended from his ministerial office in 1830 when he adamantly refused to cooperate with plans for a Union celebration of the Augsburg Confession. By this time, nearly two thousand persons had joined together to form a free Lutheran church in Silesia. Such activity, however, was illegal; the Prussian authorities attempted to break up the Silesian church. The 1830s witnessed large-scale protests and emigrations to North America and Australia by Silesians searching for religious toleration. Those who remained were often fined and their ministers suspended or transferred if they persisted in acting illegally.[20]

The actions by the Silesians amounted to a call for the spiritual independence of the church, a summons that the Prussian mon-

---

[20]See the discussion in Wallmann, *Kirchengeschichte*, 212; Kupisch, *Die deutschen Landeskirchen*, 55; Friedrich Kantzenbach, *Gestalten und Typen des Neuluthertums: beitrage zur Erforschung des Neokonfessionalismus im 19. Jahrhundert* (Gütersloh, 1968) 44-65.

archy could never accept. Nevertheless, the government needed to reach some accommodation, and in a series of royal proclamations a measure of reconciliation was reached. In 1834, Friedrich Wilhelm III issued a cabinet order in which he stated that the proposal for church union should in no way be understood as either a renunciation of earlier confessional statements nor as a diminution of their authority. Assent to the union was a matter of free choice and independent of usage of the royal agenda. The use of the Agenda was still mandated, however, and all opponents of the union were warned against forming independent sects, conventicles, or other religious societies.

In 1840 Friedrich Wilhelm III died and was succeeded by his son. Even more than his father, Friedrich Wilhelm IV was a friend to that heartfelt religion associated with pietism. Genial and sentimental in outlook, the newly crowned monarch sought to lend his personal support to the strengthening of religion in Prussia. The new king also hoped to end religious strife. In that spirit, he stopped persecutions of the separate Lutherans in Silesia and in 1841 granted them leave to establish their own church. Under the king's direction, moreover, attempts were made to make the union and Agenda more palatable to all parties. Thus, in 1846 a synod conference met to draw up a statement of consensus that both Reformed and Lutheran congregations could accept. The document, however, was not as successful as was desired and caused further estrangement between supporters and opponents of the government's policy.[21]

THE "AWAKENING"

The Silesian Lutherans' resistance and the theological renewal of the neo-Lutheran movement were both heavily influenced by the nineteenth-century revival experience known in Germany as the "Awakening" (*Erweckungsbewegung*). This neo-pietistic movement reached its height in Germany during the first half of the nineteenth century and was part of a larger parallel religious phenom-

---

[21]Schnabel, *Deutsche Geschichte*, 4:529-30; the cabinet order and statement of consensus of 1846 are reprinted in Ruhbach, ed., *Kirchenunion im 19. Jahrhundert*, 36-41.

enon taking place in Western Europe and North America. The kernel of this German revival, according to its participant-historian, Gottfried Thomasius, consisted of "the need of mankind for salvation from sin and death, the belief in the free grace of God through Christ and the justification from sin by grace through faith." An acute observer and a theologian in his own right, Thomasius realized that with its emphasis upon the importance of the individual sinner's rebirth to the Christian life through grace and faith, the *Erweckungsbewegung* shared in that longer pietistic tradition that went back through the seventeenth century. As in this earlier pietism, a concern for personal faith, a sympathy for sentiment and a disinclination to worry about dogmatic questions all colored the nineteenth-century revival movement. Moreover, the religious life, based on the personal experience of God's grace and verified in the biblical message, was one of service and love for all of God's creation. Thus, dedicated to the normative validity of the biblical message as a guide for earthly life and future hopes, this pietistic tradition bequeathed the nineteenth-century Awakening a commitment to eradicate mortal sin and to transform human lives.[22]

The Awakening was not, however, identical with its baroque predecessor. While it had its roots in the older pietistic tradition, the *Erweckungsbewegung*, as scholars have pointed out, was transformed by its encounter with romanticism. One can identify three themes that characterize romanticism's convergence with the *Erweckungsbewegung* and thereby set off this latter movement from its earlier counterpart. Above all else, German romanticism was a break from rationalism and a critique of the Enlightenment. Indeed, this anti-Enlightenment impulse can be seen in the *Sturm und Drang* and German idealism as well as in romanticism proper. Protesting against the narrowness of rationalist categories and their understanding of human nature, denying the adequacy of the Enlightenment's eudaemonistic ethics, and challenging the easy equation of morality and outward behavior, romanticism contested the ra-

---

[22]Thomasius, *Das Wiedererwachen*, 1; Martin Schmidt, *Pietismus* (Stuttgart, 1972) 12-16; F. Ernest Stoeffler, *German Pietism during the Eighteenth Century* (Leiden, 1973) ix, 38-87.

tionalist assumptions on several fronts.[23] In contrast to the rationalists, and here is a second theme, the romantics claimed that life was an ineffable mystery. In its emphasis on human affective as well as cognitive power, the romantic impulse proclaimed a vision of the whole person. Not simply the powers of reason and sentiment but the individual as a living, whole being was the object of the romantics' concern. Their celebration of creative expression, their apotheosis of artistic insight, at once concrete and universal, and their endorsement of imagination and intuition again signified a break with the Enlightenment.[24]

This romantic sense for the mysterious contained a renewed historical consciousness, one having implications for politics as well as religion. Historical consciousness or historical thinking as such was not new in the nineteenth century, for the Enlightenment had made use of historical knowledge. Not the existence of this mode of thought, but the direction it took constitutes the third theme of the romantic revolution.[25] The symbol for this new direction was the organic metaphor and the categories associated with it. Under the romantics' influence the images of Newtonian mechanics gave way to those of animate life. Models of the universe as a growing, maturing entity replaced those of a machine finished, complete, and set in motion for all eternity. The depth of this acceptance of an organic outlook in Germany is significant, for as shall be seen, in England a more mechanistic view of the universe was retained by evangelicals.

Progressive concepts supplanted static ones as the idea of 'becoming' triumphed over that of 'being'. Contained within this idea

---

[23]Max Geiger, "Das Problem der Erweckungstheologie," *Theologischezeitung* 14 (1958): 432; Schmidt, *Pietismus*, 161-63.

[24]Martin Schmidt, "Die innere Einheit der Erweckungsfrömmigkeit im Uebergangsstadium zum luth. Konfessionalismus," *Theologische Literaturzeitung* 74 (1949): 24; Rene Wellek, "The Concept of Romanticism in Literary History," reprinted in *Concepts of Criticism*, ed. Stephen Nichols, Jr. (New Haven, 1963) 160-67; Hans Hedderich, *Die Gedanken der Romantik über Kirche und Staat* (Gütersloh, 1941) 1-30; Wilhelm Lütgert, *Die Religion des deutschen Idealismus und ihr Ende*, 3d ed., 4 vols. (Gütersloh, 1929-1930) vols. 3 and 4.

[25]Ernest Cassirer, *The Problem of Knowledge: Philosophy, Science, and History Since Hegel* (New Haven, 1950) 217-18.

of development, however, was ambiguity. Was the teleology implied in the idea of growth and development directed to one or to multiple goals? If humanity, the state, and society were to be understood in terms of developmental frameworks and life cycles, in terms of integrated wholes of thought and feeling, in terms of origins and ends together, what was the nature of the process? Did the organic concept culminate necessarily in a single standard of measurement or could there be a complementary pluralism in the development? In the work of J. G. Herder, organic development led to pluralistic results, dependent, in his view, on the diverse conditions of national climate and experience. Human history could display all the varieties of organic growth while proceeding in a comprehensible manner to its fulfillment. Thus, whether the goal was divine or secular, this new concept of history with its elastic comprehensiveness and teleological presuppositions had important consequences for nineteenth-century thought.[26]

Organicism was also significant for early nineteenth-century political theory. The state was no longer a machine, and social contracts carried no validity. Rather, the state, according to organicist thinkers, was an autonomous creation, developing according to its own laws and marshaling the support of its citizens. Within such a perspective, the status of the individual was demoted beneath that of the state or community, as the state in its social, political, and cultural facets became the locus of individual fulfillment. Just as the particular could only be understood, in the organic perspective, in terms of the developmental framework of the whole, so the individual could be understood within this view only by reference to the whole, which was the state. Political change or revolution had little place within this schema, for such disruption would only impede or distort the natural growth of the body politic. Such a view of political theory, as exemplified by Adam Müller's *Elements of the Art of Pol-*

---

[26]For a discussion of the meaning and implications of organicism see Maurice Mandelbaum, *History, Man, and Reason* (Baltimore, 1974) 41-49; M. H. Abrams, *The Mirror and the Lamp* (New York, 1958) 202-25. For an illuminative study of J. G. Herder, see F. M. Barnard, *Herder's Social and Political Thought: from Enlightenment to Nationalism* (Oxford, 1965).

itics, found a receptive audience in Napoleonic Germany and the Restoration era.[27]

While the influence of romanticism was important, the complexity of the Awakening's beginning and its regional variations should not be overlooked. Although rationalist theology by the late eighteenth century was entrenched in many of the foremost German universities, a network of pietistic groups and organizations nevertheless had persisted and continued to communicate with each other. Many of these groups were associated with the German Christian Society under the leadership of Johann August Urlsperger and were active in missionary and charitable causes. Further missionary work occurred under the direction of Count Nickolaus von Zinzendorf and the Herrnhut brotherhood. Zinzendorf helped to establish Herrnhut as a settlement for Moravian émigrés in 1727. Designed as a pietist community dedicated to communal sharing, religious fellowship, and evangelism, Herrnhut was the wellspring of the Diaspora movement. The Diaspora members were reborn Christians, working for the Lord and spreading the gospel wherever they went. To Zinzendorf, such individuals were bound to one another not by allegiance to any ecclesiastical organization, but by their experience of conversion, or "heart-religion," as he called it. Accordingly, Zinzendorf's followers eschewed the technique of mass meetings in favor of quiet example and patient counsel. The challenge of such evangelism was to bring the individual into a personal relation with God. Such a relation did not consist of rational assent or syllogistic conclusions; it was grounded in feeling, not reason.[28]

Zinzendorf's emphasis on feeling and religion of the heart was consonant with general pietistic experience, while his dedication to religious fellowship and communal sharing suggest his direct proximity to other communitarian pietists such as the Philadelphians. Johann Lavater and Johann Jung-Stilling were also important fig-

---

[27]See the full discussion in F. W. Coker, *Organismic Theories of the State* (New York, 1910), and H. S. Reiss, *The Political Thought of the German Romantics, 1793-1815* (Oxford, 1955).

[28]For a discussion of Johann Urlsperger, see Erich Beyreuther, *Die Erweckungsbewegung* (Göttingen, 1963) 23; Stoeffler, *German Pietism*, 246-52. For a discussion of Count Zinzendorf, see Stoeffler, *German Pietism*, 131-67.

ures in late eighteenth-century German pietism. While informed by the pietistic tradition of Philipp Spener and August Francke, Lavater and Jung-Stilling were more profoundly influenced by the *Sturm und Drang* movement. Sentimentality, friendship, an openness to all aspects of life, these motifs appear repeatedly in the two pietists' writings. Similarly the supremacy of feeling over reason as an approach to the world and a foundation for religious life characterized both Lavater and Jung-Stilling and suggest their continuity with the romantic movement.[29]

This antirationalist bias with its elevation of feeling to ontological status characterized both the *Erweckungsbewegung* and romanticism. The appeal to a broad, nondogmatic basis for religious life, grounded above all in mystical and mundane experience, was at one with the romantic quest for integration with nature, spirit, and the world. Indeed, if Friedrich Novalis or the Schlegel brothers found a new identification with a genial and spiritualistic Christianity, their experience of a comfortable, universal, and traditionalist faith marked by an easygoing and comprehensive attitude was not unique. "We were then all one," recollected Gottfried Thomasius of the first two decades of the nineteenth-century revival, "Herrnhutter, Pietist, Lutheran, Reformed, Catholic were unanimously together and rejoiced in their Lord and Saviour. One knew nothing of confessional differences. It was really a beautiful age of revitalized faith."[30] The common feature here was the experience of rebirth, the experience of conversion to Christianity and to a faith quickened by emotions and verified by the Bible.

Such a broad-minded appeal overlooking confessional differences in the name of an allegedly uncomplicated biblical message was especially characteristic of the Awakening in the western portions of Germany. Nurtured in the traditions of Swabian pietism and local mystical movements, the areas of Baden, Württemberg, and the lower Rhine were ripe areas for the growth of the Awakening.[31]

---

[29]On Jung-Stilling and Lavater, see Stoeffler, *German Pietism*, 253-65.

[30]Thomasius, *Das Wiedererwachen*, 144.

[31]For an insightful discussion of Swabian pietism and its meaning for the religious heritage of Württemberg, see Stoeffler, *German Pietism*, 88-130.

Jung-Stilling's influence still predominated in Baden, for example, and there were noticeable exchanges in the 1820s between awakened Protestants and Catholics—especially those Catholics led by Aloysius Henhöfer. Henhöfer believed that the true church was indifferent to confessional distinctions—all reborn Christians were its members—and he preached and organized accordingly. Similar ecumenical ventures took place in Württemberg under the direction of the Protestant minister Christian Dann and the Roman Catholic priest J. M. Sailer. Dann also participated in the Stuttgart branch of the German Christian Society and regularly corresponded with nearby Herrnhuter groups.[32] Stuttgart was likewise the part-time residence of the pietistic leader, Ludwig Hofacker. An effective preacher, Hofacker throughout his ministry stressed the experience of personal sin and the call to individual repentance in faith. Conversant with Luther's works, Hofacker was more deeply influenced by the various pietist traditions of Spener, Francke, and above all, Jung-Stilling. Besides such individual leaders as Dann and Hofacker, the Württemberg Awakening was well known as the source of several chiliastic groups. Memories of the eighteenth-century pietists Johann Bengel and Friedrich Oetinger were still fresh, and eschatological hopes such as theirs prompted pietist expeditions to points as distant as North America and Russia.[33]

Finally, the pietism of southwest Germany and especially of Württemberg was known for its biblicism. The theological faculty at the University of Halle to the north, under the leadership of August Francke, had first effected the shift from systematic to biblical theology within pietist circles. This belief in a thorough and experientially corroborated study of the Bible heavily influenced the Württemberg pietist, Johann Bengel. "The Scriptures, therefore, of the Old and New Testaments," Bengel declared,

---

[32]On Henhöfer, see Beyreuther, *Die Erweckungsbewegung*, 38; F. Kantzenbach, *Die Erweckungsbewegung* (Neuendettelsau, 1957) 133-37. On Dann see Kantzenbach, *Die Erweckungsbewegung*, 141.

[33]On Hofacker, see Kantzenbach, *Die Erweckungsbewegung*, 143-44. For a discussion of Bengel and Oetinger, see Beyreuther, *Die Erweckungsbewegung*, 25; and Kantzenbach, *Die Erweckungsbewegung*, 140-41.

> form a most sure and precious system of divine testimonies. For not only are
> the various writings, when considered separately, worthy of God, but also,
> when received as a whole, they exhibit one entire and perfect body, unen-
> cumbered by excess, unimpaired by defect. The Bible is, indeed, the true
> fountain of wisdom, which they, who have once actually tasted it, prefer to
> all mere compositions of men, however holy, however experienced, however
> devout, however wise.

Within this context Bengel set out to provide a biblical text as close
as possible to the original; one that individual believers could study,
thereby helping themselves to grow in faith and understanding.
This task also led Bengel to formulate a series of chiliastic predic-
tions, including one that the world would end in 1836. It was from
this rich and diverse heritage, then, that the Württemberg Awakening developed into a vigorous and vital center of the *Erweckungsbewegung*.[34]

Although the orthodox Protestant tradition remained strong in
the lower Rhine area, the Awakening was felt there too. Discussed in
small groups or conventicles, occasionally winning over whole congregations, the Awakening in this region is linked to the names Collenbusch and Krummacher. Trained as a physician and heavily
influenced by the Württemberg pietists Oetinger and Bengel, Samuel Collenbusch was a lay leader of the Awakening. In contrast, the
Krummacher family produced three well-known Reformed ministers in the brothers Friedrich Adolf and Gottfried Daniel, and in
Friedrich Adolf's son, Friedrich Wilhelm. Although each had been
influenced by pietism, the two best known struck out in independent directions. Gottfried Daniel served as pastor for several years
in the town of Baerl and then later in Elberfeld. He was also one of
the leaders of the small neo-confessional movement within the Reformed Church in Germany. Friedrich Wilhelm Krummacher also
occupied a Reformed pulpit in Elberfeld. More at home in the revivalist tradition than his uncle, he received wide attention for his

---

[34]For a discussion of the Awakening in Württemberg, see Karl Müller, *Die religiöse Erweckung in Württemberg am Anfang des 19. Jahrhunderts* (Tübingen, 1925).
Bengel is quoted by Stoeffler, *German Pietism*, 98, and discussed more fully on 94-
106, as well as in Martin Kähler, *Geschichte der protestantischen Dogmatik im 19. Jahrhundert* (reprint; Berlin, 1962) 28-30.

homiletic skills, pastoral concern, and support for missionary work at home and abroad.[35]

A different picture of the Awakening emerges in southern and northeastern Germany. In 1810 there were approximately twenty pietist circles in Berlin. The association of persons such as Adam Müller, Clemens Brentano, Heinrich von Kleist, Johann Fichte, and Leopold von Gerlach suggests both the attraction of the Awakening for literary romantics and the upper-class character of the Berlin experience. Meeting for weekly prayer and study sessions, these Berlin groups displayed the characteristic revivalist emphases on the importance of the biblical word, the union of all believing Christians, and the availability of grace for repentant sinners. Typical in this regard and influential among the awakened circles of Berlin was Ernst von Kottwitz. Known throughout Germany for his charitable kindness to the poor, Kottwitz's pietism was summed up in the phrase, "sin and grace and Christ alone."[36] It was in this Berlin circle that the theologians August Tholuck and Friedrich Schleiermacher spent formative years. It was here that another theologian, Ernst Hengstenberg, was raised, and in his career one can follow both the continuities of emphasis and the changes of direction that characterized the Berlin Awakening.

Best known as professor of Old Testament at the University of Berlin and as editor of the *Evangelische Kirchenzeitung*, Ernst Hengstenberg was born in 1802. He helped to found the *Evangelische Kirchenzeitung* in 1827 and during his nearly forty years of editorship it remained a controversial participant in the theological discussions of the day. The choice of the word *evangelische* for the title of the journal was significant. During the 1820s and early 1830s, this word connoted sympathy for the Prussian Union and its attempt to rejoin the Lutheran and Reformed churches. During those years Hengstenberg strongly supported the Union, believing that the Confession of Augsburg provided a basis for the reunion of the two groups. In line with this position, he severely criticized all opposition to the

---

[35]On the Krummacher family, see Kantzenbach, *Die Erweckungsbewegung*, 150-53.

[36]Kottwitz is discussed in ibid., 83-87.

Union, simultaneously fighting the influences of rationalist theology in Germany.[37] By the mid-1840s, however, Hengstenberg began to alter his position on the Union. In 1839, he came out in the *Evangelische Kirchenzeitung* against what he called "false spiritualism" and expressed reservations about the heavy emphasis placed on the invisible church and the bond between all believing Christians within the circles of the Awakening. In this regard, as H. Fagerberg points out, Hengstenberg criticized the doctrinal position of pietism, while still remaining near to it in most of his daily activities and personal assumptions.[38] Consequently, by 1846, with the issuance of a new set of royal regulations concerning the Union, Hengstenberg moved into an increasingly conscious opposition to the Union and championed a strict confessional orientation.

Despite his changed position concerning union, Hengstenberg never stopped supporting the monarchy nor did he change his view that social conservatism and proper religion went together. This close identification of throne and altar was characteristic of the Berlin *Erweckungsbewegung*, and several of its leaders, especially Leopold and Ernst von Gerlach, were highly placed in royal political circles. Thoroughly opposed to the French Revolution and all vestiges of political and social liberalism, these religious politicians paraded the themes of legitimacy, restoration, and conservatism; they influenced the monarch through the 1850s. Though rarely as closely identified with the nobility as it was in Berlin, the *Erweckungsbewegung* displayed this same social conservatism and antiliberal political ideology throughout the turbulent first half of the nineteenth century.[39]

---

[37]See the discussion of Hengstenberg by Holstein Fagerberg, *Bekenntnis, Kirche, und Amt in der deutschen konfessionellen Theologie des 19. Jahrhunderts* (Uppsala, 1952) 35-39. The fullest biography of Hengstenberg is J. Bachmann, *Ernst Wilhelm Hengstenberg*, 3 vols. (Gütersloh, 1876-1892).

[38]Fagerberg, *Bekenntnis, Kirche, und Amt*, 41-45.

[39]For a discussion of the political leanings of the Berlin *Erweckungsbewegung* and their significance, see William Shanahan, *German Protestants Face the Social Question* (Notre Dame, 1954) 99-136; Hans-Joachim Schoeps, *Das andere Preußen* (Stuttgart, 1952).

The transformation from a transconfessional position to a strictly confessional one was also characteristic of the Awakening in Bavaria. The Awakening was centered in the Franconian portion of Bavaria, especially in Nürnberg and the nearby university at Erlangen. Johann Schöner and Johann Kießling led the active chapter of the German Christian Society, and their efforts ranged from the founding of the Nürnberg Bible Union in 1804 to extensive missionary and charitable works. The situation at Erlangen paralleled that in many other German universities. Its faculty had been predominately rationalist in orientation during the eighteenth century. Under the influence of the Reformed professor and minister, Christian Krafft, who joined the faculty in 1818, however, Erlangen had developed into a center for the Awakening.[40]

Descriptions of the Bavarian experience in the 1820s suggest its continuity with the Awakening in other parts of Germany, as in this appraisal:

> The external form of church life did not matter, they let them be without worry; likewise the confessional statements had little meaning for them. What inspired them was the faith in the free mercy of God in Christ, what united them was the love of Christ. What stood before them as their most desirable goal was the free association of all believers from all confessions, after the example of the community of the Brethren or the apostolic church in Jerusalem.[41]

The controversy surrounding the Prussian Union, the celebration of the Augsburg Confession, and a particularly bad harvest in 1830 all motivated Bavarians to study anew the Scriptures and the doctrinal statements and heritage of the Lutheran church. This investigation had unexpected results. Beginning with the antirationalist impulse that characterized so much of the Awakening, the Bavarians, according to Gottfried Thomasius, focused upon the doctrine of justification for their understanding of religious life. Because of this emphasis, Thomasius explained,

> We were Lutherans even before we knew it. Without reflecting very much

---

[40]Beyreuther, *Die Erweckungsbewegung*, 31; Kantzenbach, *Die Erweckungsbewegung*, 74-76; Kantzenbach, *Die Erlanger Theologie* (München, 1960) 99-114.

[41]Thomasius, *Das Wiedererwachen*, 143-44.

on the confessional peculiarity of our church nor on the confessional differences that separate it from other churches, we were Lutherans. We did
not even yet know exactly what these differences were. We read the confessions of the church as testimonies of sound teaching for the clarification and
support of our knowledge of salvation. Their symbolical meaning did not
bother us. As soon as we began to investigate the road along which God had
led us, about the testimonies out of which our faith had arisen, and about
the historical roots of our church's past and present condition, we became
aware of standing in the very middle of Lutheranism. Our Christian faith
was the Lutheran faith, exactly as the Lutheran church is and aspires to be
nothing other than an example of the one, Christian, saving truth, and as
its confessional statements intend to be nothing other than the sound scriptural confession of the gospel, which has its center in the free grace of God
in Christ. . . . In this way we became Lutherans voluntarily, from the inside
out.[42]

Thomasius's classic description of the growth of a confessional
consciousness in the *Erweckungsbewegung* of southern Germany provides a neat summary of religious life among German Protestants by
1830. Scriptural study and personal piety, Christian unity and
confessional differences, the appeal to tradition and the experience
of faith, the claims of authority and the politics of conscience—all
these features were present in this description of the dynamics of
the confessional renaissance, and all would again come into play between the years 1830 and 1866. The *Erweckungsbewegung* had a
strong but complex effect on religious life in Germany. Hardly any
geographical region of Germany went unaffected in some way by its
influence. The Awakening called some to a union of all believing
Christians, while it caused others to resist such efforts in the name
of loyalty to that very same faith. Its summons crossed lines of class
and confession, and its message was both age-old and a product of
the romantic spirit of the times. The Awakening was denounced for
its excesses and acclaimed for its enlivening results, but one of its
surest accomplishments was the renewal of church life and the reex-
amination of the nature of the church that came in its wake.

VORMÄRZ: THEOLOGY AND POLITICS

By the eve of the Revolution of 1848 the Prussian Union could
not command total cooperation or allegiance, and options and al-

---

[42]Ibid., 244-45.

ternative interpretations of the doctrine of the church within German Protestantism had appeared. Though they never directly confronted one another, Friedrich Schleiermacher and Friedrich Julius Stahl demonstrated this theological debate clearly. Their two divergent positions represent a more thorough disagreement than one simply over the question of whether to support or oppose the Prussian Union. Their division over the issue of the Union was symptomatic of a much deeper and fundamental cleavage over the nature of the church itself. Likewise, the forcefulness with which they each argued their respective positions provided the general outlines and identified the salient issues within which the entire debate over the nature of the church between confessionalists and Unionists, conservatives and liberals alike could be understood. Thus, while Schleiermacher and Stahl participated directly in the German discussion, their influence on the early nineteenth-century debate of the "church question" affected more than just Germany. For in their dispute the major issues were posed with a rigor, clarity, and depth that no one in England or America matched. Consequently, they deserve close attention.

Friedrich Schleiermacher's position is ably represented in his masterpiece, *The Christian Faith, presented systematically according to the fundamental doctrines of the Evangelical Church*, first published in 1822. Out of this treatise the doctrine of the church emerged first as a series of dogmatic propositions, and then second, as a series of guidelines for practical affairs. The importance of the doctrine of the church to Schleiermacher is clear from the outset, for the definition of dogmatics as a theological discipline is possible only "when we have become clear as to the conception of the Christian church."[43] In filling out this portrayal of the church Schleiermacher announced, "Now the general concept of 'Church,' if there really is to be such a concept, must be derived principally from ethics, since in every case the 'Church' is a society which originates only through free human action and which can only through such continue to exist." The same point is firmly reiterated in paragraph 115: "the

---

[43]Friedrich Schleiermacher, *The Christian Faith*, trans. H. R. Mackintosh and J. J. Stewart (New York, 1963) 3.

Christian church takes shape through the coming together of regenerate individuals to form a system of mutual interaction and cooperation." Note that Schleiermacher emphasized the associational nature of the church. The church is a society of regenerated individuals joined together through their own volition for common goals and purposes. While these individuals express themselves through their actions, the association as such has a different basis. That basis, for Schleiermacher, consisted of piety, for "that a Church is nothing but a communion or association relating to religion or piety is beyond all doubt for us Evangelical (Protestant) Christians."[44]

As Schleiermacher developed this point in paragraphs 3-5, he sketched out his famous discussion of the essence of all those diverse expressions of piety, and indeed, the essence of the religious experience, "the consciousness of being absolutely dependent, or, which is the same thing, of being in relation with God."[45] Neither a "knowing nor a doing," the feeling of dependence is uniquely experienced as a religious self-consciousness. The significance of the existence of this feeling of religious piety consisted in that "the religious self-consciousness, like every essential element in human nature, leads necessarily in its development to fellowship or communion, a communion which, on the one hand is variable and fluid, and, on the other hand, has definite limits, i.e. is a church."

At this point Schleiermacher had gathered all the necessary elements for what he called "the general concept of the Church." For in postulating the religious self-consciousness of absolute dependence Schleiermacher established the foundation for a religious feeling in human nature that was neither a function of morality nor of deductive logic. Furthermore, the nature of this religious feeling was associational and while the forms of such associations varied within certain stipulations, the nature of all such associations corresponded to the general concept of the church. As Schleiermacher put it,

---

[44]Ibid., 3, 532, 5.

[45]Ibid., 12.

Every such relatively closed religious communion, which forms an ever self-renewing circulation of the religious self-consciousness within certain definite limits, and a propagation of the religious emotions arranged and organized within the same limits, so that there can be some kind of definite understanding as to which individuals belong to it and which do not—this we designate a church.[46]

Out of this same basis Schleiermacher elaborated his view of the Christian church. He began by noting that every "particular form of communal piety" had both an outward and an inward unity that when taken together provided the essence of that particular form of piety. With the groundwork laid, Schleiermacher proceeded to define Christianity. "Christianity is a monotheistic faith, belonging to the teleological type of religion," he stated, "and is essentially distinguished from other such faiths by the fact that in it everything is related to the redemption accomplished by Jesus of Nazareth."[47] What was the essence of the Christian church and in what way did it express its own particular unity? To this question Schleiermacher responded, "the Christian church, animated by the Holy Spirit, is in its purity and integrity the perfect image of the Redeemer, and each regenerate individual is an indispensable constituent of this fellowship."[48] Reflecting its constitutive event of the redemption by Jesus and its particular relation to the Holy Spirit, the Christian church still remained a freely chosen association of regenerate individuals. In this particular form of piety the touchstone of religious piety was grounded in the life and death of Jesus of Nazareth. This basis provided the outward unity that distinguished the Christian church from that of other religions.

The meaning of the activity of the Holy Spirit was a complex and crucial aspect of Schleiermacher's doctrine of the church. The Holy Spirit propelled the inward unity that was likewise essential to a true church. This striving for unity was a characteristic of the Christian church at the same time it was akin to that operative in other forms, such as the nation. Schleiermacher specifically pointed out this

---

[46]Ibid., 26, 29.

[47]Ibid., 44, 52.

[48]Ibid., 578.

analogy to the nation, saying, "the Christian church is one through this one Spirit in the same way that a nation is one through the national character common to and identical in all."[49] Consequently, both the church and the nation state experienced "the common bent found in all who constitute together a moral personality, to seek the advancement of this whole." Once again the consciousness of the individual was the indisputable starting point for an analysis of the church. Yet, in the church was a twofold unity that attracted individual self-consciousness. This associational communion of regenerate individuals was motivated by the very fact of its collective regeneration to further grow in cooperative activity and mutual influence through the agency of the Holy Spirit.[50] In this way the bond between the regenerate individual and the collective fellowship could be strengthened and reinforced. While Schleiermacher never undercut the centrality of the regenerate individual as the basis of his doctrine of the church, he always provided a means to facilitate the "striving for unity" that he likewise regarded as so important.

The call for unity among the different branches of Christendom had a timely aspect to it. For Friedrich Schleiermacher more than any other individual deserved to be called the theologian of the Prussian Union. In the preface to the second edition of the *Christian Faith*, published in 1830, Schleiermacher wrote that he hoped his book might contribute to a wider understanding of the evangelical faith that the Union claimed to represent. His very choice of a title for the book, directed as it was to the Evangelical Church, reflected sympathy for the task of the Prussian Union. As with many of the themes in Schleiermacher's doctrine of the church, his interest in church union could be traced back to several of his earlier works.[51]

---

[49]Ibid., 563.

[50]Ibid., 562.

[51]For a discussion of the centrality of the Union question in Schleiermacher's theology, see Martin Stiewe, *Das Unionverständnis Friedrich Schleiermachers* (Witten, 1969) and the older study, E. L. Henke, *Schleiermacher und die Union* (Marburg, 1860). Both the second and third editions of *The Christian Faith* contain cross-references to *On Religion*, much of which bears on the issue of union and its wider implications for Schleiermacher. In this context the following discussions of Schleiermacher's theology have been helpful: Karl Barth, *Protestant Theology in the Nineteenth Century*; Holgar Samson, *Die Kirche als Grundbegriff der theologischen Ethik*

It is in *Christian Faith*, however, with its partial purpose of justifying the Prussian Union, that one finds the clearest presentation of
the Union within the overall context of Schleiermacher's ecclesiology. The fundamental issue of church union was the nature of the
relationship between the Lutheran and Reformed confessions and
ultimately the Protestant and Roman Catholic branches of Christianity as well. Interestingly, Schleiermacher took the difference between Protestantism and Roman Catholicism to lie in their relation
to the doctrine of the church. "Insofar as the Reformation . . . was
the origination of a distinctive form of the Christian communion,"
he wrote, "the antithesis between Protestantism and Catholicism
may provisionally be conceived thus: the former makes the individual's relation to the church dependent upon his relation to Christ,
while the latter contrariwise makes the individual's relation to
Christ dependent on his relation to the church."[52] Schleiermacher
believed that the dogmatic differences between Protestantism and
Catholicism resolved into different views of the church. Where a
definite split existed between Catholic and Protestant communions,
Schleiermacher regarded the separation of Reformed and Lutheran confessions as lacking "sufficient grounds, inasmuch as the
differences in doctrine are in no sense traceable to a difference in
the religious affections themselves, and the two do not diverge from
each other, either in morals and moral theory or in constitution, in
any way which at all corresponds to those differences of doctrine."
Indeed, with regard to Lutheran and Reformed views of the nature
of communion, Schleiermacher claimed that the differences were
"quite negligible" and insufficient in "excusing a breach of church
fellowship."[53]

Schleiermachers (Zollikon-Zurich, 1958); Klaus-Martin Beckmann, *Der Begriff der
Häresie bei Schleiermacher* (Bonn, 1959); Hans Joachim Birkner, *Schleiermachers christliche Sittenlehre im Zusammenhang seines philosophisch-theologischen Systems* (Berlin,
1964); Richard R. Niebuhr, *Schleiermacher on Christ and Religion* (New York, 1964);
Yorick Spiegel, *Theologie der bürgerlichen Gesellschaft: Sozialphilosophie und Glauben-
lehre bei Friedrich Schleiermacher* (München, 1968).

[52]Schleiermacher, *The Christian Faith*, 103.

[53]Ibid., 107, 657. For a further discussion of Schleiermacher's view on the split
between Protestants and Roman Catholics as well as between Lutherans and Reformed, see Beckmann, *Der Begriff der Häresie bei Schleiermacher*.

Committed both to Protestantism and to the Union, it is no wonder that Schleiermacher developed these two points. Grounding his understanding of religion in the religious self-consciousness enabled him to transcend dogmatic differences in a way that illustrated his debt to pietist and romantic influences. Furthermore, in elaborating a tolerant and elastic view of the religious context, the "system of mutual interaction and co-operation" that the church embodied and within which the regenerate individual developed, Schleiermacher provided a theological system that combined the new historical and philosophical impulses of the nineteenth century with the older Protestant dogmatic.

A characteristic aspect of that older orthodox tradition dealt with the essential features of the church, the so-called *notae ecclesiae*. As set out in paragraph 127, Schleiermacher characterized the Christian church as the witness to Christ found in the Scriptures and ministry of the word of God, in the ordinances of baptism and holy communion, and as displayed in the power of the keys and prayer in the name of Jesus. While admitting that this list of features was open to dispute, he suggested that the features' apologetic value lay in their demarcation once again of the Roman Catholic and Protestant doctrines of the church. Adhering to his belief that the relation of the individual to Christ distinguished Protestantism, Schleiermacher stressed the integral dependence of all these features on Christ's activities as these activities are continued in those of the church. These differences of interpretation over the essential features that did arise were, to him, only a testimony to the further proposition that the visible church was indeed a divided one and subject to error, while the invisible church was infallible and undivided.[54]

As noted, Schleiermacher favored a decentralized pattern or organization built upon a synodical foundation. In proposing this scheme he articulated two themes—the need for a legal separation of church and state and the importance of the local congregation as the focus for the administration of church authority. He believed that, within the context of the reform movement, the need to estab-

---

[54]Schleiermacher, *Christian Faith*, 586, 678.

lish a church free from state control and unified against enervating confessional differences paralleled the need for a free and unified German nation. To Schleiermacher, both the church and the state occupied independent spheres of activity. Each had a responsibility as part of the nation, a nation conceived organically as a convergence of ethical, social, and political purposes. The church and state, moreover, derived their authority from different aspects of divine authority. Accordingly, while they might cooperate with each other, they should always be legally independent of one another. To be sure, as early as 1803 Schleiermacher had argued that the church owed the state and society a large measure of support. Such an endorsement was not a call for the subjugation of the church to the state, though it did recognize the preponderance of state authority in most cases. Similarly, this position did not insist upon the union of Protestant confessions, but it did stress that a union of the Reformed and Lutheran churches would facilitate those churches' ability to mediate the grace of God in their proper relationship to the state.[55] The separation of church and state also entailed for Schleiermacher a division of proper responsibilities. An example of this division was the new responsibility of the Prussian government for the education of its citizenry. In Schleiermacher's opinion the state should take over all educational activities except religious and theological. The church would be freed of state interference, and any potential compromise between the needs of state and the message of the gospel could be avoided.

Note, too, the importance for Schleiermacher of the local congregation within the ecclesiastical administration. As already seen in the liturgical controversy, Schleiermacher broke with the king's

---

[55]See ibid., 438-75; Schleiermacher, "Zwei unvorgreifliche Gutachten in Sachen des protestantischen Kirchenwesens zunächst in Beziehung auf den Preußischen Staat," *Sämmtliche Werke*, ed. G. Reimer, 31 vols. (Berlin, 1834-1864) 1/5:41-156; and the general discussion of Schleiermacher's nationalism and political philosophy in Günther Holstein, *Die Staatsphilosophie Schleiermachers* (Bonn, 1923); Johannes Bauer, *Schleiermacher als politischer Prediger* (Gießen, 1908); Gerhard Kaiser, *Pietismus und Patriotismus im literarischen Deutschland* (Wiesbaden, 1961); Jerry Dawson, *Friedrich Schleiermacher, the Evolution of a Nationalist* (Austin, 1966); H. Samson, *Die Kirche als Grundbegriff der theologischen Ethik Schleiermachers*, 65-73; H. J. Birkner, *Schleiermachers christliche Sittenlehre*, 132-41.

supporters when he felt that the king's liturgical innovations tres-
passed on the prerogatives of church authority. Liturgical reform
should be carried out with the aid of properly constituted synodical
assistance. Yet these powers of counsel as well as other ecclesiastical
powers "derive ultimately," Schleiermacher noted, "from the congregation."[56] For it was in the local congregation, composed of baptized and confirmed individuals, that most of the ministerial
authority and powers of the church resided. Here again, the centrality of the regenerate individual in composing the congregation
through his own volition as well as the equality of each member
within the congregation gained significance for Schleiermacher,
and it was over this issue and its implications for a doctrine of the
church that Friedrich Schleiermacher and Friedrich Julius Stahl
would so completely disagree.

Stahl was every bit the match for Schleiermacher in such a dispute. Born in Munich in 1802 and educated at the universities of
Würzburg, Heidelberg, and Erlangen, Stahl was called to the University of Berlin in 1840. There he quickly identified himself with
conservative monarchists and rose to increased prominence within
that circle.[57] In regard to the doctrine of the church there was a continuity in Stahl's ideas throughout his career. The major themes
were thus recorded by 1848, even though he continued to write until his death in 1861.[58] Consequently, while most of his philosophical
positions can be traced to his major study, *Die Philosophie des Rechts*,
first published in 1830, it is from a later book, *Die Kirchenverfaßung
nach Lehre und Recht der Protestanten*, that Stahl's doctrine of the
church emerges most succinctly. In this book, published the same
year that he was called to Berlin, Stahl articulated three premises
concerning the church. First, "the Church," Stahl argued, "is the

---

[56]Schleiermacher, *Christian Faith*, 667.

[57]See Gerhard Masur's biography of Stahl, *Friedrich Julius Stahl. Geschichte seines
Lebens* (Berlin, 1930) and Peter Drucker's study, *Friedrich Julius Stahl. Konservative
Staatslehre und geschichtliche Entwicklung* (Tübingen, 1933).

[58]The most thorough discussions of Stahl's doctrine of the church are Werner
Srocka, *Der Kirchenbegriff Fr. Julius Stahls* (Erlangen, 1927) and Reiner Strunk, *Politische Ekklesiologie im Zeitalter der Revolution* (München, 1971) 154-229.

visible, revealed institution (*Anstalt*) for the Kingdom of God. . . ."[59]
As such, and here was Stahl's second contention, this institution
contained both the visible and invisible aspects of the church in one
indissoluble bond. This "organic institution," this "community of
faith united in Christ" was simultaneously one church containing
these two essential features. Any suggestion that the true church
could be divided without acknowledging the unity of the parts,
which would include both halves, was false in Stahl's view. For it was
in the "identity of both of these sides," of the church, in that unity
that included not only the communion of saints through all time but
also the "true doctrine of the Gospel and the true administration of
the Sacraments," that the church was to be found. Moreover, the visible church was the medium through which the invisible church was
revealed, a statement which led to Stahl's third contention—the visible church was distinguished by its confessional statement and constitutional polity.[60]

Taken together, these three premises provided not only the
foundation of Stahl's doctrine of the church, but also a clear alternative to Schleiermacher's position. The kernel of the first premise,
that the church was a visible institution, an *anstalt*, which existed
prior to the formation of any given parish or congregation, directly
confronted Schleiermacher's individualistic assumption. For Stahl,
the church was an institution founded by God, not an association established through the free choice of regenerate individuals. Similarly, in accenting the visible nature of the church Stahl stressed a
view divergent from any that exclusively emphasized the invisible
church construed either in pietist or rationalist terms. Consequently, when he turned to a discussion of confessional standards
and church polity, Stahl could suggest several important ways in
which this third contention continued and extended the meaning of
the first two.

Stahl's emphasis in 1840 on the importance of creedal statements later would be the basis upon which he would criticize the

---

[59] Friedrich Stahl, *Die Kirchenverfassung nach Lehre und Recht der Protestanten* (Erlangen, 1840) 53.

[60] Ibid., 49-51.

Prussian Union. Nevertheless, even in 1840, he explicitly called for allegiance to a confessional standard, one grounded in correct doctrine and providing a common and consistent standard by which questions of faith might be decided. Stahl presented the difference between the Protestant and Roman Catholic churches in terms of their relation to creed and church polity. For "according to protestant doctrine the creed is the first and highest moment in the visible church, the issue of polity is secondary; however all this is reversed in Catholicism."[61] Nevertheless, Stahl took great pains to discuss the three systems of church polity as used and understood within Protestant church history. As the visible church was both derived from the invisible church and its revealed medium (both of which attested to the divine establishment of the true Church) any specific form of church polity must adequately express this complex set of relations.[62] Stahl identified three historic systems of church polity that he wished to discuss—the episcopal, the territorial, and the collegial. Indeed, he not only found the tripartite division adequate to encompass all major examples of church polity, he also argued that they directly corresponded to different time periods in history:

> The episcopal system is a reflection of that time, in which the independence of the institution of the church, as with all other corporate bodies, was maintained throughout the land. The territorial system belongs to the period in which the authority of the prince was all powerful. The collegial system, finally, is of that period in which the masses and their authority were established as rulers, it is in the church the analogy of popular sovereignty.[63]

Interestingly, Stahl viewed both the territorial and collegial systems as appeals fundamentally to the inner subjectivity of the pious life and opposed to any organically conceived and institutionally grounded notion of the church. In the former system the prince was granted his authority in return as much for civil and religious peace as for any notion of divinely ordained powers. This relinquishment of authority in outward things, in exchange for social tranquility and freedom of undisturbed individual religious belief and prac-

---

[61] Ibid., 49.

[62] Ibid., 52.

[63] Ibid., 46.

tice, Stahl ascribed to pietist influence and teachings. In short, he argued that the territorial system of church organization still viewed the church as a free association of regenerate believers. In such a situation the dignity and true nature of the church was in danger of compromise. On the one hand, the church was threatened with diminution into nothing more than an association of individuals, blind to a proper sense of its historical past and future missions. On the other hand, the prince, rather than being situated within a proper hierarchy of offices and orders, could always attempt to appropriate illegitimate power, thereby surpassing his authority.[64]

While he pointed out both dangers, it was the former of these that worried Stahl more, and it was his dislike for this stunted view of the church that formed the bulk of his criticism of the collegial system. In his discussion, he took the eighteenth-century theologian, Christian Pfaff, as his point of departure, but it was clear that his remarks applied equally to the ecclesiological assumptions and premises of Schleiermacher. According to the collegial system, "the visible church is a free society which stands under no other authority than that of the will of the individual members who freely choose to associate together."[65] The basis of their association thus amounted to a social contract. Nor should this be surprising, for "the collegial system," Stahl contended, "is a result of rationalism. The rejection of a higher authority, of given powers, the dependence of all proper orderliness and all laws on the will of the individual, these are indeed the characteristics of rationalism." All authority was developed as a result of popular will rather than episcopal succession or territorial sovereignty. The church was only an association, identical in status with any other free society or group.[66]

Of the three systems of church polity, Stahl found the collegial to be the most flawed. Indeed, he praised the episcopal organization for its properly constituted division of state and ecclesiastical powers and commended it as "the system of church polity in ortho-

---

[64]Ibid., 32-36.

[65]Ibid., 37.

[66]Ibid., 44, 38.

dox Protestantism." The collegial system knew of no other church
than that "of a society of men met through convenience . . . dependent upon the will of the majority." In contrast to this associational
idea, the church was "an organic institution, necessarily arising out
of the Kingdom of God, and preserving itself as such." Established
by Jesus Christ and continuing until the end of time through the
power of the Holy Spirit, populated by persons called to it rather
than formed by it, the visible church was as little established by the
work of humans as was the invisible church.[67]

Here, then, were two clear theological alternatives on the interpretation of the Protestant church. The church could be seen as an
institution divinely established and preexistent to any given congregation or parish, unified in both its visible and invisible natures and
ordered in a hierarchy of properly constituted offices. Or it could be
seen as an association that had special membership requirements
and whose very process of association testified to the important part
it played in society as the harbinger of the message of salvation and
the moral life.

Schleiermacher and Stahl laid out the general contours of the
nineteenth-century examination of the "church question" in ways
paralleled in England and America, even while they discussed its
specific application in Germany. If theology posed alternative con-
structions of the nature of the church, then the ecclesiastical politics
of Germany from the 1830s to the 1860s framed equally important
interpretations of the relations of church and state. The question of
the separation of the church and state, for example, figured as the
most important ecclesiastical issue during the deliberations of the
Frankfurt Parliament in 1848. This question concerned the acceptable extent of state power in religious affairs. Was the interpretation
correct that allowed the king, as prince of the land and prince of the
church, authority in internal church matters? Or was the king the
spiritual equal of all other members and responsible additionally
only for civil peace?

These questions had been raised on two different occasions between 1837 and 1845. In Cologne in 1837 the Prussian government

[67]Ibid., 21, 54-55.

and the Catholic archbishop seriously disputed the question of mixed marriages. Earlier in 1825 the Prussian government had drawn up an agreement with the Catholic hierarchy that stipulated that in cases of mixed marriages the children should follow the religion of the father. In 1837, however, the archbishop of Cologne, Clemens August von Droste-Vischering, after initial compliance had refused to follow the agreement. To Droste, the church could never be subordinated to the state, and any such prescribing of its internal affairs was an extravagant trespass by the state of its authority. Unfortunately, Droste's convictions directly contradicted those of Karl vom Altenstein, the Prussian cultural minister, and he had the archbishop jailed.[68] The conflict over mixed marriages further strained the already tense relations between the Catholic church and Prussian government. The monarchy of Friedrich Wilhelm III clearly favored the Protestant religion though it did not persecute Catholics. The king believed that Catholicism could be tolerated so long as that toleration did not interfere with the efficient operation of the Prussian state. In his personal affairs Friedrich Wilhelm was less understanding, refusing to bless his son's marriage for four years because the prospective bride was Catholic. As seen in the case of the Silesian Lutherans, Friedrich Wilhelm IV was more flexible in dealing with ecclesiastical conflicts than his father. Nevertheless, he too felt that Droste had broken his word and that the Catholic hierarchy in Cologne deserved little sympathy.[69]

The strife at Cologne was not the only example of conflict between state and church authorities. In Bavaria in 1838, a dispute developed that occupied ecclesiastical officials for seven years. In August 1838, Ludwig I, the Catholic king of Bavaria, ordered all soldiers, both Catholic and Protestant, to kneel as the elements of

---

[68]For a discussion of the dispute at Cologne, see H. Schrörs, *Die Kölner Wirren* (Berlin, 1927); Rudolf Lill, *Die Beilegung der Kölner Wirren* (Düsseldorf, 1962); and Schnabel, *Deutsche Geschichte*, 4:106-43.

[69]See Schnabel, *Deutsche Geschichte*, 119-21; *Aus dem Briefwechsel Friedrich Wilhelms IV mit Bunsen*, ed. Leopold von Ranke (Leipzig, 1874) 11-24; Emil Friedberg, *Die Grundlagen der Preußischen Kirchenpolitik unter König Friedrich Wilhelms IV* (Leipzig, 1882); Ewald Schaper, *Die geistespolitischen Voraussetzungen der Kirchenpolitik Friedrich Wilhelms IV von Preußen* (Stuttgart, 1938).

communion passed their parade ranks at the festival of Corpus Christi. Ludwig had witnessed similar displays by Napoleon's troops and with the support of his chief staff minister, Carl von Abel, and the Catholic theologian, Ignaz von Döllinger, he now insisted that his troops follow the French example. To the Protestant minority in Bavaria, soldiers and civilians alike, obedience to this order compromised faith. As such feelings grew, frequent petitions by people ranging from Protestant soldiers through Adolf von Harless, the administrative head of the Protestant church in Bavaria, asked for a withdrawal of the order. The king refused. When in March 1844, Reverend Wilhelm Redenbacher called on all Protestant soldiers to disobey the royal order, he was arrested and jailed. Finally, in December 1845 the king revoked the order.[70] The incidents at Cologne and Munich aroused animosity between Protestants and Catholics there. They had also raised the issue of the relation of church and state, and the proper relation of religiously mixed populations to each other and to the state.

Despite the ironic twist that saw Prussian Protestants ordering about Catholics, and Bavarian Catholics ordering about Protestants, both situations provoked displeasure with state involvement in ecclesiastical matters. By 1848 and the Frankfurt Parliament this displeasure had found many more voices. While the tenor of the deliberations at Frankfurt favored adjusting church and state relations, the motivations for wishing to do so reflected the ideological background of the several groups represented in the assembly. Although a series of parties composed the Frankfurt Parliament, essentially four groups evolved during the deliberations regarding the church. Significantly, three of these favored at least an administrative separation of church and state, and none were so inimical to the church as to call for its abolition on the model of the French Revolution.

To begin, there were those liberal Catholics, influenced by the events at Cologne, who wished to separate the church from state control and involvement. Fearful of just the sort of contest they had

---

[70]Matthias Simon, *Die Evangelische-Lutherische Kirche in Bayern im 19. und 20. Jahrhundert* (München, 1961) 36-38.

seen in Cologne, these politicians hoped to safeguard the church by strictly defining the responsibilities and prerogatives of both church and state. A different position was advanced by a larger group of moderate liberals, who believed that religious freedom meant freedom to follow conscience. In their view, it was the business of the Frankfurt Parliament to insure this freedom of religious choice; thus, they argued for civil marriage and secular education. Finally, among the advocates of a separation of church and state were radicals indifferent to the claims of religion and desirous of a state free from its influence. Contrasting with these three groups were conservative defenders of the status quo who favored for various philosophical reasons the continued domination of the church by the state.[71]

The focus of discussion for these various contingents was the much heralded bill of fundamental rights. In the final version of the bill Germans were assured of their freedom of belief, the separation of church from state apparatus, and their right to form religious organizations, even non-Christian ones. Each of these points was consonant with the aspirations of the moderate liberals, though for tactical reasons both liberal Catholics and radicals supported the bill. Even in those cases in which previous royal edicts had provided such freedoms—such as the guarantees for all religious organizations—these resolutions of the Frankfurt Parliament once again proclaimed that particular faith in the individual so dear to German liberalism.[72] As noted, however, the failure of the liberals' revolution left their religious reforms as much in limbo as the rest of their program.

Although they failed in large measure, the revolutionaries of 1848 dramatically presented the hopes of German liberals. Propos-

---

[71]Walter Delius, *Die Evangelische Kirche und die Revolution 1848* (Berlin, 1948) 43-52; James Sheehan, *German Liberalism in the Nineteenth Century* (Chicago, 1978) 68-70; Eberhard Amelung, *Die demokratischen Bewegungen des Jahres 1848 im Urteil der protestantischen Theologie* (Marburg, 1954).

[72]For a discussion of the tolerance edict of Friedrich Wilhelm IV in 1847, see Delius, *Die Evangelische Kirche*, 19; for a commentary and text of the relevant resolutions regarding the church and state question, see Heinrich Hermelink, *Das Christentum in der Menschheitsgeschichte*, 3 vols. (Stuttgart, 1951-1955) 2:70-73.

als for religious reform built once again on the premise that unleashing an individual from antiquated restraints while harnessing that individual's energies to the building of a unified German state would unlock vast untapped social potentials. Here again, the liberals' commitment to emancipating the individual found a specific context for application. For if German liberals objected to the capricious interference of state power in private lives, the three decades prior to 1848 provided ample instances for their protest and concern. Yet the inability of the liberals to manufacture a sufficiently broad, deep constituency spelled the end of their experiment and cleared the way for the reaction of the 1850s.

The foundations of German Protestantism had begun to shift during the first half of the nineteenth century. Cracks in an older framework of religious exclusivity and control appeared during the Enlightenment and were furthered by the various union movements in 1817. In their turn, defenders of the older ways tried to retard what they regarded as the desecration of proper religion. Significant among these forces for conservatism and restoration was the neo-Lutheran party, championed by Wilhelm Löhe of Bavaria, August Vilmar of Hesse, and Theodor Kliefoth of Mecklenburg. It is to their conservative response to these innovations in religion, epitomized above all by the Frankfurt Parliament, that we now turn.

CHAPTER THREE

THE NEO-LUTHERANS

The singular clarity with which the Revolution of 1848 defined liberal goals helps to explain the forcefulness of the subsequent counterrevolution. In this regard the views of the neo-Lutheran churchmen, Wilhelm Löhe, August Vilmar, and Theodor Kliefoth should be seen in contrast to the aspirations of the revolution. Considered as part of the reaction to 1848, these conservative theologians were aligned not only against liberal developments in theology, but also against the more general liberal tendencies in German society as a whole. As such they were part of wider cultural forces of traditionalism arrayed against the forces for change in nineteenth-century German society. They saw signs of the changing times in the theological reformulations of Friedrich Schleiermacher, the political innovations made at Frankfurt, and the ecclesiastical plans of interconfessional union. The neo-Lutheran party thus was a continuation of the strict confessionalism in the spirit of the Bavarian Awakening that Thomasius described. One of its geographical strongholds was, in fact, Bavaria in the person of Wilhelm Löhe, as well as members of the Erlangen faculty itself. Yet this group had followers throughout Germany, August Vilmar of Hesse and Theodor Kliefoth of Mecklenburg being the best known, while Ludwig Petri of Hannover and Franz Delitzsch of Rostock were also associated.

Drawing on the rich content of nineteenth-century philosophy and theology in Germany, one can see four central features emerging as characteristic of the neo-Lutherans. First, in the spirit of Claus Harms's ninety-five theses, the neo-Lutherans strongly opposed proposals for church union, believing these compromised traditional Lutheran doctrine. Second, influenced by the Awakening, the neo-Lutherans emphasized the need for a spiritual rebirth or conversion to the new life in Christ. Such a view demonstrated the antirationalist assumptions of the neo-Lutherans. It also suggested the importance to the neo-Lutherans of experience and of the reinterpretation of the meaning of experience undertaken by the romantic movement. Building on the centrality of the experience of spiritual rebirth, the neo-Lutherans, third, developed a theology focused on the Word and the creed. This theology began with a concept of revelation, understood as divine activity evidenced in the specific person of Jesus and the whole of Creation and human history. The content of divine revelation was mediated or transmitted through the biblical message, through the Word. Here in the biblical message was the summons to spiritual rebirth, to conversion to the life in Christ. For such a rebirth could only be properly understood within the context or circle of faith, that faith which is the union of God and mankind. Within this perspective, human experience—for example, that of conversion and the forgiveness of sins—was not simply subjective. Rather, according to the neo-Lutherans, such experiences were objective in that they were controlled and made comprehensible by the authority of the Bible. In this regard, confessional statements were important as clarifications and explanations of that experience given in divine revelation. Last, and drawing on this theology of the Word and creed, the neo-Lutherans heavily emphasized the church and in the 1840s and 1850s seriously reexamined this doctrine. An examination of the three foremost spokesmen for the neo-Lutherans—Wilhelm Löhe, August Vilmar, and Theodor Kliefoth—will illustrate the unity of their theological positions and the meaning of their broader conservative philosophy.[1]

---

[1] The neo-Lutheran movement has received attention in many of the standard accounts of nineteenth-century German theology. See, for example, Emanuel Hirsch, *Geschichte der neuern evangelischen Theologie im Zusammenhang mit den allge-*

WILHELM LÖHE OF BAVARIA

Wilhelm Löhe was born in 1808 in Fürth near Nürnberg and spent his whole life in his native Bavaria.[2] Although he was one of thirteen children, his mother provided him with enough money to insure his schooling. He attended the nearby University of Erlangen and there came under the influence of the Reformed minister and teacher, Christian Krafft. As noted, Erlangen was a center of the Bavarian *Erweckungsbewegung* and Löhe felt its influence. After graduating from the university and completing his ministerial training, he served in several parishes before accepting a call in 1837 to the small village of Neuendettelsau. He remained at Neuendettelsau for the remainder of his life and died there in 1872.

Although he lived far from a major city, Löhe was well aware of ecclesiastical developments throughout Germany. He sympathized with the situation of the Lutherans in Silesia who opposed the Prussian Union, concluding to a friend in 1834, "I mean Scheibel is correct, not Friedrich Wilhelm III."[3] Löhe was also a personal friend of Wilhelm Redenbacher, the Protestant minister arrested for his opposition during the "kneeling controversy" in Bavaria. And while he did not openly attack the Bavarian king's pronouncement, Löhe

---

meinen Bewegungen des europäischen Denkens, 2d ed., 5 vols. (Gütersloh, 1960) 5:145-231; Horst Stephan and Martin Schmidt, *Geschichte der deutschen evangelischen Theologie seit dem deutschen Idealismus*, 3d ed. (Berlin, 1973) 202-27; Martin Kähler, *Geschichte der protestanischen Dogmatik im 19. Jahrhundert* (Berlin, 1962) 167-92; Claude Welch, *Protestant Thought in the Nineteenth Century* (New Haven, 1972) 190-98.

[2]Löhe's full name was Johann Konrad Wilhelm Löhe, but he seldom used the first two names. The standard biography of Löhe is J. Deinzer, *Wilhelm Löhes Leben: Aus seinem schriftlichen Nachlaß zusammengestellt*, 3 vols. (Gütersloh, 1880-1901). Two shorter studies by Hans Kressel are *Wilhelm Löhe: ein Lebensbild* (Erlangen, 1954), and *Wilhelm Löhe, der lutherische Christenmensch: ein Charakterbild* (Berlin, 1960), as well as biographical articles on Löhe in *Religion in Geschichte und Gegenwart* and *Lexicon für Theologie und Kirche*.

[3]Löhe to Chr. K. Hornung, 16 January 1834, Wilhelm Löhe Papers, Löhe Archiv, Neuendettelsau, Bavaria. Löhe also corresponded with the leaders of the Old-Lutheran movement in Silesia. See the discussion in Friedrich Kantzenbach, *Gestalten und Typen des Neuluthertums: beitrage zur Erforschung des Neokonfessionalismus im 19. Jahrhundert* (Gütersloh, 1968) 75-77; Matthias Simon, *Evangelische Kirchengeschichte Bayerns*, 2 vols. (München, 1942) 2:609.

sided with those Bavarian Protestants who regarded the order as state interference in the affairs of the church.

Löhe's concern with the church formed the center of his theology, and took up his intellectual and pastoral energies throughout his life. Writing in 1843 to his friend, Karl von Raumer, he confided that two issues, a proper understanding of the church and missionary activities, lay at the basis of his theological concerns.[4] Two years later these interests found expression in two important publications, *Three Books about the Church* and *A Call from the Homeland to the German-Lutheran Church in North America*. Both pieces reflected Löhe's involvement in contemporary ecclesiastical affairs and marked him as a central figure within the German neo-Lutheran movement.

Three different events motivated Löhe to set down his thoughts on the church. The first was the repercussions from the controversies between Protestants and Catholics, notably in Cologne and Bavaria. The second was the information sent back by German missionaries in North America concerning the various challenges that they faced. Third, a series of deaths in Löhe's family, above all that of his wife, caused him to reflect on the nature of the church, both visible and invisible.[5]

Although Löhe's treatise on the church was written early in his career, nearly all of his major ideas can be found in it. Three themes formed the basis of *Three Books about the Church*. Fighting against religious individualism, Löhe first argued that humans were created for fellowship and community. "As long as a man is alone he cannot even be blessed," he stated. Moreover, "a desire for fellowship with other men is born in us," and that real fellowship was found in the divinely established institution of the church.[6] Humanity, then, was made for the church, but human needs were not the foundation for the church. Instead, the grounding of the church lay in its divine

---

[4]Löhe to K. von Raumer, 25 May 1843, Löhe Papers.

[5]See the discussion of Löhe's motivation for writing these pieces in *Gesammelte Werke*, ed. Klaus Ganzert, 7 vols. (Neuendettelsau, 1951 ff.) 5/2:964. (Hereafter cited as *Werke*).

[6]Löhe, *Three Books about the Church*, trans. and ed. James Schaaf (Philadelphia, 1969) 47, 50.

establishment as attested in the apostolic world.[7] Here was Löhe's second major theme. He argued that neither tradition, duration, extension, nor succession, none of these features were more fundamental than the basis established in the apostolic word.

In his emphasis on the Word, Löhe drew out three subsidiary points. First, the church was both invisible and visible. Löhe compared the church to a continuous succession of pilgrims all united heavenward to Zion by the Word. Here, too, emphasis on fellowship could be found, though now cast in a more eschatological light. Indeed, Löhe was always aware of the church triumphant, and though its expression might be subdued at times, recognition of the church, both temporal and eternal, always remained in his thinking.[8]

Second, Löhe emphasized that in spite of these dual features, the church was indeed one, unified in the apostolic word. Likening the church to a river that flows through time, or a flower that lives through many seasons, Löhe sketched out a history of the church full of organic images. While he wanted to guard against exclusive emphasis upon tradition or succession, Löhe was still too deeply marked by romanticism and the *Erweckungsbewegung* to escape an indebtedness to their organic imagery.[9]

Last, by basing his doctrine of the church in the Word, Löhe demonstrated his compatibility with those theologians, such as Friedrich Stahl, who emphasized the divine foundation of the church. Indeed, Löhe had considered naming his book, "the church as the holy institution" (*die Kirche als Heilsanstalt*).[10] Thus he had no sympathy for those who based the ministerial offices on the will of the congregation, nor for those, such as Schleiermacher, who emphasized the volitional and associational character of the church.

Löhe's third major theme concerned the visible church and the significance of confessional statements of faith. He believed that there was a visible church wherever there was a call issued and a

---

[7]Ibid., 62-63, 75, 116, 123, 131.

[8]Ibid., 54-55.

[9]Ibid., 56.

[10]See the discussion in *Werke*, 5/2:1140.

people called. This belief led to the obvious corollary that the visible church, though centered in the apostolic word, was nevertheless divided into several branches. These divisions reflected important doctrinal differences. The implications these assumptions had were clear in Löhe's mind. "What distinguishes the church from all other groups in the world," he remarked, "is its possession of the pure Word and Sacraments, and that which distinguishes each denomination (*partikularkirche*) from all others is the way it understands the word and administers the sacraments. . . . Therefore, the distinguishing mark of a denomination must be its confession."[11]

From this statement it was a short step to asserting that the Lutheran church was the purest church because it had the confessional statements most faithful to the Scriptures. Here was a strong affirmation of confessional consciousness. Löhe's remarks on succession and tradition were clearly a polemic against the Roman Catholics. Now with his emphasis upon the superiority of the Lutheran confessional statements, he struck at the Reformed doctrine of communion and the concept of election. More than that, he reaffirmed his opposition to Unionist proposals as had taken place in Prussia. Charging that the age was one "when union is everyone's slogan," Löhe decried those who attempted to create "an external union by the unfortunate method of ignoring and disregarding undeniable differences and then childishly hoping that somehow an inner unity will be found." Instead, he complimented the Silesian Lutherans whose example "started many others thinking and today from the North to the deep South of Germany there is a great multitude united by its confession and for the sake of its confessions."[12] Confessional clarity and adherence to pure doctrine, study of the Scriptures and proclamation of their message—these were the bulwarks against error and the safeguards for the future that the church possessed.

From this foundation Löhe explained his position on most of the important ecclesiastical and theological concerns of the day.

----

[11]Löhe, *Three Books*, 106.

[12]Ibid., 157, 161. See the previous chapter for a discussion of the Prussian Union.

None of these were more significant in his mind than that of missions. "For mission is nothing but the one church of God in motion," he declared in the *Three Books*, "the actualization of the one universal, catholic church."[13] It is interesting in this context to note that Löhe originally considered appending the *Call . . . to the German-Lutheran Church in North America* to the *Three Books*. Instead, he issued it separately in 1845 as a pastoral letter for the German Lutheran congregations in America. Löhe had been involved since 1840 in missionary activities in America. In that year, responding to a plea for more aid by the German missionary, Friedrich Wyneken, Löhe began organizing missionaries for America. In 1842 he sent his first two. From then on, Löhe was closely connected to the growth of the Lutheran church in the United States.[14]

In his charge to the Lutheran churches in America, Löhe again sounded two familiar themes—the importance of joining together in the community of the visible church and of remaining faithful to the confessions of the Lutheran church. Upon these two premises he predicated all his further suggestions.[15] Much as he had in the *Three Books*, Löhe explicitly advised against any Unionist proposals, no matter what exigencies the missionary church might face. Likewise, he cautioned against that other feature so prominent on the American religious scene, the revival meeting and the use of "new measures." In the *Three Books* Löhe had admonished against "stimulations of emotions," or "the impure means of exciting nerves to win friends for the Lord Jesus." Indeed, "the preacher of the church," Löhe continued, "is therefore no friend of 'new measures,' as the Methodists call them, but he sticks to the old measures of patient, faithful loyalty to Word and pure doctrine."[16] Finally, in a series of specific suggestions, he recommended that careful attention

---

[13]Ibid., 59.

[14]See the excellent discussion by James Schaaf, "Wilhelm Löhe's Relation to the American Church: A Study in the History of Lutheran Mission" (Heidelberg, 1961).

[15]Löhe, "Zuruf aus der Heimat an die deutsch-lutherische Kirche Nordamerikas," *Werke*, 4:74, 81.

[16]Löhe, "Zuruf," 4:69; Löhe, *Three Books*, 168-69.

be given to the schooling of all children in both secular and religious matters. To that end he stressed the importance of proper teachers, daily Bible study, and above all, the preservation of the German language through its continued use. In this last item Löhe was not only appealing to a German audience, but also was taking sides in an important issue concerning American Lutheranism.[17]

In a wide-ranging letter written in April 1845 to his friend and publisher, Samuel Liesching, Löhe gauged the response to his treatise on the church and continued reflecting upon the stiff challenges facing the church. Noting that the theological faculty at Erlangen had given his book a mixed reception, he ruefully concluded that the church would never be saved through the efforts of university professors. His relationship to the faculty at Erlangen continued to be a stormy one throughout his lifetime, with each party despairing of the other's faithfulness. In another context, Löhe ruminated over the fortunes of the church in the hands of the state; his conclusions were equally pessimistic. Allowing that his perspective might be too gloomy, he disagreed with both finding refuge for the church in the hands of the state, as well as adopting the perspective of the Reformed church, "which instead of recognizing martyrs, supports the sins of revolution. The resistance of the Dutch against the Spanish is always an example of what and how it should not be."[18]

It was, however, exactly this question of the nature of the relationship between church and state that the Revolution of 1848 posed, a question as pressing in Munich as in Frankfurt or Berlin. On 20 March 1848, Ludwig I, king of Bavaria, abdicated in favor of his son, Maximilian II. Ludwig's relationship to the dancer, Lola Montez, and the ultramontane policies of his ministers, especially Carl von Abel, were chief among the causes for his and his government's fall. Abel was not the only one to lose his position. In a complicated series of maneuvers, the people of the Bavarian lands on the east side of the Rhine, as well as of the Bavarian lands in the Rhineland Palatinate, demanded ecclesiastical independence from

---

[17]Löhe, "Zuruf," 4:70-74, 84.

[18]Löhe to S. Liesching, 25 April 1845, Löhe Papers.

the predominantly Lutheran Bavarian Protestant church. While the Palatinate Protestants were largely Unionist, the Bavarian Protestant Rhinelanders were overwhelmingly Reformed. Their demands were granted by Maximilian and they were allowed to set up their own ecclesiastical administrations on a par with the Bavarian Lutherans. While these decisions were taking effect, the king accepted the resignation of Friedrich von Roth and the other leaders of the prerevolution Protestant church administration.[19]

Wilhelm Löhe's basic premise throughout the turmoil of 1848 was that the church should be a spiritually independent body, free from interference by the state. At the same time the church owed the state its allegiance and support to the extent that the state preserved order and allowed the church to carry out its spiritual responsibilities. Thus, while Löhe suggested in a letter on 7 March 1848 that "the church has nothing to say in politics," he was well aware that the times boded changes for the church as well as for the state.[20] It was with news of the events in Berlin and Vienna, events he characterized as "frightful," that Löhe organized a pastoral conference to take place in late March at Neuendettelsau. Declining invitations to similar conferences in Leipzig and Wittenberg, he suggested that the conference address the proper role of the church in the political affairs of the day and the role, if any, of local ministers.[21] Not surprisingly, he led the conference in adopting a statement emphasizing the independence of the church in all spiritual matters. The church ought to remain neutral, and institutionally and through its ministers it should remain dedicated to its heavenly and spiritual responsibilities. Desire for "freedom and equality of all confessions and religious persuasions rules the day," Löhe noted, but even such a situation as that could be better accommodated than

---

[19]Simon, *Evangelische Kirchengeschichte Bayerns*, 2:634-35.

[20]Löhe to J. F. Wucherer, 7 March 1848; Löhe to Chr. Hornung, 11 March 1848, Löhe Papers.

[21]On Löhe's reaction to events in Berlin and Vienna, see Löhe to U. von Maltzahn, 22 March 1848, Löhe Papers. On the background to the conference of March 27-28, see Löhe to K. von Raumer, 15 March 1848, Löhe Papers.

to allow state domination and its consequent interference in internal ecclesiastical matters.[22]

Löhe's observation about the ubiquitous desire for religious equality serves as an apt reminder of the support for the Frankfurt Parliament within clerical ranks. As noted in the previous chapter, both Roman Catholic and Protestant clergymen attended the deliberations at Frankfurt. One of these, the Erlangen professor of theology, Johannes von Hoffman, was well known to Löhe. Hoffman participated in the Frankfurt Assembly and supported the work of the Assembly throughout its deliberations. He was also a collaborator with Johann Wichern in his nondenominational Inner Mission. Hoffman's warm support for Wichern's work with its appeal to Christians of all creeds, contrasted sharply with Löhe's position that all missionary work must proceed along confessional lines. It is interesting to note that Wichern was one of the main speakers at the pastoral conference at Wittenberg that Löhe declined to attend. In contrast to what they heard at the meeting at Neuendettelsau, the ministers at Wittenberg heard Wichern plead for confessional unity and challenge all to become involved in the social problems facing Germany. No clearer contrast to Löhe's position could be found within Lutheran clerical circles than that articulated by Wichern at Wittenberg.[23]

The meaning of a reconstruction of the relationship of church and state understood within the context of confessional clarity and adherence would occupy Löhe's attention for the next several years. More than that, by 1866 he would have not only contributed to the private and public discussion of these church affairs, he would have clashed with the faculty at Erlangen, courted secession from the Lutheran church, endured accusations of holding Roman Catholic beliefs, and suffered suspension from his ministerial duties only to be reinstated by his ecclesiastical superiors two months later.

---

[22]Löhe, "Mitteilung über eine Pastoralkonferenz," *Werke*, 5:205-12.

[23]On Hoffman see Kantzenbach, *Die Erlanger Theologie* (München, 1960) 179-208; Kantzenbach, *Gestalten und Typen des Neuluthertums*, 243-55. On Wichern and the Wittenberg conference, see Shanahan, *German Protestants Face the Social Question* (Notre Dame, 1954) 205-206.

As the Revolution continued in Bavaria and throughout Germany, Löhe became increasingly dissatisfied with the course of events. "The entire edifice of new hopes," he lamented in April 1848, "appears to me to be built on shaky grounds. I will have no part of it." Later that month he reflected upon the reports of the deliberations in Frankfurt. "What sort of Parliament is this, dear God," he wrote in his journal, "it seems to be quite clear that we can expect little for the church from this body!"[24] In private correspondence, he often deplored the revolutionaries' exclusive concern with temporal affairs rather than spiritual ones. By late summer of 1848, he could only conclude, "Germany has never been so godless as now."[25]

In spring of 1849 the synodical meeting of the Protestant church in Bavaria was held at Ansbach. In line with the reforming spirit of the times, laymen as well as ministers attended as voting representatives. Here would be the first opportunity within official ecclesiastical circles to take control of the dynamic moment that the revolution offered and to remodel the organization of the church. Löhe realized the potential of the circumstances, voicing the hope that some new arrangement would come out of the instability of the situation.[26] In this spirit of guarded expectations he submitted the first of a series of petitions to the church synod. The petition sounded the familiar themes of allegiance to confessional standards and need for a spiritually strong and independent church. In this context it called more specifically for strict adherence by all Lutheran ministers to the creeds or symbolic statements of orthodox Lutherans. Beyond that, it protested the current untenable situation of a Roman Catholic king serving as titular head of the Bavarian Lutheran church. Ever since the complete recognition and administrative formation of the Bavarian Protestant church in 1818, the king had been recognized as the *summus episcopus*. Löhe's objec-

[24]Löhe to S. Liesching, 10 April 1848, Löhe Papers; journal entry of 26 April 1848, quoted by Deinzer, *Wilhelm Löhes Leben*, 2:247.

[25]Löhe to C. Alt, 9 June 1848; Löhe to K. von Raumer, 21 August 1848, Löhe Papers.

[26]Simon, *Evangelische Kirchengeschichte Bayerns*, 2:638; Löhe to S. Liesching, 24 July 1848, Löhe Papers.

tion was thus directed less at the legal relationship of episcopacy than it was at the religion of the ruling family. How could the Lutheran church observe its confession in complete faithfulness when its ruling head did not share its faith and in fact, as in the "kneeling controversy," ordered actions in direct contradiction to that faith? Similarly, Löhe complained that Lutheran pastors were often expected to serve Reformed congregations or to serve alongside Reformed ministers. Finally, the ruling administration of the Protestant church in Bavaria was staffed in part by Reformed ministers who ought to have no authority over Lutheran pastors although they obviously did. Again the twin issues of fidelity to pure doctrine and the spiritual sovereignty of the church over its own internal affairs formed the basis of Löhe's position. The challenge within the church posed by lax standards and slack discipline, in Löhe's opinion, was equaled by the damage resulting from state intervention.[27]

Nothing came of Löhe's petition. In late February 1849, shortly after the synod disbanded, he published a further statement evaluating the synodical proceedings. Not surprisingly, he expressed disappointment with the outcome of the synodical convention. Characterizing the majority of the delegates as "distant from a recognition and consciousness of the church, when they were not consciously inimical to that direction," he saw the meeting as symbolic of the current indifference to confessional standards and opposition to strict discipline within the church. It had not challenged or even recognized the objectionable circumstances that the petition had enumerated. The result would be comical if it were not so serious. "Here crowd together the orthodox Lutherans, the moderates, the pietists, the rationalists," Löhe lamented in describing the Bavarian situation, "all united through one synod and through one church administration. The *summus episcopus* is Roman Catholic, the church administration is Unionist, the church is Lutheran, Reformed, Unionist, Rationalist."[28]

---

[27]Löhe, "Petition, 1849," *Werke*, 5/1:333-49.

[28]Löhe, "Eine Beleuchtung der Synodalbeschlüße," *Werke*, 5/1:353.

In the aftermath of 1848 and throughout the 1850s, as the Bavarian church drifted farther toward the unionism that Löhe had always contested, Löhe's opposition took two forms. Through the first two years of the new decade, he attempted to rally wider support, especially from the Erlangen faculty, for the cause of higher confessional standards. By mid-1851 this strategy was failing. Sensing his own isolation, Löhe resolved to carry on his battle even if it meant leaving the church. He met with members of the Erlangen theological faculty several times between April and June 1849. Previously, he had expressed his dissatisfaction with the low level of confessional consciousness at Erlangen, and as late as February 1849 he had identified Erlangen's leading theologians as a chief source of opposition at the Ansbach conference.[29] Löhe knew and esteemed these men from Erlangen—Adolf von Harless, Gottfried Thomasius, Johann Höfling, and Franz Delitzsch—though he differed from them on several important points. The respect was mutual. For example, in 1847, while still in Mecklenburg, Delitzsch had written a treatise, *Four Books about the Church*, which in content as well as title took up many of Löhe's major contentions.

The overtures to Erlangen came to no avail, and in April 1850 Löhe published a small essay, "Our church situation in Protestant Bavaria and the efforts of several Bavarian Lutheran ministers in the years 1848 and 1849." Similar in tone and content to the piece on the synod conference at Ansbach, "Our church situation" represented another attempt by Löhe to rally support for his cause though his growing distance from the centers of ecclesiastical power appeared more and more obvious. In January 1850, he chided a friend, "You call me a 'sect-leader,' but that doesn't bother me because I have never been one nor desired to become one. That, which I seek, is not a sect, nor do I want to separate from the Bavarian church."[30] Sectarian or not, Löhe's opposition to the direction of church administration was clear. Condemning policy decisions for the Lutheran church made in the aftermath of 1848 by "agitators

---

[29]Löhe to K. Ehlers-Liegnitz, 24 February 1849 and 27 March 1849, Löhe Papers.

[30]Löhe to J. Schlier, 6 January 1850, Löhe Papers.

who were in part neither Lutherans nor even baptized, the mass were seduced and blindly led," Löhe charged that they sacrificed all to the banner of freedom with no awareness of its meaning or limitations.[31] The insidious influence of such democratizing tendencies was not all. There could be found even in Löhe's own Frankish Bavaria a complete indifference to sacramental and liturgical veracity. "The sacrosanct host and simple bread, Lutheran and Reformed formulas for distribution, all on the same altar and promiscuously distributed by the same minister": this was the scandal under which the church suffered.[32] Though he had emphasized previously in the *Three Books* the importance of the sacraments and the correctness of the Lutheran interpretation of their meaning, Löhe here directed his appeal primarily to those within the Lutheran church. Consequently, after reiterating the importance of confessional differences, he called for a total reconstruction of the Lutheran church on confessional principles. Noting his own efforts over the last several years, he pleaded for a reaffirmation of the cardinal tenets of discipline, community, and sacrifice as a basis for church life. Reviewing the mixture of confessional affiliations within the ruling church administration, he appealed for their separation along confessional lines. Finally, he requested a complete reorganization of missionary efforts, both in Germany and abroad, in addition to support for new catechisms that could educate the young toward this churchly direction.[33]

This essay had no visible effect in drawing adherents either to Löhe's standard of confessional consciousness or to his dream of a reconstructed Lutheran church. Consequently, in July 1850 Löhe struck out in a dramatic new direction. In a petition to the Bavarian church authorities he raised the possibility of seceding from the church with those who shared his confessional opinions. In framing this alternative, he noted his previously unanswered addresses to

---

[31]Löhe, "Unsere Kirchliche Lage im protestantischen Bayern und die Bestrebungen einiger bayerisch-lutherischen Pfarrer in den Jahren 1848 und 1849," *Werke*, 5/1:374, 379.

[32]Ibid., 388.

[33]Ibid., 406, 413, 422-24, 426-30, 433-36.

the church officials, which called for a separation of the Lutheran and Reformed confessions within the Bavarian church. Citing the inclusion of the Palatinate and Rhineland congregations in church administration and, more importantly, in common celebration of the sacraments, Löhe charged that as a Lutheran such indiscriminate practices not only taxed his conscience, they endangered it. Displeased with having to oppose the administration but refusing to compromise his beliefs further, Löhe asked the church officials if he had any option other than to leave such a church.[34] Later that month while waiting for an answer to his petition, he attended a conference at Bamberg. He submitted for the consideration of the other attending ministers a series of theses in support of two propositions: "The Bavarian church is not Lutheran and Lutherans, such as ourselves, cannot remain in it without committing sins." The concerns Löhe voiced here could be traced back to his publication of the *Three Books* in 1845. However, now after repeated protestations, conferences, and attempted mediations, the circumstances appeared to call for a break from the established church much as the Silesian Lutherans had done earlier in the century.[35]

The years between 1851 and 1856 saw a personal accommodation, if not a final adjudication, of the differences between Löhe and the Bavarian church authorities. On 19 September 1851, the church officials responded to Löhe's July petition of the previous year. In their reply, the consistory argued that no legal or factual union of Reformed, Unionist, and Lutheran confessions existed in Bavaria. Any instances in which either ministers or congregations of these confessions jointly celebrated communion or otherwise worshiped together were purely by chance, due to extraordinary circumstances and thus, should in no way imperil Löhe's conscience or those of his fellow believers.[36] Löhe, of course, completely disagreed with the consistory's interpretation. In October 1851 he issued a re-

[34]Löhe, "Eingabe von 2 Juli 1851," *Werke*, 5:514-15.

[35]Löhe, "Thesen für die Pastoralkonferenz zu Bamberg," *Werke*, 5:516-19.

[36]See the response by the consistory, reprinted in *Werke*, 5/2:1244-46.

buttal to their reply. In November he gave notice that he would no longer administer communion to Reformed and Unionist laity, and that he considered any Lutheran minister who did so to be in error and sin. For his part, he would administer communion only to those Lutherans who agreed with him and desisted from all such mixed confessional practices.[37]

The controversy over communion appeared to have come to a head. Loyalty to confessional standards had led Löhe virtually to abandon his ministerial duties. Similarly, his challenge to the consistory was of a nature that could hardly be ignored. It came as no surprise, then, when a preliminary report to the consistory in December 1851 concluded that Löhe was no longer fit to perform his ministerial duties and that he should be suspended from office. In April of the following year proceedings for his suspension were begun and an address by the minister of culture recommending suspension was given to the king, Maximilian II. At first, no action was taken. Another address was submitted in June. Still the king delayed. On 9 September 1852, Löhe's case took an unexpected turn—the king offered Adolf von Harless, formerly of the Erlangen faculty, the presidency of the superior consistory. Harless had been forced from Bavaria for his part in the Protestant opposition during the "kneeling controversy" and had gone to Leipzig to teach. Throughout his years in Leipzig he had kept abreast of developments in Bavaria and had corresponded with Löhe. Thus, Löhe could greet the news of Harless's return to Munich with pleasure. His sentiments proved appropriate when Harless quashed the suspension proceedings.[38]

Löhe and Harless respected each other though they shared no unanimity of opinion or doctrine. Hence, though Harless's appointment was mutually agreeable, Löhe could not expect instant backing for his beliefs. Indeed, Löhe shrewdly informed a North German friend in November, "Here in Bavaria we wait in expectation of improvement. We wait, however we do not sleep. We have

---

[37]See the "Erklärung," *Werke*, 5/1:609-13.

[38]See the discussion of this episode in *Werke*, 5/2:1025-33.

been too long and earnestly in struggle to do that."[39] Harless's entry into the controversy served to diminish tensions on both sides, though it provided no real resolution. Harless's desire to keep Löhe within the church, and Löhe's friendship with Harless brought the two sides together. Built on such a bond, however, the resolution of the conflict for Löhe represented more of a personal accommodation than a full accomplishment of his stated goals. In spring of 1855 he became severely ill. His illness exhausted him, and he turned his energies more and more to work in his own parish. His ideas had not changed though. As he told Harless in September of that year, he was happy to be in the Lutheran church, though he was still "a servant of his conscience."[40]

By 1855 Löhe's battles over the doctrine of the church were largely over. He did have one further conflict, which revolved around questions of liturgical practice and which occupied his attention between 1858 and 1860. Between 1856 and 1858, Löhe had given last rites to several of his parishioners. In addition, throughout his ministry he had given private confession and absolution to those who requested it. In February 1858 he was called upon by the consistory to account for these practices and to provide "a simple open explanation of his position relative to the Roman Catholic Church." In spring of 1858 and again in January 1859, he provided the consistory with a full explanation of the circumstances surrounding each of the practices, as well as biblical and confessional statements that he believed justified their use. The consistory responded by issuing a reprimand telling him to desist from such practices.[41]

Löhe's troubles with the consistory were not yet over. Although he had never produced his statement on Roman Catholicism, it was not fear that his high church practices verged into Catholicism that finally caused his superiors to suspend him. Rather, it was his traditional interpretation of church discipline that was his undoing. As

---

[39]Löhe to U. von Maltzahn, 10 November 1852, Löhe Papers.

[40]Löhe to A. von Harless, 8 September 1855, Löhe Papers.

[41]The consistory's address is quoted in *Werke*, 5/2:1048. Löhe's explanations are reprinted in *Werke*, 5/2:721-30, 735-43.

a champion of high confessional standards Löhe had occasionally withheld certain ministerial offices, such as church burial, from those individuals whom he believed were obstinate troublemakers in the parish or flagrantly lax in attending church or maintaining proper church discipline. Such a case occurred in November 1856, and a protest against Löhe had been filed with the consistory by the refused party. A similar episode happened in the spring of 1860. In this case Löhe refused to marry a previously divorced man and woman. Appealing to the sanctity of a consecrated marriage and to the powers to loosen as well as to bind, which he considered inherent in his ministerial office, Löhe categorically refused to reconsider his position. Several laymen from Löhe's church testified in his behalf before the local church authorities, and Löhe himself petitioned in his own defense. However, on 5 July 1860, he was suspended from his ministerial duties.[42]

The episode was yet unfinished. Due to the unpopularity of the bridegroom and the extensive support for Löhe in his parish, there was much local sentiment against the marriage taking place. Finally the consistory compromised. Despite increased reluctance to sanction such a union, the couple was married in a church in the bride's hometown. At the same time, Löhe was reinstated in his parish of Neuendettelsau. Thus concluded the final battle in Löhe's lifelong conflict with the authorities of the Bavarian church.

AUGUST VILMAR OF HESSE

Löhe once described himself as a Don Quixote, one who fought for his ideals no matter how distant they appeared, a gadfly who persistently irritated the established powers.[43] In contrast to Wilhelm Löhe, August Vilmar of Hesse found a much more comfortable association with the authorities of his church. Recognized within his native Hesse as a staunch conservative and a loyal defender of Lutheran confessionalism, Vilmar served in a number of official capacities during his lifetime. A close advisor to H. D. L.

----

[42]See Löhe's defense of his actions, *Werke*, 5/2:781-89 and the further discussion on 1054-59.

[43]Löhe to K. von Raumer, 1 February 1845, Löhe Papers.

Hassenpflug during Hassenpflug's two terms as minister of the Interior, Vilmar was also a member of several ecclesiastical committees within the Hessian church hierarchy. Beyond such governmental activity, he was director of the *gymnasium* in Marburg from 1833 to 1850, and later professor of theology in Marburg University. He died in Marburg in 1868 as old as the century in which he had so actively taken part. Vilmar's academic reputation rested on his studies in German literature and in theology. In addition he wrote numerous short pieces on contemporary religious and political topics, many of which appeared in his journal, *Hessischen Volksfreund*.[44]

His strident criticisms of democracy and confessional indifference, particularly in the aftermath of 1848, marked Vilmar as an ardent supporter of the counterrevolutionary movement in Hesse. Ironically, this champion of traditionalism had been something of a liberal in his youth. Reared in the heady days of the war of liberation from Napoleon, he had been a member of a nationalistic student fraternity (*Burschenschaft*) in Marburg. Hearing the news in 1819 of the murder of the diplomat August von Kotzebue by the German theology student Karl Sand, Vilmar had toasted the murderer in front of his fellow students and fraternity brothers. Equally surprising, given his later theological positions, was Vilmar's deep attraction to theological rationalism and his expressed aversion to Claus Harms's criticism in 1817 of the Prussian Union. Calling Harms a fool and indignant at the prevalence of what he called "catholicizing and non-catholicizing mystics" whose ideal was the Middle Ages, Vilmar commended his own rationalist system as a more credible approach to the questions of theology.[45]

Vilmar's transformation into a political and religious conservative happened slowly during the 1830s and was confirmed by his experiences in 1848. Indications of a shift in his theological perspective appear first. In a letter to his brother, Wilhelm, August Vilmar wrote of his preoccupation with the ideas of Friedrich

[44]The standard biography of Vilmar is W. Hopf, *August Vilmar*, 2 vols. (Marburg, 1913). Short articles on Vilmar also appear in *Religion in Geschichte und Gegenwart* and *Lexicon für Theologie und Kirche*.

[45]Hopf, *August Vilmar*, 1:78-81, 94-99. The quotation occurs on page 95.

Schleiermacher and of his respect for him. "I am of the opinion," August wrote, "that outside of Schleiermacher's *Christian Faith*, we have absolutely no system of theology."[46] In 1830, in Hesse as throughout Germany, celebrations of the three hundredth anniversary of the Augsburg Confession took place. Vilmar took this occasion to study anew the confessional statements of the Lutheran church. The results of his study were apparent in an address that he delivered on 25 June 1830. As if to signal a personal resolution to his troubles through a public testimony to the importance of confessional statements, Vilmar told his audience that the celebration that day marked a new era in the history of the Christian faith in Germany. The time in which one could base faith either in speculative reason or in unmediated feeling was now past. Instead, the new era of faith must now build itself out of the totality of the life of humanity. To him, an indication of the success of this direction was the renewed interest in the doctrine of the church, "one of the most important interests of our time," and one that all classes of Germans were taking up seriously and successfully.[47]

Continuing on this theme, Vilmar drew attention to the Augsburg Confession, a bulwark for the purity of the Lutheran faith, and in whose name many in 1817 as in 1530 had sacrificed.[48] The explicit references to the importance of a confessional standard and the more subtle mention of resistance in the name of confessions spelled a clear break for Vilmar from his former theological position. The implications of this new confessional foundation became increasingly evident to him. Writing to his brother on 27 February 1831, Vilmar remarked, "it becomes even clearer to me that we have to come forward right now in behalf of the church." Such a defense would include many points but in the face of recent attacks, "the one single theme in which all variations come together is that any improvement must come from within the church. It is the downfall of

---

[46]August Vilmar to Wilhelm Vilmar, 15 December 1829, August Vilmar Papers, Hessisches Staatsarchiv Marburg, Marburg.

[47]Quoted in Hopf, *August Vilmar*, 1:163.

[48]Ibid., 163-65.

the church if it is placed within the state without equal attention to the church's own independent resources of faith."[49]

Vilmar's linking of politics and religion would remain characteristic of him throughout his life. The context for his concern in 1831 can be traced to his involvement with proposals for constitutional reform in Hesse in 1831-1832, and to his disillusionment with his liberal colleagues. The liberals' proposals were framed in the spirit of the July Revolution of 1830 in Paris, and Vilmar found them to be completely misguided. By January 1832, his esteem for conservative Hessians such as H. D. L. Hassenpflug grew proportionately greater. Vilmar applauded Hassenpflug's strong antiliberal stance. He "was able not only through his sharp invective, but also through his convictions to recognize the inner connection between religious liberalism—rationalism in every form—and political liberalism," Vilmar noted, "Hassenpflug belonged to that minority of ministers in Germany, indeed in Europe, who made absolutely no concession to revolution."[50]

Agitation to change the constitution came to nothing, but before the decade was over, another contest would again pose the question of creedal adherence or compromise. In 1839 a controversy over the interpretation of the Augsburg Confession developed within the Hessian Lutheran church. One group, led by the church administrator, F. W. Bickell, advocated greater flexibility in understanding the confessional statements and executing their statutes. Arguing that times had changed since these documents were first written, Bickell and his faction in the Hessian church called for clerics to adhere to the confessions only insofar as the creed agreed with their consciences. For Vilmar and his followers, such a lessening of required allegiance amounted to private judgment of the worst sort, and the ruin of the distinctive tenets of Lutheranism. The Augsburg Confession, indeed the whole Reformation legacy, provided a standard for doctrinal truth against both liberal Protestants and Roman Catholics. Mediation by the Hessian crown avoided a rupture

---

[49]August Vilmar to Wilhelm Vilmar, 27 February 1831, Vilmar Papers.

[50]August Vilmar to Wilhelm Vilmar, 2 January 1832, Vilmar Papers; Hopf, *August Vilmar*, 1:225

within the church, but left both liberals and conservatives unsatisfied and biding their time.[51]

As Vilmar's biographer notes, conservatives in Hesse continued throughout the 1840s to consolidate their forces and meet together in the hopes of stemming the tides of liberalism. Vilmar eagerly gave his support to these conservative efforts, especially to his fellow Marburger, Aimé Huber, the author of the pamphlet, "Concerning the Elements, Possibility, or Necessity of a Conservative Party in Germany."[52] Even more significant for Vilmar was the new unity to his thinking, particularly as it concerned his doctrine of the church. For in Vilmar's thought on the doctrine of the church could be seen the results of his transformation into a political conservative and a confessional Lutheran. Beyond that could also be seen the seeds for his conflicts with Hessian liberalism and his attempt to respond to the challenge of the new social order in Germany, a development abetted by liberalism, but one, in his view, that these same liberals scarcely understood.

Fundamental to Vilmar's view of the church was the premise that the church was a divine institution. Just as Wilhelm Löhe had done, August Vilmar emphasized that the church was an *anstalt*, an institution always more than the individuals composing it. Speaking in 1847, Vilmar continued the theme he had first articulated in his tercentenary address celebrating the Augsburg Confession. The present era was "the age of the Church," he said in a speech entitled, "On the Future of the Church." It was the age of "the seventh sign" when the millennium would arrive and the church visible and invisible would come into its own. The eschatological tone of Vilmar's reflections was not unusual for him, and this manner of construing the meaning of the present age as well as the schematic periodization of human history was shared by other theologians of his day,

---

[51]See the discussion in Johann Kißling, *Der Deutsche Protestantismus*, 2 vols. (Münster, 1917-1918) 1:261-63; Hopf, *August Vilmar*, 421; and more generally Heinrich Steitz, *Geschichte der Evangelischen Kirche in Hessen und Nassau*, 4 vols. (Marburg, 1961-1977) 3:340-47.

[52]Hopf, *August Vilmar*, 418.

notably Theodor Kliefoth.[53] Contained within this eschatological perspective was the influence of organic thinking. This influence had been evident since the late 1820s and the early 1830s. On 6 October 1828, August Vilmar wrote to his brother Wilhelm of that unity of feeling and reason, that "animated whole" that made up the human being.[54] Here was the same emphasis on the totality of experience that Vilmar had spoken of in his tercentennial address in 1830. In line with the emphasis on unity and wholeness was his insistence that the church be understood not as an association of atomistic individuals, but as a corporation. Vilmar's developmental scheme assumed that the present stage, that of the age of the church, fulfilled all past stages. In this teleological conception the last stage encapsulated and culminated all previous efforts.[55]

Vilmar believed that the church as *anstalt* was further demarcated by proper doctrine and correct use of the sacraments as these were set out in its creed. His position in the confessional controversy of 1839 and his later statements demonstrate that he saw symbolic writings such as the Augsburg Confession as functioning in important ways. First, such creeds provided sources for identification and for the establishment of distinctly Lutheran theological doctrines. Second, they acted to maintain the purity of those doctrines, to guard against revision and a subsequent loss of precious truth. Finally, he emphasized the objective status of such confessional statements, their unchanging nature and their sufficiency as bulwarks against error. According to Vilmar, confessional statements were not as liable to the vagaries of interpretation as was personal experience. Instead, tradition acted to set the proper framework for understanding. Indeed, it had been in the return to a strict

---

[53]Ibid., pages 421-26 discuss this address and reproduce the text. For Vilmar's view of the church as *anstalt*, see Vilmar, *Die Theologie der Tatsachen wider die Theologie der Rhetorik* (Marburg, 1857; reprint 1938) 50; Vilmar, *Kirche und Welt oder die Aufgaben des geistlichen Amts in unserer Zeit*, 2 vols. (Gütersloh, 1872) 1:96. For a discussion of the similar eschatological emphasis in Kliefoth and the Irvinginers, see Kantzenbach, *Gestalten und Typen des Neuluthertums*, 101-104.

[54]W. Maurer, *Aufklärung, Idealismus, und Restauration*, 2 vols. (Gießen, 1930) 1:217.

[55]See ibid., 224.

confessionalism in 1817 and 1830 that the twin perils of rationalism and Unionism had been contested. The easy recourse to individualistic experience remained, however, and such a challenge could be adequately met, Vilmar suggested, only if strict adherence to the confessions and proper discipline within the church were maintained.[56]

Just as the church was threatened by the dissolution of its confessional bonds, so too was society menaced by the social disintegration that Vilmar believed was so much a part of the times. "Our age is in many ways an age of atomism," he declared, "each wants to be for himself, no one can stand to be with or under anyone else."[57] Here, in society, was the same danger of exclusive reference to personal authority that rationalism posed in theology. Vilmar's interweaving of religion and politics, his capacity to see dangerous subjective influences at work as much in theology as in social theory, and his desire to denounce them both insured that he would have volatile encounters with Hessian liberalism. "The old Tower of Babel has again poured out its whore's wail," Vilmar wrote his son-in-law, Leonard Schilling, on 3 March 1848, "and perhaps it will be even more dreadful than 1789; the dull waters of 1830 can hardly compare [with the present.]"[58] Later that month, Vilmar began publishing the *Hessischen Volksfreund*. Its counterrevolutionary perspective was clear from the first issue with its castigation of impiety and unbelief, and its identification of true German character with those who sided with the monarchy.[59]

Reactions to Vilmar's frenzied diatribes against "republicans and communists" were immediate. A colleague in the *gymnasium* publicly denounced him in March as the "scandal of the school." By midsummer Vilmar spoke of receiving several verbal threats; once, in June his house was stormed. In that instance, Vilmar's own *gymnasium* students, much to his surprise and delight, circled his house

---

[56]Vilmar, *Theologie der Tatsachen*, 50; *Kirche und Welt*, 1:40-42.

[57]Vilmar, *Kirche und Welt*, 1:40-42.

[58]Quoted in Hopf, *August Vilmar*, 2:4.

[59]Ibid., 12.

to stand guard and prevent any further disturbances. Amidst this disorder with "ministries changing as often as one changes gloves," and with the prospect of blood flowing in the streets, Vilmar pinned his hopes on the emergence of a strong leader, perhaps a Prussian, to restore order and establish a true German nation. Until that time, though, he continued to criticize the revolutionaries in the pages of the *Hessischen Volksfreund* and in turn continued to receive threats.[60] The controversy raged so furiously that Vilmar erected barricades within his house and took to arming himself whenever he went out. Before the year was over, his house was attacked twice more. In reporting one of the attacks to his brother, Vilmar suggested "the people must now break completely with the revolution, or the devil will certainly take them. The challenge which the people have to solve is not revolutionary, if they would only realize it." Instead of following the banner of that "satanic thing, the sovereignty of the people," Germans should be rallying to the standard of the "sovereignty of the prince."[61]

Throughout 1849 while continuing vocally to support the monarchy and those forces opposed to the revolution, Vilmar privately expressed thorough discouragement. Despite his initial hopes, nothing positive had materialized in Prussia. "Phrases and more phrases, but no deeds" was his verdict on Prussian developments. Similarly, the Parliament at Frankfurt had disappointed any expectation that nationalists, even conservative nationalists, might have placed in it.[62] By 1850, however, Vilmar's outlook had brightened. The liberals were losing ground and as his friend, Hassenpflug, once again took up a ministerial post, Vilmar could suggest that the conservatives had won the day. The public and private attacks on Vilmar in 1848-1849 had soured his estimate of the governmental officials in Hesse, most of whom he dismissed as "state eunuchs."

---

[60]Ibid., 14, 20-22; August Vilmar to Wilhelm Vilmar, 27 August 1848, Vilmar Papers. The Marburg authorities took precautionary measures on Vilmar's behalf, see "Anweisung des Marburger Bürgermeisters Uloth an die Bürgergarde, betr. Schutz für August Vilmar," 26 June 1848, Vilmar Papers.

[61]August Vilmar to Wilhelm Vilmar, 1 October 1848, Vilmar Papers.

[62]Hopf, *August Vilmar*, 2:41-45. The quotation occurs on 43-44.

But as order was restored during the 1850s Vilmar found new support from these sources for his continuing attacks on religious and political liberals.[63]

In 1848 when he began publishing the *Hessischen Volksfreund*, Vilmar indicated that the journal would comment "on the relationship of the Christian church to the political movements of the present." In 1851 as he closed out his editorship of the magazine and reviewed the intervening years he continued to connect religion and politics. It had been God himself, Vilmar suggested, who had brought about the undoing of the "democrats and communists" who had supported the revolution. Likewise, it was through God's agency that the church had survived the several assaults leveled against it.[64] It is unsurprising, then, that through the 1850s and until his death, Vilmar continued to assail German democrats and charge them with desiring not only to abolish the monarchy but also "to destroy inheritance, property, and the family."[65] Similarly, his publications during these years railed against egalitarian tendencies in the church. In his book, *The Theology of Facts against the Theology of Rhetoric*, first published in 1856, Vilmar strongly warned against any interpretation of the church that would emphasize the importance of the church as an association at the expense of its divine and institutional creation. And later in 1863 he struck out against "congregational constitutions," which he saw as "exact parallels to that universal suffrage which already rules the world."[66]

Although personally he was comfortably accommodated to royal power, Vilmar did not favor domination of the church by the state. As early as 1831, he stated that the Lutheran church should not give itself into the hands of the state. Through the years of strife and dissension with the liberals, Vilmar argued that the only satisfactory separation of church and state was one that could safeguard the

---

[63]Ibid., 105; August Vilmar to Wilhelm Vilmar, 10 November 1849, Vilmar Papers.

[64]Ibid., 12, 183-88. The quotation occurs on 185.

[65]Vilmar, *Kirche und Welt*, 1:54.

[66]Vilmar, *Theologie der Tatsachen*, 70; *Kirche und Welt*, 1:34. See also the discussion by William Shanahan, *German Protestants Face the Social Question*, 237-38.

rights of the faithful and insure the spiritual independence of the church. Participating in the deliberations at Jeseberg in February 1849, he said that "only such men as belong with the deepest convictions to the church, and who are truly equipped to follow out these convictions unconditionally can lead the church." Later that same year as the prince of Hesse capitulated to further demands for religious freedom, Vilmar publicly contradicted the monarch. For this opposition he was later passed over for ecclesiastical preferences and office.[67]

Thus from the 1840s until his death in 1868, August Vilmar sought to understand the changes occurring in Germany, and in so doing to analyze the failures, as he saw them, of German liberalism. Repeatedly, whether in 1848 or later, Vilmar returned to the problem of eroding traditional social bonds and the atomizing of society. Instead of an organically conceived whole, society had degenerated until there was an exclusive emphasis on individuality and a thorough disregard for divine creation.[68] The villains of the story remained those democrats, republicans, and radicals who attempted to loosen the bonds of authority and tradition in the name of progress. But Vilmar also recognized the influences of industrialism, and he had sharp words for those captains of industry, "who reduce all property relationships to money."[69] In such a social context the challenge was to reach "the industrial masses of today and the industrial slaves of tomorrow," and to lead them under the church's auspices to a vigorous reconstruction of corporative and communal institutions within German society. By reversing this process of individualization and by strengthening the ligatures of society—above all, the family—Vilmar hoped to administer the necessary antidote for the liberal poisons he saw spreading throughout society.[70]

---

[67]See "Angelegenheiten der hess. Kirche, vor allem Kirchenkonferenzen von Kassel, Jeseberg, Marburg, Homburg, Treysa, 1848-1850," Vilmar Papers; Hopf, *August Vilmar*, 1:175, and 2:59-61, 76-78, 90.

[68]Vilmar, *Schulreden über Fragen der Zeit*, 3d ed. (Gütersloh, 1886) 83-90.

[69]Vilmar, *Kirche und Welt*, 1:97, 127.

[70]Ibid., 103.

It was to these ends as professor of theology that Vilmar instructed his university students at Marburg in lectures on the Augsburg Confession, moral theology, and pastoral care. He also sought out allies among his fellow Lutherans. He was in contact with Ludwig Petri of Hannover regarding home missions, and he helped to found the *Pastoral-theologischen Blättern* to which Wilhelm Löhe contributed. Vilmar also expressed appreciation for Friedrich Julius Stahl. He agreed totally with Stahl's analysis of the church as *anstalt*. Furthermore, Stahl's attack on Unionism in 1860—Unionism is rationalistic and an abandonment of distinctive Lutheran truths—resonated with Vilmar's own opinions. Finally in his series of lectures, "The Present Day Parties in the State and Church," Stahl distinguished between the forces of legitimacy and those of revolution. Much as Vilmar had done, Stahl saw the conflict between these parties centering in the doctrine of popular sovereignty with its implications for the reordering of traditional society.[71] Clearly, whether or not Vilmar drew his ideas directly from Stahl, Stahl's work significantly influenced him.

THEODOR KLIEFOTH OF MECKLENBURG

Friedrich Stahl also influenced the third of the neo-Lutherans considered in this study, Theodor Kliefoth. In their common emphasis on the church as an *anstalt*, a divine institution, and in their mutual opposition to popular sovereignty, understood as collegialism within the church and democracy within the secular sphere, clear thematic parallels are evident between Kliefoth and Stahl. Yet Theodor Kliefoth was more than a pale imitator of Friedrich Julius Stahl. Born in 1810 at Körchow, Mecklenburg, Kliefoth was an active leader of the Lutheran church in Mecklenburg and a vigorous defender of Lutheran confessional standards throughout his life. During his lifetime and after his death in 1895, assessments of Kliefoth's theological and ecclesiastical contributions varied widely. The

---

[71]Stahl's view of the church as *anstalt* can be found in *Die Kirchenverfassung nach Lehre und Recht der Protestanten* (Erlangen, 1840). For his attack on the Union, see *Die lutherische Kirche und die Union* (Berlin, 1860), and for his evaluation of contemporary politics, *Die gegenwärtige Parteien in Staat und Kirche* (Berlin, 1863). See Vilmar's recommendation of *Die gegenwärtige Parteien* in *Kirche und Welt*, 1:134.

charge of "church dictator" and the tribute of defender of the Lutheran faith in Mecklenburg suggest the sharp feelings that he aroused.[72]

Kliefoth attended the University of Berlin where he most liked the lectures of Friedrich Schleiermacher and August Neander. A good student, Kliefoth late in life reminisced that "when I was young, I had it in my head to become a professor of theology, especially in the area of church history . . . but God took my life in a totally different direction."[73] After only one year at Berlin, he returned in 1830 to his native Mecklenburg and completed his education at the University of Rostock. Shortly thereafter the course of Kliefoth's life began to change. In 1833 he was appointed instructor to Duke Wilhelm of Mecklenburg, and in 1837 he became tutor to the Grand Duke, Friedrich Francis. The relationship between Kliefoth and his student developed into a close friendship as Friedrich Francis happily informed his father. Consequently, although Kliefoth's services as tutor were no longer needed after 1839, his personal relationship with the royal house continued and would have a significant effect upon his later life.[74]

Between 1840 and 1844 Kliefoth served as a pastor for a small congregation at Ludwigslust in Mecklenburg. Just prior to accepting this position, perhaps still hoping for an academic position, Kliefoth published his *Introduction to the History of Dogma*. This study, which Adolph Harnack later spoke of as "thoughtful and instruc-

---

[72]The standard biography of Kliefoth is E. D. Haack, *Theodor Kliefoth, ein Charakterbild aus der Zeit der Erneuerung des christlichen Glaubenslebens und der lutherischen Kirche im 19. Jahrhundert* (Schwerin, 1910). Shorter biographical articles on him also appear in *Religion in Geschichte und Gegenwart* and *Lexicon für Theologie und Kirche*. The charge of "church dictator" occurs in Walter Nigg, *Kirchliche Reaktion* (Leipzig, 1939) 57, while H. Stoll's study, *Theodor Kliefoth als Kirchenführer* (Göttingen, 1936) lauds Kliefoth. As one commentator put it regarding Kliefoth, "Many heeded him, even more hated him, some loved him, all feared him," quoted in Karl Schmaltz, *Kirchengeschichte Mecklenburgs*, 3 vols. (Schwerin and Berlin, 1935-1952) 3:441.

[73]Kliefoth's estimate of Schleiermacher and Neander is shown in Haack, *Theodor Kliefoth*, 70. For his reminiscences on his youth, see Kliefoth to R. Rochvoll, 30 December 1886, quoted by Stoll, *Theodor Kliefoth als Kirchenführer*, 13.

[74]See the correspondence between Friedrich Francis and Kliefoth bearing on their friendship as quoted by Stoll, *Theodor Kliefoth*, 19-20.

tive," attested to Kliefoth's continued interest in church history.[75] Kliefoth stated there that the task of the church historian was "to comprehend history and in so doing, to recognize the unity within the diversity of its forms, the order within its variegated multiplicity, the abiding laws within its transient variations."[76] Within this context Kliefoth articulated several themes significant for his doctrine of the church. He castigated the methodology of "crude empiricism," which he said "can never discover the spirit behind the outward appearances, which can research the heavens and earth and never find God therein. It knows only singularities and can never find laws or rules of history."[77] Instead, he stated, one's approach must be able to account for the spiritual, as "the Christian spirit is the living source out of which springs everything Christian, including dogmas as well." This Christian spirit could be seen as both objective and subjective. Its objective side was the Holy Spirit; its subjective side was the spheres upon which the Holy Spirit worked. In this way the historian of dogma investigated the history of the promise of salvation as that history was attested to in the Bible and in human history.[78] And out of the interaction of spirit and world, sacred and profane, came those materials that it was the historian's task to assemble, periodize, and comprehend.

Within this conceptual framework were the two further themes of development and unity within church history. In the *Introduction to the History of Dogma* Kliefoth discussed the formation of the Greek church at Alexandria and Antioch, its succession by the Roman church, and the subsequent appearance of the Protestant church. In this historical course Kliefoth saw a process that suggested the influence of the Hegelian dialectic, for just as the Greek church gave way to the Roman, so too did "every negation necessarily presuppose something positive." Indeed, "every period brings forth an essential side of Christianity into appearance and consciousness, and

---

[75]Adolph Harnack, *History of Dogma*, trans. Neil Buchanan, 7 vols. (London, 1894) 1:35.

[76]Kliefoth, *Einleitung in die Dogmengeschichte* (Parchim und Ludwigslust, 1839) v.

[77]Ibid., vi.

[78]Ibid., 43-44, 50.

the latter always takes on the results which have been developed to that point and adds them to the new development."[79] Yet if his emphasis on history resembled that of Hegel, Kliefoth's replacing of reason with the divine promise of salvation in the revelation of Jesus suggests an essential difference between the two systems. That both men stressed the logical necessity of development should not obscure the contradiction between Kliefoth's additive view of development (*annehmen*) and Hegel's more synthetic one (*aufheben*).[80]

In placing Protestantism within this historical schema Kliefoth made it clear that he saw the history of Christianity as a unified one. Protestantism thus represented a modification of certain doctrinal themes and not a completely new beginning in the sixteenth century. While he did not want to de-emphasize the degree and significance of these doctrinal modifications, he did emphasize the unity throughout history of the Christian church. In this way Kliefoth sounded many of the themes—the Christian experience as both subjective and objective, the concept of unity understood within a developmental framework—that would appear in his theological reflections in the 1850s.

If in 1843 he had thought he was destined to become a university professor like Vilmar or to remain the pastor of a small congregation like Löhe, Kliefoth was to be greatly surprised. For in 1844, two years after succeeding his father to the throne, Friedrich Francis appointed Kliefoth as superintendent or chief administrator of the Lutheran church in Mecklenburg. His assumption of the superintendency marked a turning point in Kliefoth's life. From that point on, his career was identified with the religious and political struggles of the Mecklenburg church.

The young superintendent summarized the conditions facing the church in a short essay published in 1844. Above all, the church was being called to reinvigorate itself, to renew itself and rededicate its energies to spiritual battle. In this conflict the church could find spiritual support in the resources of confessional orthodoxy, a Lu-

---

[79] Ibid., 221, 133.

[80] See the discussion in G. Kehnscherper's excellent study, "Das Wesen der Kirche nach Kliefoth." Ph.D. diss., Leipzig, 1955, 8-9.

theran stronghold that was to be dearly protected.[81] Kliefoth took seriously the task of regenerating all facets of church life. Within two years of assuming office he had begun measures to reform liturgical practices and the examination of ministerial candidates in accordance with what he considered the high standards of Lutheran orthodoxy.

From 1844 into the 1880s Kliefoth remained active as a leader of the Mecklenburg Lutheran church. During the years covered in this study, those from 1848 to roughly 1858 emerge as especially interesting. This decade not only contained the revolutionary experience of 1848, it witnessed in Kliefoth, as in Löhe and Vilmar, a deepening of confessional commitment and a clearer articulation of the doctrine of the church.

The dynamics and effects of the revolution of 1848 in Mecklenburg were similar to those throughout Germany. Sporadic outbursts of popular resentment occurred. The Torgelow castle was burned in protest of its owner's agrarian policy. In response to the burning the military was brought in and order restored. Orderliness was the keystone of the call for reform by the middle-class liberals of Mecklenburg. This approach appeared to pay off handsomely. In March 1848 Friedrich Francis convened a constitutional convention; in October 1849 a new constitution was unveiled. As in the deliberations at Frankfurt, attempts to secure civil rights featured prominently in the discussions. Beyond that, the delegates were much concerned with the relationship between church and state. After much debate over the church-state question, a moderate coalition established a majority in the assembly and secured a statement endorsing the free and independent development of religious life in Mecklenburg and the right to self-government by the local congregations.[82] But the liberals' apparent success would be as impermanent in Mecklenburg as elsewhere in Germany. In September 1850, pressured by Friedrich Wilhelm IV of Prussia, Friedrich Francis revoked the new

---

[81]Kliefoth, *An die Geistlichkeit und den Lehrstand des Superintendent Schwerin* (Hamburg, 1844) unpaginated.

[82]Schmaltz, *Kirchengeschichte Mecklenburgs*, 3:359-61; Stoll, *Theodor Kliefoth*, 24.

Mecklenburg constitution and replaced his liberal aides with conservatives as Mecklenburg entered an era of reaction.[83]

The course of religious developments in 1848 in Mecklenburg paralleled developments in politics. December 1848, Friedrich Francis set up a church commission, with Kliefoth as one of its members, that was to make recommendations on church-related topics.[84] From the outset this commission favored moderate, if not decidedly conservative, resolutions to all issues placed before it. Just prior to the establishment of the commission, in a piece entitled "Our Task"—which served as the foreword to the first issue of the *Zeitblatt für die evangelische-lutherische Kirche Mecklenburgs*, a publication coedited by Kliefoth and other commission members—Kliefoth set out a representative view of the situation in 1848. Writing of the movements for liberal reforms in Germany, he asserted that they "had changed little, and improved even less," for "whatever desires to have an influence upon the church, must have a religious content to it." Instead, these reform movements were "nothing other than a political attempt of the radicals to destroy or to seize the state from the vantage point of the church." The forces of conservatism and tradition might be forced to bide their time, but "everyone has had more than a mouthful of slogans about freedoms of belief, the rights of conscience, etc., not to mention the establishment in every locale and parish under the influence of these same alluring notions of societies free from faith and creed in which atheism, irreligiosity, indifference, and immortality are legalized."[85]

Predictably, the commission in two of its early recommendations underscored the state's financial obligation to the church and demanded that all primary education be retained under the direction of religiously licensed teachers. The commission discussed the topic of education in a memorandum composed in June 1849. In this document the commissioners disagreed with those who advocated

---

[83]Ibid., 365-66.

[84]See the letter of Friedrich Francis to G. Garlitz, 14 December 1848, Kliefoth Papers, Staatsarchiv Schwerin, Schwerin.

[85]Kliefoth, "Unsere Aufgabe," *Zeitblatt für die evangelische-lutherische Kirche Mecklenburgs*, 7 October 1848, 4-5.

the teaching of children by instructors holding no religious certifi-
cation. Even in those cases where such certificates were enforced,
one often found the scarcely preferable situation of Christians of
every stripe indiscriminately mixed together along with Jewish believers. In these circumstances a return to strict confessional standards would be the proper step to take.[86]

The commission in its memorandum also discussed a proposal
to hold a synodical meeting to revise the practices of the Lutheran
church in Mecklenburg. The revisions suggested were of the same
spirit as those outlined for reforming the practice and constitution
of the secular state. Conservative churchmen in Mecklenburg were
apprehensive of such a meeting—they feared that such a convocation would revise church organization along more broadly democratic lines and further entangle the church in political discussions.
In the memorandum the church commission warned against the effects of a synodical meeting in which "unchurched and incapable
elements" of the laity would take part. Such a synodical meeting, to
the extent that it included lay participation, would inevitably "bring
a great mass of individuals into the synod, and thereby into participation in church governance, who have no other relationship to the
church than their membership, and perhaps only a passive membership at that." Rather than allowing such a situation to develop, it
was far better, the commission advised, to allow the collected ministers instead of the local congregation to choose representatives to
any proposed synodical conferences.[87]

Despite these admonitions a preliminary conference was called
for 5-17 September 1849. Kliefoth participated in the conference,
and he and other conservatives were able to curtail all democratizing aspirations for church governance. In fact, within four months,
as liberalism in Mecklenburg increasingly lost power, Kliefoth and
his fellow commissioners were able to reconstruct their position into
a superior church advisory council (*Oberkirchenrat*). Their reorganization quashed any attempt at reform through synodical convoca-
tions. Indeed, the advisory council undertook the actual

---

[86]Kliefoth et al., *Denkschrift* (Schwerin, 1849) unpaginated.

[87]Ibid.

administration of the Lutheran church in Mecklenburg, centralizing day-to-day governance under its authority and initiating further procedures to insure fidelity to high confessional standards.[88]

The activities of the *Oberkirchenrat* provoked protests, but as the political climate in Mecklenburg shifted away from liberalism such protests as did occur were strongly rebutted by the conservatives. In one case, the advisory council answered a criticism of its policies with a small pamphlet. Not above polemic extravagance of its own, the council proclaimed that "the single basis of the diverse oppositions to the *Oberkirchenrat* lies in enmity or indifference to the church." Scarcely better were those advocates of collegial democracy within the church, "men for whom the church was nothing more than an association . . . [men] who could think with regard to church authority of none other than that which the state has over any other association or corporation." Such a truncated view of the church was lamentable though unsurprising, for such believers "in the area of the church just as in that of secular affairs were adherents to the social contract of Rousseau."[89]

By the beginning 1850s, Theodor Kliefoth had pointed out the dangers of democracy within the church, and renewed his call for the reappropriation of a confessional understanding of church life. He had admonished his fellow Lutherans against adopting either collegial governance or mixed religious practices. Like Wilhelm Löhe, Kliefoth saw these tendencies embodied in American church practices, and he warned specifically against their use. Like August Vilmar, Kliefoth's theological perspective was evident before 1848, but it was the revolution that deepened his confessional orientation and political conservatism. As in the case of the Hessian, Kliefoth's experience of the revolution and his analysis of its implications would result in a series of theological reflections.

These reflections appeared in 1854-1855, first in a set of pamphlets directed against the theology faculty of the University of Göttingen, later in Kliefoth's theological treatise, *Eight Books about the*

---

[88]See the letter of Kliefoth to Friedrich Francis, December 1849, Kliefoth Papers; Stoll, *Theodor Kliefoth*, 31-32.

[89]Kliefoth et al., *Beleuchtung . . . des historische Bericht* (Schwerin, 1851) 24, 6-7.

Church. Kliefoth described the background of his position in these terms:

> We came from a subjective feeling about Christianity to a new sense of the church, and indeed to a new conscious understanding of the Lutheran church. Clearly we stand here now quite different from when we left school: we had not to dream about the church of the future, but rather to worry about the future of the church.[90]

Concern for the state of the church was the foundation of Kliefoth's position, and as he drew out his argument he attacked the Göttingen theologians for supporting the Prussian Union of 1817 and for taking part in what Kliefoth regarded as a widespread dilution of confessional standards.

In line with other neo-Lutheran theologians Kliefoth opposed the Prussian Union. Hence, he criticized the support that earlier Göttingen theologians had given it. Where the liberal theologians of Göttingen portrayed the differences between Lutheran and Reformed congregations as one of opinion, Kliefoth retorted that much more was at stake. "We must stand upon the position which our church had held for three hundred years," Kliefoth wrote, "that the Lutheran and Reformed church stand in proportion to one another as truth does to falsity. The Lutheran church may have internal differences of opinion . . . however, it has correct and accurate administration of the means of grace." He emphasized that members of Reformed churches unquestionably had led upright lives in the past and could certainly continue to do so in the future. Nevertheless, where the Reformed church "through its public doctrine has erred," the Lutheran church had remained faithful to the truth. Thus, the proper administration of the means of grace through the Word and sacraments was the crucial difference between Lutheran and Reformed or Roman Catholic practices, and over this issue no compromise of principle could be reached.[91]

---

[90]Kliefoth, "An die hochwürdige theologische Fakultät der Georg Augustus Universität zu Göttingen," *Kirchliche Zeitschrift* (1854): 44.

[91]Kliefoth, "Die Erklarung der theologischen Fakultät zu Göttingen in Veranlassung ihrer Denkschrift . . . über die gegenwärtige Krisis des kirchlichen Lebens," *Kirchliche Zeitung* (1855): 133-36.

As historical proof that such union proposals were unacceptable, Kliefoth pointed to the persecution of the Silesian Lutherans, claiming that no Western church but the Lutheran had had martyrs in the nineteenth century.[92] But Göttingen liberalism, rather than helping the Silesians, had only produced a situation in which "the confessional differences had lost their power to distinguish churches and build them up . . . so that the differentiation between churches no longer exists. Instead one finds now a 'new theology' on one side, and on the other side a disorganized Protestant people in whom a sense of the church must be reestablished."[93]

As he admonished the Göttingen faculty for helping to lower confessional standards, Kliefoth chided them for "struggling so vigorously against the right, that you have not paid enough attention to those on the left." Kliefoth then again assaulted the liberal political stance in 1848, charging that the liberals, in the name of freedom, had called for the abolition of the state as well as for all confessional distinctions.[94] Returning to theological concerns, Kliefoth pointed to pietism as a danger that had been overlooked. "With Spener began the great war of conquest by the Reformed church against the Lutherans," Kliefoth claimed, "since then under various names, first piety, then tolerance, then union, then confederation, it has continued even through the present day."[95]

Yet, if Kliefoth was dismayed with the pietists' success, he was even more discouraged with the doctrines and practices of the liberals:

> For you, my learned gentlemen, are good old ideologues. For you, the church is an idea, or an ideal . . . you never speak of the church itself, only of the idea of the church. For you, the existence of the church lies in the future, you belong to a church of the future. . . . By contrast we are sober realists, for whom the church is a real thing created by God at the first Pentecost

---

[92]Kliefoth, "An die hochwürdige theologische Fakultät," 32.

[93]Ibid., 43.

[94]Ibid., 10; Kliefoth, "Die Erklarung," 127-28.

[95]Kliefoth, "An die hochwürdige theologische Fakultät," 22.

and thereafter objectively existing in the world, indeed for the last three hundred years in the concrete, historical form of the Lutheran church.[96]

Continuing his attack, Kliefoth charged the liberals with having no understanding of the church as a "living organism." To them, he maintained, it was only a *tabula rasa* upon which the theologians thought it proper to inscribe "the results of their research in the form of constitutions, liturgical services, and somewhat new creedal statements."[97] Furthermore, concentration upon the "church of the future" had allowed individuals who were not concerned primarily with Lutheran theology—indeed who were not necessarily even members of the Lutheran church—to become members of Lutheran theology faculties. To Kliefoth, such a situation was intolerable. It was a complete misunderstanding of the right to academic freedom and an insult to the Lutheran church in whose service the faculty supposedly labored.[98]

Kliefoth's pamphlet war with the Göttingen faculty was short-lived, but its polemic nature served to highlight Kliefoth's theological position. Where the tone of Kliefoth's remarks to the Göttingen faculty was negative and vitriolic, his treatise, *Eight Books about the Church*, attempted to discuss thoroughly the doctrine of the church, and thus to correct the many errors that he accused his liberal colleagues of holding. In common with his fellow neo-Lutherans August Vilmar and Wilhelm Löhe, Kliefoth saw his era as the age of the church, not simply because of contemporary interest in ecclesiastical issues, but rather in an eschatological sense, for the present age waited upon the fulfillment of the messianic promise and the return of Jesus to earth.

Kliefoth called the church a "living organism" established by God and as such more than a "collection of believing souls," or "an atomistic total of equal individuals." The church was an institution ordained to preach the message of salvation through its properly

---

[96]Ibid., 31.

[97]Ibid., 12-13.

[98]Ibid., 58-59, 70.

constituted orders, offices, and members.[99] Such a theme clearly resonated with the *anstalt* views of theologians like Vilmar, Löhe, or Stahl. In addition to emphasizing the objective nature of the church, Kliefoth allowed for its subjective nature as well. As in his *Introduction to the History of Dogma* with its declaration of the objective and subjective nature of the spirit, Kliefoth insisted in this latter work on the dual nature of the church. His use of organic imagery in his discussion of the church was indicative of his beliefs. Not only did Kliefoth call the church a "living organism," he likened it to an embryo, which "does not develop the single parts out of the whole, but rather through God's creative power is there originally in its constituents and grows in its parts through its mutual effort." Such an organism "is a body not in the way of an aggregate or conglomerate, that is not through a mechanical pinning on of parts to a whole. Instead it has a liveliness and personality, it is something which none of its parts in themselves or the sum total of the parts added together can be. As such a whole, it has properties which neither the single parts nor the sum of them together contains."[100]

Within this organic framework, Kliefoth argued, the church was both a *gemeinde*, the believers gathered together in a collectivity, and an *anstalt*, a holy institution through which the means of grace were administered and the faithful drawn together. Beyond that, it was clear that the relationship of individuals to the subjective side of the church, the *gemeinde*, was determined by their relationship to the objective side, for the "church as a divine institution gathers together the church as a collectivity of believers."[101] Nevertheless, the status of the *gemeinde* was such that any given individual could depart without destroying the unity of the whole. Also, the unity of the subjective features occurred not in a commonality of purpose but in the bonds of a shared moral understanding or ethical perspective. For even when construed in this subjective manner, the church was more like a family bound together by divine word and spirit rather than flesh and blood. Indeed, to compare the church to "an

---

[99]Kliefoth, *Acht Bücher von der Kirche* (Schwerin, 1854) 26-27.

[100]Ibid., 351-52.

[101]Ibid., 238.

association on a par with a railroad society or an industrial company, and differentiated from such associations only in material content," was to misunderstand the nature of the situation.[102]

Kliefoth's emphasis on the Word as a bond was important. As such, the Word was a palpable means of joining together the subjective sphere and insuring its unity. The divine word acted as a bond for the objective side of the church, the *anstalt*, as well. In addition to the Word, the means of grace as they were administered by properly constituted officials served to identify the unity and correctness of the objective side and, hence, to guarantee them. Word, sacraments, and ministerial office properly understood and performed were the critical defenses against error. Again, while Kliefoth allowed for the subjective side of the church, he clearly gave priority to the objective factors.

> The objective existence of the *gemeinde* does not depend upon the subjective faith of the believer. Rather in every case it is brought into being by God's actions through the means of grace. Properly understood this does not mean that "where two or three are gathered," there is the *gemeinde*: but rather where God works through his means of grace, there are the faithful and so there is the *gemeinde*.[103]

For Kliefoth, the church in its dual but unified nature was a vessel for the transmission of divine grace. In itself, it could neither create nor prepare this grace because, according to Kliefoth, grace was already complete. Instead, the church could witness and make means of grace available and properly administer them. Given Kliefoth's stress on the proper performance of the means of grace, it was unsurprising to find him again assailing the Prussian Union as "nothing more than the Calvinization of the Lutheran church."[104]

In discussing the doctrine of the church, Kliefoth expanded upon the themes of availability and of proper administration of the means of grace. Central to his ecclesiology was the concept of the church as a *volkskirche*, a church related to a history and to a people. Along with his image of the *gemeinde* as a family, he spoke of the sub-

---

[102]Ibid., 328-29, 354.

[103]Ibid., 241.

[104]Ibid., 217-18, 416. For Kliefoth's criticism of Roman Catholicism, see 316-19.

jective side of the church in terms of communal and ethnic identity. In this manner Kliefoth affirmed that the individual believer was enmeshed in a series of human ties and ethical responsibilities. Beyond that, however, the means of grace now, after the resurrection of Jesus, were available to all persons and the church conceived of as the *gemeinde* was larger than the body of regenerate believers. Indeed, just as the promise of salvation was a universal one, so had God created the church for all humanity.[105]

In commenting on the church as an institution of a people, Kliefoth reiterated that his construction should not be understood as advocating democracy or popular sovereignty. Indeed, in every discussion of the correct execution of church practice, he clearly differentiated between those in spiritual authority and those in spiritual obedience. It was necessary to set up a church authority in order to establish a proper church order. Such an authority was not a secondary derivative of the means of grace; it was equivalent to them, for it too had been created by divine activity.[106] The Lutheran church, in Kliefoth's view, was properly organized in a hierarchical and episcopal arrangement that recognized that "the church consists only of teachers and listeners, of pastors and parishioners."[107] He disagreed with the legitimacy and applicability of a collegial understanding of the church. Finally, he insisted on the independence of the church from state authority, for the authority of the state and that of the church were two separate spheres of authority in the world. This separation of church and state, he thought, must be maintained in order to preserve the spiritual autonomy and independence of the church.[108] Much as his neo-Lutheran colleagues, Wilhelm Löhe and August Vilmar had done, Theodor Kliefoth in-

---

[105] Ibid., 329-30. For further discussion of the concept of *volkskirche*, see H. Fagerberg, *Bekenntnis, Kirche, und Amt in der deutschen konfessionellen Theologie des 19. Jahrhunderts* (Uppsala, 1952) 265-67; Alfred Adam, *Nationalkirche und Volkskirche in deutschen Protestantismus* (Göttingen, 1938).

[106] Kliefoth, *Acht Bücher*, 369, 397, 29.

[107] Ibid., 416.

[108] Ibid., 29.

sisted upon the spiritual freedom of the divinely established church and the illegitimacy of state interference in internal church affairs.

Responding to the political, social, and above all, religious innovations taking place throughout their society, the neo-Lutherans developed their blueprint of confessional religion and conservative politics. Opposed to the subversion of doctrinal content and creedal adherence furthered by rationalism and pietism alike; critical of attempts at religious union, nondenominational missions, and the diminution of religious obligations; the neo-Lutherans called for a return to confessional statements of faith. Consistent with this stance, they tried to discourage democratizing tendencies within their society and sought to restore and revive an older corporate conception of society. Their position was not simply one of theological and political repristination. In their insistence that the Lutheran church was part of the Christian church as a whole, that it was part of a theological tradition and institution older than Luther, the neo-Lutherans betrayed their indebtedness to romanticism as well as to other prominent nineteenth-century intellectual trends. Their support for the spiritual independence of the church, even if it meant financial as well as administrative separation from the state, also signaled their entrance into the modern world.

PART THREE

ENGLAND

CHAPTER FOUR

THE ESTABLISHMENT BESIEGED

A CONSTITUTIONAL REVOLUTION, 1828-1832

On the evening of 18 June 1828, a gala banquet filled the great hall of the Freemason Tavern in London. The occasion was the celebration of the recent repeal of the Test and Corporation Acts. Over four hundred guests attended, with the Duke of Sussex, accompanied by nine peers and forty-three Members of Parliament, presiding over the festivities. In the midst of the dinner the duke rose and proposed a toast to his fellow guests in the name of "the event we are met to celebrate . . . the triumph of Religious Freedom and Christian Charity in the abolition of the Sacramental Test." Upon finishing this round he motioned in the direction of one of the peers and proposed another, "Speedy and effectual relief to all His Majesty's Subjects who still labour under any legal disabilities on account of their Religion." He was alluding to the Roman Catholics' situation in England and Ireland, and his meaning was clear to all present that evening. The whole company rose and applauded the duke's words.[1]

The religious climate in England was changing. The years 1828-1832 witnessed important ecclesiastical alterations as the winds of reform buffeted the stronghold of Anglican orthodoxy. In rapid succession the repeal of the Test and Corporation Acts in 1828, Roman Catholic emancipation in 1829, and the Reform Bill in 1831-1832 all signified a revolution in church-state relations. Those events also symbolized a frank recognition of religious diversity, which marked the end of the assumption of uniformity within English religious life. While these constitutional changes were taking place, Tories and Whigs alike undertook a comprehensive revision of the parish system, addressed the problems of education, and modified the Protestant church in Ireland. As the following chapter demonstrates, these changes represented a major transformation of centuries-old ecclesiastical arrangements, which many thought were overdue. Religious reforms paralleled political ones as politicians inside and outside the government joined other groups in pressing for reform. Within the sphere of religion, demands for reform ranged from acknowledgment of the need for slight adjustments to militant appeals for complete disestablishment. Similarly, the reform effort attracted participants from a wide spectrum of beliefs. Evangelicals, Benthamite radicals, and Anglican liberals (along with their Dissenting brethren) found themselves working toward similar goals.

The celebrants in June 1828 might well have been satisfied with the direction ecclesiastical reform was to take from 1828-1832. They probably would have agreed with those who hoped that these reforms would continue after the Reform Bill was passed. Not all Britons, however, exultantly hailed these innovations and their implications. Bemoaned one observer in 1834:

> Three of the great embankments of our constitution have recently been cut through, one in 1828, another in 1829, and a third in 1831. The first broke down the long-established qualifications for office in our Christian state; the second *let in*, as *legislators*, men implacably hostile to the one great living

---

[1]See the account given by Bernard Manning, *The Protestant Dissenting Deputies* (Cambridge, 1952) 248.

principle of all our institutions; the third, as a natural consequence of the two former, poured into the House of Commons . . . the turbid waters of sheer *mammonry*, democracy, and republicanism.[2]

The writer's fears for the House of Commons were exaggerated, but there is no doubt that his observations were consonant with the feelings of many High Churchmen and that they correctly signaled a profound shift in English political and religious experience. For the passage of Dissenter and Catholic relief bills marked a crucial stage in England's transition from an age of toleration to an age of religious equality. In so doing, it testified to the collapse of two assumptions: 1)that England's Christian, or at least Protestant, population shared a unity of practice, and 2)that church and state were equal partners in authority. Religious diversity, institutional expansion among an exploding population, and reevaluation of the relation of church and state appeared as hallmarks of the day. And before these social tremors had ceased to shake the Anglican church and hierarchy, not only would a renovated church emerge, but out of the University at Oxford a movement for religious restoration would arise.

This was to be the battle, but in 1828 the lines of opposition were still forming. The repeal of the Test and Corporation Acts was a significant advance for non-Anglican Protestant (Dissenter) Englishmen and their struggle for religious and civil equality. The core of the Dissenters was made up of Presbyterians, Congregationalists, and Baptists, with Quakers, Unitarians, and later, Methodists, allied to their cause. Ever since the Elizabethan Settlement of the sixteenth century, the Anglican church had been recognized as the official national church of the realm. Uniformity of religious practice was expected and the church and state were, at least in theory, inextricably linked and coextensive in authority. Toleration of Dissenting practice was deemed neither advisable nor correct. A crisis occurred with the English Civil War, as James II turned against the national Anglican church, thereby questioning its privileged position and

---

[2]See the anonymous letter in the *British Magazine* 6 (September 1834): 273. Norman Gash further discusses the nature of English society in his recent study, *Aristocracy and People: Britain 1815-1865* (Cambridge, 1979).

destroying the illusion of a unified religious practice. The Toleration Act of 1688 officially recognized the existence of Dissenters but did not remove the burdens of civil disabilities and the social stigma of exclusion. The Corporation Act of 1661, for example, barred from membership in municipal, commercial, and charitable corporations anyone refusing to receive communion according to the rites of the Church of England. If such a person had not taken communion in this manner within a year before his election to such a corporation, his election was void. Under the Test Act of 1673 Dissenters were disqualified from holding offices under royal, civil, or military authority. Here again, taking the sacraments according to the rites of the Church of England, in this case within three months prior to assuming office, was the criterion of eligibility. Neither of these statutes was affected by the passage of the Toleration Act in 1688. Further restrictive legislation was passed forbidding groups of more than four persons from assembling within a private household for non-Anglican religious worship (Conventicle Act, 1664), excluding Dissenting ministers and schoolmasters from towns (Five Mile Act, 1665), and making illegal all weddings except those celebrated by Anglican clergy (Hardwicke Act, 1753). Finally, the Occasional Conformity Act of 1711 defeated the strictures of the Corporation and Test Acts by allowing the Anglican orthodoxy to punish Dissenters who occasionally received communion in the Church of England. The Occasional Conformity Act imposed heavy fines on municipal or royal officeholders who attended Dissenting services after they had received communion in the Anglican church.[3]

The ascendancy of the Whigs in the wake of the Jacobite disturbances in 1715 brought about the repeal of the Occasional Conformity Act and the passage of the first Indemnity Act in 1727. Passed almost every year thereafter, the Indemnity acts reduced the difficulties of the Dissenters by suspending for a year at a time the provisions and penalties of the Test Act. The Dissenters won a significant legal victory in 1767 in the so-called Sheriff's Cause. It had

---

[3]See the discussion in Ursula Henriques, *Religious Toleration in England, 1787-1833* (Toronto, 1961) 5-13.

been the practice of certain municipal corporations to harass Dissenters by appointing them to offices, such as that of sheriff, which they could not legally or conscientiously discharge, and then fining them for their refusal. In a suit between the city of London and a group of Dissenters, the court ruled that Dissenters were allowed to object to these appointments without fear of fine or reprisal. Similarly, in 1811 a bill proposed by Lord Sidmouth restricting licensing of Dissenting ministers was defeated. After Sidmouth's bill failed, both the Five Mile Act and the Conventicle Act were repealed. In the case of the Conventicle Act the limit of persons able to meet for non-Anglican religious purposes within a private dwelling was raised to twenty.

Despite these legal victories, the forces of heterodoxy were still subject to waves of popular outrage, such as occurred in the 1790s. In the wake of the reaction against the French Revolution, the assaults by Dissenters, especially Unitarians, on the Anglican establishment were not taken lightly. In Birmingham in July 1791, three Dissenting meetinghouses were torn down; Joseph Priestley's house, complete with manuscripts and scientific instruments, was burned; and the homes of other known Dissenters were threatened. Destruction of this sort was not often repeated, but the pointed warning of a Manchester address in 1795 was clear enough:

> They who disregard their maker, and the duty they owe to him—revile the sacred writings—despise religious ordinances—contemn the adorable Redeemer of men—and scoff at revealed religion, have but very little claim to tenderness of conscience.[4]

After the furor of the 1790s had died down, the Dissenters returned to their efforts to repeal the Corporation and Test Acts. A petition of 1820 submitted by Lord Henry Holland and William Smith articulated nicely the basic premises of the Dissenters' claim to repeal. The Dissenters' argument was fourfold. First, they built a historical case by recalling Dissenter loyalty to the House of Hanover, particularly during the Jacobite incidents still fresh in popular

---

[4]See Raymond Cowherd, *The Politics of English Dissent* (New York, 1956) 24-25; W. R. Ward, *Religion and Society in England, 1790-1850* (New York, 1972) 23-24. The Manchester address is quoted by Ward on page 24.

memory. Then, they developed a theory of absolute natural rights, central to which, they claimed, was the principle of private judgment in religious matters. Holland and Smith then noted that dispensation through the Indemnity acts left the Dissenters insecure and shamed them publicly as persons unworthy of office. Finally, the Dissenters argued that using the sacraments as the criterion for officeholding was a travesty and a scandal. It debased the sacrament in the eyes of many sincerely religious individuals, and ridiculed its sacred meaning. The use of this test, moreover, while it deterred the honest and scrupulous, was no bar to the fraudulent and unprincipled.[5]

Thoughtful, reasonable, and in tune with the times, the Dissenters' case was a strong one. But their opponents both within and without the Anglican hierarchy also had a well-constructed position, one that turned on more than an appeal to past practice and one that included its own set of historical and theoretical arguments. Defenders of the existence of a closed established religion argued that establishment promoted salvation by maintaining uniform religious practice and unified religious belief. Reminiscent of past generations that saw in the sufferance of heterodoxy an invitation to heresy and discord, these nineteenth-century defenders were slow to admit that changing times demanded changing viewpoints. Grudgingly they conceded that changed circumstances demanded recognition of religious dissent and the toleration, if not equality, that it implied. "To tolerate is to allow that which is not approved—to suffer that which is not and ought not to be encouraged," wrote the conservative social commentator, Robert Southey, "and no more dissenters ought to expect or ask, more being inconsistent with the fundamental principles of any constitution whereof religion is part."[6] Southey clearly expressed the second orthodox assumption, that by encouraging social and political authority in town and country, an established church promoted social order. "Nothing is more certain than that religion is the basis upon which civil government rests," Southey declared, "And it is necessary that this re-

[5]Manning, *Protestant Dissenting Deputies*, 221-22.

[6]Robert Southey, *Quarterly Review* 38 (July-October 1828): 550.

ligion be established for the security of the state, and for the welfare of the people."[7] From these two premises conservatives drew the corollary that just as there is or ought to be only one religious truth, and just as sacred and civic authority were confirmed in one another, so established religion provided the necessary and visible unity of church and state authority.

For Tory theorists of the established church the institutions of church and state were linked—indeed, they covered the same ground. And membership in the secular commonwealth ought to imply simultaneous membership in the religious community. Against those charges, brought especially by revivalists and Methodists, that the church was failing to meet the pressing challenge of social dislocation, urban growth, and political unrest, conservative defenders replied, with no small degree of pique and smugness, that the old ways were best and would yet serve the church in this latest struggle. To Tory apologists for the Church not popular ferment nor accountability to an electorate but the wisdom and stability of tradition were the beacon lights by which public and ecclesiastical policy ought to be guided. Moreover, as Lord Liverpool more directly stated, "in truth many of the staunchest Friends of the Establishment have a sort of Religious Respect for whatever is old, and connected with established Habits or preconceived Opinions, and they dread all Changes for this further Reason, that they are aware what Advantages may be taken of them by those whose only object is to destroy."[8]

The debate appeared stalemated. The situation, however, changed dramatically when a bill to repeal the Corporation and Test Acts was passed and was given the royal assent on 9 May 1828. Debate over the bill had echoed the arguments and pamphleteering of the preceding decades. In the broad view of Bishop John Kaye, "the Repeal of the Sacramental Test was a concession, not exclusively to the feeling and wishes of our Dissenting brethren, but also to the

---

[7]Robert Southey, *Sir Thomas More: or, Colloquies of the Progress and Prospects of Society*, 2 vols. (London, 1829) 2:47-48.

[8]Liverpool to Peel, 24 January 1821, as quoted by G. F. Best, *Temporal Pillars* (Cambridge, 1964) 177. See the general discussion, 172-79.

conscientious scruples of many sincere Churchmen."[9] In its final form the Repeal Act was a compromise in which the sacramental test was replaced by an oath "on the true faith of a Christian" not to subvert or disturb the established church during the length of holding office. Consequently, the bill contained a residual discrimination against Dissenting Protestants and provided no relief at all to Jews or, on account of other complications, to Roman Catholics. Yet a telling blow had been struck against the Anglican establishment, and its significance was agreed upon, even if its implications were disputed. "It really is a gratifying thing," Lord John Russell wrote in 1828, "to force the enemy to give up his front line, that none but churchmen are worthy to serve the state, and I trust we shall soon make him give up the second, that none but protestants are." Less sanguine by contrast was the High Churchman, Reverend Walter Hook, when he gloomily concluded in 1831, "I refer our calamities to the repeal of the Test Act; for then the State *virtually* renounced any connection with religion."[10]

As Lord Russell implied, defenders of the established church retreated and regrouped, preparing to do battle once again over the issue of Catholic relief from civil disabilities. Many more than Lord Russell saw the link between concessions to Dissenters and relief for Roman Catholics. And the successful repeal of the Test and Corporation Acts, seen in conjunction with the several years of Catholic appeal, suggested to advocates of extended religious equality that the time was ripe for reform. Most participants in the debate over Roman Catholic emancipation recognized that the situation and issues concerning the Catholics were not the same as those concerning the Dissenters. Catholic citizens had not been subject to the Indemnity acts as their Dissenting counterparts had been. Furthermore, Catholics were debarred from officeholding not only by the Test and Corporation Act, but by the provisions of the royal coro-

----

[9]Kaye is quoted by John Overton, *The English Church in the Nineteenth Century* (London, 1894) 307.

[10]Russell to Thomas More, 31 March 1828, as quoted by G. I. T. Machin, *The Catholic Question in English Politics, 1820-1830* (Oxford, 1964) 115. Hook to A. P. Perceval, 25 May 1831, *The Life and Letters of W. F. Hook*, ed. W. R. Stephens, 2 vols. (London 1879) 1:221.

nation oath wherein the sovereign agreed to uphold the Church of England by law established. Finally, the Catholic question involved the issue of Ireland, and it was to be this factor that finally precipitated a parliamentary crisis and applied the leverage necessary to win passage of a relief bill.

The political groups involved, pro or con, with the issue of Catholic emancipation were more diverse than those that had been involved with the Test and Corporation Acts. To be sure, there were the ultra-Protestant Tories, who were as opposed (if not more opposed) to relief of Catholics as they had been to relief of Dissenters. To them, the attack on the Anglican character of the English constitution had been an unconscionable assault, but the move against the Protestant foundation was a blow at the constitution's very roots.[11] The settlement of 1689 with its Protestant ascendancy, its popular cries of "No Popery," and its belabored equations of English success and Roman Catholic defeats pervaded this argument. Furthermore, supporters of the idea of the Protestant constitution charged that Catholics, like Dissenters, not only enjoyed liberal toleration, but were more widely indulged than they themselves would have permitted of other religions had the Catholics been in power. Roman Catholicism, they charged, prohibited diverse religious practices and belief where it ruled; Catholic claims to religious equality were thus little more than hypocrisy. Finally, they said, Roman Catholic citizens were always torn between their allegiance to their English sovereign and their allegiance to the Pope. "The admission of Papists into Parliament is contrary to the fundamental laws of our Protestant constitution," Bishop Burgess wrote to the Duke of Wellington in 1829, "the admission of persons into Parliament who are subjects of the Pope, and refuse to acknowledge the King's ecclesiastical supremacy, is to recognize in these realms that foreign jurisdiction which by the laws of Church and State we deny to exist."[12] Consequently, as a group, the ultra-Protestant Tories

---

[11]See the discussion by G. F. Best, "The Protestant Constitution and Its Supporters, 1800-1829," *Transactions of the Royal Historical Society*, 5th ser., 8 (London, 1958):105-27.

[12]Burgess to Wellington, 26 February 1829, as quoted by Best, "The Protestant Constitution," 113.

consistently opposed any liberalizing of their demand for religious uniformity; their arguments, varying little over the years, resonated with a popular anti-Catholicism that continued into the mid-nineteenth century.[13]

The evangelical, or revivalist, portion of the Church of England was the Anglican counterpart to German pietism. While generally they had supported the campaign for relief of Dissenter disabilities, prominent individuals such as Granville Sharp, Zachary Macaulay, and Hannah More opposed Catholic emancipation. Yet for every Macaulay or More there was a William Wilberforce favoring relief, and by 1829 evangelicals in Parliament strongly supported emancipation.[14] As for the Dissenters themselves, there was a variety of opinion. Almost unanimously, Methodists opposed any measure of relief for Catholics. Many other Dissenters, above all the Dissenting Deputies, a political vanguard located in London, recognized the common interests demonstrated by Dissenting and Catholic claims, and supported the Catholic cause after their own had been won.[15] As for the Whigs, they consistently supported relief for both causes. The Whig commitment to religious liberty was prominent and undiscriminating. Members hoped that with the amelioration of religious strife, energies might be turned to serving the state.[16]

Yet ever since 1801 and the Act of Union between Ireland and Britain, the issue of Roman Catholic emancipation had taken on a new color. Throughout the first two decades of the nineteenth century all attempts to secure emancipation had failed. Anger over the failure boiled among Irish and English Catholics, and friction be-

---

[13]See the discussion by G. F. Best, "Popular Protestantism in Victorian Britain," in *Ideas and Institutions of Victorian Britain*, ed. Robert Robson (London, 1967) 115-42.

[14]See J. H. Hexter, "The Protestant Revival and the Catholic Question in England, 1778-1829," *Journal of Modern History* 8, no. 3 (September 1936): 306-307.

[15]See R. W. Davis, "The Strategy of 'Dissent' in the Repeal Campaign, 1820-1828," *Journal of Modern History* 38, no. 4 (December 1966): 374-93.

[16]See G. F. Best, "Establishment in the Age of Grey and Holland," *History* 95, no. 154 (June 1960): 103-18.

tween the militant Catholic Association and the ultra-Protestant Orange Society threatened civil war in Ireland.[17] Election of Daniel O'Connell for county Clare in 1828 precipitated the confrontation between supporters and foes of the Catholic cause. O'Connell's election forced the hand of the ministry at Westminster and presented Wellington with a dilemma. He could support the Protestant ascendancy and risk civil war in Ireland. Probably, if O'Connell could get elected so could other Irish Catholics. These would-be representatives together with their supporters, drawn largely from the forty-shilling freehold class, could tear apart the Union if their claims were not met. Alternately, both Wellington and Robert Peel publicly opposed Catholic relief and ardently supported the Protestant church in Ireland. In the end, however, Wellington and Peel reversed their position, hoping to avoid war and realizing that practical statesmanship required as speedy a settlement as possible.

With fear of an uprising in Ireland uppermost, the Wellington ministry brought forward a bill for emancipation. Given Wellington's previous opposition to such a measure, his sponsorship perplexed many fellow Tories, as one pro-Catholic Member of Parliament described it:

> All the High Church Tories, Peers, Bishops and M.P.s are in a quandary—some facing about at the Duke's command and without hesitation, though with evident shame—others pretending to be squeamish . . . only waiting for time to come round decently, others more bigoted and therefore more honest. We Liberals are dying with Laughter at the just confusion and shame, to which . . . Selfishness and Intolerance are at length met.[18]

In the end, a majority in both Houses did come round, but not before other issues had been settled. First had been the development of some sort of security measure that would insure that Catholic

---

[17]For a full discussion of the Irish situation see James Reynolds, *The Catholic Emancipation Crisis in Ireland, 1823-1829* (New Haven, 1954); Donald Akenson, *The Church of Ireland: Ecclesiastical Reform and Revolution, 1800-1835* (New Haven, 1971). For a discussion of the situation of English Catholics, see Robert Linker, "The English Roman Catholics and Emancipation: The Politics of Persuasion," *Journal of Ecclesiastical History*, 27, no. 2 (April 1976): 151-80.

[18]For an analysis of Wellington's pragmatic stance on emancipation, see G. I. T. Machin, "The Duke of Wellington and Catholic Emancipation," *Journal of Ecclesiastical History*, 14, no. 2 (October 1963): 190-208. The quotation is on page 205.

Parliament Members, once seated, would not disturb or weaken the Anglican church. While plans of vetoes, concordats with the Vatican, and other means of control had been discussed, the following arrangement was proposed. Any Catholic renouncing the temporal power of the Pope and promising not to harm the church would be eligible for any parliamentary office but Regent, Lord Chancellor both of England and Ireland, Lord Lieutenant of Ireland, and certain other offices attached to church establishments, ecclesiastical courts, and schools. In exchange for such emancipation, a second major bargain was struck. Wellington insisted on and received authorization to suppress the Catholic Association and to raise the electoral qualifications in Ireland from forty shillings to ten pounds.[19]

Such securities as these would not satisfy the ultra-Protestants. Having failed to prevent the bill's progress or to win exhaustive safeguards, they still hoped to influence the king to refuse consent to any such relief bill. Opponents of emancipation argued that the royal coronation oath to support the established church prevented George IV from consenting to the bill. George IV, though, was hardly a stronghold of moral and spiritual certitude. Mocked by Wellington as an "old fool sometimes tormented by the gout, at others stupified by laudanum," the king vacillated, finally acceding to the duke's pressure and giving his consent on 13 April 1829.[20] When it was settled, emancipation of Catholics—like relief for Dissenters—represented a compromise. For in 1829 it was clear that wishes for religious liberty and age-old fears of divided allegiance and Jesuitical subversion both fell before the pragmatic desire to avoid strife in Ireland. So too did emancipation come at the cost of the suppression and disenfranchisement of the very forces, the forty-shilling freeholders, who had finally brought about relief. If the Parliament was now to include non-Anglicans, dissolving the assumption of identity between secular and religious establishments, then Tory statesmen such as Wellington and Peel were going to in-

---

[19]Machin, *Catholic Emancipation*, 160, 169, 173.

[20]Wellington is quoted in Hexter, "The Protestant Revival," 303.

sure that authority would still reside securely in the hands of respectable property owners.

The passage of the Reform Bill in 1832 affected the Church of
England. Although the bill did not alter the church as immediately
as had the two repeal acts of 1828 and 1829, it nevertheless por-
tended changes as thorough. Summarizing the significance of the
electoral reforms, especially as they followed upon the relief efforts,
the Duke of Wellington commented:

> The revolution is made, that is to say, that power is transferred from one
> class of society, the gentlemen of England, professing the faith of the
> Church of England, to another class of society, the shopkeepers, being dis-
> senters from the Church, many of them Socinians, others atheists. . . . I do
> not think that the influence of property in this country is in the abstract di-
> minished, that is to say, that the gentry have as many followers and influence
> as many voters at elections as ever they did. But a new democratic influence
> has been introduced into elections . . . these are all dissenters from the
> Church, and are everywhere a formidably active party against the aristo-
> cratic influence of the Landed Gentry.[21]

The emergence of this politically powerful middle-class voting
strength coincided with a current low public esteem for the Church.
Indeed, in the aftermath of the campaign for Catholic emancipation when the ultra-Protestants had withdrawn support from Wellington's ministry, the Whigs assumed control of the government
with a mandate to carry out additional societal reform. That such
reform would continue and that it would include further ecclesiastical revision seemed self-evident to many observers. For with the
passage of the Reform bill the Whig majority demonstrated its interest and determination to carry out an ecclesiastical houseclean-
ing. If Tory theorists had earlier argued that church and state were
coextensive, then Whig reformers in the 1830s saw political reform
requiring religious reform as well. In short, a rotten borough could
refer as easily to an ecclesiastical living as to a political safety, and
thus when Lord Grey told the bishops to set their house in order, he
was only making explicit what many assumed the church's future
agenda already contained.

---

[21]Wellington to J. Wilson Croker, *The Correspondence and Diaries of John Wilson
Croker*, ed. Louis Jennings, 3 vols. (London, 1884) 2:205-206.

PRESSURES FOR REFORM: DISSENTERS, EVANGELICALS, AND LIBERALS

A whole raft of major issues filled the reformer's program for the church. Central to these was the sorry state of the parish system in general. Under this heading came the abuses of nonresidence and pluralism (that is, holding more than one church living simultaneously), the virtual abandonment of tithe collection, the abysmal record of church-rate payment, and the more diffuse problems seen most poignantly in the new towns with their sprawling populations—a problem simply referred to as "the condition of England question." Related to the problem of the parish system yet separate from it was the problem of education. Whether one considered the competition between religious societies over primary education or the competition between Dissenters and Anglicans over entrance requirements for Oxford and Cambridge universities, education seemed ripe for reform. Then there was the nagging question of the Protestant church in Ireland. In its own way the Irish church exemplified all the problems besetting its English counterpart, yet its minimal membership made its problems more intense and its existence more precarious.

Pressure for these church reforms came from several sources. There was the popular backlash directed at the episcopal hierarchy. Because the bishops in the House of Lords had opposed the Reform bill in 1831, they became the target of popular animosity and outrage. In October 1831 the House of Lords had rejected the bill by a substantial majority, a margin swelled by the overwhelming opposition of the bishops. For their actions the episcopal hierarchy was roundly criticized by Whigs and Dissenters. "Englishmen—remember that it was the bishops, and the bishops only, whose vote decided the fate of the Reform Bill"—this was the message of placards, handbills, and Whig newspapers alike. The bishops were heckled, hooted, and shouted down in meetings, the bishop of Carlisle was burnt in effigy by a crowd of eight thousand, and the episcopal residence at Bristol was burned to the ground. The bishops' intransigence had further repercussions. After the bill was defeated in 1831, Whig politicians lobbied the king to create a new bloc of peers who might overrule the clerics. Initially the king refused to intervene in this manner. Lord Grey resigned and the Whig government fell. Wellington, however, found himself unable to form a new government. Grey returned with the assurance that the king would cooperate. The threat of the creation of new peers, however, was sufficient to cow the opposition in the House of Lords. In June 1832 when the Reform bill again reached the House of Lords, it passed without a single bishop opposing it.[22]

Compulsory support of the Anglican clergy and church through church-rate and tithe was another mark against the established church. As signs of the times and symbols of discontent, these issues alone could have marshaled anti-ecclesiastical sentiment. Tithe collection was, even in the best of years, dependent in its practical operation on smooth relations with the parson's neighboring farmers. Yet as the 1830s began, farm harvests and prices were as low as they had been in the immediately preceding years. This situation spelled trouble. With prices dropping and no relief in sight, tempers rose. At the start of the 1830s rural unrest broke out in Kent and spread north as far as Norfolk. "Things are still in a bad way down here," wrote the Tory churchman Hurrell Froude from his home at Dartington,

> the labouring population, as well as the farmers, seem thoroughly indifferent to the welfare of the parsons and squires: and this does not seem at all to depend on their situation in respect to poverty, or in the way in which they have been treated. . . . Two very great fires have taken place in our neighborhood, and, for three or four nights, we expected that our threshing machine would be set on fire.[23]

Country parsons faced a sensitive situation, especially when the farmers convinced the laborers that any wage increases were blocked by the size of the tithe. The farmers in East Kent, for example, petitioned, "That at the present alarming crisis, it is the duty of the landowners and clergy, by a liberal abatement of rent and

---

[22]See Owen Chadwick, *The Victorian Church*, 2 vols. (London, 1966-1970) 1:27-32; W. Mathieson, *English Church Reform, 1815-1840* (London, 1923) 50.

[23]R. Froude, *Remains of the late Reverend Richard Hurrell Froude*, ed. John Newman and John Keble, 4 vols. (London, 1838-1839) 1:245-46.

tithes, to assist the farmers."[24] Such an agricultural alliance would not last very long, but it affected rural church establishment.

The church-rate, by contrast, was largely an urban problem, born of the tremendous expansion of the cities and the growth of Dissenting bodies. The church-rate was a tax to maintain the church and churchyard in good repair. It was voted on each Easter in the local parish vestry meeting. The parish was legally liable to keep the church in good condition; however, if a majority of the parish refused to approve the tax at the vestry meeting, it was not clear if they could be compelled to do so. The Anglican establishment in Ireland had long faced opposition over rates. Now in 1832, a majority of the vestry of St. Martin's church in Birmingham registered their discontent and refused to vote a church-rate for the following year.[25]

The anger of non-Anglicans at the Church of England was not necessarily new nor was it always well focused. In the hands of the growing Dissenter population, however, the cry for disestablishment of the church was articulated in a manner that none could mistake. "I do not want to reform the church," a Dissenting minister in Leeds said, "I want to pull it down."[26] A new militancy on the part of Dissenters was apparent. This group, now emboldened and enfranchised by their recent parliamentary victories, pressed further their claims for full civic and religious equality. The number of Dissenters was growing in England. By 1820 they formed thirty percent of the Protestant population of England and Wales; by mid-century the number of their chapels and buildings approximated that of the established church. A Dissenter by the name of Faithfull secured sixty-seven votes in the House of Commons for a motion to dismiss bishops from the House of Lords. The Protestant Dissenting Deputies likewise championed the separation of church and state and exerted pressure for the cause at their London center. The Dissent-

---

[24]Quoted by Ward, *Religion and Society in England*, 123. For a full discussion see W. R. Ward, "The Tithe Question in England in the Early Nineteenth Century," *Journal of Ecclesiastical History* 14, no. 1 (April 1965): 67-81.

[25]Ward, *Religion and Society in England*, 178-82.

[26]*British Magazine* 5 (February 1834): 257.

ers' new vitality found clear expression in these lines by a group of Unitarians:

> Besieged as the Church of England is on all sides, her defenders would do well to capitulate, whilst honorable terms may be had, and not to wait from indolence or obstinacy or false pride until the Establishment is stormed by popular indignation which is fast gathering around the dilapidated edifice.[27]

Allied to the Dissenters in their agitation for change were the "philosophic radicals" or Benthamite utilitarians. The utilitarians had consistently supported relief for Dissenters and Roman Catholics, but such programs were in fact only initial measures toward their ultimate goal of complete disestablishment. Among the voluminous writings of Jeremy Bentham, two short pieces, *Church of Englandism and the catechism examined*, first published in 1818, and *Analysis of the influence of natural religion on the temporal happiness of mankind*, which appeared in 1822, contain the Benthamite critique of religion. Bentham believed that religion was above all a system of supernatural and posthumous rewards and punishments. Yet because, according to him, religion had produced more harm than good for humanity, it did not pass the utilitarian test requiring the greatest good for the greatest number. Also, he argued, religion was used as a means of enforcing social order—it was the spiritual arm of the temporal constabulary. Such an effect not only bred passive citizens deaf to the reformist appeals of the utilitarians, it furnished an opportunity for the growth of that "sinister influence," the clergy.

Invested with the authority to interpret this system of eternal bliss or damnation, the clergy was naturally allied with the forces of the state. As such, these twin powers collaborated, for "all sinister interests have a natural tendency to combine together and to co-operate, inasmuch as the object of each is thereby most completely and easily secured. But between the particular interest of a governing aristocracy and a sacerdotal class, there seems a very peculiar affin-

---

[27]Quoted by Ward, *Religion and Society in England*, 126. See the general discussion by Ward, 125-31; Chadwick, *Victorian Church*, 1:61-62; Gash, *Aristocracy and People*, 63-64.

ity and co-incidence."[28] The result of this alliance was the miserable story of persecution and intolerance in which "all *powers* are *real* and all *checks* are *nominal*."[29]

To Bentham, religion had two lamentable consequences for society. First, individuals were often punished for allegedly harmful beliefs, rather than for actual deeds committed against society. Second, religious belief tended to divide societies, splitting them up into believers and unbelievers, and then further into mutually antagonistic sects. These consequences made disestablishment necessary. The Benthamites added their voices to the chorus of those calling for church reform. With the establishment besieged and the armies of voluntaryism and disestablishment all but storming the ramparts, many churchmen agreed with the liberal theologian, Thomas Arnold, when he scornfully concluded, "the Church, as it now stands, no human power can save."[30]

To the Dissenters' and Benthamites' calls for reform were added the voices of evangelicals and liberals. The evangelicals were the descendants of an early eighteenth-century revivalist movement, first associated with John Wesley and later strengthened with the Methodist separation from the established church. Breaking with what they regarded as the cold abstract rationalism of Anglican theology and its numbingly ritualized devotional practices, evangelicals preached a simple message of the recognition of sin, faith in Jesus, and sanctification by the Holy Spirit. In *The Complete Duty of Man*, an esteemed counsel of piety written by Henry Venn, the elder, in 1763, is found a clear admonition not to confuse the truth and practice of "the national religion," no matter how fervently believed or practiced, with real religious concerns. For unless religion confronts the individual with his or her own sinful nature and calls upon the sinner to beseech Jesus for mercy and forgiveness, only a charade of

---

[28]Jeremy Bentham [Philip Beauchamp, pseud.] *Analysis of the Influence of Natural Religion on the Temporal Happiness of Mankind* (London, 1822) 137.

[29]Jeremy Bentham, *Church of Englandism and its Catechism Examined* (London, 1818) 246. For an analysis of Bentham's views on religion, see E. Halevy, *The Growth of Philosophic Radicalism* (Boston, 1955) 293-94.

[30]*The Life and Correspondence of Thomas Arnold*, ed. A. P. Stanley, 2 vols. (Boston, 1860) 1:283.

religious truth has been represented.[31] Not faithful attendance at church but heartfelt recognition of sin and forgiveness—this was the mark of the real Christian in the eyes of the evangelical. For "it is the peculiar glory of the gospel," Venn maintained, "to humble every believer in the dust, and to fill him with the most dreadful apprehension of sin, in order to raise him from his dead state, and to establish him in obedience from love to God, from holy admiration of his perfections, and from an earnest desire to be partaker of his blessedness."[32]

Venn's invective against formalist or nominal Christianity was a standard feature of evangelical diagnosis of the state of English religion. As often as real and nominal Christianity was contrasted, so was that contrast followed with a call to the "saving faith" that would place this earthly life into its proper perspective. Venn called on his readers to realize the insignificance of "every thing which the children of men seek with the greatest anxiety to enjoy," and recognize that the salvation of the soul was humanity's true concern. Venn enjoined the supplicant to read and study the Scriptures, the only infallible source of knowledge concerning faith and grace. No longer need one turn to abstract systems of reasoning. Within the evangelical framework, empirical observation interpreted by way of Scripture could provide cosmological understanding. The evangelical system thus built upon this premise of human sinfulness a theory of mercy and righteousness that all could understand and follow.[33]

Henry Venn was a pioneer of the evangelical movement, along with John Hervey, William Grimshaw, John Berridge, and William Romaine. Each of these men was familiar with the story of John Wesley and his founding in 1729 of the Holy Club at Oxford for prayer and study of the Scriptures, as well as with Wesley's conversion experience at the Moravian meetinghouse on Aldersgate Street ten years later. Like many early evangelicals these men shared with

---

[31]Henry Venn, *The Complete Duty of Man* (London, 1763; reprint, New York, 1836) 32-33.

[32]Ibid., 4-5.

[33]Ibid., 6, 10.

the Wesleyan movement several of the same revivalistic techniques and faced many of the same ecclesiastical challenges. Indeed, whether it was preaching out of doors or praying within the home, suffering harrassment and persecution under the Conventicle Act or striking a balance over the Calvinist controversy of the 1740s, first-generation evangelicals and Methodists shared much in common. The one issue that most clearly distinguished the two groups was that of itinerancy versus loyalty to the parochial system of the Church of England. Could ministers be permitted to preach beyond the boundaries of their own parish without proper authorization, or should all clergymen be restricted to efforts in their own churches? John Berridge forcefully defended itinerancy for "sure there is a cause," he wrote, "when souls are perishing for lack of knowledge. Must salvation give place to a fanciful decency, and sinners go flocking to hell through our dread of irregularity?"[34]

Whatever the merits of Berridge's depiction of the state of England's soul, itinerancy and circuit riding remained the mark of the Methodists; upon John Wesley's death and the loss of his powerful and dominant personality, the forces for separation finally and officially broke with the Church of England. Both the potential of the evangelical movement and the problems that characterized it could be seen in its formative period. William Grimshaw in the north and John Berridge in the midlands were strong, somewhat eccentric personalities. Both maintained a moderate Calvinism, typical of evangelicals, and itinerated from their own parishes. They were on familiar terms with both Methodist and evangelical leaders, and both camps claimed them for their own. Other evangelical preachers were John Newton of Olney and his successor, Thomas Scott. Newton's adventurous life, in which he deserted from the British navy, became a slave-trader, was sold as a slave himself, was converted in 1748, returned to England, and married his childhood sweetheart, was hardly the prototype for most evangelicals. Yet in his vivid and forceful sermons, Newton's descriptions of his early

---

[34]Berridge to John Thornton, 10 August 1774, as quoted by Charles Smyth, *Simeon and Church Order* (Cambridge, 1940) 250. For the early history of revivalism in England, see John Walsh, "Origins of the Evangelical Revival," in *Essays in Modern Church History*, ed. G. V. Bennett and J. D. Walsh (New York, 1966) 132-62.

life and rescue from barbarism were but a metaphor in the minds of evangelicals for every individual's battle against the slavery of sin.[35]

Thomas Scott succeeded Newton at Olney but his curacy was short-lived; he soon moved to London. In this era London was not an especially hospitable venue for evangelicals. William Romaine was probably the best-known evangelical centered at London in this early period. He was associated with Methodism early in his life but remained within the Church of England when the Methodist secession took place. Romaine's situation typified the dilemmas facing many evangelical churchmen. If they stayed within the Church, as Romaine did, they might find it difficult to obtain a parish. The bishops might refuse to assign them or the parishioners might balk at accepting the strict regimen associated with evangelicalism. Dissenting chapels were an alternative but, while they did exist, preaching in them amounted to breaking with Mother Church. Beyond that, there was the problem of licensing the chapels and the ministers in order to avoid being prosecuted under the conventicle legislation. One way out of this quandary was to be appointed a lecturer to a church or private chapel. This was an avenue often used by evangelicals, and it was in this capacity that Romaine served for nearly forty-six years as the lecturer at St. Dunstans in London. When Thomas Scott arrived in London in 1795, he followed this route, attaching himself as a chaplain to Lock Hospital and as a lecturer to St. Mildred's. Yet Scott's reputation rests as much on his biblical commentary as it does on his pastoral activities. Indeed, his commentary was well received in contemporary evangelical circles

---

[35]The story of Methodism is beyond the compass of this study. See the discussion in Robert Wearmouth, *Methodism and the Working-Class Movements of England, 1800-1850* (London, 1937); Maldwyn Edwards, *Methodism and England: a study of Methodism in its social and political aspects during the period, 1850-1932* (London, 1944); Bernard Semmel, *The Methodist Revolution* (New York, 1973). For discussion of the early evangelical movement see Charles Abbey and John Overton, *The English Church in the Eighteenth Century* (London, 1887); John Overton and Frederick Relton, *The English Church from the accession of George I to the end of the eighteenth century* (London, 1906); G. R. Balleine, *A History of the Evangelical Party* (London, 1908); L. E. Elliott-Binns, *The Evangelical Movement in the English Church* (London, 1928); L. E. Elliott-Binns, *The Early Evangelicals* (London, 1953).

and stands as one of the few examples of scholarship in this period of English evangelicalism.[36]

At approximately the turn of the century, during what might be called the second generation of English evangelicalism, several developments took place. First, while a fervent preaching style was still associated with evangelicals, preaching out of doors and conducting ecstatic revival meetings ceased to be characteristic. Evangelicals tended to concentrate their efforts on the middle and upper classes and to leave the lower classes, urban and rural, to the Methodists. Second, although evangelical pastors continued to fan out all over England, the evangelical strongholds became London, the small but influential parish of Clapham, and Cambridge University. Last, though the strength of the evangelical movement increased during this period, its contributions were seen not in the area of theological studies, but in its nurturing and furtherance of its gospel of "saving faith."

The message of the second generation of English evangelicalism was still very much that of its predecessors. That message, indeed, the message of nineteenth-century English evangelicalism can be seen in a well-known piece of homiletical advice, *A Practical View on the Prevailing Religious System of Professed Christians in the Higher and Middle Classes Contrasted with Real Christianity*, written by William Wilberforce in 1797. In it are the religious reflections of a person so influential that a study of nineteenth-century evangelicalism aptly bears the subtitle, "the Age of Wilberforce."[37] The very name of Wilberforce's tract demonstrated his wish to reach the centers of power and influence with his message of salvation. Contrasting real and nominal Christianity once again Wilberforce advised that the "grand radical defect in the practical system of these nominal Christians is their forgetfulness of all the peculiar doctrines of the religion which they profess—the corruption of human nature, the

---

[36]For a discussion of William Romaine and Thomas Scott, see Overton and Relton, *The English Church*, 150-53, 175-76, 189-91, 236-37; Balleine, *A History of the Evangelical Party*, 51-53, 113-20.

[37]Ford K. Brown, *Fathers of the Victorians: The Age of Wilberforce* (Cambridge, 1961).

atonement of the Saviour, and the sanctifying influence of the Holy Spirit." Disregard of these precepts, he continued, led to "the grand distinction between the religion of Christ and that of the bulk of nominal Christians in the present day."[38] In laying out, within the evangelical framework, the importance of these themes, Wilberforce was on common ground with Henry Venn. Similarly, when he took up the question of Scripture, Wilberforce articulated the evangelical fundamental that the Bible is a self-sufficient and self-contained authority.

It is interesting to note, however, that while he maintained that the Scriptures needed no philosophical system within which to be interpreted, Wilberforce in his account did put forth his, and his movement's, philosophy that biblical accounts stressed the importance of feeling. "We can scarcely indeed look into any part of the sacred volume," Wilberforce wrote of the Bible, "without meeting abundant proofs that it is the religion of the affections which God particularly requires. Love, zeal, gratitude, joy, hope, trust are each of them specified."[39] Here was that refrain so dear to English evangelicalism, a description of a vital and heartfelt religion. To evangelicals, such a religion rebuked the arctic rationalism of Deists such as John Toland and Matthew Tindal or the smug self-confidence and distance of John Locke and John Tillotson. But Christianity was not only a religion of the heart. Instead of triumphant victories of reason over feeling or vindications of the heart over the head, it was the glory of Christianity, Wilberforce continued, "to bring all the faculties of our nature into their just subordination and dependence; that so the whole man, complete in all his functions, may be restored to the true ends of his being and be devoted to the service and glory of God."[40]

This description of the incorporation of feelings, if somewhat mechanistically depicted by Wilberforce, reflected the influence of those enthusiastic, spontaneous, and emotional conversion experi-

---

[38]William Wilberforce, *Practical View of the Prevailing Religious System* (London, 1797; reprint New York: American Tract Society, n.d.) 245.

[39]Ibid., 69.

[40]Ibid., 68.

ences that many evangelicals had experienced and even more had witnessed. Their influence was also revealed in Wilberforce's attempt to define the relevancy of such emotion. In so doing, Wilberforce cautioned against the "mistaken supposition, that the force of the religious affections is to be mainly estimated by the degree of mere animal fervor, by ardors, and transports, and raptures, of which, from constitutional temperament, a person may be easily susceptible." Instead of searching the experience itself for signs of authenticity, one should look to the subsequent conduct, the only sure test, to see if the individual faithfully discharged "the duties of life: the personal, and domestic, and relative, and professional, and social, and civil duties."[41]

A sense of duty permeated all of Wilberforce's religious views. He strongly believed in righteous acts as well as righteous thoughts. And while he realized that it was often harder to get persons to act than it was to get them to believe, he still insisted that there was an indestructible link between religion and moral activism, between belief and service to God. For it is true of Christianity that "she values moral attainments at a far higher rate than intellectual acquisition, and proposes to conduct her followers to the height of virtue rather than of knowledge." In this way he led his readers from the admission of human sin in the sight of God to the recognition that an equally stern Jehovah demanded that they participate in the great evangelical reforming causes of the day. Once again the call was to the fulfillment of divine law and the discharge of human responsibilities. Christianity for Wilberforce meant recognition of sin and belief in forgiveness, but the genuineness of each was always attested to in the active course of Christian witness in all spheres of life. Thus, although in Wilberforce's evangelical rendering Christianity was never completely identified with morality, its doctrinal content was radically diminished.

Following the assertion that morality takes preeminence over knowledge, came Wilberforce's declaration that "the distemper of which, as a community we are sick, should be considered rather a moral than a political malady." Morality triumphed over politics as

---

[41]Ibid., 71-72.

well as learning. The Christian reformer coveted neither admiration nor sought power and affluence as did too many politicians. Indeed, just as individuals needed to be confronted with the gospel of saving faith in order that thereafter they might believe in individual grace, so too in the social sphere was it individuals who should engage in the work of reform. "A nation consists of individuals," Wilberforce pointed out. "True national prosperity is no other than the multiplication of particular happiness." "If any country were indeed filled with men," he continued,

> each thus diligently discharging the duties of his own station without breaking in upon the rights of others, but on the contrary endeavoring so far as he might be able, to forward their views and promote their happiness, all would be active and harmonious in the goodly frame of human society. There would be no jarrings, no discord. The whole machine of civil life would work without obstruction or disorder.[42]

Reform was individual and cumulative, the sum of single actions. If this claim was in part an appeal to the conscience of the powerful and mighty in the upper classes of England, it still exposed Wilberforce's stress in both religion and social reform on individual belief and action. Wilberforce always believed that effective change had to spring from a change in an individual's heart. Admittedly, Parliament could pass social legislation that coerced individual behavior. However, the result of such legislation must be morally acceptable (abolition of the slave trade in England being the prime example), and the coercion used to enforce the legislation must be designed to safeguard the moral welfare of the community and allow delinquents to receive the full blessings of Christian wisdom and charity.[43]

Wilberforce hoped that his book would win over the upper class to evangelicalism, for he believed that the upper class needed to set a proper example. Thus, he directed his closing thoughts to its members. In line with the view that a good society was a properly ordered and harmonious one, he reaffirmed Christianity's opposition to political or religious factionalism. Ascribing political dissen-

---

[42]Ibid., 300-301.

[43]See Brown, *Fathers of the Victorians*, 385.

sion to selfishness rather than to differences of interest or principle, Wilberforce stated that it was the mark of genuine Christianity to promote benevolence and to counteract evidences of narrow-mindedness or self-seeking. Finally, he remarked that two dangers still stood before his readers—inactivity and failure to do one's duty, and the loss of that spirituality, that vital religion, that made all such activity comprehensible and worthwhile. In reminding his readers of these twin perils, Wilberforce outlined the dilemma of his evangelical generation and cautioned that the path between Mammon and service to true faith was an arduous and complicated one.[44]

A review of this second period of evangelicalism reveals its growth and consolidation of influence. Since the days of William Romaine, London had become an important evangelical center. Josiah Pratt was the first editor of the evangelical newspaper, the *Christian Observer*, and one of the founders of the Church Missionary Society. Henry Blunt, known in London as an active pastor and talented devotional writer, was curate at St. Luke's Church in Chelsea, while Daniel Wilson, later Bishop of Calcutta, had transformed his parish at Islington into an evangelical stronghold.[45]

The village of Clapham—today part of London but in the nineteenth century situated outside the city boundaries—was a citadel of evangelical beliefs, and its residents provided the major evangelical voice within Parliament. Clapham was the home of Charles Grant, Zachary Macaulay, Granville Sharp, John Shore (later Lord Teignmouth), James Stephen, Henry and John Thornton, Henry and John Venn, and the indomitable William Wilberforce. The "Clapham Sect," as they became known, was in the forefront of a wide range of reform activities both inside and outside British government circles. Still, whether it was emancipation for slaves, or missionaries and Bibles for the subcontinent of India, moral reform built on Christian conversion provided the underlying premises of their efforts.[46]

---

[44]Wilberforce, *A Practical View*, 308-11.

[45]Overton, *English Church in Nineteenth Century*, 81-85.

[46]See E. M. Howse, *Saints in Politics: The 'Clapham Sect' and the Growth of Freedom* (London, 1953); James Stephen, *Essays in Ecclesiastical History* (London, 1875) 523-84.

The third locale of evangelical growth during this period was Cambridge University. Oxford, though the university of John Wesley, had a reputation for strong anti-evangelical prejudices. In part this derived from the expulsion of six students in 1768 on charges of religious enthusiasm and ecclesiastical irregularity. Aside from Isaac Crouch's leadership, and later Daniel Wilson's, of St. Edmund's Hall, Oxford was indeed hostile to any evangelical forays into its precincts. The situation at Cambridge was better. More than anything, it was the presence of Charles Simeon, a well-known evangelical, that had established an evangelical ambience within the university. Simeon combined the revivalist solicitude for individual salvation with loyalty to the established church. Isaac Milner also helped root evangelicalism at Cambridge. Milner was president of Queen's College in the university and dean of Carlisle Cathedral, and under his aegis evangelicals found a supportive atmosphere of prayer and study.

His brother Joseph, though not attached to Cambridge, was important for his study, *History of the Church of Christ*. Evangelicals found in this work an accounting of the ministry of the church designed to answer their questions and fulfill their needs. Here was the story of the invisible church of true believers, that body populated by real (versus nominal) Christians, among whom every evangelical hoped to be counted. Milner's volumes gained a wide audience, going into multiple editions and several translations. If his treatment lacked a sense of historical development and his periodization appeared arbitrary at times, Milner's work still provided evangelicals with an awareness of their theological heritage at a time when these insights were sorely lacking.[47]

Other features besides growth characterized English evangelicalism during this era. First, driven by the command to engage in moral activism and to remake the world in the evangelical image, evangelicals formed dozens of voluntary religious societies, often nondenominational. Early on, John Berridge had recognized that

---

[47]See J. S. Reynolds, *The Evangelicals at Oxford, 1735-1871* (Oxford, 1953); Smyth, *Simeon and Church Order*, 97-147; John D. Walsh, "Joseph Milner's Evangelical Church History," *Journal of Ecclesiastical History* 10, no. 2 (October 1959): 174-87.

"preaching kindles the fire, but societies nurse and keep the flame alive."[48] Consequently, from Wesley's time onward, but especially when directed and financially supported by the Clapham Sect, voluntary religious societies proliferated. Again, their projects were diverse, but their logic and message were as old as the evangelical movement itself. For one of the favorite evangelical passages of Scripture enjoined believers to go and preach the gospel to every creature throughout the world. As Rowland Hill said in consideration of this demand, "in preaching through England, Scotland, Ireland, and Wales, I always conceived I struck close to my parish."[49] Here was an argument that overlooked national and territorial boundaries in the same way that earlier disputants had argued about the boundaries of a parish. Jurisdictional contentions arose between denominational and nondenominational agencies, but throughout it the reforming zeal of the evangelicals remained constant. Their loyalty to the task of witnessing individual conversion and the gospel of saving faith never wavered. Furthermore, Wilberforce and his colleagues never tired of struggling to remove the temptations of irreligion and immorality (though the categories might not be that distinct) in the hopes of ushering in the evangelical millennium.

Although these religious societies operated within the Church of England, it should be noted that the evangelicals' attitude to the established church was an ambivalent one. Concerning its liturgy and practice they were as loyal as orthodox clergymen. Regarding its power to reform and to increase righteousness throughout the land they were hopeful. Yet the history of the evangelicals within the church had been a stormy one; establishment power had been used against them more than once. Even more unsettling was the fact that no evangelical would revere an established church, *qua* establishment, as the only means of grace. For behind all outward activities lay the deeply held attachment of evangelicalism to a doctrine of the invisible church.[50]

---

[48]Balleine, *History of the Evangelical Party*, 156.

[49]Smyth, *Simeon and Church Order*, 264.

[50]See the discussion of G. F. Best, "The Evangelicals and the Established Church in the Early Nineteenth Century," *The Journal of Theological Studies*, new series, vol. 10 (April 1959): 63-78.

The significance of the invisible church was agreed upon by all evangelicals. John Berridge had spoken of his high regard for "neither high church, nor low church, nor any church, but the Church of Christ, which is not built with hands, nor circumscribed within peculiar walls nor confined to a single denomination." Joseph Milner included all whom he judged to be real Christians within the scope of his *History*, for "it is of no consequence with respect to my plan, nor of much importance I believe in its own nature, to what External Church [real Christians] belonged."[51] Indeed, focus upon the invisible church allowed evangelicals the latitude to recognize all other "real Christians" whatever their religious affiliation. Moreover, it suggested the easy camaraderie and sympathy that could grow up between evangelicals and those Dissenters who shared the evangelical quest for conversion and social reform. Within this context, nondenominational religious societies provided an ideal vehicle for promoting those moral ends cherished by evangelicals and Dissenters alike.

The concept that fundamental unity existed beneath denominational difference illustrated Wilberforce's desire to avoid factionalism. "Policies not parties" was the motto of evangelical statesmen such as Wilberforce or Henry Thornton. Yet while the evangelicals' proximity to power suggested the possibility that they might accomplish their moral crusade, the results of their efforts reflected the problem they had of remaining above party politics in an age when "party" held growing meaning.[52] In addition, appeals to social harmony and a unity of true believers could reintegrate believers, after their solitary conversions before God, into a communal fellowship. Yet these attempts were always predicated upon the irreducible confrontation of sinner and sacredness. In a religion that traded so heavily upon individual sin and the ineffectualness of personal effort to win faith, the burden placed upon solitary individuals could be enormous. Neither institutional bulwarks nor friendly support could help, hinder, promote or quicken conversion. In the end,

---

[51]Berridge to Lady Huntingdon, 26 April 1777, as quoted by Smyth in *Simeon and Church Order*, 181; Milner, *The History of the Church of Christ*, 4 vols. (Boston, 1809-1811) 1:ix.

[52]See Best, "The Evangelicals and the Established Church," 76-77.

nothing but the subjective correctness of the soul's relation to God would count.

Thirsting for that experience of rebirth and the assurance of salvation, revivalists of early nineteenth-century England and Germany partook of a common bond of faith. Yet a common purpose masked crucial differences. Occasionally German pietists, such as the Moravians, worked in England, Scotland, and Wales, but on the whole their efforts were not successful. Turn-of-the-century evangelicals shared with their German brethren an earnestness and sobriety that set each apart within their societies. English evangelicalism during this period, however, appears less affected by romanticism than the German *Erweckungsbewegung*. To be sure, English evangelicals participated in that antirationalist stance so characteristic of nineteenth-century romanticism. Similarly, they acknowledged the importance of feelings in their account of religion. Yet, when he spoke of the nature of society, William Wilberforce pictured it as a "number of different circles of various magnitudes and uses." Within such a social physics, it "should be the desire and aim of every individual to fill well his own circle, as a part and member of the whole, with a view to the production of general happiness."[53] In contrast to German pietists such as Jung-Stilling or Gottfried Thomasius, Wilberforce was clearly indebted to a mechanistic cosmology of spheres and orbits rather than to an organic one. Likewise, English evangelicalism was almost blind to progressive revelation or development through history. The central plank of the evangelicals' greatest historian, Joseph Milner, was the continuity of historical experience and the centrality of original sin. The English movement with its emphasis upon an invisible church and a fundamental unity of all Christians had none of the pronounced confessional consciousness distinguishing portions of the German (and particularly Bavarian) Awakening. Instead, a trans-confessional standard of saving faith in Jesus cushioned individual English evangelicals in their nineteenth-century pilgrimage of faith.

---

[53]Wilberforce, *A Practical View*, 303.

The influence of the evangelical movement on church reform was matched by the influence of liberalism. Religious liberals among early nineteenth-century English churchmen comprised an extraordinarily diverse group for whom political sympathy with the Whigs acted as an important bond. "Whig Christianity seems to have been largely a blend of the classical precepts of morality and the moral sense of the Scottish philosophers," Professor Best has written, "improved by Christ's special injunction to tolerance and forbearance and substituting for the dreamy ambition of establishing Christ's Kingdom on earth, the nearer but no less desirable objective of the Reign of Liberty."[54]

Though it might seem surprising, some liberal pronouncements had an evangelical ring to them. Indeed, their appeals to tolerance and their emphasis on moral duty were not the only themes that demonstrated an affinity between liberalism and evangelicalism. Whig clerics often invoked a broad view of Christianity in which Anglicans, Dissenters, and Roman Catholics, too, were called brethren in faith. While they recognized the legitimacy of a religious establishment, their view of the derivation of any given congregation was reminiscent of evangelicalism though it sprang from Locke rather than the Bible. "A church," John Locke wrote in his *Letter Concerning Toleration*, "I take to be a voluntary society of men, joining themselves together of their own accord in order to the public worshipping of God in such a manner as they judge acceptable to him, and effectual to the salvation of their souls."[55] Locke's opinion was well suited to Whig sensibilities, at once explaining the origins of sacred congregations and justifying the existence of religious voluntary associations.

Despite these and other similarities, religious liberals in England differed from their evangelical colleagues in important respects, nowhere more than in their understanding of Scripture. Richard Whately and Thomas Arnold were not only two of the most articulate spokesmen for the liberal cause, their lives illustrate

---

[54]Best, "Establishment in the Age of Grey and Holland," 107.

[55]John Locke, *A Letter Concerning Toleration*, ed. Mario Montuori (The Hague, 1965) 23; Ibid., 103-107.

clearly the complicated interface that liberalism and evangelicalism shared. Whately was born in 1787, eight years prior to Arnold. Both were associated with Oriel College at Oxford, particularly with a group there known as the "Noetics." Under the leadership of Edward Copleston and Edward Hawkins, the Noetics developed a reputation for incisive discussions informed by new developments in logic and history. Later, writing with regard to other concerns, Thomas Arnold might well have been thinking of the Noetics' ideal when he spoke of "a sober freedom of honest and humble inquiry," neither irreverent nor "too little accustomed to question old opinions to be able fairly to judge when they are questioned without reason."[56]

In 1831 Lord Grey nominated Whately as Archbishop of Dublin, but by the time Whately left Oxford for that post he had written a series of pieces that provided a valuable index to the concerns of religious liberals. If the Whigs had a penchant for forbearance, then Whately in his Bampton lectures of 1822, entitled *The Use and Abuse of Party Feeling in Matters of Religion*, made it the hallmark of proper Christian conduct. Acrimony and divisive sectarianism not only contradicted the examples of Gospel meekness and charity, they were a "matter of scornful triumph to the infidel, and a stumbling-block to the weak." As a consequence, the history of Christianity appeared too often to be an account of strife, animosity, and dissension.[57] Such party spirit was divisive. In the spurious name of orthodoxy and doctrinal standards, fellow Christians were blinded to the truth of the gospel. Whately believed that the antidote to this malady was a conscious renewal of charity towards opponents and a search for areas of agreement rather than disagreement. One should refrain from imputing ignoble motives to religious adversaries until further investigation had confirmed the facts under dis-

---

[56]For a discussion of the Noetics, see John Tulloch, *Movements of Religious Thought in Britain during the nineteenth century* (New York, 1893) 41-74; E. Jane Whately, *Life and Correspondence of Richard Whately, D.D.*, 2d ed. (London, 1868) 10-12; Thomas Arnold, *The Miscellaneous Works of Thomas Arnold: first American edition with nine additional essays* (New York, 1845) 398.

[57]Richard Whately, *The Use and Abuse of Party Feeling in Matters of Religion* (London, 1833) 65-71. The quotation appears on page 67.

pute. One should avoid speculating on seemingly insoluble questions, and refrain from extreme positions. Rather, one should concern oneself with questions of moderate tenor and practical consequence. To Whately, a believer should hold fast to the fundamental truths and doctrines of faith but should eschew the "badges of a party" or the merely "technical terms" which so noticeably aggravated party spirit and strengthened each side in its contentiousness.[58]

In applying his principles, Whately cited the contemporary debate over Dissenters' rights. It was difficult but necessary, Whately wrote, "to steer the middle course between lukewarmness and repulsive severity—to oppose Dissenters as such, without being wanting in charity towards them as men, and as Christians; to be steady in maintaining the sinfulness of schism, yet without censuring as unpardonable those who fall into it."[59] Concluding, Whately noted that it was inappropriate to use civil coercion in order to enforce religious conformity. Christ's kingdom was not of this world, the future archbishop declared, and exemplary lives, a firm but conciliatory attitude towards those with whom one disagrees, and internal unity within the church were the true and effective means for spiritual contention.[60]

In line with this principle and in keeping with Whig policy, Whately favored Roman Catholic emancipation in 1829. Civil exclusion on account of religious belief, he believed, was a throwback to a bygone era and an impediment to contemporary progress. Prior to the resolution of the Catholic question, however, Whately had offered a series of thoughtful suggestions regarding the plight of the Church of England. In a book entitled *Letters on the Church by an Episcopalian*, published anonymously in 1826 but conceded to be his work, Whately astutely criticized the current alliance of church and state. He argued that the present relationship harmed the state as much as religion. Civil enforcement of religious belief was immoral,

---

[58]Ibid., 262.

[59]Ibid., 238.

[60]Ibid., 240-43.

state interference in internal ecclesiastical matters injurious. Alienating Dissenters from the state on religious grounds was as unwise as government meddling in religion was blasphemous. In Whately's view the connection between church and state should be severed, but the establishment of the church—that is, its possession of property and discharge of services—should continue. Whately's book influenced John Henry Newman, but it had more immediate import. It proposed a separation of church and state, while claiming to strengthen the two and bind them more closely together. The anomalies of the Whig theory of church establishment were evident in Whately's proposals. The strains upon the theory would become even more acute before long.

If Whately's suggestions pleased neither Tories nor disestablishment-minded Benthamite radicals, his researches into scriptural interpretation demonstrated a similar distance from evangelicals. In two studies, *Essays on Some of the Peculiarities of the Christian Religion* (1825) and *Essays on Some of the Difficulties in the Writings of St. Paul* (1828), he demonstrated that although liberals and evangelicals might share a concern for moral duty and public and private virtue, there were important differences between them. In keeping with his injunction to concentrate on practical issues, Whately claimed that the very character of the Gospel's message was "practically instructive." Like William Wilberforce, he maintained that "every doctrinal discourse should lead the Christian hearer to its proper moral result." Like evangelicals, he believed that Christianity demanded an activistic program of moral reform. Yet Whately edged away from evangelicalism when he claimed that the Apostle Paul alluded "*occasionally* only to the rewards and punishments of a future state, and the folly of not preparing for it; but he insists *continually* on the mercies which God has *already* shown us." To evangelicals, such a de-emphasis of the eschatological theme would coddle unrepentant sinners by softening the message of eternal damnation.[61] In his analysis of Paul's writings, Whately controverted those evangelicals who believed that the four Gospels alone

---

[61]Richard Whately, *Essay on Some of the Peculiarities of the Christian Religion* (London, 1831) 312, 247, 192.

were all that was required for understanding Christianity. More telling, however, was his assertion that simple proof-texts displayed less
than a full understanding of biblical writings, and should be aban-
doned in favor of systematic study of the Bible. Beyond that, he
scrutinized the doctrine of election, perseverance, assurance, and
imputation; his results were decidedly at variance with common
evangelical views.[62]

Whately was creative and affable, and his years at Oxford were
productive. His appointment as archbishop of Dublin must have
seemed a cruel joke to some conservatives, for the man who had
called for severance of church and state now benefited from that
very alliance. Yet the Irish church was in trouble, and no one knew
this better than Whately himself. In his episcopal Charge of 1834 he
surveyed the strength of those forces in Ireland calling for the disestablishment of both the political and property connection between church and state. "I will only remark," he concluded to his
fellow prelates,

> that I really believe the very best thing that can be done—at least, the best
> that can be done by *us*—with a view to the safety and permanence of the
> Establishment—is, to use in every way our utmost exertions to give it effi-
> ciency—to make it both to appear, and to be, a useful institution—worthy
> of public confidence and protection, as being of substantial benefit to the
> nation, in the inculcation of the knowledge and practice of religion: and
> that, of such religion as, by its fruits, may command the respect and esteem
> even of those who have little or nothing of religious feeling themselves.[63]

Other Whig reformers would be found to appeal to efficiency,
but Whately's fellow liberal, Thomas Arnold, did not stress that feature. In describing the purpose for his activities, Arnold once
wrote:

> My object is moral and intellectual reform which will be sure enough to
> work out political reform in the best way, and my writing on politics would
> have for its end, not the forwarding any political measure, but the so puri-
> fying enlightening, sobering, and, in one word, *Christianizing* men's notions

---

[62]Richard Whately, *Essay on Some of the Difficulties in the Writings of St. Paul* (London, 1833) 89; Tulloch, *Movements of Religious Thought*, 48-50.

[63]Richard Whately, *Charges and other Tracts* (London, 1836) 10.

and feelings on political matters, that from the improved tree may come hereafter a better fruit.[64]

The fulfillment of Christian duty—earnestly, soberly, and responsibly—this was what Arnold asked for and what he believed would best direct church reform. Born in 1795, Arnold received high academic honors and recognition as a student at Corpus Christi College and later as a fellow at Oriel College. During these years at Oxford Arnold developed his interest in the classics and became well known as one of the Oriel Noetics. It was as headmaster of Rugby and later as Regius Professor of Modern History, however, that Arnold was best known. His premature death in 1842 silenced one of the more creative participants in the Church-reform controversy. The sources for Arnold's scholarship were as wide-ranging as his reading and travels. Competent in German, he maintained a close friendship with the Prussian diplomat, Christian Bunsen, and familiarized himself with the biblical criticism of Friedrich Schleiermacher, Karl Ullman, and Friedrich Umbreit. He was on cordial terms with both the Wordsworth and Coleridge families, despite the two families' political differences, and Samuel Taylor Coleridge and William Wordsworth both influenced his work.[65] Finally, as a critic of High Church policies, Arnold was a skillful opponent of the Tractarian movement.

Although Arnold wrote about most of the major ecclesiastical issues of the day, most pertinent to this study are his views on Roman Catholic emancipation and reform of the Church of England. In 1829 Arnold published a pamphlet appropriately entitled "Christian Duty of conceding the Roman Catholic Claims." He wanted to address the problem in terms of duty and not just in terms of the oft-emphasized political expediency. "For as parties and public are made up of individuals morally and religiously responsible," Arnold

---

[64]Thomas Arnold to John Ward, *Life of Arnold*, 1:263.

[65]For a discussion of the influences on Arnold's thought, see Merton Christensen, "Thomas Arnold's Debt to German Theologians: A Prelude to Matthew Arnold's *Literature and Dogma*," *Modern Philology* 55, no. 1 (August 1957): 14-20; Eugene Williamson, *The Liberalism of Thomas Arnold* (University AL, 1964) 40-52; Basil Willey, *Nineteenth Century Studies* (New York, 1949) 51-72.

stated, no Christian should ignore an issue if it was sinful to do so. Arnold claimed that there were two reasons why Christians should support emancipation. First, further exclusion of Catholics was unjust, and it was "a want of faith in God and an unholy zeal to think that he can be served by injustice, or to guard against contingent evil by committing certain sin." Second, emancipation would benefit Christianity, specifically by "purify[ing] the Catholic Religion in Ireland from its greatest superstitions, and gradually . . . assimilat[ing] it more and more to Protestantism."[66] Arnold was not enamored with the Irish people, "but with this unpromising race and with this dreadful religion we have chosen to connect ourselves"; thus, it was the moral responsibility of English Christendom to set the situation right.[67]

Built into Arnold's arguments was the assumption that the established church must and could be saved. Calling the Christian church "one of the greatest blessings with which England has been favored," and saying that disestablishment, should it come about, would be "a national sin," Arnold envisioned a situation in which civic equality for Catholics would diminish their animosity and thus coax them into the establishment's fold. Should assimilation at first prove impossible, then, said Arnold in terms reminiscent of Whately's strictures against party feeling, "we should substitute inquiry for controversy; not wishing to bring them over to our side, but that both they and we should be on the side of truth, renouncing our errors, and clearing our views when indistinct and imperfect."[68]

In his belief that civil power should not be used to coerce religious minorities, and in his disavowal of the partisanship that characterized much of the debate over emancipation, Arnold demonstrated his indebtedness to his mentor, Whately. In 1826, however, Arnold reviewed Whately's *Letters on the Church by an Episcopalian* and with his remarks exhibited his independence. After summarizing Whately's arguments fairly, Arnold concluded that

---

[66] Arnold, *Miscellaneous Works*, 161.

[67] Ibid., 181.

[68] Ibid., 200.

Whately's proposals for severing the alliance between church and state were "no more than the dreams of a warm imagination."[69] Then Arnold proffered his own plan for church reform (a plan later expanded into his well-known essay, "Principles of Church Reform").

> It is evidently most desirable, that the church should be completely identified with the people; that it not only should be uncorrupt, but should be generally acknowledged to be so; that while its terms of Communion were made as comprehensive as possible, so as to include conscientious members of almost every denomination of Christians, it should be most uncompromising in the standard of moral excellence, to which it required its ministers to conform; and should watch over their previous education as well as their subsequent course of life, with the most zealous care.[70]

Arnold did not wish for a separation between church and state. Rather, he looked to "the attention and reforming hand of the national Legislature" for improvement of the Church of England. Here in this small review was the kernel of Arnold's reform program. In 1833, as pressures for ecclesiastical change increased, he published an expanded version of his recommendations.

Arnold's concern with a proper reorganization of the church had been growing since 1826. By 1831, with reform agitation intensifying, Arnold predicted that the church could keep aloof for only so long. "Reform [of the church] would now prevent destruction," Arnold wrote the Prussian diplomat, Christian Bunsen, "but every year of delayed reform strengthens those who wish not to amend, but destroy." Later that year Arnold wrote to Whately, "I cannot get over my sense of the fearful state of public affairs—is it clean hopeless that the Church will come forward and crave to be allowed to reform itself?"[71] Would the church be reformed by those outside forces who were increasingly hostile and who seemed increasingly powerful, or would the church's friends within be allowed to effect remedies in this time of trial and need? Arnold hoped for the latter, and it was to further this dream that he submitted his plan.

---

[69]Ibid., 221.

[70]Ibid., 224.

[71]Arnold to C. Bunsen, *Life of Arnold*, 1:260; Arnold to Whately, ibid., 1:273.

"These principles I believe to be irrefragable," he began,

> That a Church Establishment is essential to the well-being of the nation; that the existence of Dissent impairs the usefulness of an Establishment always, and now, from peculiar circumstances, threatens its destruction; and that to extinguish Dissent by persecution being both wicked and impossible, there remains the true but hitherto untried way, to extinguish it by comprehension.[72]

As others had done before him, Arnold defended the national establishment for its social utility and historic precedence. But more importantly, he admitted the full significance of non-Anglican Christians and proposed a radical remedy for their situation. Exclusion of Dissenters from the establishment was counterproductive to national progress, setting up an opposition between those within and without the establishment. As the strength of Dissent grew, so did the threat to the religious establishment. Yet differences of religious belief and ritual were too deep to be eliminated through wish or fiat. Arnold recommended that rather than devise a new liturgy and worship service (as the Prussian church had attempted), the problem of Dissent could be resolved by incorporating Dissenters into a reconstructed and inclusive church establishment. "To constitute a Church thoroughly national, thoroughly united, thoroughly Christian," Arnold wrote, "which should allow greater varieties of opinion, and of ceremonies, and forms of worship according to the various knowledge, and habits, and tempers of its members, while it truly held one common faith, and trusted in one common Saviour, and worshipped one common God."[73] The platform upon which Arnold proposed to build his comprehensive church contained four planks: belief in one God, faith in Jesus Christ and the resurrection, acceptance of the Old and New Testaments, and recognition of a broadly based sense of right and wrong. Arnold readily agreed that historically, the interpretation of these four points had been disputed, but he swept aside such objections. "The real question is, not what theoretical articles a man will or will not subscribe to," he contended, "but what essential parts of Christian

---

[72]Arnold, *Miscellaneous Works*, 73.

[73]Ibid., 88.

worship he is unable to use."[74] Remedial action to meet the present crisis at hand, rather than arguments over nonessential points of dogma—this was what Arnold believed was needed. Whether Christianity could be boiled down to a few fundamental assertions posed no problems in Arnold's mind. Realistic concessions to make the establishment as inclusive as possible was his concern.

The first half of the nineteenth century witnessed a massive attack on the traditional view of the Bible and its place within divine revelation. The twin blows of higher criticism in Germany and advances in the physical sciences, notably geology, seemed to weaken familiar assumptions about the veracity of the Bible. Conversant with the research of German biblical critics such as David Friedrich Strauss and with the research of English geologists such as Charles Lyell, Arnold tried to reassure his fellow Christians by stressing the importance of the moral and religious truths within the Bible, truths that were independent of scientific discovery. "Christian doctrine," Arnold maintained, "is no more than a law of duties, a statement of what we ought to do, and what we ought not to do." Arnold's concept of the Bible paralleled his concept of the church. As he saw the ideal church stressing a fundamental set of doctrines, moral precepts, and duties; so did he see an ideal interpretation of the Bible stressing its doctrinal simplicity and uniformity. Such interpretation would reemphasize the importance of individual ethically and religiously directed acts.[75]

Out of these principles Arnold derived specific suggestions for reform. In the spirit of Whately's suggestions of 1822, Arnold's advice was that there be moderation in trying to press Quakers, Roman Catholics, and Unitarians into a new comprehensive church.

---

[74]Ibid., 88-89, 92.

[75]Ibid., 450. For a discussion of Arnold's views on biblical criticism, see Williamson, *Liberalism of Thomas Arnold*, 68-73. A full examination of the rise of higher criticism and its impact is beyond the compass of this book. Helpful recent studies of this question include James R. Moore, *The Post-Darwinian Controversies* (New York, 1979); Herbert Hovenkamp, *Science and Religion in America, 1800-1860* (Philadelphia, 1978); Horton Harris, *The Tübingen School* (Oxford, 1975); and Günter Altner, *Schöpfungsglaube und Entwicklungsgedanke in der protestantische Theologie zwischen Ernst Haeckel und Teilhard de Chardin* (Zurich, 1965).

Whereas it appeared that Presbyterians, Baptists, and Independent-Congregationalists differed with the establishment principally on issues of church polity, the obstacles to including Quakers, Catholics, and Unitarians, Arnold admitted, seemed greater. Yet because "extravagance in one extreme provokes equal extravagance in the other," he advised that "reasonable and moderate men" could meet together with the intent of being "comprehensive and conciliatory, rather than controversial" and work out even these difficulties.[76]

Other problems besides the Dissenters beset the church. The accelerated growth of the Dissenter population during 1780-1830 suggested to Arnold that the church was failing to meet its responsibilities. The challenges issued by social need, religious ignorance, and personal despair had not been met in burgeoning new manufacturing centers such as Manchester and Birmingham. For example, in 1812 the bishop of Chester had confirmed 8,000 children in one twelve-hour period, while in Manchester, with a population of 136,000, there was but a single parish.[77] Similarly, the problems of nonresidence and plural livings were long standing, but no less tragic. The famous though unusually obvious example of Richard Watson illustrated the lengths to which the problem could go. In the course of his life Watson was successively professor of chemistry at Cambridge, Regius Professor of Divinity at Cambridge, and Bishop of Llandaff. Watson himself admitted that he knew absolutely no chemistry when elected to the first post and that he only began his theological studies when he was nominated as professor of divinity. His view of theological education was simple and straightforward. "I determined to study nothing but the Bible," he wrote, "being much unconcerned about the opinions of councils, fathers, churches, bishops, and other men as little inspired as myself." Adjourning from Llandaff for a country estate in Westmoreland, Watson had the curious distinction of being both a nonresident professor and a nonresident bishop. He candidly described his tenure as bishop in these terms: "Having no place of residence in my diocese, I turned my attention to the improvement of land. I

---

[76]Arnold, *Miscellaneous Works*, 90.

[77]Mathieson, *English Church Reform*, 17.

thought the improvement of a man's fortune by cultivating the earth was the most useful and honourable way of providing for a family. I have now been several years occupied as an improver of land and planter of trees." A planter of trees rather than a fisher of men, Watson still accepted his annual church income of two thousand pounds, thereby highlighting the problem of nonresidence and plural livings.[78]

These were the challenges facing the church and threatening its establishment. Having spelled out his principles for reform and having acknowledged the church's old and new structural problems, Arnold concluded with a series of administrative recommendations. He insisted that lay participation in the ordinary governance of the church be increased. He suggested that diocesan boundaries be realigned, that advisory councils for bishops and diocesan general assemblies be created, and that Dissenting ministers be included as assistant ministers on the staff of local parishes.[79] In keeping with his desire for a common national faith, albeit one expressed in a variety of forms, Arnold advised that "different services should be performed at different times of the day and week within the walls of the same church. . . . there seems to be no reason why the National Church should not enjoy a sufficient variety in its ritual to satisfy the opinions and feelings of all." To him, this plan had the advantage of simplicity and eliminated the need for a new liturgy that in attempting to include all, would satisfy none.[80]

Administrative reform was not the central concern for Arnold. Rather, it was "the monstrous evil of sectarianism." And to Arnold, the religious situation in the United States most clearly depicted the disasters concomitant with sectarianism. Indeed, America, particularly its southern and western regions, was, to Arnold, an example of the wrong paths taken, a threat of what would come about should religious establishment be dissolved in Great Britain. "The world has as yet produced," he morosely observed, "no instance of society

---

[78]Watson is quoted by Abbey and Overton, *English Church in the Eighteenth Century*, 27-28.

[79]Arnold, *Miscellaneous Works*, 96-101.

[80]Ibid., 107.

advancing under a less promising aspect, intellectual, moral, and religious than in the new states and territories of the American union." In his private correspondence Arnold confessed that he was most occupied with the lessons England could learn from America's mistakes. Writing to Whately, he indicated that his plan of reform grew from his opposition to other proposals and "because I have heard the American doctrine of every man paying his minister as he would his lawyer, advanced and supported in high quarters, where it sounded alarming. I was also struck by the great vehemence displayed by Dissenters at the late election, by the refusal to pay Church-rates at Birmingham."[81] The conditions in America were wrought with dangerous implications. If the situation in New York and New England was somewhat better than in the newly settled areas, this state of affairs only reflected the existence in those states of what Arnold regarded as a religious establishment. Taken as a whole, the voluntary quality of religion in America was a pernicious and insidious disease, one that had to be exposed for the spiritual malady it was. A national religious establishment was a national blessing, "an instrument," as Arnold phrased it, "of national good." In terms appropriate for his many sermons, Arnold concluded his "Principles" by challenging his readers to "convert many merely nominal Christians into hearty friends of the Establishment."[82]

If Arnold's injunction to convert nominal Christians sounded faintly evangelical, so too was his vision of a Christianity based solely on faith in Jesus and the fulfillment of moral duties. Similarly, Arnold based his policy recommendations on the assumption of the primacy of individual reform effort. For Arnold, as for William Wilberforce, the challenge was to awaken individual consciences and to raise their awareness of the human situation. From this individual reform, social reform would follow. But evangelicals were chary of the prominence national establishment was given in Arnold's proposal. Ironically, had Arnold been understood, neither his conviction in the inseparability of church and state, nor his desire to see religious values illumine everyday life, nor his wish for an establish-

---

[81]Ibid., 112; Arnold to Whately, *Life of Arnold*, 1:301.

[82]Arnold, *Miscellaneous Works*, 118-19.

ment that would reflect "real Christianity" should have caused evangelical readers concern.

PARLIAMENTARY REFORM OF THE CHURCH

In the aftermath of the Reform Act of 1832, amidst calls for change from dissenting, evangelical, and liberal critics alike, reform of the church was a foregone conclusion. Thomas Arnold believed that Parliament was the appropriate vehicle for saving the church from disestablishment and strengthening the state in the performance of its joint secular and religious duties. Whatever the infeasibility of his latitudinarian ideas, Arnold correctly recognized the importance of Parliament's role in any reform. As the years from 1830 to 1860 clearly demonstrated, most assumed that the state would be involved in ecclesiastical reform. Only conservative churchmen questioned the Erastian premise of such a view. Informally or officially, the various parties interested in ecclesiastical affairs assembled their ideas, drew up their proposals, and traded for votes in the Houses of Parliament.

Yet, as if designed for dramatic effect, the prologue to Parliament's involvement was acted out not in the English church, but in its nearby Irish neighbor. The year was 1833; the topic was the Irish Church Temporalities Act. Admittedly, it was not the first time Ireland had served as an experimental model for English reform. Neither was the Irish situation identical with the English. Nevertheless, the debates in Westminster concerning the established church in Ireland prefigured those concerning the established church in England.

The United Church of England and Ireland had been formed out of the Act of Union in 1800. While its title suggested that the two nationalities shared equally in rank and honor, actually, what the Irish church mainly shared with its English counterpart was problems. Many of the parishes of the Irish church contained few or no Protestants, with as many as one-third of the parish incumbents not in residence. Consequently, church revenues were diminished. Tithes had virtually ceased to be collected, while church-rates (called church cess in Ireland and levied on Catholics and Presbyterians as well as on Anglicans) were sporadically received at best. Relations between Protestant clergy and Catholic residents could be polite, but it was a cordiality based on an implicit agreement that both sides ignore financial obligations and religious practices. If the clergy broke that agreement, recriminations and even violence could erupt.[83]

In February 1833 the Irish Church bill was introduced into the newly reformed House of Commons. Its provisions contained proposals to abolish through merger upon vacancy ten episcopal sees (out of twenty-two); to reduce two archbishoprics to bishoprics while suspending appointments to parishes where services had not taken place during the preceding three years; to restructure ecclesiastical revenues and tenancy requirements; and to create an ecclesiastical commission to administer the surplus money thereby gained. The bill caused quite a stir. Most questioned was the propriety of suppressing episcopal sees and dispensing their income for nonreligious purposes. The *Christian Observer*, the voice of English evangelicalism, assailed the proposed reduction of ten bishoprics. The government appeared to treat the Protestant establishment in Ireland as "an evil to be borne with and mitigated," the *Observer* caustically remarked, "rather than a blessing of which we should wish the extension and perpetuity." In contrast, some Catholics and Dissenters demanded complete disestablishment and the appropriation of ecclesiastical funds for pressing Irish social problems. Thus, while the Whig government had proposed the bill, support for it belied a fundamental split over the issue of ecclesiastical funds and their use. Finally, the need for an immediate remedy to the chronic problems of the Irish situation held the supporters of the bill together. It was passed in June 1833.[84] With its enactment, an ecclesiastical commission with powers of distribution and management was established, and a program significant to the English church itself began. The measures did not solve the Irish problems, but they did provide a precedent for future ecclesiastical legislation, especially once the focus returned to England.

---

[83]Mathieson, *English Church Reform*, 75; Chadwick, *Victorian Church*, 1:49-51; Machin, *Politics and the Churches*, 31-32.

[84]Mathieson, *English Church Reform*, 78; Olive Brose, "The Irish Precedent for English Church Reform: The Church Temporalities Act of 1833," *Journal of Ecclesiastical History* 7, no. 2 (October 1956): 204-25.

The debate over the church in the 1830s and 1840s dealt with one central question: should the church, in line with the arguments of utilitarians or voluntarists, be disestablished and disendowed, or should it be reshaped with the aid and advice of reforming elements within it? With the Whigs in power, buoyed by electoral gains from constituencies newly enfranchised by the Reform Act, conservative churchmen expected a full-scale assault on the English church. Yet the Whigs were as divided on the issue of church property in England as they had been over the issue in Ireland. Lord John Russell, who had favored a plan for the Irish church with "concurrent endowment" of Catholic, Presbyterian, and Anglican clergy based upon appropriation, expected equally fundamental change in the English church. Russell's sentiments, however, were far ahead of Whig leaders such as Grey and Althrop. In 1834, with little more than the Irish Church Act accomplished, the Whigs were dismissed. The ministerial change brought the Tories and Sir Robert Peel back into office. Because of his involvement in Roman Catholic emancipation, Peel's reputation among many churchmen was tainted, yet he was at least a Tory. For that, conservative churchmen were glad. Like many of his Whig counterparts in Parliament, Peel recognized the existence of problems facing the church. In December 1834, just days after assuming office as prime minister, he signaled his commitment to moderate ecclesiastical reform. In an address to the constituents of Tamworth, Peel called for "a careful review of institutions, civil and ecclesiastical, undertaken in a friendly temper."[85]

Three features characterized Peel's interest in reordering the ecclesiastical situation in England. First, Peel believed equally in the needs for reform and establishment. In a letter to John Crocker regarding parish reform, Peel asked,

> But is this right—that there should be no provision whatever for spiritual duties in some of the largest, most populous, most important, most dissenting districts of the country? . . . Is the Church to be a provision for men

---

[85]On Russell's plan and Peel's Tamworth address, see Machin, *Politics and the Church*, 36-37, 48-49. For a comprehensive account of Peel's career, see the studies by Norman Gash, *Politics in the Age of Peel* (London, 1953), *Mr. Secretary Peel* (London, 1961), *Sir Robert Peel* (London, 1972).

of birth, or for men of learning? or is its main object the worship of God according to the doctrines of the Reformed faith?

"Some of our Tories," Peel continued with regard to opposition within his own party to his plan, "who now profess their exclusive friendship for the Church, will find their friendship the severest measure of hostility from which the Church ever suffered."[86] Concerning establishment, Peel similarly tried to ward off what he regarded as the extravagances of the ultra-Tory position. While some Tories believed that any changes made to ecclesiastical property or structures would ruin the church, Peel did not. "In these times it is not being prudent," Peel wrote, "to lay down general and unqualified doctrines with respect to the essential attributes of the Church." "It is safe to say," he continued,

> that *Church* is the Established Church of *England* to which the King must conform, whose Chief ministers have a right to seats in the House of Lords, which has an inalienable Claim to the Ecclesiastical Property but I should be sorry, for the sake of the Church to argue that she would infallibly cease to be the Established Church if you have once to admit equality of Civil Privilege. We might be taken at our word.[87]

Thus, just as in 1829 and the Catholic emancipation issue, Peel could concede certain political issues, in the hope that a pragmatic compromise could retain the central premises of establishment and still mollify those outside it.

In line with this flexible approach, Peel second sought the aid of sympathetic clergymen in his reforming efforts. Reminding churchmen of the calls for change from those outside the establishment, Peel asked that the church "avail itself of this, possibly the last, opportunity of aiding its true friends in the course of judicious reform, to enable us to go all the lengths we can go with perfect safety, and

---

[86]Peel to John Croker, *The Correspondence and Diaries of John Wilson Croker*, 2:264-65.

[87]Peel to Charles Lloyd, Bishop of Oxford, *Memoirs of the Right Honourable Sir Robert Peel*, ed. Lord Mahon and Edward Cardwell, 2 vols. (London, 1856-1857) 1:80.

to make, if possible, a satisfactory and final establishment."[88] In this spirit he approached influential churchmen, curried their favor, and solicited their opinions in the hopes of cajoling them into supporting his ecclesiastical plans. Prominent on his list were Bishop Charles Blomfield, Bishop John Kaye, and Bishop Charles Lloyd. Peel's tactics were as wise as they were sincere. In forming such an alliance the nature of reform was assured of moderation and of the appearance, if not the reality, of cooperation by church officials.

Third, Peel's management of the ecclesiastical issues was marked with his own self-confidence and the Tories' diffidence towards public opinion. Compromise in the face of political reality was one matter, truckling under to popular agitation was another. "There are, as might indeed naturally be expected," Peel wrote Archbishop Howley, "some eminent authorities who will think that we do not go far enough, as well as some who may probably deprecate the extent to which we do go. In this as in all other matters, the true course to be taken is to do what upon the whole we ourselves believed to be best for the permanent interests of the Church."[89]

Directed by the Tory party and Peel, ecclesiastical reform would proceed, but always in an orderly and measured fashion. Peel's approach was designed to prune extravagances, shore up weakened joints, and allow the blessings of established religion to reappear. In short, it attempted to answer Dissenters in their own language—the language of utility. Bishop Blomfield did the same when he called for ecclesiastical changes designed "to enhance and give lustre to the true beauty of the Church—the beauty of its holy usefulness."[90] This alliance between reformers in church and state characterized the administration of Whigs and Tories alike, but it was Peel's initial

---

[88]Peel to Bishop of Exeter, *Sir Robert Peel: from his private papers*, ed. Charles S. Parker, 3 vols. (London, 1891-1899) 2:265-66.

[89]Peel is quoted by Olive Brose, *Church and Parliament* (Stanford, 1959) 64.

[90]Blomfield, *Charge of 1832*, as quoted by ibid., 36. For an analysis of his utilitarian viewpoint see ibid., 35-36, 93-94, 190-91; for a discussion of the relationship between Blomfield and Peel, see P. J. Welch, "Blomfield and Peel: A Study in Cooperation Between Church and State, 1841-1846," *Journal of Ecclesiastical History* 12, no. 1 (April 1961): 71-84.

efforts that set the tone, if not the policy, for most of the subsequent ecclesiastical legislation.

AN AGENDA FOR REFORM

A variety of bills were proposed in Parliament from 1832-1852, yet the measures that ultimately passed remained within the perimeters Peel had set in his Tamworth Manifesto of 1834—reform within the limits of established religion. A review of this legislation shows it falling into three categories: parish revision, education, and societal reform. Significantly, all three had figured first in the debates over the Irish church.

First, parliamentary acts were passed designed to remedy many of the abuses persisting in the local parish. Most significant of these was a series of acts focusing upon church property and revenues. Lord Grey had established a commission of inquiry in 1831 to investigate ecclesiastical revenue, but it was not until 1835 that a full-scale report on the subject was delivered and an ecclesiastical commission established. That the composition of the commission demonstrated Peel's desire for cooperation between church and state was clear: included were seven laymen and five clergymen. Similarly, it illustrated the rationale of greater utility: Peel pronounced that the sole purpose of the commission was "to extend the sphere of [the Church's] usefulness, and to confirm its just claims upon the respect and affection of the People."[91]

The ecclesiastical commission was responsible for the passage of four important acts dealing with parochial and diocesan reorganization and revenues. The first of these acts, the Established Church Act of 1836, streamlined certain diocesan boundaries, merged other units, and moved towards equalization of episcopal incomes. The second, the Pluralities Act of 1838, strengthened the laws prohibiting concurrent holding of church benefices. The third, the Ecclesiastical Duties and Revenues Act of 1840, abolished all nonresident prebends and all sinecure rectories attached to cathedrals, and simultaneously diminished other cathedral offices. The revenues gained thereby were to go to poorer parishes and to the

---

[91]Peel is quoted by Machin, *Politics and the Churches*, 51.

creation of new urban parishes. In keeping with the spirit of the Ecclesiastical Duties and Revenues Act, a fourth act was passed in 1847
creating a new episcopal see at Manchester. Interestingly, this act
compromised between the demands of churchmen and the demands of those outside the establishment. Although it created a
new see, that see's bishop was forbidden to sit in the House of Lords
until a vacancy occurred. Had the second stipulation not been
made, the act would have meant a rise in ecclesiastical influence.[92]

Further legislation reforming the parish concerned rates and
tithes as well as church extension. In 1836, because church-rate and
tithe collections were very low, a law commuting tithe requirements
into corn-rent passed in Parliament after extended debate.[93] An attempt the following year to abolish mandatory church-rates failed,
giving conservative defenders of ecclesiastical practice a small sense
of victory. Yet although that attempt failed, the Braintree case of
1837 would have implications further unpinning the legality of
mandatory payments. In this episode, the vestry, with Dissenters in
the majority, refused to vote a church-rate. The churchwardens
then appropriated the vestry's power and levied a church-rate
themselves. Their action was declared illegal, so in 1841 the churchwardens and a minority of the vestry tried to vote a rate. However,
the House of Lords invalidated this procedure in 1853. If a majority
of the vestry refused to levy a church-rate, there seemed to be no
way to force them. Resulting from these decisions and from increased Dissenter growth and resistance, rate refusal increased
through the 1850s and early 1860s. In 1868 mandatory payment of
church-rate was abolished.[94]

While mandatory church-rates had caused problems of conscience for Dissenters for decades, the prominence of that issue

---

[92]See the discussion in ibid., 57-59, 63-64, 69-70, 150-51; P. J. Welch, "Contemporary Views on the Proposals for the Alienation of Capitular Property in England
(1832-1840)," *Journal of Ecclesiastical History* 5, no. 2 (October 1954): 184-95.

[93]See the discussion by Ward, "The Tithe Question in England," pass.

[94]Manning provides a full discussion of church-rates—see *Protestant Dissenting
Deputies*, 175-98. He estimates that in 1859, 1,525 areas had refused to levy church-
rates.

from 1830-1860 was due to its close connection with the issue of church extension. The demographic explosion in England between 1780 and 1840, accompanied by a population flight from rural areas into urban industrial areas, posed problems for the established church. At first willing to concede the new cities to the Methodists and evangelicals, the church by 1835 began to face the demands for increased spiritual and social services engendered by these changes. One typical call was for clergy to be sent "to divide the moral wilderness of this vast city into manageable districts, each with its place of worship, its schools, and its local institutions."[95] It was believed that the sanctified oasis of the parish would part and cast out the sinful influences of the urban wilderness, providing respite and education for its residents.

Such demands for church extension were immediately challenged by nonestablishment groups. While Anglicans might believe it entirely natural that public taxes be used to support new state churches, Dissenters heartily disagreed. Dissenters resented the double duty of supporting their own chapels and paying church-rates for the parish where they lived. To augment this situation with additional charges, first to build new Anglican churches and then to maintain them, riled them. Consequently, they opposed rates assessed for new parish structures as much as they opposed parliamentary subsidies for church extension. The latter was less direct but every bit as offensive. Although Dissenters argued for the use of private funds to pay for churches, initial legislation, such as the Church Building Act of 1818, blasted their hopes. This act mandated the building, where needed, of new parish churches in populated areas. Public revenues, approximately one million pounds, were appropriated for the task and a commission set up to oversee the project. In addition, the Church Building Society, formed the year before, contributed private donations. Roughly ten years later, however, Dissenting strength in Parliament increased—with immediate results. Another church building bill was passed in 1829, this time stipulating that any new churches should be constructed entirely out of private sources. By 1830, the increase in the number

---

[95]Quoted by Brose, *Church and Parliament*, 200-201.

of churches was apparent. Almost twice as many new churches were built during 1811-1826 as were built during 1801-1811. Between 1821 and 1831, 276 new churches appeared.[96]

The shift from government subsidy to private voluntary support was finalized by the passage of the New Parishes Act in 1843. Instigated by Robert Peel, it reversed the policy of the 1818 legislation by abolishing expenditures of public money in favor of stipulated advances from specific sources, such as the Queen Anne's Bounty. While these revenues were administered by a central ecclesiastical commission, they were intended to induce further private funding. Peel himself contributed, but he was adamantly opposed to the additional use of public moneys. "For the sake of the Church and its best interests," he refused to "stir . . . up that storm which large demands on the public purse would inevitably excite." Nonetheless, between 1801 and 1851, 2,529 churches were built at a total cost of roughly nine million pounds. Of this amount more than one and a half million pounds came from public funds, and Dissenters could only feel that disestablishment, or short of that, abolition of church-rate and public subsidy, would correct their situation.[97]

"On every hand, in some shape or other, the Church and State question meets the politician." These were the words of Bishop Blomfield. As he explained them, he neatly summarized the situation most prominent during the mid-1830s. "It is the Tithe question in Ireland; the Church extension question in Scotland," Blomfield said, "the Church-rate and the Education question, and the University question in England."[98] Blomfield's linking of the issues of church-rate and education was apt and prescient. Education was the second arena for parliamentary reform of ecclesiastical affairs. At the start of the nineteenth century the main issue discussed was the

---

[96]See the discussion in Best, *Temporal Pillars*, 195; Machin, *Politics and the Churches*, 17.

[97]Peel to James Graham, *Life and Letters of Sir James Graham*, ed. Charles Parker, 2 vols. (London, 1907) 1:347. Manning discusses church building in *Protestant Dissenting Deputies*, 176; Best, *Temporal Pillars*, fully investigates the Queen Anne's Bounty.

[98]Blomfield's comment appears in *The Parliamentary Debates*, ed. T. Hansard, 3d series, 48: 1,296.

necessity of a plan for national education. Concerning this point two separate approaches developed. One favored a strictly interpreted and implemented denominational scheme for education, the other favored a nondenominational orientation. It was assumed by advocates of both approaches that proper education included a religious component, but it was over the precise meaning of this religious component that differences arose.[99]

The National Society (founded 1811) and the British and Foreign School Society (founded 1814) represented the contrasting approaches to education. Unlike the High Church orientation of the National Society and its founders, Henry Norris and Joshua Watson, the British and Foreign School Society was supported primarily by evangelical sources, although large numbers of sympathetic Dissenters were also members. A disinclination to interpret Christian doctrine in rigorous and creedal terms made the evangelicals and Dissenters compatible, but their alliance within the British and Foreign School Society was a convenience caused by the facing of a common enemy rather than the endorsing of shared principle. Significantly, the battle line between the two national organizations had been drawn earlier. Two educational reformers, Andrew Bell and Joseph Lancaster, had struggled over the same issue of religious instruction in their own attempts to develop model schools. Bell's system employed older students as aides and monitors for younger ones and made religious instruction clearly Anglican. Lancaster shared Bell's views regarding monitors but designed his religious instruction "on general Christian principles, and on them only. Mankind is divided into sects, and individually think very differently on religious subjects. . . . but the grand basis of Christianity alone is broad enough for the whole bulk of mankind to stand upon, and join hands as children of one family." In 1808, with the receipt of royal patronage and the establishment of the Royal Lancaster Society, the contest appeared to turn in Lancaster's favor. The Royal Lancaster Society, based on Lancaster's idea of "general Christian

---

[99]See G. F. Best, "The Religious Difficulties of National Education in England, 1800-1870," *The Cambridge Historical Journal* 12, no. 2 (1956): 155-73.

principles," was the direct predecessor of the British and Foreign School Society.[100]

Just as the membership of the British and Foreign School Society crossed denominational lines, its educational efforts extended outside the classroom. Especially under the auspices of evangelical leadership, the society's educational work joined with the labors of the Religious Tract Society, the Bible Society, and the Church Mission Society. Indeed, prominently featured within the concept of proper religious education was instruction for the poor, especially in reading the Bible. Thus, home missionary societies were often seen working in adjunct capacities with members of educational societies.

But if strict Anglicans and less creedal evangelicals both agreed on the need for literacy and domestic missionary works, they were again split on a correct approach to meeting those needs. Where the British and Foreign School Society might offer the Bible alone, or perhaps only the four Gospels, the worker for the National Society would counter that ideally the Prayer Book and authorized commentaries as provided by the Society for Christian Knowledge and the Society for Propagating the Gospel ought to be included. The latter two societies were the strict-creedal counterparts to the Tract and Mission groups. They were likewise directed to educational and missionary tasks but understood these within a denominational framework in a way that strikingly paralleled evangelical and dissenter efforts.[101]

Consequently, as Blomfield had intimated, two issues, public subsidies for education and admission of dissenters to the universities, made up the bulk of legislation and focused the discussion between members of the two rival education groups. In 1833,

---

[100]For a full discussion of the situation in education, see F. W. Cornish, *The English Church in the Nineteenth Century*, 2 vols. (London, 1910) 1:89-93; John Adamson, *English Education, 1789-1902* (Cambridge, 1930); David Wardle, *English Popular Education* (Cambridge, 1970); M. Vaughan and M. Archer, *Social Conflict and Educational Change in England and France, 1789-1848* (Cambridge, 1971); R. A. Soloway, *Prelates and People: Ecclesiastical Social Thought in England, 1783-1852* (London, 1969) 349-431.

[101]See the discussion in Best, "The Evangelicals and the Established Church," 72.

utilitarian radicals proposed a scheme for secular national education, but their plan foundered and the debate rearranged itself along religious lines. In 1833 the government granted twenty thousand pounds for national education. As with other legislation this was foreshadowed by action taken in Ireland, where a grant for education had been made in 1815. Now in 1833 the money was to be divided evenly between the National Society and the British and Foreign School Society with the stipulation that each society match the government grant with an equal amount from private sources. This system of matching grants persisted until 1839. In that year Lord John Russell proposed to increase the subsidy to thirty thousand pounds a year, establish inspectors to check on religion instruction, and open a National Training College for teachers. Russell's plan was fiercely opposed by many sources. He revised his suggestion about inspectors and dropped the idea of the teacher training college altogether. Officially at least, governmental neutrality in education had been preserved.[102]

One of the problems with Russell's proposed inspectors was that originally he had suggested they be chosen by a secular legislature rather than a clerical authority. When that plan had been opposed, he had then modified it, specifying that church authorities would inspect National Society schools instead. However, the issue reappeared. In 1843 James Graham introduced a bill stipulating that schools be established in industrial factories and that young children spend three hours a day receiving instruction. Graham's bill also called for state inspection and for Anglican churchmen to act as headmasters of the new schools. Dissenters objected to this provision, of course, as well as to the inroads such instruction would make into their strongholds of industrial and laboring congregations. Graham tried to soften his bill, but his concessions were repudiated—the bill failed to pass. Once more an uneasy balance had been struck between the forces of church and Dissent, though the struggle over education would continue into the twentieth century.[103]

---

[102]See Machin, *Politics and the Churches*, 64-68.

[103]See ibid., 151-60; J. T. Ward and J. H. Treble, "Religion and Education in 1843: Reactions to the Factory Education Bill," *Journal of Ecclesiastical History* 20, no. 1 (April 1969): 79-110.

The deadlock over the issues of primary education was duplicated in the controversy surrounding university admission. Many Anglican churchmen regarded the universities of Oxford and Cambridge as theirs. Traditionally, Oxford had trained the majority of Anglican clergy and the lectures of its professors of divinity had interpreted Anglican orthodoxy and kept it safe. Cambridge insisted that students subscribe to the Thirty-nine Articles upon graduation, thereby allowing in principle for Dissenters to pursue studies, though stopping them short of receipt of degrees. The requirements at Oxford were stiffer, calling for subscription at matriculation. Under these circumstances Dissenters were forced to go either north to Scotland or across the Channel to the Continent in order to obtain degrees. In 1834, hard on the heels of the debate over subsidies to primary education, a petition was presented from Cambridge calling for abolition of the subscription test. This petition produced countermeasures from supporters of the test. Some advocates of test abolition lost their appointments. The Cambridge petition failed to gain much support at Oxford. Soon the episode faded before other concerns. Two years later in 1836 Dissenters saw their University of London finally awarded a charter and thereby given the capacity to award degrees. This development enabled them to pursue their educational obligations; however, the two great universities of Oxford and Cambridge remained closed to them. It was not until 1854 that Dissenters were allowed to receive the baccalaureate degree without subscription at Oxford. Cambridge dropped its subscription requirements in 1856. It was not until the 1870s that all religious tests at Oxford and Cambridge were abolished.[104]

Admission to the universities was not the only bone of contention between Dissenters and the established church. In 1833 a group of prominent Dissenters issued a petition outlining six major grievances. They asked relief from the law making legal only marriages conducted according to Anglican rites, from laws making them liable for church-rate and responsible for poor rates; they asked that religious tests at the universities be abolished and

---

[104]See the discussion by Manning, *Protestant Dissenting Deputies*, 372-84.

stressed the need for a charter for the University of London; they asked for civil registration of births and deaths and for permission to be buried by their own rites within their parish churchyards.[105]

The issues of church-rate, religious tests at Oxford and Cambridge and the charter for the University of London have already been discussed. The remainder of these grievances illustrates the third area of reform legislation: that concerned with social problems, including the problem of church relations with the Roman Catholic Church. Dissenters pressed for relief from their complaints and happily noted that the parliamentary session of 1833 exempted their chapels from liability for poor rates. Similarly, in 1836 bills were passed providing for civil registration for births, marriages, and deaths. Indeed, while the Anglican church remained established, Dissenters could observe with satisfaction that they had forced the establishment to acquiesce to their demands—even if it had done so only to prevent disestablishment. Nevertheless, the more intractable issues of rate relief and educational opportunity provided the Dissenters with material for struggle for several more decades.[106]

Added to these political victories were other indications of growing Dissenter strength. Dissenter power in confronting the establishment could be glimpsed in the discussion over ecclesiastical patronage. Patronage claims comprised an area as full of precedent and tradition, defensive pride and arbitrary authority as any. Somewhat obliquely these privileges were curtailed through the Municipal Reform Act of 1835. In line with the Reform Act of 1832, the Municipal Reform Act increased popular involvement in local government. In large urban areas where Dissent was extensive and powerful, these enfranchising measures brought Dissenters prominently into local electoral politics. For ecclesiastical patronage this situation caused certain ecclesiastical positions, disposed of by municipal corporations, to fall into the hands of local councils whose composition was often overwhelmingly Dissenter. Conservative churchmen, such as Lord Lyndhurst, tried to insist on limiting ec-

---

[105]Machin, *Politics and the Churches*, 42-43.

[106]Ibid., 43, 56; Manning, *Protestant Dissenting Deputies*, 254-332.

clesiastical patronage exclusively to Anglicans, but such measures smacked of renewed religious tests. His measure failed. Finally, churchmen and Dissenters usually cooperated with one another. Sometimes ecclesiastical positions, particularly in smaller boroughs, remained in Anglican hands; other times they were auctioned to the highest bidder, falling quite often to evangelicals who for generations had acquired livings in this manner.[107] Patronage on the local and national levels continued much as before though the gains made by Dissenters further highlighted them.

If many of the precedents for English church reform could be found in Irish reform, the fundamental issue behind the Irish question—the relation between the Protestant and Catholic churches—also figured in the English scene. The years between 1829 and 1845 were generally quiet insofar as England's Roman Catholics and Parliament were concerned. From the mid-1840s until the passage of the Ecclesiastical Tithes Act in 1851, a change in mood, a more acrimonious tone, characterized the kinship between Catholics and Protestants. For by 1845, with the new Irish immigrants fleeing the famine and crossing St. George's Channel in search of jobs and security, English Catholicism underwent a marked cultural shift. The transfusion of Irish Catholicism into the traditions of its English counterpart affected the subsequent course of Catholicism during the remainder of the century. A new and invigorated spirit took hold of English Catholicism in the 1840s and 1850s. It was a spirit that, though pulled in many cultural and political directions, rallied Catholics to a new self-awareness.[108]

Two pieces of parliamentary legislation passed in 1845 and 1846 directly affected Roman Catholics. In 1845 after fierce debate, the parliamentary subsidy to the Irish Catholic college of Maynooth finally passed. This dispute emphasized the ever-present arguments over religious education and suggested that the embers of anti-

---

[107]See Machin, *Politics and the Churches*, 54-55; Chadwick, *Victorian Church*, 1:108-12; G. B. Finlayson, "The Politics of Municipal Reform, 1835," *English Historical Review* 81 (1966): 673-92.

[108]See the discussion in B. Ward, *The Sequel to Catholic Emancipation, 1840-1850*, 2 vols. (London, 1915).

Catholic sentiment in England had not completely died out. The following year a bill aimed at the existing restrictions placed on Catholics and Jews was debated and passed. This legislation, the Religious Opinions Relief Act, still did not remove all complaints, yet its concessionary nature and its intention to remove obsolete recusant articles pleased Catholics.[109] The next major encounter between Catholics and Parliament would not be so pleasant. In 1851, in response to a papal proposal for reintroducing the Catholic hierarchy into England and in response to the worsening relations between Westminster and the Vatican that ensued, Parliament passed the Ecclesiastical Titles Act. This legislation fined any clergyman who assumed a title duplicating one existing in the established church. The confrontation that this legislation posed to the Catholic hierarchy was intended, and it signaled government support for the spirit of anti-Catholicism again growing in England.[110]

In 1838 in the midst of Parliament's reforming activity, Henry Manning took stock of that activity's immediate and implied effects. Manning was disgruntled with what he found, but nothing so distressed him as the implications he believed Parliament's activity held for relations between church and state. "The next patriarch of the English Church will be Parliament," Manning wrote, "and on its votes will hang our order, mission, discipline and faith; and the Pontificate of Parliament is but the modern voluntary principle in disguise."[111]

If Manning was dismayed by the drift of Parliament's efforts, he and other like-minded clergymen were shocked by the outcome in 1850 of the famous Gorham case. George Gorham was an evangelical clergyman who had been denied an ecclesiastical position by the

---

[109]See the discussion by G. I. T. Machin, "The Maynooth Grant, the Dissenters, and Disestablishment, 1845-47," *English Historical Review* 82 (1967): 61-85.

[110]For an analysis of this issue see Machin, *Politics and the Churches*, 210-28; G. I. T. Machin, "Lord John Russell and the Prelude to the Ecclesiastical Titles Bill, 1846-51," *Journal of Ecclesiastical History* 25, no. 3 (July 1974): 277-95; G. A. Beck, ed., *The English Catholics, 1850-1950* (London, 1950); Best, "Popular Protestantism in Victorian England."

[111]Henry Manning, *The Principles of the Ecclesiastical Commission Examined* (London, 1838) 38.

conservative bishop, Henry Phillpotts. As with most good evangelicals, Gorham placed the spiritual birthdate of believers at their time of conversion rather than at baptism. For Phillpotts, Gorham's belief denied the validity of baptismal regeneration, and he blocked Gorham's candidacy. Gorham in turn first appealed his case to the Court of Arches, which ruled against him. Then he appealed the ruling of the Court of Arches to the Judicial Committee of the Privy Council, which had become the court of highest appeal in ecclesiastical matters when the High Court of Delegates was abolished in 1832 as part of a reform program. In 1850, the Privy Council overturned the previous decision and ruled that Gorham should be allowed his position. While evangelicals were vindicated, conservative Anglicans were outraged at what they considered illegitimate state interference in the church's internal affairs. To conservatives like Phillpotts, a secular judicial body had just ruled on a point of doctrinal interpretation. Had he known of Manning's words he would have agreed with them completely.[112]

The controversies between church and state and between established religion and Dissent produced another movement of note: the attempt from 1852-1855 to revive the convocation of Canterbury as an autonomous ecclesiastical body.[113] Convocation had been prorogued in 1717. With the exception of a session in 1741, it was suspended in each succeeding year before it could carry out any significant business. By the 1850s, however, with on the one hand the possibility of the reestablishment of a Catholic hierarchy and on the other the ever-growing dissatisfaction among certain clergymen over Parliament's legislation, it seemed apparent to many church members that there was a need for a synodical body to represent the church's interests. Indeed, after the Gorham case, conservative church members believed that Parliament (whose members might or might not be Anglican) had interfered in ecclesiastical adminis-

---

[112]On the Gorham case, see Machin, *Politics and the Churches*, 202-205; Chadwick, *Victorian Church*, 1:250-70.

[113]See P. J. Welch, "The Revival of an active Convocation at Canterbury (1852-1855)," *Journal of Ecclesiastical History* 10, no. 2 (October 1959): 188-97.

tration and that this group of secular jurists had dictated to them on matters of church doctrine.

To these clerics the notion that Parliament represented the interests of the church was no longer tenable, if ever it had been. In 1852 Samuel Wilberforce, Bishop of Oxford and son of William Wilberforce, began his campaign to revive convocation. Sporadic attempts had been made over the years, but now under Wilberforce's direction, energetic new efforts were reapplied. In so doing, Wilberforce, through formal and familial avenues, pressured the government to accept convocation. Finally, with the help of Blomfield, Wilberforce brought the recalcitrant Archbishop of Canterbury, John Sumner, into his camp, and in 1855 convocation resumed its deliberations.

The renewal of convocation in 1855 symbolized an equilibrium that had been struck in ecclesiastical affairs. The church had been neither disestablished as some had hoped, nor had Dissent, as others had hoped, been eradicated. Instead, moderate reforms had taken place. Throughout the twenty years following the Reform Act of 1832, Whigs and Tories alike had avoided disestablishment by enacting legislative reform. Bodies such as the Ecclesiastical Commission begun by Peel in 1835 had helped effect these changes. Churchmen and Dissenters had contended with one another over solutions to the problems of education, social need, and spiritual destitution—problems that were lumped together as the "condition of England question." Dissenters had seen many of their grievances answered. Conservatives, if tamed, were not completely subdued. Victory, if it could be called that, belonged to the advocates of parliamentary ascendancy. The implications of the parliamentary reforms were clear. They transformed an older view of "the Church of England as by law established" into something quite new. "In what way the Church of England is established," observed Walter Hook in 1846, "is very difficult to say. . . . It exists, therefore, now, simply as one of the great corporations of the country, claiming from the State, like every other corporation, protection for its rights and its property."[114] Hook was one of those who believed that church rights

---

[114]Walter Hook, *A Letter to the Lord Bishop of St. David's* (London, 1846) 37-38.

had been poorly guarded and church property stolen by its very defenders. Yet his assessment of the status of the Church of England was as relevant to the institution on the eve of the Reform Bill of 1867 as when he first said it.

If modifications had been made, they had not come about without a contest. Indeed, if Parliament was ultimately to become the new patriarch of the Church of England, as Henry Manning maintained, its assumption of power was strongly opposed by groups within the church. And no section of the church resisted this redefining of Erastian prerogatives more vocally than did a clerical cadre at Oxford.

CHAPTER FIVE

THE OXFORD MOVEMENT

"A CALL TO CHURCH PRINCIPLES"

When the House of Parliament caught fire in 1834, many churchmen interpreted it as a sign of divine displeasure with the ecclesiastical reforms of recent years. Conservative clerics of the 1830s did not depend on God, however, for a demonstration of displeasure with those reforms. In Oxford, in the midst of the university known for its close association with the Church of England, a movement appeared whose self-proclaimed purpose was to rouse a defense of the church's spiritual claims.

On October 1831, Hurrell Froude, a firebrand within the Oxford movement, wrote John Henry Newman concerning the Whig reformers. While he opposed the Whigs, Froude was equally wary of certain contented Anglican Tories. For Froude, it was not enough to resist outside pressure; a proper defense of the church's integrity required agitation and education within the church. As Froude put it, "the Church can never right itself without a blow up." Newman had earlier voiced his own disappointment with the lassitude enveloping the church. Instead of great leaders, Newman said, the Church party "is poor in mental endowments. It has not activity, shrewdness, dexterity, eloquence, practical powers. On what then does it depend? on prejudice and bigotry."[1]

The need to reawaken Anglicans to a proper sense of spiritual heritage was a goal shared by Newman's colleagues at Oxford. Indeed, although John Henry Newman, John Keble, Hurrell Froude, Edward Pusey, and Robert Isaac Wilberforce came from different backgrounds, their efforts during 1833-1845 demonstrated a unity of purpose. The Oxford movement evolved as a means of resisting what was seen as encroachment and spoliation of the church by the state—an illegitimate interference in internal ecclesiastical affairs by individuals who had no stake in the life or future of the church. Supporters of the movement wished to reassert the importance of the church as a visible institution holding the power and responsibility of administering the sacraments. They wished to restore a proper respect for faith: the faith expressed in the tradition of antiquity, the faith standing above mere private judgment, the faith containing eternal truth and the message of salvation.

The common efforts of this group, and the series of tracts most often associated with it, represented a junction in lives otherwise disparate. Wilberforce and Newman, for example, were both raised in families influenced by evangelicalism. Robert Isaac Wilberforce was the second son of William Wilberforce. Born in 1802, Robert spent his childhood in the warm intimacy of his well-known family. In 1820 he left for Oxford and matriculated in Oriel College. That the son of William Wilberforce should be sent to this citadel of orthodoxy surprised many. Nevertheless, Robert's older brother, William, had had a disastrous career at Cambridge. Robert's father greatly esteemed Edward Hawkins, tutor at Oriel, and wanted his son to be broadly educated. He determined to send Robert to Oxford.[2] In 1823, the paths of Wilberforce and his future colleagues,

---

[1]Hurrell Froude to John Newman, 4 October 1831, Froude Papers, Birmingham Oratory, Birmingham, England; Newman to his mother, 13 March 1829, Newman Papers, Birmingham Oratory, Birmingham, England. See also the description in Richard Church, *The Oxford Movement, 1833-1845* (London, 1892) 27-32.

[2]See the excellent study by David Newsome, *The Parting of Friends* (London, 1966) 57-62; and the memories of Thomas Mozley, *Reminiscences chiefly of Oriel College and the Oxford Movement*, 2 vols. (Boston, 1882) 1:100-101.

Hurrell Froude and John Keble, crossed. In that year Keble invited Froude, Wilberforce, and Isaac Williams to spend the Long Vacation with him. Wilberforce accepted and during the course of that session was won over, as many others had been, by Keble's charm, humility, and learning.

After graduating, Robert Wilberforce spent the next two years preparing to stand for one of the coveted Oriel fellowships. He gained one in 1826 but left Oxford for Cambridge the following year in order to study Hebrew. He returned to Oriel before the year was out. Another of those significant experiences during the 1820s that drew the future Tractarians into closer personal acquaintance-ship was about to occur.

In 1827 the provostship of Oriel became vacant. The two candidates for the post were Edward Hawkins and John Keble. Both men were respected and had a circle of friends and alliances wide enough to make the decision a perplexing one within the small confines of the college. After long deliberation Wilberforce cast his vote for Hawkins, the eventual winner. But this episode had hardly concluded when Wilberforce found himself again embroiled in college politics, this time directly at odds with Hawkins. Beginning in 1827, Wilberforce served as a tutor at Oriel along with Newman and Froude. All three were dissatisfied with the nature of the tutorial system. In 1828 they attempted to revise its operation and to gain more direct control over their students' education. The reform plan was carried out without Hawkins's knowledge. Upon discovering the operation, the provost refused to assign further students to these tutors unless they returned to the former tutorial methods. The result of this turn of events was that Newman, Froude, and Wilberforce, bound together by their collaboration in reforming the tutorial system, became even closer when they accepted the provost's ultimatum and gave up teaching. Consequently, in 1830 while still attached to Oriel College, Robert Wilberforce was ready to strike out on new paths. Although he was disturbed by events in Europe including the abdication and flight of Charles X from Paris, Wilberforce decided to revive an earlier plan and travel to Germany to resume his language studies.[3]

---

[3]Ibid., 82-84, 94-96.

In contrast with Robert Wilberforce and the other leaders of the Oxford movement, John Newman came from a middle-class family. The son of a London banker, Newman was born in 1801 into a family of moderate evangelical leanings. An important turning point in his young life occurred in 1816 when he experienced religious conversion and became assured of living in a state of grace. In a famous passage from the *Apologia*, Newman wrote that he came to "rest in the thought of two and two only absolute and luminously self-evident beings, myself and my Creator."[4] The following year Newman went up to Oxford and studied at Trinity College. In 1822, though his undergraduate studies had been undistinguished, he was elected a fellow of Oriel College. Newman was exhilarated with the atmosphere of Oriel; he grew in intellectual self-confidence among colleagues such as John Keble, Richard Whately, and Edward Hawkins. Ironically, it was the liberal, Whately, who first influenced Newman to view the church as a corporative body. In keeping with his evangelical leanings, Newman served as co-secretary in the Oxford branch of the Church Missionary Society. He continued to study Anglican theology, especially the work of Joseph Butler. It was during these years at Oriel that Newman also met Edward Pusey and Hurrell Froude. Pusey left in 1825 to pursue his studies in Germany, but Newman's friendship with Froude grew from this point onward.[5]

The personal relationship that developed between Newman and Froude further evidenced the gradual process of events and influences that welded a diverse group of individuals into a united whole. The Froude family into which Hurrell was born in 1803 was steeped in a particular brand of Tory Anglicanism deserving of its nickname, "High and Dry." Hurrell's younger brother, James Anthony, described their father, Archdeacon Froude, as

---

[4]The biographical material on Newman is extensive. See, for example, Maisie Ward, *Young Mr. Newman* (New York, 1948); R. D. Middleton, *Newman at Oxford* (London, 1950); Louis Bouyer, *Newman: His Life and Spirituality* (London, 1958); and Meriol Trevor, *Newman: The Pillar of the Cloud* (London, 1962). Newman is quoted from *Apologia Pro Vita Sua*, ed. A. Dwight Culler (Boston, 1956) 25.

[5]Newman, *Apologia*, 31-33, 36-37, 43-44; T. C. Stunt, "John Henry Newman and the Evangelicals," *Journal of Ecclesiastical History* 21, no. 1 (January 1970): 65-74.

an excellent parish priest of the old sort, with strong sense, a practical belief in the doctrine of the Church of England as by law established, which no person in his right mind would think of questioning. As a country gentleman and a landowner himself, he was looked up to by the tenants and the parishioners with affection and reverence. . . . He was perpetually occupied with business, but always silently, never I believe in his whole life appearing to make a speech on a platform, and despising and distrusting the whole race of popular orators. He never spoke even in private, of feeling and sentiment, and never showed any in word or action.[6]

Consequently, twenty years later when Hurrell Froude first met Newman at Oriel, he felt as though they were two different breeds. To Froude, Newman was stained with the beliefs of his evangelical upbringing and his association with the liberal crowd surrounding Richard Whately. As for Froude, he still identified with the Tories, though he was moving away from the stuffiness of his own family traditions, especially as he grew to know John Keble. Froude, like Robert Wilberforce, had spent the Long Vacation of 1823 at Keble's. Both he and Keble felt the impact of the meeting. Froude wrote of Keble in glowing phrases to his father, while Keble declared of Froude to a friend, "I assure you I miss him not a little—he is one of the best tempered, and in scenery one of the most romantic fellows I know; but idle, or given to reveries a little too much."[7] But although his encounter with Keble raised new questions for Froude about the meaning and direction of his Tory Anglicanism, he was still acutely aware of the differences between himself and Newman.

These feelings changed under the pressure of events. In 1827 Froude and Newman both had been Fellows at Oriel; now they were elevated together as tutors. At first their differences seemed most apparent, as Newman voted for Hawkins, and Froude for Keble, in the election for provost. Their mutual efforts towards the reform of the tutorial system and the opposition they encountered from Hawkins, however, bound them more closely and deepened their admi-

---

[6]Archdeacon Froude is described in Waldo H. Dunn, *James Anthony Froude*, 2 vols. (Oxford, 1961-1963) 1:14-15. For a thorough discussion of Hurrell Froude, see the excellent study by Piers Brendon, *Hurrell Froude and the Oxford Movement* (London, 1974).

[7]Hurrell Froude to Archdeacon Froude, 10 August 1823, Froude Papers; John Keble to J. T. Coleridge, 27 September 1823, cited in Brendon, *Hurrell Froude*, 49.

ration for each other. Political events outside the college also strengthened their friendship—they found themselves allied against the reelection of Robert Peel. It was after the passage of the Catholic emancipation bill of 1829 and Peel was hoping to continue to represent Oxford in the House of Commons. When news reached Newman of Peel's defeat at Oxford, his happiness was unbounded. "We have achieved a glorious Victory," Newman wrote his mother. "It is the first public event I have been concerned in, and I thank God from my heart both for my cause and its success. We have proved the independence of the Church and of Oxford."[8] Newman's involvement in Peel's defeat was both personally and politically significant. It marked Newman's break with liberals such as Whately and Hawkins, and signaled his shift towards the type of conservatism that would typify the Oxford movement. In a letter to his sister, Newman tried to explain his opposition to Peel. "I am in principle Anti-Catholic," he wrote,

> i.e., I think there is a grand attack on the Church in progress from the Utilitarians and Schismatics—and the first step in a long train of events is *accidentally* the granting these claims. Thus it is to me a matter of subordinate consequence whether they are granted or not—if granted, something fresh will be asked; say, the unestablishing of the Irish Protestant Church.

Continuing, Newman emphasized that the fight against Peel represented "an opportunity of showing our independence from the world." He believed that the church was under attack, and in a follow-up letter to his mother Newman more clearly defined the nature of the enemy. "We live in a novel era," he stated,

> one in which there is an advance towards universal education. Men have hitherto depended on others, and especially on the Clergy, for religious truth; now each man attempts to judge for himself. . . . Christianity is of faith, modesty, lowliness, subordination; but the spirit at work against it is one of latitudinarianism, indifferentism, republicanism, and schism, a spirit which tends to overthrow doctrine, as if the fruit of bigotry, and discipline as if the instrument of priestcraft.[9]

---

[8]Newman to his mother, 1 March 1829, Newman Papers.

[9]Newman to Jemina Newman, 4 March 1829; Newman to his mother, 13 March 1829, Newman Papers.

From 1829 on, as the distance widened between Newman and his former liberal and evangelical associates, he and Froude grew closer. Froude not only supported Newman in his shift away from liberalism, he communicated that rich strain of Anglican Caroline theology that was the legacy of his studies under Keble. By 1830, Newman had resigned from the evangelical Church Missionary Society. In doing so, he began to define the themes that were to become the trademarks of the Tractarians. "The Society recognizes no *Church principles* on which the friends of the Church who join it can fall back," Newman explained in defense of his resignation. "If it were recognized, e.g., that the Church were the divinely-sanctioned system, or that dissent were per se an evil, or that reading the Bible is not (ordinarily) sufficient for salvation, there would be something for Churchmen to cling to."[10] Long dissatisfied with the missionary society, Newman now believed that reform from within this society was impractical and meant eventual compromise of personal values. Instead, a clean break was needed and church principles somehow advocated in a fresh and pure manner. In the aftermath of the battle with Hawkins over the Oriel tutorial system and in the midst of his confusion about the proper way to pursue church principles, Newman accepted an offer by Froude's father to accompany him and his son Hurrell on a trip to the Mediterranean. The voyage was to have important consequences for both John Newman and Hurrell Froude, but as they left England in 1832 the ecclesiastical horizons seemed to them stormy and uncertain indeed.

John Keble was the exception that proves the rule with regard to the varied backgrounds of the Oxford movement's leaders. If Wilberforce and Newman both shed their evangelical backgrounds in some fashion, and if Hurrell Froude sloughed off his carapace of "High and Dry" Anglicanism, it was Keble's fortune to be the one raised in the traditions most in sympathy with the eventual aims and ethos of the Oxford party. Furthermore, Keble proved to be the linchpin in the organization and development of those early associations and relationships from which the Oxford movement of the

---

[10]Newman to Samuel Pope, 15 August 1830, Newman Papers; Stunt, "Newman and the Evangelicals," 65ff.

1830s and 1840s grew. Keble, of course, did not consciously plan such developments. Nevertheless, his influence on Wilberforce, Froude, and Newman was great, and the opportunity for conversation and exploration that his vacation reading sessions provided enabled ideas to be discussed and values explored in a way that proved immensely fruitful in subsequent years.

Keble was something of a legend at Oxford. Born in 1792, he was educated at home by his parson father, and grew up within a close-knit family thoroughly steeped in the piety of the Caroline divines and the politics of the nonjuring bishops. In 1810 Keble graduated with a double first in mathematics and classics. The next year he was elected to a fellowship at Oriel. All Oxford stood in awe of his intellectual achievements.[11] In 1818 Keble was named a tutor at Oriel, and it was under these auspices that he first met Froude and Newman. In 1823 Keble resigned his position at Oriel, however, and returned to Lincolnshire to assist his father in parish work. Keble's removal from Oxford to the country did not mean that he had cut all his Oxford connections. The university had not heard the last of him. In 1827 Keble published his well-known collection of poems, *The Christian Year*, and was proposed as a candidate for the Oriel provostship. The election split the future Tractarians. Froude actively canvassed on Keble's behalf, while Newman supported Hawkins quipping, "If we were electing an Angel, I should, of course vote for Keble, but the case is different." Keble, for his own part, thought he was quite capable of doing the job but wished to avoid contention. He withdrew his name rather than force a tally of the votes.[12]

In 1829 when the issue of Peel's election arose, Keble wrote a short pamphlet urging that Peel be opposed. The pamphlet dealt less with the issue of Catholic emancipation and more with the fact that Peel had changed his mind. When Peel was defeated, Keble's

[11]For biographical details see J. T. Coleridge, *A Memoir of the Rev. John Keble*, 2 vols. (New York, 1869); Walter Lock, *John Keble* (London, 1893); Georgina Battiscombe, *John Keble: a Study in Limitations* (London, 1963).

[12]*The Letters and Diaries of John Henry Newman*, ed. C. S. Dessain, Ian Ker, and Thomas Garnall, 33 vols. (Oxford, 1961-) 30:107; Battiscombe, *John Keble*, 119.

verdict reflected the particular blend of values that he brought to politics. Writing to Newman shortly after the election, Keble stated,

> On moral grounds I am disposed to respect and admire him; but on political grounds I am more and more pleased that he was not elected. To say the truth, I never wish to see a minister of state, or leader of a party, representing the University again; I had rather have a straight forward country gentleman.[13]

His invoking the virtues of a country gentleman at a time when many social and political problems were developing out of the complexity of an increasingly industrial society may sound anachronistic of Keble. Nevertheless, it was this ethos of respect, reserve, and tradition that Keble exemplified in his own life and looked for in others. These virtues were tempered in him by a mixture of humility, optimism, and self-confidence, an ability to see wisdom in the old answers while avoiding the pomposity and self-righteousness typical of "High and Dry" churchmen. They were qualities that earned Keble many lasting friends, friends that stuck with him even during future times of turmoil and recrimination. Thus, in 1830 when it seemed that the church was being attacked from all sides, Keble wrote to his brother, Thomas, "I cannot help hoping from all I can observe that there is a sort of under-current of Toryism gaining strength which sooner or later will set things right again."[14]

Newman and Froude's trip to the Mediterranean provided the pair with an opportunity to observe Roman Catholicism in a way not previously available. The encounter was revealing for them both. In February 1833 Froude wrote an impassioned letter from Naples describing the low state of religious life in Sicily, and detailing a situation in which the state garnered one-third of church revenues and priests laughed aloud during confessions. "The Church of England has fallen low, and will probably be worse before it is better," Froude concluded, "but let the Whigs do their worst, they cannot sink us so deep as these people have allowed themselves to fall." Newman's let-

---

[13]Keble to Newman, 28 March 1829, John Keble Papers, Keble College, Oxford. For Keble's pamphlet, see Battiscombe, *John Keble*, 125.

[14]John Keble to Thomas Keble, ca. 1830, Keble Papers.

ters expressed some of the same despair, though his rage was sharpest against developments at home.[15]

Despite their Sicilian experiences, both Newman and Froude looked forward to visiting Rome. During their stay they met with Nicolas Wiseman, rector of the English College at Rome, and explored the issue of reconciliation between the Anglican and Roman churches. In his typically direct manner, Froude spoke of his frustrations with the meeting. "We found to our dismay that not one step could be gained without swallowing the Council of Trent as a whole," Froude remarked. "We found to our horror that the infallibility of the Church made the acts of each successive council obligatory for ever." Thus the naive ecumenical overtures of the young Newman and Froude ran up for the first time against the dogmatic solidity of the Catholic tradition. Froude's disappointment was clear in his letter; he could not resist one final pointed comment. "So much for the Council of Trent, for which Christendom has to thank Luther and the Reformers."[16]

Froude and Newman were both back in England by July 1833, though neither of them attended the event that many consider to be the beginning of the Oxford movement. On 14 July 1833, forty-four years to the day that the Bastille was stormed, John Keble ascended a pulpit and delivered his famous sermon on "National Apostasy." Keble took this occasion to protest the suppression of the ten Irish bishoprics by the Whigs, and the advertisement to the printed edition of his sermon spoke of this issue forcefully. Since the legislature, which need no longer be composed of church members, had ratified the view that the Church of England was but one sect among others, had not the church, Keble asked, become a creature of the state, "a mere Parliamentarian Church." Keble answered his question, concluding "there was once here a glorious Church, but it was betrayed into the hands of Libertines for the real or affected love of a little temporary peace and good order." Here was the na-

---

[15]Froude, *Remains of the late Reverend Richard Hurrell Froude*, ed. John Newman and John Keble, 4 vols. (London, 1833-1839) 1:294-95; Newman to his mother, 28 February 1833, Newman Papers. When he heard of the Irish Church Reform Bill, Newman was nearly apoplectic:"Well done! my blind Premier, confiscate and rob, till like Samson, you pull down the Political Structure on your own head."

[16]Froude, *Remains*, 1:306.

tional apostasy, in Keble's view. The process in which the "apostolical church" had become a slave of state bondage had to be reversed.[17]

If Keble had trumpeted a call, the next step required that forces be marshaled in defense of this apostolic church. Yet there is no greater testimony to the cross-purposes and competition that characterized the first stages of the Oxford movement than the group that assembled to begin this task. Shortly after Keble's sermon Hugh James Rose invited a small group of individuals to meet at his parsonage at Hadleigh. Rose earlier had expressed the desire for some form of action, and his position as editor of *The British Magazine* gave the conference an air of respectability. The attendance at the meeting, however, was not particularly promising. Newman was not there, and Keble preferred to return to work in his rural parish. Consequently, Froude, Rose, William Palmer, Arthur Perceval, and R. C. Trench formed the war council that was to organize resistance to state interference.[18] By the end of the conference the participants had agreed to make a unified effort, emphasizing the importance of the doctrine of apostolic succession and preserving the prayer books from revision. Upon this broad ideological consensus two strategies were undertaken. First, an address supporting these twin points and signed by approximately seven thousand clerics was delivered to the Archbishop of Canterbury. Second, a similar appeal designed to garner adherents among the laity was drawn up and contained 230,000 signatures from heads of households when it was delivered to Canterbury.[19]

RAILROADS FOR THE DIFFUSION OF APOSTOLICAL KNOWLEDGE

Even this tactical agreement was soon to break up though, for by August 1833, Froude, Newman, and Keble were pushing for a more

---

[17]Keble, "National Apostasy," *Sermons, Academical and Occasional* (Oxford, 1847) 127-28, 138.

[18]For an account of the meeting, see A. P. Perceval, *A Collection of the Papers Connected with the Theological Movement of 1833* (London, 1842) 10-11; for Rose's earlier call for action, see Hugh Rose to William Palmer, 1 February 1833, in William Palmer, *A Narrative of Events Connected with the Publication of the Tracts for the Times* (New York, 1843) 18.

[19]Perceval, *Papers Connected with the Theological Movement*, 11-12.

comprehensive statement of principles, and disagreeing with Palmer and Perceval over the wisdom of forming an association to defend the church. Froude sent Perceval a draft statement in August which among other things suggested enhancing the popularity of the church, and contemplated a possible separation of church and state. In a follow-up letter by Newman explicit discussion of controversial points such as disestablishment was dropped, and mention was made for the first time of a plan to circulate books and tracts intended to educate the public in proper church principles and history.

Ever the agitator, it was Froude who first objected to the idea of an association. He feared that such a body would be too slow-moving and, in the hands of the High Churchmen, Palmer and Perceval, too conservative. Froude derided the idea of "a *union* between *excellent* men of *all parties*" uniting in defense of the church, as pure "mawkishness." On the whole he thought Perceval and Palmer too attentive to Tory opinion in London and too unwilling to strike out in a bold and advanced way. Froude previously had demonstrated his penchant for taking the avant-garde position. He had said of a group of influential but conservative potential allies, "it seems to me quite evident, that those whose services must be bought by *concession*, can have no authority as advisors."[20] Newman, in turn, tried to moderate Froude's impetuousness and wrote to Keble in August 1833 that the resources available from their association with the university had not yet been thoroughly explored. Two months later in a letter to Palmer, Newman sided completely with Froude, categorically rejecting the formulation of a supervisory association.[21]

As events turned out, the tracts were to be the medium of education in church principles and the mode of agitation. In a letter to his friend, R. F. Wilson, then living in Bonn, Newman summarized the situation as it stood in the autumn of 1833. "Our first duty is the defence of the Church," Newman wrote,

---

[20]Ibid., 12-14; Palmer, *Narrative*, 29-30; Church, *Oxford Movement*, 95-99; Froude, *Remains*, 1:144, 189.

[21]Newman to Keble, 5 August 1833; Newman to Palmer, 24 October 1833, Newman Papers.

therefore expect on your return to England to see us all cautious, long-headed, unfeeling, unflinching radicals. . . . we have begun to print tracts. We intend to have nothing to do with party-politics. . . . we shall do nothing *against* the Monarchy, we intend to be quiet subjects and obedient, but *loyalty* is almost an impossibility now. Our political affections are now centered in the Church.[22]

By September 1833, the *Tracts* had begun. While Perceval still thought a formal committee was needed to approve the content of each of the tracts as they appeared, Keble, Newman, and Froude adamantly opposed the idea. The Oxford triumvirate distrusted the conservatism of Perceval and his friends and thus successfully argued that each tract was to be the work of an individual. This was the tone and stance that Newman struck in the opening of Tract 1: "I am but one of yourselves,—a Presbyter; and therefore I conceal my name lest I should take too much on myself by speaking in my own person."[23]

Two central themes can be seen in the three volumes of tracts that appeared between 1833-1836—the nature of the visible church and the nature of faith. Both themes were important within the overall theological posture of the Oxford movement. These doctrines provided the framework for the Tractarian attempt to ward off the state on the one hand, and to ward off the evangelicals and Roman Catholics on the other. In both cases this attempt revolved around Tractarian efforts to define a via media in politics as well as in theology, and it was over exactly these issues that rupture and collapse would come in 1845.

Three underlying elements supported the Tractarian concept of the visible church: the importance of apostolic succession; the importance of medialism; and the need for a spiritually independent church. In Tract 15, for example, Newman sketched the contours of clerical and lay duties: "The Clergy have a commission from God Almighty through regular succession from the Apostles, to preach the Gospel, administer the Sacraments, and guide the Church. . . . The people are bound to hear them with attention, receive the Sac-

---

[22]Newman to R. F. Wilson, 8 September 1833, ibid.

[23]See Keble's argument against association, Keble to Perceval, 15 November 1833, Pusey Papers, Pusey House, Oxford.

raments from their hands, and pay them all dutiful obedience."
Newman's list of duties was standard; what was at stake was the importance of the visible church and the apostolic succession. For it
was the visible church that made the sacraments available. Its existence was therefore vital. Yet even more important to Oxford theologians was that people recognize that this church derived its
authority from its relation to the apostolic legacy. "Why should we
talk so much of an *Establishment*, and so little of an APOSTOLIC
SUCCESSION?" Keble asked in Tract 4. Said Newman in Tract 1, "I
fear we have neglected the real ground on which our authority is
built—our Apostolical Descent." Here was a reference point for all
ecclesiastical thought. The Tractarians balanced any undue emphasis upon a spiritual and invisible fellowship of believers, with a stress
upon the church as a divinely commissioned visible institution. Furthermore, no "mere voluntary ecclesiastical arrangement," as Keble
phrased it in Tract 4, but a successive transmission of power and authority from the apostles through to the present was the basis of the
church's charter for salvation.

The Anglican church, as a result of its political history and theological heritage, held a special position. "I like foreign interference,
as little from Geneva, as from Rome," Newman wrote in Tract 38;
"the glory of the English Church is, that it has taken the VIA ME-
DIA, as it has been called. It lies between the (so called) Reformers
and the Romanists." The via media reflected the unique historical
situation of the Church of England, at once related to both Rome
and the Reformation, yet distant from both. While the Tractarians
insisted that the Anglican Church stood midway between Rome and
the Protestant Reformers of the sixteenth century, they also maintained that it was still part of the Catholic tradition that contained
the legacy and meaning of the apostolic succession. Such a contention ran counter to popular religious sentiment in England, and
Newman admitted that "men seem to think that we are plainly and
indisputably proved to be Popish, if we are proved to differ from the
generality of Churchmen now-a-days." Yet in the same tract, 38, he
asked about his opponents: "what if it turns out that they are silently
floating down the stream and we are upon the shore?" As far as
Newman was concerned, the allegation of popery was misplaced,

for in Tract 15 he had disputed the right of the pope to any dominion over the church bishops.

In the early 1830s Newman and the other Tractarians felt less need to fight the charge of Romanism than they did to call attention to state intervention. In the Tractarian view, if any were floating down the river to perdition, it was those who acquiesced in the Whig ecclesiastical reforms. Here, then, was their third concern—the defense of the church's prerogatives and the consideration of disestablishment. The Tractarians were outraged at the series of ecclesiastical reforms proposed and enacted by the Whigs. "We must make a stand *somewhere*," Newman declared in 1834. "Things are rolling down hill so gradually that, wherever we make a stand, it will be a harsh measure—but I am determined (please God) that, as far as I am concerned, the Church shall not crumble away without my doing in my place what I can to hinder it." Froude wrote in the same tone to Samuel Wilberforce, citing fears that "some foul deterioration of the Liturgy, some wretched compromise of the Apostolical Doctrine" would be conceded to the liberals.[24]

The first volume of tracts blazed with the call to action, a call borne of wrath and righteousness. In terms reminiscent of Keble's "National Apostasy" sermon, Newman in Tract 2 asked his fellow clerics, "are we content to be accounted the mere creation of the State, as school masters and teachers may be, or soldiers or magistrates, or other public officers? Did the State make us? can it unmake us?" Newman anticipated a battle, one that might martyr the bishops and cause their goods to be confiscated. He spoke of this possibility as a "blessed termination," a view in which few on the episcopal bench would have joined him. Along these lines, in Tract 1, Newman appealed to his fellow clergymen to renew their faith in their divine commission, but more importantly, to involve themselves in the crisis. "*Choose* your side," he said, "since side you shortly must, with one or another party, even though you do nothing."

The contenders were preparing to join the fray. As Newman wrote to John Bowden in August 1833, "Agitation is the order of the

---

[24]Newman to John Bowden, 13 July 1834, Newman Papers; Froude to Samuel Wilberforce, 1 October 1832, quoted by Brendon, *Hurrell Froude*, 82.

day." But though he might be sure there was to be a fray, he was not so sure of all the topics it might concern. For one, the Tractarians had no long-standing consensus about the wisdom of separating church and state. Were it to happen, it was possible that the church would be thrown on popular shoulders for its support. In the summer of 1833 with events moving rapidly and the Tractarians flushed with the excitement of their war cry of apostolic succession, Newman vacillated on the issue of disestablishment. In his letter to Bowden he wrote:

> I do not at all fear for the result were we thrown on the people, though for a while many of us would be distressed *in re pecuniaria*—not that I would advocate a separation of Church and State unless the nation does more tyrannical things against us; but I do feel I should be glad if it were done and over, much as the nation would lose by it; for I fear the Church is being corrupted by the union.[25]

Froude more strongly supported disestablishment, writing to his father in 1830,"I cannot but believe that the Church will surprise the people a little when its latent spirit has been roused; and when the reasons for caution have been removed by disconnecting it with the State."[26] In Tract 59, "The Position of the Church of Christ in England, Relative to the State and the Nation," Froude insisted that the union of church and state in practical terms meant only state protection and state interference. The state, he believed, had done little to protect the church but much to interfere with it. But in his public pronouncement Froude struck a balance, declaring that the union of church and state was a mixture of good and evil. In conversation with close associates, he continued to hold out for a radical break with the state.[27]

John Keble's beliefs illustrated the mood of uncertainty that, much more than Froude's bravado, typified the Tractarian position on disestablishment. In 1829, Keble told Perceval that after much thinking on the matter, he had decided that the benefits of continued connection with the state outweighed the liabilities. Four years

---

[25]Newman to John Bowden, 31 August 1833, Newman Papers.

[26]Froude to Archdeacon Froude, 28 November 1830, Froude Papers.

[27]See Brendon, *Hurrell Froude*, 112-13, 144-45.

later, in the wake of the Reform Bill and the Irish Church reform, Keble reversed his position, telling Perceval, "Anything, humanly speaking, will be better than for the Church to go on in unison with such a state." Yet, in continuing Keble expressed a fear that attested to the still fragile base of support on which the Tractarians operated. "But how to conduct a separation without producing a schism in the church," Keble wrote, "even *that* I am not sure that I would deprecate, if I were sure of getting rid of the right persons."[28] Keble's assessment reflected the concern that the Tractarians might indeed lose any direct contest with evangelicals or Dissenters that took place in Parliament or ecclesiastical councils. If the Tractarians could grab the reins of power, dictate episcopal appointments, and direct theological education; if they could get rid of the "right people" and put their own in; then an establishment might not be so bad. But so long as the liberals held the upper hand, separation remained a possibility, if only a rhetorical one.

These remarks put Tractarian appeals for popular support into context. The ethos of the Oxford movement was always too paternalistic and condescending to allow its adherents to rely seriously on the public. While Newman or Froude could chastise those who equated a comfortable parsonage and ample patronage with the discharge of their ministerial duties, the tone of the Tractarian appeal was far from democratic. Throughout the Tractarian anti-Erastianism ran a deep stream of ambivalence. While all agreed on the desirability of a spiritually strong and independent church, none could agree on how to go about attaining such a goal, and none could agree on such a goal's implications.[29]

In Tract 3 Newman rebuked those persons who, caught in the present spirit of reform, wished to revise the liturgy. He conceded that insignificant features of the liturgy might be changed without damage but said that such actions once begun would only stop when

---

[28]Keble to Perceval, 25 March 1829, Pusey Papers; Keble to Perceval, 1 March 1833, Pusey Papers.

[29]See the discussion by Cyril Gloyn, *The Church in the Social Order* (Forest Grove OR, 1942) 66-68; Terence Kenny, *The Political Thought of John Henry Newman* (London, 1957) 108-109.

the criticisms of all parties were answered. In raising this question of liturgical revision Newman bridged the gap between the Tractarians' anti-Erastian defense of the church and their concern for the nature of faith. As he argued, Newman made it clear he was apprehensive not only about the possibility of unlawfully delegated individuals making changes to the liturgy. He was equally fearful of the repercussions such maneuvers might have on religious faith itself. Amending the liturgy, even in small details, gave one an appetite for criticism, Newman charged. This appetite led to an unsettled mind and to doubt, two conditions Newman considered inimical to belief. The result, as Newman saw it, was that these reformers, "worldly men, with little personal religion, of lax conversation and lax professed principles," would never be satisfied with a few small revisions. The great body of faithful believers, meanwhile, would be confused and skeptical. The discussion of liturgical reform was thus a parry to the slashing attacks of the liberals. It was also an attempt to gather and shield the orthodox behind the Tractarian view of piety.

In attempting to explain the nature of faith, the Tractarians explored the implications of rationalism, the place of the Bible, and the direction of religious education. As with the discussion of the visible church, these three subsidiary points filled in the meaning of the Tractarians' position. Yet underneath these points lay a central premise—faith meant obedience. Faith entailed obedience, it symbolized a trust in the message of salvation, as that message was delivered by divinely commissioned clergy and guaranteed by apostolically warranted bishops. Faith implied submission in spiritual and secular matters alike. The latter of these circled back to the church-state question, for the state was established by God. Hence, when operating in its proper sphere, the state was, like the church, entitled to the obedience of its subjects. The problem, of course, was to determine the state's proper sphere.

As that debate raged, so did the one over obedience in spiritual matters. Both Newman and Froude contributed to this topic in their discussions of rationalism. Much like the critical mind that desired liturgical reform, the rationalist mind, when concerned with religious affairs, Newman wrote in Tract 73, sought "to make our reason the standard and measure of the doctrine revealed . . . and thus a rationalistic spirit is the antagonist of Faith; for Faith is, in its very nature, the acceptance of what our reason cannot reach, simply and absolutely upon testimony." To Newman, rationalism tended to elevate the facilities of reason beyond their proper boundaries. This misplaced emphasis on reason led to false pride, for "the rationalist makes himself his own centre. . . . he does not go to God, but he implies that God must come to him." Furthermore, rationalism was blind to the mysteries of the religious world, those "truths faintly apprehended and not understood," that formed an integral part of divine revelation.

In Newman's depiction, rationalism corroded faith and shallowly approached the entirety of earthly experience. In his "Essay on Rationalism" written in 1834, Froude reached similar conclusions, though not by the same route. For Froude, reason and faith were not enemies. Rather, faith was opposed to a philosophy that relied on empirical evidence and denigrated all other sources of authority. Froude illustrated his point with the example of the Eucharist. In so doing, he returned to the argument of the Anglican church as the via media. He contended that Protestants in their desire to refute the Roman Catholic concept of transubstantiation had robbed the Eucharist of all its mystery and reduced it to a mere commemorative and empirically comprehensible shell. In contrast, the Roman Catholics had equally erred in "explaining precisely wherein the miraculous consisted and how it was brought about." Again only Anglican theology at its best had represented both the mysterious and the sensible in their correct proportions.[30]

In Newman's and Froude's analyses, rationalism figured more as a codeword for a certain approach to reality than as a systematic set of epistemological propositions. Their discussion of the place of Scripture built on their previous discussion of rationalism in that they maintained that the Bible was not a rationalist document but instead teaches "matters of faith." In Tract 8 Newman spoke of how important the deposit of faith was—those doctrines revealed in the

---

[30]Froude, "Essay on Rationalism," *Remains*, 1:18-23, 61, 146. See the thorough discussion of this matter in Alf Härdelin, *The Tractarian Understanding of the Eucharist* (Uppsala, 1965).

Scripture that were necessary to salvation. These revelations did not spell out systems of church governance nor other secondary matters, but they did support the foundation of faith in apostolic succession and provide examples of correct practice. The precise meaning of the deposit of faith would become a larger issue in coming years, but even in the early 1830s, the importance of "primitive tradition" and the development of an authoritative referent other than Scripture could be seen.

Similarly, an emphasis upon a particular approach to religious education could be seen in these early years. It would not be until Isaac Williams's tracts "On Reserve in Communicating Religious Knowledge" that the notion of the gradual revelation of doctrine would be fully discussed. Yet for Newman and Keble especially, concern with this concept could be traced to this earlier period. Fundamentally, the concept of reserve maintained that knowledge would be revealed gradually to a supplicant as that supplicant's moral life evidenced that he or she could understand and make use of that knowledge. Contrasting with the evangelical style and its profuse and elaborate discussions of spiritual life, this ideal of reserve held that reticence about holy subjects was more befitting them. Garrulousness about deeply held matters of faith with those unprepared and uninitiated was wrong.[31]

Behind this concept was the influence of Joseph Butler, to whom both Keble and Newman acknowledged their indebtedness. Butler's emphasis upon the moral faculty and his belief in the close correspondence between the natural and supernatural world, especially as expressed in his treatise, *The Analogy of Religion*, deeply impressed Keble.[32] In Newman's case, Butler's influence joined that of the Alexandrian Platonists, such as Clement and Origen. Combined, these philosophies caused him to develop a particular view of "economy," which was both a means of imparting knowledge and a testimony to the harmony of the moral and earthly worlds. As Newman testified in the *Apologia*, Butler taught him that "the very idea of an

---

[31]Stephen Prickett, *Romanticism and Religion* (Cambridge, 1976) 95.

[32]W. J. A. Beck, *John Keble's Literary and Religious Contribution to the Oxford Movement* (Nijmegan, 1959) 48-52.

analogy between the separate works of God leads to the conclusion that the system which is of less importance is economically or sacramentally connected with the more momentous system." Thus when he studied the Alexandrians he understood them "to mean that the exterior world, physical and historical, was but the manifestation to our senses of realities greater than itself. Nature was a parable: Scripture was an allegory." As far as Newman was concerned, the connection between Butler's beliefs and the writings of the Alexandrian Fathers was striking.[33]

Newman's invoking of the principle of economy raises a further issue—that of the relationship between Tractarian theology and romanticism. This feeling that the supernatural permeated the natural, this acceptance of mystery as an important part of total human experience, was shared by both Tractarians and romantics. In addition to honoring the ineffable mystery of life, the Tractarians emphasized intuition and imagination in a manner typical of romanticism's opposition to the Enlightenment. Also, they shared a third element of romanticism—a renewed historical consciousness.[34]

Clearly, the Oxford movement both conceptually and as regards personal relations shared a bond with English romanticism. John Keble, for example, was a close friend of William and Dorothy Wordsworth, and was acquainted with Samuel Taylor Coleridge through the poet's nephew and son. Keble dedicated the set of lectures he delivered as professor of poetry at Oxford between 1832-1841 to Wordsworth; his lectures, in turn of phrase and in content, reflect several common concerns with Wordsworth.[35] Later in life, as he searched for the major influences upon the Tractarians, Newman likewise listed Coleridge and Walter Scott. Scott's authority was

[33]Newman, *Apologia*, 31, 45-47; Charles Harrold, "Newman and the Alexandrian Platonists," *Modern Philology* 37, no. 3 (February 1940): 279-91; Jaak Seynaeve, *Cardinal Newman's Doctrine of Holy Scripture* (Louvain, 1953) 109-14; Klaus Dick, "Das Analogieprinzip bei John Henry Newman und seine Quelle in Joseph Butler's 'Analogy'," *Newman-Studien* 5: 9-228.

[34]See the prologue for a further discussion of romanticism.

[35]M. H. Abrams, *The Mirror and the Lamp* (New York, 1953) 144-48.

also highly regarded by Hurrell Froude. Froude's love for the Middle Ages and Gothic architecture first arose from his reading of Scott. Indeed, Scott probably more than anyone else helped to revive and strengthen the sense of historical awareness so characteristic of the romantic revival in England.

To cite the importance of Scott or Coleridge is to underscore the difficulties posed in assessing romantic influence on the Tractarians. For there is little evidence that the Tractarians adhered strictly to Scott's, Coleridge's, or even Wordsworth's views. Moreover, while Scott's vision was of the Middle Ages, the Tractarians (even with allowances for Froude) were more taken with the Apostolic era. Consequently, the issue between the Tractarians and romantics, as one scholar has judged it, "is obviously a question of affinity rather than influence."[36]

Out of this welter of sources, then, came the first volume of tracts and the other literary productions of the young movement. With the watchwords *Apostolical Succession* emblazoned on their banners, the Tractarians had joined battle with their liberal opponents in defense of the church's prerogatives. The return reports were not optimistic, Newman conceded in 1834, but he still retained his hopes. "I see a system *behind* the existing one, a system indeed which will take time and suffering to bring us to adopt, but still a firm foundation."[37] Here was that same sense of assurance and optimism to be found in John Keble. Unlike Keble, however, Newman was later to find his confidence slipping away and his foundations shifting beneath him. In the early years of the movement, however, between 1833 and 1836, there were reasons for satisfaction. The tracts had made a vigorous beginning and were spoken of within clerical assemblages. Newman had emerged as a visible leader, leaving behind his chrysalis of shyness and uncertainty. He had also begun that vast flood of books, essays, epistles, and lectures which he would continue to write until the end of his life. Keble for his part

---

[36]L. A. Willoughby, "On Some German Affinities with the Oxford Movement," *Modern Language Review* 29, no. 1 (1934): 61; Yngve Brilioth, *The Anglican Revival* (London, 1933) 56-76; Brendon, *Hurrell Froude*, 26-37.

[37]Newman to R. F. Wilson, 31 March 1834, Newman Papers.

had moved into the background. Comfortable with the format of the tracts, now that the tactical battles of the first four months had been won, Keble resided at his parish in Hursley. Near to his family and removed from the glare of Oxford, Keble contributed to the tracts and acted as senior counselor for the groups as a whole on matters of tone, approach, and strategy. Froude, soon to die of tuberculosis in 1836, left Oxford in November 1833 for a trip to the warmer climate of Barbados, searching for ever-elusive, better health. During his sojourn there Froude composed his "Essay on Rationalism" and several other pieces, and upon his return to England continued working to the extent that his health permitted.

In 1833 with tracts underway, Froude had jocularly asked Perceval about their distribution. Calling for the development of "railroads and canals for the diffusion of Apostolical Knowledge," Froude suggested that a network of allies be contacted who could send the tracts to their friends. The circulation of the tracts remained a problem, but in 1834 the movement no longer suffered from a lack of ecclesiastical recognition. In that year the Tractarian movement was boosted by the inclusion of a new member in its inner circle of leaders, Edward Bouverie Pusey. In December 1833 when Pusey contributed a tract on fasting and broke with the tradition of anonymous authorship by signing his initials to it, he was known within the university community as a person of high integrity and exhaustive knowledge. Newman gleefully conceded that as a member of a well-known family and as professor of Hebrew and canon of Christ Church, Pusey was able to provide the movement with "a name, a form, and a personality, to what was without him sort of a mob." Nevertheless, that Pusey should be tapped for leadership by Newman or that the Oxford movement would be known in some circles as "Puseyism" was ironic.[38]

Pusey was born in 1800 to a titled family of landowners whose religious sympathies were moderate and evangelical. As with the other Tractarian leaders, Pusey won an Oriel fellowship and in 1823 first met Newman. The two stayed in contact, although in 1825 at

---

[38]Froude to Perceval, 14 August 1833, quoted by Brendon, *Hurrell Froude*, 136; Newman, *Apologia*, 77.

the urging of his mentor, Charles Lloyd, Pusey left for Germany to pursue linguistic studies. Pusey set out for Göttingen to study under Johann Eichhorn, professor of theology and oriental languages, and lived in Germany intermittently through the spring of 1827. In addition to studying languages and German critical methods Pusey became acquainted with many of the preeminent German theologians and churchmen of the day. Besides working with Eichhorn, Pusey traveled to Berlin and Bonn and met August Tholuck, Friedrich Schleiermacher, August Neander, and E. W. Hengstenberg, among others.[39]

The results of Pusey's encounter with German theology soon became apparent. In 1828 his volume, *An Historical Enquiry into the Probable Causes of the Rationalist Character lately predominant in the Theology of Germany*, was published. Pusey's book was a response to his future Tractarian colleague, Hugh James Rose. In 1825 Rose had delivered four lectures that were published together as *The State of Protestantism in Germany*. In them, Rose pictured German Protestantism as overrun by rationalism, its church life in poor health, and its theology floundering without any clear authority. Had the German churches developed a strong episcopacy or been controlled through some stable restraint, like the Thirty-nine Articles, they might have had a basis from which to counter this rationalist inundation. Lacking such securities Germany was defenseless. Rose only hoped that the problem would not spread to England. Pusey responded that the specter of German rationalism did pose a severe threat to English faith. But he hoped to show that the battle was not yet over, and that true friends of English piety existed in Germany and should not be overlooked.[40]

In carrying out this task Pusey sketched a developmental view of human history. Pusey charged that civic and religious history, rather than a tale of "irregular, undefined, and often jarring principles,"

---

[39]The standard biography of Pusey is H. P. Liddon's *Life of Edward Bouverie Pusey*, ed. J. O. Johnston and R. J. Wilson, 4 vols. (London, 1893-97). See 1:70-114, for a full discussion of his trip to Germany.

[40]Rose, *The State of German Protestantism* (Cambridge, 1825); Vernon Storr, *The Development of English Theology in the Nineteenth Century* (London, 1913) 118.

was a uniform system with the "contest of faith and unbelief" at its base. This system was dynamic, not static—in the sense that it progressed until it reached a point of crisis. More specifically, each era of history embodied some principle or idea; as these principles interacted, smooth progress or turbulent contention resulted. Pusey claimed that from this contest of spiritual forces two simple lessons were clear: each new era was the result of the struggle of preceding forces; and any investigation of a given period should look to the anterior age for an explanation of its origins.[41] In a bow to German critical method Pusey had testified not only to the legacy of romanticism's new historical consciousness, he had also established the foundation for his rejoinder to Rose. As he detailed the situation in Germany with its "abstract and unpractical" theology, "presented in a dry and dialectic form" and "without reference to the practical religious value," Pusey traced the causes of rationalism back to the Reformation. Where Rose had concluded his analysis with an observation of the deficiency of ecclesiastical authority in Germany and an admonition to the faithful in England, Pusey showed that a dead "orthodoxism" had gripped Lutheranism in the seventeenth and eighteenth centuries and deflected the path of its theological development. Where Rose saw only disaster, Pusey discerned glimmers of hope. Just as human history always involved a contest between opposing forces, so in this concrete example were there bearers of the living Gospel message. Pusey believed that these true witnesses had been the groups of German pietists centered around Arndt and the Spener circle at Halle. English churchmen could learn from the German experience what to avoid, Pusey agreed, but they should also acknowledge and honor those who had sought to protect the integrity of Christian faith. Beyond exemplifying his historical method, Pusey's esteem for pietism was a component in his appreciation for evangelicalism. Indeed, despite theological differences Pusey never lost his respect for the evangelical effort, as his biographer put it, "to make religion a living power in a cold and gloomy age."[42]

---

[41]Pusey, *An Historical Enquiry into the Probable Causes of the Rationalist Character Lately Predominant in the Theology of Germany* (London, 1828) 3-6.

[42]Liddon, *Pusey*, 1:255.

When Pusey's book first appeared in 1828, Newman reported to his sister that it was "sadly deformed with Germanisms—he is wantonly obscure and foreign." His syntax would not be the only characteristic setting Pusey off from the rest of the Tractarians. For Pusey was regarded by many to be a political liberal. He had supported Edward Hawkins in 1827 for provost of Oriel. He had endorsed Roman Catholic emancipation, as had his friend, Charles Lloyd, and sided with Peel in the subsequent election battle.[43] Thus, both his liberalism and his sympathy for evangelicalism initially distinguished Pusey from the Tractarians. A deep strain of piety and devotional humility ran through Pusey, though, and these aspects were never forgotten, especially by Newman. From his diary observation in 1823, "That Pusey is Thine, O Lord, how can I doubt," through the glowing accolades inscribed in the *Apologia*, Newman cherished the quest for holiness and sanctification that formed such a large part of Pusey's approach to life.[44]

In late 1832 Pusey wrote a small pamphlet defending the preservation of cathedral institutions as a means of religious education. Appearing during the time of the Reform bill's passage and amidst talk of a radical reform of the established church, the essay supported the same principle of nonintervention by the state in spiritual affairs that the Tractarians were fighting for. Newman praised the pamphlet in a long letter written during his Mediterranean trip with Froude. It was a short step then, once Newman had returned and the tracts had begun, to enlist the efforts as well as the sympathies of Pusey in the Tractarian movement.[45]

A PROTESTANT PALLADIUM

In a prophetic observation on the contemporary ecclesiastical situation, Thomas Sikes is reported to have said in 1833,

> There is no account given anywhere, so far as I can see of the one Holy Catholic Church . . . , the doctrine of the Church Catholic and the privileges

---

[43]Newman to his sister, Harriett, 4 June 1828, Newman Papers; Liddon, *Pusey*, 1:199-202.

[44]17 May 1823, *Letters and Diaries*, ed. Dessian et al., 1:163.

[45]Liddon, *Pusey*, 1:225-34, 248-52.

of Church membership cannot be explained from pulpits; and those who will have to explain it will hardly know where they are, or which way they are to turn themselves. They will be endlessly misunderstood and misinterpreted. There will be one great outcry of Popery from one end of the country to the other. It will be thrust upon minds unprepared and on an uncatechized Church. Some will take it up and reject it; and all will want a guidance which one hardly knows where they shall find it.[46]

The prescience of Sikes's remarks would become evident in the coming years. By 1836, with the Tractarians assembled, publishing literature, and making public statements and private gestures all designed to rally support for their cause, they began to draw criticism. The Oxford apostolics' rebuttals during the second phase of the Tractarian movement—1836-1839—appeared in the controversy over the appointment of R. D. Hampden as professor of divinity and in the continued and increasingly polemical run of pamphlets, essays, and books that flowed from their pens.

The clash over Hampden occurred in 1836, when the Melbourne government named him to the vacant Regius professorship. When news of his nomination first became known at Oxford, opposition grew up on two related fronts. Hampden was regarded as a liberal at Oxford and in 1834 had led the push to abolish undergraduate subscription to the Thirty-nine Articles. Toward this aim, he had written a pamphlet, *Observations on Religious Dissent*, calling for Dissenters to be admitted to the university. Above all, Hampden believed that religion was a matter of feeling, piety, and conduct—not doctrinal adherence.[47] Hampden's position on subscription with its de-emphasis on the importance of doctrine could be traced back to a series of lectures he had given in 1832, and published as *The Scholastic Philosophy considered in its Relation to Christian Philosophy*. Consequently, as both his position on subscription and his views on religion were anathema to the Tractarians, they turned to his lectures of 1832 to mount their case. Hampden's lectures argued that Christian truth was separable from the form in which it was presented in any given age. This premise cut two ways. First, Hamp-

---

[46]Ibid., 1:257-58.

[47]For a discussion of Hampden, see C. H. Smyth, "R. D. Hampden," *Theology* 18 (1929): 259-65, 312-22; Storr, *Development of English Theology*, 100-105.

den's claim suggested that there was a set of essential Christian truths, available in the Scriptures and easily understood by all sincere readers. Such a proposition also meant that all theological formulations, all creeds, and all confessional statements were merely representative statements of their own time, and hence had no binding authority for future generations.[48]

In Tract 73 Newman had argued with rationalism's tendency "to accept the Revelation, and then to explain it away; to speak of it as the Word of God, and then treat it as the word of man." The charge of rationalism would thus become the rallying cry among those opposed to Hampden. At first Newman hesitated to take too visible a role. Hampden had been Hawkins's ally and tool during the tutorial affair of 1828, and Newman himself had been nominated for provost; thus he wanted to avoid the appearance of a personal squabble.[49] Soon, though, he put aside his reservations and wrote an anonymous pamphlet against Hampden, while Pusey took charge of a petition to the university convocation. Newman's essay, "Elucidations of Dr. Hampden's Theological Statements," was composed of extracts from Hampden's writings. As these selections were lifted out of context, the volume justifiably can be regarded as a hatchet job on Hampden. In contrast, Pusey's petition took issue with the theme of rationalism or "the assumption that uncontrolled human reason in its present degraded form is the primary interpreter of God's word," and alleged that this was "the root of all errors in Dr. Hampden's system."[50]

To the Tractarians, the Hampden appointment was yet another example of state interference in ecclesiastical affairs; the university was being forced to accept a questionable candidate as one of its premier professors of divinity and defenders of the faith. Yet Newman was sanguine enough to see gains for the Tractarians whether Hampden was appointed or not. "If he is not appointed, we have gained a victory," Newman declared. "On the other hand, if Hamp-

---

[48]R. D. Hampden, *The Scholastic Philosophy considered in its relation to Christian theology* (Oxford, 1833) 6, 86-94.

[49]Newman to Keble, 30 January 1836, Newman Papers.

[50]Copy of petition (n.p., n.d.), Pusey Papers.

den is appointed . . . the Ministry will be at open war with the Church; the Archbishop will be roused; and a large number of waverers in this place will be thrown into our hands."[51] As it happened, Hampden gained the appointment but not before a vote of no confidence from the university convocation revoked certain of his powers as professor.

Writing to his brother, Samuel, in April 1836, Robert Isaac Wilberforce described Hampden's Bampton Lectures as "unsound in principle from one end to the other." By the mid-1830s Wilberforce was back within the Tractarian fold. In the aftermath of the tutorship dispute, Wilberforce had left for Germany to study theology and Eastern languages. During his stay he retraced some of Pusey's steps and took advantage of some of Pusey's earlier contacts. Yet Wilberforce never felt comfortable in Germany, and when cholera broke out, Robert took advantage of that pretext to return to England. By December 1831 he was back at home with his family. Within six months he had married and soon took up duties as vicar at East Farleigh in Kent. Although he did not attend the conference at Hadleigh nor the subsequent meetings at Oxford, Wilberforce kept abreast of the latest developments by corresponding with Newman. He also helped distribute tracts in the district where he lived, and collaborated with Newman, Froude, and Keble in producing the well-known volume of poetry, *Lyra Apostolica*. In May 1836 he attended the convocation meetings and voted with the majority to condemn Hampden's teachings.[52]

In March 1836 amidst the excitement of the Hampden affair, Newman wrote Wilberforce of graver tidings. On February 28 Froude had died. As Newman said to Wilberforce, "As to our present loss, I cannot speak of it—as you may well understand. I never on the whole can have a greater."[53] Out of Newman and Keble's grief and their desire to produce some tribute to their friend's memory came one of the more controversial literary pieces of the move-

---

[51]Newman to J. W. Bowden, 17 February 1836, Newman Papers.

[52]Robert Wilberforce to Samuel Wilberforce, 16 April 1836, Wilberforce Papers, Bodleian Library, Oxford; Newsome, *Parting of Friends*, 137-43, 164-68.

[53]Newsome, *Parting of Friends*, 168.

ment's history, Hurrell Froude's *Remains*. The *Remains* appeared between 1838 and 1839 and contained Froude's journal, a series of essays, and a collection of sermons. The journal was the first volume of the set and its appearance both sounded the themes and elicited the criticisms that would be associated with the *Remains* as a whole. Many of the themes that Froude articulated—outrage with state interference in ecclesiastical affairs, the insufficiency of rationalism or dissatisfaction with Protestantism—could be found in earlier Tractarian writings. Yet where Newman had been tactful in his presentation of the concept of the via media, Froude was not, blurting out, "The Reformation was a limb badly set—it must be broken again in order to be righted."[54]

Such statements could only rupture Anglicanism and send many, who had previously respected the Tractarians' piety and anti-Erastianism, into opposition. Although he was firmly committed to publishing the *Remains* and served with Keble as coeditor of the manuscript, Newman was shrewd enough to foresee problems. "I am very anxious about Froude's *Remains*," Newman wrote immediately prior to its publication. "They will arrest and bring forward many, I doubt not, but they will much scandalize and I fear throw back some persons by their uncompromising Anti-protestantism."[55] Froude's "Anti-protestantism" was not the only sore point. In "Remarks on Church Discipline" Froude had written, "If a national Church means a Church without discipline . . . the best thing we can do is to unnationalize ours as soon as possible. . . . let us give up a *national* Church and have a *real* one." This concern for a fuller and more rigorous spiritual life was a familiar feature of Tractarian writings. What emerged in Froude's journal, however, were his attempts to foster spiritual discipline and penance in his personal life. Newman understood that the journal would be the object of criticism and the source of greatest misunderstanding, but he seemed to have

---

[54]Froude, *Remains*, 1:433.

[55]Piers Brendon, "Newman, Keble, and Froude's Remains," *English Historical Review* 87, no. 345 (October 1972): 697-716. The quotation is on page 706; William J. Baker, "Hurrell Froude and the Reformers," *Journal of Ecclesiastical History* 21, no. 3 (July 1970): 243-59.

underestimated the easy target Froude's inner dialogue would pose.[56]

One of the sharpest critics of the *Remains* was Thomas Arnold. "After all I had seen of the Newmanites," Arnold wrote in 1838,

> I own Froude's book did surpass all that I had conceived possible. It is I think, considering the writer's age and qualifications, the most impudent book I ever read. . . . And yet really I believe that the policy is good, and that with readers so greedy after error as the Newmanite Disciples the strength of the dose will not revolt them but only complete the infatuation.[57]

Thomas Arnold was no stranger to the Tractarians. From the time Newman first questioned Arnold's Christianity through the Hampden crisis to the publication of Froude's *Remains*, Arnold and the Oxford movement were at odds.

Arnold had won his Oriel fellowship in 1815. While there, he came under the influence of the Oriel Noetics, among whom Hampden was included. Arnold's political views and theory of Scripture were closer to those of Hampden than to those of the Tractarians. Furthermore, Arnold believed that the Tractarians, and especially Newman, had dealt unfairly with Hampden. In April 1836 Arnold published an essay, which the editors of the *Edinburgh Review* entitled "The Oxford Malignants and Dr. Hampden." Here Arnold assailed Newman for ripping Hampden's statements out of context in Newman's "Elucidation" essay. He charged that "the Oxford conspirators," the "Judaizing fanatics," had indulged in "the fanaticism of mere foolery. A dress, a ritual, a name, a ceremony;—a technical phraseology;—the superstition of a priesthood, without its power."[58]

In a less rhetorical and feverish moment Arnold expressed his disagreements in these words, "Newman and his party are idolators; they put Christ's Church and Christ's Sacraments, and Christ's min-

---

[56]Froude, *Remains*, 1:272-73; Brendon, "Froude's Remains," 701-702, 711.

[57]Arnold is quoted by Brendon, "Froude's Remains," 716.

[58]Thomas Arnold, *The Miscellaneous Works of Thomas Arnold: First American Edition with Nine Additional Essays* (New York, 1845) 140-41.

isters, in the place of Christ Himself."[59] To Arnold, this "idolatry" lay in the Tractarians' emphasis upon a mythical primitive tradition that Arnold's own historical studies found neither as internally consistent nor as readily available as did Newman and company. Arnold saw the publication of Froude's *Remains* as only further confirming Tractarian errors. With its castigation of the Reformation and with Christ's name missing from the journal, the *Remains* symbolized both a pernicious trend toward Rome, and an ignorance of the nature of the problems the church faced.[60]

The Tractarians' response to their critics during this second phase of the movement contained both familiar themes and others. In hindsight some of these revisions appeared more fundamental than perhaps intended at the time, some of them more polemical and strident than necessary or prudent. But as the title page of the second volume of the tracts proclaimed, "If the trumpet give an uncertain sound, who shall prepare himself to the battle?" The Tractarians did not want to be caught short. Hence, the introduction to the second volume also identified for its readers "the main doctrine in question, that, namely of the One Catholic and Apostolic Church," and thereby specified the three issues central to this period. For the themes of catholicity, apostolicity, and universality encapsulated not only Tractarian ecclesiological thought, but the very kernel of the movement.

The concept of catholicity had always figured prominently in the Oxford movement's attempt to represent an English theology, "Catholic but not Roman." In carrying out this task the Tractarians enlarged upon the concept of the via media and sharpened their disagreements with both Protestants and Roman Catholics.[61] In analyzing the contemporary church, Newman divided Anglicanism

---

[59]Thomas Arnold to A. P. Stanley, 24 May 1836, *The Life and Correspondence of Thomas Arnold*, ed. A. P. Stanley, 2 vols. (Boston, 1860) 2:47.

[60]See the discussion of Arnold in the preceding chapter. It had been in response to Arnold's *Principles of Church Reform* that Newman had asked, "But is he a Christian?" *Apologia*, 52.

[61]Newman, "Lectures of the Prophetical Office of the Church viewed relatively to Romanism and Popular Protestantism," in *The Via Media of the Anglican Church*, 2 vols. (London, 1895-1896) 1:20.

into three groups—apostolic, latitudinarian, and puritan. All three of these parties were opposed to Roman Catholicism, although to Newman, latitudinarians such as Hoadly or Arnold and puritans or evangelicals were at some points indistinguishable. As he charted the path between Roman Catholicism and "Popular Protestantism," Newman first faced the problem of scriptural authority. Where the Protestant position considered the Bible the only standard of appeal in doctrinal questions, Newman indicated that the Anglo-Catholic opposition viewed Scripture as a satisfactory but not sole informant of divine truth. As for Roman Catholicism, it recognized a tradition wider than simply Scripture, yet this tradition had been corrupted, Newman charged, through practical abuse and popular superstition. In a conclusion echoing the thoughts of the late Froude, Newman insisted that the controversy with Rome "turns more upon facts than first principles; with Protestant sectaries it is more about principles than facts."[62]

As he continued to assess popular Protestantism Newman hammered away at its individualistic tone and assumptions. First, there was the issue of private judgment, or "the prerogative, considered to belong to each individual Christian, of ascertaining and deciding for himself from Scripture what is Gospel truth and what is not. This is the principle maintained in theory, as a sort of sacred possession or palladium, by the Protestantism of the day." In personal and private study, the individual Protestant was to form his judgment. Where previously Newman had assailed "mere Protestants" for their ignorance of tradition, now he berated them for the untenable burden they placed on each believer. "There is something so very strange and wild," Newman wrote, "in maintaining that every individual Christian, rich and poor, learned and unlearned, young and old, in order to have an intelligent faith, must have formally examined, deliberated, and passed sentence upon the meaning of Scripture for himself."[63]

Newman skeptically concluded that even if a normally educated person could get the drift of debates such as took place at Nicea, still

[62]Ibid., 1:19, 26-28, 38-41. The quotation is on page 40.

[63]Ibid., 1:128, 145.

"few have minds tutored into patient inquiry, attention, and accuracy sufficient to deduce it aright from scripture."[64] Sometimes literal, sometimes figurative, the meaning of Scripture was a complicated affair. Even an individual familiar with ecclesiastical history would be impeded by the absence of an external guide.

A second example of popular Protestantism's atomism concerned its view of the nature of the church. Newman pointed out that to evangelicals, the doctrine of divine illumination was a primary aid to scriptural interpretation. The corollary to this position was that "everything else is human": rites and sacraments, creeds, confessions, primitive faith, and most of all, the church. For "the Church, according to this view of it," Newman wrote, "is not and never was, more than a collection of individuals."[65]

In an interesting tangent to this critique of individualism, John Keble surveyed the current state of missionary societies. He warned that church societies were "not to be regarded as merely charitable voluntary associations, standing each on its own merits, independent of all other institutions, like the body of subscribers to a hospital, or a charity school." Rather, church societies shared in the same traditions that ruled and regulated the whole church. Hence, Keble's strictures reaffirmed the consecrated and creedal nature of missions. Newman etched Keble's point in sharper relief:

> Fancy any model Protestant of this day in a state of things so different from his own! With his religious societies for the Church, with his committees, boards, and platforms instead of Bishops, his *Record* and *Patriot* newspapers instead of Councils . . . his niggardly vestry allowances for gold and silver vessels, his gas and stoves for wax and oil, his denunciation of self-righteousness for fasting and celibacy, and his exercise of private judgment for submission to authority—would he have a chance of finding himself at home in a Christianity such as this?[66]

In this way Newman sketched how assumptions that the Scriptures could be interpreted through private judgment led to as-

---

[64]Ibid., 1:149.

[65]Ibid., 1:160.

[66]Keble, *Sermons*, 234; Newman, "Primitive Christianity," in *Essays and Sketches*, ed. Charles P. Harrold, 2 vols. (London, 1948) 1:177.

sumptions that the church was a voluntary association. He would return to these points when proposing an Anglo-Catholic alternative. Newman admitted that the Tractarian option was viewed with misgivings. To the Protestants the Tractarians were masquerading papists; to the Roman Catholics they were typically inconsistent Protestants. Nevertheless, the Tractarians retorted that their concept of apostolic tradition remedied the deficiencies of Protestantism and Roman Catholicism alike. Moreover, its power could be seen nowhere better than in the issues of scriptural authority and the nature of the church. John Keble, for example, claimed that the "faith once for all delivered to the saints, in other words, Apostolical Tradition, was divinely appointed in the Church as the touchstone of canonical Scripture itself." Such a tradition drew on Scripture and the writings of the apostles, as well as on the unwritten tradition of the primitive church regarding governance and certain doctrinal points. Recognition of these resources of authority and instruction shielded the church from the dangers of rationalism, nominalism, and Erastianism that were assaulting her and undermining her power.[67]

Here then was the second theme of apostolicity, for if the Anglican church was Catholic, the very meaning of that attribute implied participation in an apostolic tradition. Newman portrayed this tradition as providing the external reference needed for scriptural interpretation—a guide more adequate than the evangelicals' dependence on Scripture alone or the Roman Catholics' dependence on the uniformity of tradition. Continuing his discussion, Newman argued that much of the difficulty encountered in scriptural exegesis was due to a lack of moral rather than intellectual preparation. In 1822 Keble had written that "moral rather than intellectual proficiency" was the appropriate qualification for properly understanding the Scriptures; now Newman reiterated the point. Consistent with the Tractarians' concept of reserve was their insistence that the path to spiritual insight was predominantly moral. Contradicting the ideas of popular Protestantism, they stressed that

---

[67]Keble, *Sermons*, 194, 199, 213-16.

that path was arduous and narrow as well.[68] Beyond discussing the road to scriptural understanding, they provided a standard measure by which true apostolic tradition could be recognized. "*Quod semper, quod ubique, quod ab omnibus*: Antiquity, Universality, Catholicity," these were the tests, Keble declared, by which apostolic tradition could be faithfully discerned and genuinely established. Newman developed Keble's point, adopting two of his terms and substituting "consent of the Fathers" for universality. Later, however, Newman stipulated in another essay that the Fathers of the Church were primarily witnesses to the faith, not authoritative of it.[69] Last, Newman expanded upon the issue of authority by focusing on the meaning of the Thirty-nine Articles. These were articles of religion, not of faith, Newman alleged; as such, they were not necessary for salvation except insofar as they embodied the Apostles' Creed. Their authority grew from their adoption by venerable individuals past and present, from their consonance with Scripture, and from contemporary subscription. Above all, the Thirty-nine Articles were instruments of Catholic teaching and a witness to the deposit of faith revealed in apostolic tradition. Again, apostolicity was seen as the bedrock for the church's foundation.[70]

Universality of doctrinal tradition was integrally related to catholicity and apostolicity. This theme surfaced in Newman's discussion of the problem: how could there be one tradition when the church was visibly divided? He answered that the apostolic tradition was substantially the same for the entire church, though local areas might disagree over minor points. Invoking a "branch theory" that recognized Roman, Greek, and Anglo-Catholic descendants from the common stock of apostolic truth, Newman steadfastly argued

---

[68]Newman, "Lectures on the Prophetical Office," *Via Media*, 1:38, 158; Keble, *Sermons*, 24, 115.

[69]Keble, *Sermons*, 199; Newman, "Lectures on the Prophetical Office," 1:51; Newman, "Primitive Christianity," *Essays and Sketches*, 1:126.

[70]Newman, "Lectures on the Prophetical Office," 1:136-39, 234-37; Keble, *Sermons*, 210.

that the apostolic church provided a model for contemporary Anglican practice and theology.[71]

Implicit within Newman's discussion of the universal church was the hope that the several branches might one day reconcile with each other and heal the divisions within the church. For the present though, Newman recognized the reality of separation and continued to insist on the via media as the proper path for the Anglican church. To some it seemed as if this road was only a theological conjecture. Yet the Tractarians maintained their faith in the lodestar of apostolic tradition, ever mindful that their way lay between Rome and Geneva, and ever convinced of their ability to move forward and avoid pitfalls even though their eyes were lifted skyward.

THE WRATH TO COME

Newman believed that in 1839 he was at the height of his powers, but before long he and the whole Oxford party found themselves tripped up and stumbling.[72] During 1839-1845, three sets of events rocked the self-confidence of the Tractarian leaders and the public's estimation of the movement. Newman, in an important essay written in 1839, took stock of Anglo-Catholicism and looked forward to its future. Once again he sought a middle position between evangelical Protestantism and Roman Catholicism. Calling the Protestants "puritans," he said that despite their present popularity they would have no staying power. The puritans' first principle, Newman claimed, was "that in spirituals no man is really above another, but that each individual from high to low, is both privileged and bound to make out his religious views for himself." Here was the Tractarian nemesis—private judgment. As before, Newman saw it leading to a rationalism incompatible with genuine religious faith. As he contemplated the roots of the present Anglo-Catholic revival, Newman recalled the beliefs of previous theologians, such as Alexander Knox

---

[71]Newman, "Lectures on the Prophetical Office," 1:201-203, 212; Newman, "Apostolical Tradition," *Essays: Critical and Historical*, 2 vols. (London, 1910) 1:127. See also Christopher Dawson, *The Spirit of the Oxford Movement* (New York, 1933) 103-104.

[72]Newman, *Apologia*, 104.

and Bishop Jebb—theologians who had sounded themes similar to those of the Tractarians. Yet in this essay Newman looked beyond Anglican resources, claiming concordance with poets such as Coleridge and Wordsworth and alliances with similar renewals on the European continent.

Newman's knowledge of specific developments in Europe, especially in Germany, was rather limited. He was most familiar with events in France and the struggle over ultramontanism associated with Lamennais. Nevertheless, he made his claim and returned to his main contention: "Surely then our true wisdom now is to look for some *Via Media* which will preserve us from what threatens."[73] Anglo-Catholicism need not mean a slavish and ritualistic imitation of antiquity nor a forgetfulness of past events. Yet if such a movement for "catholic tradition" was so widespread, then it was simplistic to allege that it was a function of this or that individual person. "The current of the age cannot be stopped," Newman intoned, "but it may be directed; and it is better that it should find its way into the Anglican port, than that it should be propelled into Popery, or drifted into disbelief." These were the spiritual forces at work, these the options of faith. Making his final point, Newman queried, "would you rather have your sons and daughters members of the Church of England, or of the Church of Rome? That is the real alternative, if we follow things to their results."[74]

Some feared that the Oxford movement's answer to the question would increasingly favor Rome, and they wished to expose that suspected disloyalty. One of those most concerned with the possibility of faithlessness was Charles Golightly, a former confidant of Newman and Pusey, but by 1839 one of the movement's fiercest opponents.[75] Golightly had sided with the Tractarians in the Hampden

---

[73]Newman, "Prospects of the Anglican Church" [original title: "The State of Religious Parties"] *Essays and Sketches*, 1:362, 337, 371. See also Newman, "Fall of De la Mennais," *Essays: Critical and Historical*, 1:138-72; W. G. Roe, *Lamennais and England* (London, 1966) 93-114; E. A. Knox, *The Tractarian Movement* (London, 1933) 332-57.

[74]Newman, "Prospects of the Anglican Church," *Essays and Sketches*, 1:353, 372.

[75]R. W. Greaves, "Golightly and Newman, 1824-1845," *Journal of Ecclesiastical History* 9, no. 2 (1958): 209-28.

dispute and later had served as Newman's curate at Littlemore, an adjunct of St. Mary's parish outside of Oxford. But Golightly had continued to hold certain evangelical views, particularly on baptism, and consequently had resigned his position after maintaining it for a year. The separation was none too amicable, adding questions of personality to questions of principle. By 1838 and the publishing of Froude's *Remains*, Golightly and others were hardened in their opposition to the Tractarians. Their counterattack came in the context of a larger plan to build a memorial to the memory of Thomas Cranmer, Nicholas Ridley, and Hugh Latimer, all of whom had been martyred by Queen Mary. Subscriptions were taken out to help build the suggested Martyr's Memorial, and all Oxford waited to see how the Tractarians would respond. If they subscribed, it would appear that the Tractarians had backed off from their censures of Protestant individualism; if they did not subscribe, it would confirm their opponents' worst fears regarding Tractarian attachment to Roman Catholicism. Newman and Keble adamantly refused to contribute in any way. Pusey would not desert his colleagues but tried to explain their sentiments to Richard Bagot, Bishop of Oxford. "One should have thought it very natural and a right feeling, had the place, where they yielded up their souls been inclosed long ago," Pusey demurely wrote to the bishop, "but this plan of a monument was *devised* only to serve a party purpose: it was, in fact, (as some of themselves avow) a counter movement against Froude's 'Remains,' or as one of them said, 'It will be a good cut against Newman.' " Pusey struck at the divisiveness of the proposal and concluded with oratorical fervor,

> It has seemed to me, for some years, the great blessing of our Reformation that we are not (as the Lutherans and Calvinists are) connected with any human founder, or bound up with his human infirmities: we are neither Cranmerites nor Ridleyites but an Apostolic branch of the church Catholic; and I fear lest this plan should tend to increase the vulgar impression that we were a new Church at the Reformation, instead of being the old one purified.[76]

The Martyr's Memorial episode dried up whatever remaining respect some evangelicals held for the piety of the Tractarians as in-

---

[76]Pusey to Bishop Bagot, 12 November 1838, Pusey Papers.

dividuals. It also appeared to ratify increasing suspicions that the Tractarians were papists in disguise. In the autumn of 1838 Pusey had written to Keble conceding that such stories abounded, yet concluding "when all the red dye which they have laid on to make us look like the Church of Rome, is washed off, (as it must be sooner or later) people will be the more taken with what they thought ugly. So I enjoy much every absurd report I hear. Some folks' lethargy could not be raised any other way."[77]

In 1841 other events occurred that in different ways provoked a crisis within the movement, destroying its self-confidence and precipitating its dissolution. These were the condemning of Tract 90 in the spring and the Jerusalem bishopric affair in the fall. Tract 90 was published in late February 1841. In it Newman argued that the Thirty-nine Articles were not contrary to Roman Catholic doctrine and practice but rather condemned popular abuses. Additionally, he came out for the real presence of Christ in the Eucharist, and made room for purgatory and the invocation of the saints. His point was to show how Catholics could subscribe to the Thirty-nine Articles; however, many read it as a call for secession to Rome.[78] On 17 March 1841, Bishop Bagot wrote to both Pusey and Newman expressing his anxiety over the content of the recent tract. While complaining to Pusey of the "alarms and offense" disturbing the church, the bishop conceded to Newman that "the *object* of the Tract is to make our *Church* more Catholic (in its true sense) and more unified"; the result, however, had been quite different. Accordingly, the bishop requested that there be no further discussion of the Thirty-nine Articles in the Tracts.[79] Bagot was a personal friend of Keble, Pusey, and Newman and was loath to criticize their work. As for the Tractarians, the furor over Tract 90, with its claim that the Articles

---

[77]Pusey to John Keble, Autumn 1838, Pusey Papers; Keble to Pusey, 18 January 1839, Pusey Papers.

[78]R. D. Middleton, "Tract Ninety," *Journal of Ecclesiastical History* 2, no. 1 (1951): 81-100; Church, *The Oxford Movement*, 266-95; Marvin O'Connell, *The Oxford Conspirators* (New York, 1969) 320-39.

[79]Bishop Bagot to Pusey, 17 March 1841; Bagot to Newman, 17 March 1841, Pusey Papers.

could be interpreted in a manner allowing for Catholic meaning, came as a surprise. John Keble had written his sister about an early draft of the tract that Newman had shown him. "The drift of it being to shew," he related, "that the objections sometimes made to parts of them on Catholic views ought not to hinder anyone from signing or adhering to them. . . . Well I was very glad of it. . . . So I returned it with an Imprimatur, making one or two slight alterations."[80]

Pusey responded to Bagot's letter by pointing out that Newman had already criticized Roman Catholicism and consequently "he did not think it necessary to speak against . . . [it] again."[81] Nevertheless, Pusey concluded that despite the present misunderstanding, both he and Newman maintained their pledge of absolute obedience to the bishop. Such loyalty might appear unnecessary or even extreme, but for a movement that had made so much of apostolic authority, episcopal declarations were no light matter. Furthermore, there had been an episode in 1838 in which Bagot had appeared to criticize the Tracts. As it happened, reprimand was not his intention, and the whole incident turned into a mire of mutual apologies, explanations, and epistles.[82] Now in 1841 Newman was indeed ready to obey, though he insisted that "matters would not have gone better for the Church had I never written." Bagot persisted in requesting balance, although by then, with supporters and opponents of the Tractarians jousting with one another in public papers and private pamphlets, a *status quo ante* was irretrievable. Finally on 22 March 1841, the Archbishop of Canterbury wrote to the Bishop of Oxford that "it seems most desireable that the publication of the *Tracts* should be discontinued forever."[83]

---

[80]John Keble to his sister, Elizabeth, 14 March 1841, Keble Papers.

[81]Pusey to Bishop Bagot, 18 March 1841, Pusey Papers.

[82]See "The Charge of the Bishop of Oxford, 1838," *The Judgment of the Bishops upon Tractarian Theology*, ed. W. Simcox Bricknell (Oxford, 1845) 150-51; Pusey to Bishop Bagot, 5 September 1838; Bagot to Pusey, 10 September 1838; Bagot to Pusey, 10 November 1838, Pusey Papers.

[83]Copy of a letter from Newman to Bishop Bagot, 20 March 1841; draft of a letter from Bagot to Newman, ca. 21 March 1841; copy of a letter of Archbishop of Canterbury to Bishop Bagot, 22 March 1841, Pusey Papers.

The embers of the controversy over Tract 90 continued to send out an occasional shower of sparks, but with the archbishop's pronouncement it was clear that the Oxford movement had lost. The Tractarians had tried to expand the context and doctrinal meaning of the Articles; it was no more than the rationalists, such as Hampden, had attempted. But to their dismay, they found their bid for doctrinal endorsement blocked. When they were censured by the university and episcopal misgivings were finally expressed, they knew they were badly beaten.[84]

Before the year was over, the Oxford movement would be beaten yet again, this time in ecclesiastical politics. In the summer of 1841 Baron Christian Bunsen on behalf of Friedrich Wilhelm IV, king of Prussia, proposed that a new bishopric be established in Jerusalem. Under this plan the new bishop would superintend any Anglicans or German Protestants in the area and discharge a special missionary commission to convert the Jews. In addition, the bishop would be empowered to ordain any German who subscribed to the Thirty-nine Articles and the Confession of Augsburg. The British and Prussian crowns would alternately nominate the bishop, although the Archbishop of Canterbury would have permanent veto power over any candidate. Similarly, funds for the position would be supplied by both English and Prussian sources.[85] The proposal was politically and religiously appealing. Politically, such an outpost would establish a mutually beneficial alliance between the two countries and would help weight the political balance in the Middle East in favor of England and Germany and lighten it with regard to France and Russia. Friedrich Wilhelm's desire for the new bishop was not only political, but figured in a larger plan, inherited from his father,

---

[84]Greaves, "Golightly and Newman," 220-24; Church, Oxford Movement, 266-95.

[85]For a discussion of the establishment and history of the bishopric, see W. H. Hechler, The Jerusalem Bishopric (London, 1883); P. E. Shaw, The Early Tractarians and the Eastern Church (London, 1930); R. W. Greaves, "The Jerusalem Bishopric, 1841," English Historical Review 64, no. 252 (July 1949): 328-53; P. J. Welch, "Anglican Churchmen and the Establishment of the Jerusalem Bishopric," Journal of Ecclesiastical History 8, no. 2 (October 1957): 193-204; Kurt Schmidt-Clausen, Vorweggenommene Einheit: die Grundung des Bistums Jerusalem im Jahre 1841 (Berlin, 1965).

to unite all believing Christians in a bond of simple piety, oblivious to confessional differences.[86]

In Bunsen, the Prussian king had chosen an excellent representative. Poised and well connected, fluent in English, and personally committed to the success of the project, Bunsen had the qualifications necessary for success. Upon arriving in England in 1841 he began to contact influential persons and soon could boast of Archbishop Howley's and Bishop Blomfield's active support. Equally important, Bunsen developed backing in both High Church and evangelical circles. Not only did that curmudgeon of Anglican orthodoxy, Walter Hook, write a pamphlet endorsing the bishopric, but both Lord Ashley and Samuel Wilberforce, leading lights among the evangelicals, championed it as well.[87] With this auspicious start, events moved quickly. In October 1841 Parliament passed an act overcoming a series of legal hurdles connected to the proposal. On 7 November 1841, the new bishop was consecrated and left to take up his post.[88]

There had been little opposition in Parliament to the bill expediting the Jerusalem project. Only the Earl of Randor had spoken out, and he chided the Anglican hierarchy for championing apostolic succession and then irresolutely seeking permission in Parliament from the Crown.[89] That the bishopric project had not been reviewed by the bishops in formal convocation was also one of the grievances the Tractarians pointed out. It was not the only complaint, however. The Prussian emissary, Christian Bunsen, was well known to many of the Oxford group. Pusey had first become acquainted with him in 1825 during his trip to Germany. Newman and Froude had met Bunsen in Rome during their visit in 1833. Accounts of Newman's and Froude's conversations in Rome reflect their appreciation of Bunsen and indicate their interest in the Prus-

---

[86]See chapter 2, "Unions, Awakenings, and Revolution," for discussion of the Prussian monarchy and its plans for religious reform.

[87]Desmond Bowen, *The Idea of the Victorian Church* (Montreal, 1968) 76; Newsome, *Parting of Friends*, 289.

[88]Greaves, "Jerusalem Bishopric," 344-45.

[89]Ibid., 344.

sian Union. Bunsen evidently portrayed the Union to them as an extension of episcopacy, for Newman's and Froude's approval of Friedrich Wilhelm's efforts is ironic given the campaign the two waged a few short months after they returned to England.[90]

The Oxford leaders' initial appreciation of Bunsen withered under the pressure of fighting his proposed bishopric. "Have you heard of this deplorable Jerusalem matter," Newman wrote Samuel Woods on 10 October 1841. "There is not a single Anglican at Jerusalem, but we are to place a Bishop (of the circumcision expressly) there, to collect a communion of Protestants, Jews, Druses, Monophysites, conforming under the influence of our war steamers, to counterbalance the Russian influence through Greeks and the French through Latins."[91] Newman's reaction to the Jerusalem bishopric was perhaps more vitriolic than that of his fellow Tractarians, but it was not unique. Keble called the proposal "a sad business"; Robert Wilberforce confessed that although he did not know all the details of the project, he could not "understand why the council of the Bishop of the Greek Church was not solicited." Robert's brother, Samuel, could not understand the Tractarians' antipathy to the project. "I confess I feel furious," he candidly wrote to Robert, "at the craving of men for union with idolatrous, material, sensual, domineering Rome and their squeamish anathemizing hatred of Protestant Reformed men."[92]

Pusey alone among the Tractarian foursome initially had been inclined to approve the establishment of the bishopric. Soon after Bunsen arrived in England, he met with Pusey and emphasized the missionary aspect of the enterprise, speaking of congregations struggling in the wilderness without leadership. By November 1841 Pusey's views had altered considerably; he agreed with Newman. In

[90]Liddon, *Pusey*, 1:77; Froude, *Remains*, 1:301-302; Newman to his sister, Jemina, 20 March 1833, Newman Papers.

[91]Newman to John Keble, 5 October 1841; Newman to Samuel Woods, 10 October 1841, Newman Papers.

[92]Battiscombe, *John Keble*, 227; Robert Wilberforce to Newman, 25 November 1841, Newman Papers; Samuel to Robert Wilberforce, 2 February 1842, as quoted in Newsome, *Parting of Friends*, 289.

that month Newman and William Palmer (of Magdalen College, Oxford) both issued protests against the bishopric offer. In a letter to Bishop Bagot, Palmer condemned the proposal in words consonant with the views of Newman. "If it is to involve an interconnection with the Lutherans," Palmer wrote, "they not being required to renounce what is considered to be the fundamental principle of modern dissent, nor to admit the Church's doctrine and practice of the Laying on of Hands in Confirmation, it will appear to involve the Church of England in both heresy and schism."[93]

For his part Pusey wrote a long letter to the Archbishop of Canterbury attacking this new "experimental Church" with its congregation of persons "sound or unsound, pious or worldly bound together by no associations, accustomed to no obedience."[94] Heresy and schism, blindness to confessional standards, and dictation by the state—the Jerusalem bishopric provided the Oxford party with an opportunity to articulate their protests once again and once again they were soundly defeated. Pusey's change of opinion was marked with a profound sense of consternation, if not betrayal. In 1846 in a letter to William Gladstone, Pusey wrote of how he had hoped to extend episcopacy and nurture a diasporic people, and of how his hopes had been stillborn in the reality of the bishopric. "It is a piece of Prussian Diplomacy," Pusey ruefully concluded, "not a people asking us to bestow upon them a gift which they have not, nor a want of the people at all, but a sort of experiment on the part of the Civil Government." Bunsen finally became a target for Pusey, much as he had earlier for Newman, and Pusey cursed him as a rationalist.[95]

Beyond its immediate significance for the Oxford movement, the Jerusalem bishopric episode caused an indirect encounter between the English Oxford movement and the German neo-Lutheran confessional movement. In 1842, Ignaz Döllinger wrote a warm and sympathetic letter to Pusey. "All eyes—of Protestant as

---

[93]William Palmer to Bishop Bagot, 5 November 1841, Pusey Papers.

[94]Liddon, *Pusey*, 2:257.

[95]Pusey to W. E. Gladstone, 9 April 1846, Pusey Papers. His views of Bunsen are noted in Welch, "Jerusalem Bishopric," 199-200.

well as of Roman Catholics—are turned in fear and hope towards Oxford," he said. "It becomes more and more probable that your great and memorable movement will have essential influence also on the course of religious development in Germany." Continuing, Döllinger referred to the current religious situation in Germany and mentioned the struggle (probably that of the Silesian Lutherans) "to assert again the old Protestantism of the Symbolical Books; but the Union, established by Prussia, has struck it a deep wound."[96] Among the leaders of the Oxford party, Pusey was the best informed as regarded religious developments in Germany. Not only his book on German Protestantism but his continuing correspondence with Döllinger, August Tholuck, August Neander, and E. W. Hengstenberg attest to his interest. There is no evidence, however, that Pusey was aware of the neo-Lutherans; and if Pusey was not, then chances are that the rest of the Oxford leaders were ignorant of them as well. Germany, in short, remained an enigma for most of the Tractarians, one in which speculation and rationalism seemed too often to have the upper hand, while faith seemed to play little or no role at all.

If these English theologians were theologically isolated from certain continental developments, the same cannot be said for the neo-Lutherans. In August 1844 Wilhelm Löhe quipped that his work was seen as the "product of German Puseyism." The following month he told a friend that he did not mind if he was called a Puseyite, for his antagonists had no understanding of the true church. Later in his study, *Three Books About the Church*, Löhe attacked the Jerusalem bishopric. Finally, in 1849 in words reminiscent of the complaints of Newman, Pusey, and Palmer, Löhe assailed the situation in which an Anglican bishop could evaluate and ordain Lutheran candidates for the ministry as was taking place in Jerusalem.[97]

---

[96]I. Döllinger to Pusey, 4 September 1842, Pusey Papers. For an assessment of Newman's influence, principally as a Catholic, see Werner Becker, "Newman in Deutschland," *Newman-Studien* 2: 281-306.

[97]Wilhelm Löhe to K. Raumer, 21 April 1844; Löhe to Ludwig Petri, 9 May 1844, Löhe Papers, Löhe Archiv, Neuendettelsau, Bavaria; Löhe, *Three Books About the Church*, trans. and ed. James Schaaf (Philadelphia, 1969) 137; Löhe, "Petition to the Generalsynod, 1849," *Gesammelte Werke*, ed. Klaus Ganzert, 7 vols. (Neuendettelsau, 1951-) 5/1:335-36.

Löhe's colleague, Theodor Kliefoth, also took up the cudgel against the Jerusalem bishopric, though he misunderstood who supported it in England. Protesting against the failure to adhere to confessional standards, Kliefoth lashed out at the bishopric, calling it "puseyistic" and denouncing its intermixed ordination. Thus these Anglo-German opponents of the Jerusalem project, separated by distance, traditions, and inaccurate information obliquely engaged one another. Had their alliance been stronger and more timely, they would in all likelihood still have been unable to prevent the establishment of the bishopric. However, this episode provided another opportunity for each group in their separate contexts to proclaim the themes of ecclesiological discipline, spiritual independence, and allegiance to doctrinal standards.[98] Furthermore, to knowledgeable and sympathetic Germans, the Oxford movement appeared to be fighting for the spiritual independence of the church, though it did so in the exclusively English terms of episcopacy. The perceived singularity of those terms made them difficult to export; thus even those Germans friendly to the Oxford priests had a hard time explaining and defending what German critics repeatedly castigated as "Puseyismus."

If Pusey initially felt betrayed at Bunsen's hands, after the Jerusalem episode he and the other Tractarians were completely bewildered. It is well known that the Jerusalem bishopric affair was a main contributor to John Newman's decision to leave the Anglican church and become a Roman Catholic. Similarly, his retirement to Littlemore, his retraction of his previous anti-Roman statements, his resignation as vicar of St. Mary's, and his transfer to the Roman Catholic Church—all these are familiar and well documented.[99] In the context of the present study, Newman's move raised personal questions for each of the Tractarian leaders about the viability of the via media and the standing of the Anglican church. In May 1841 Pusey entertained the idea of writing a pamphlet against the Roman Catholics, and solicited information from his sister concerning pop-

---

[98]Theodor Kliefoth, "An die hochwürdige theologische Fakultät . . . Göttingen," *Kirchliche Zeitschrift* (1854): 160-62.

[99]See the accounts in Church, *Oxford Movement*, 384-408; O'Connell, *Oxford Conspirators*, 365-415; and Newman's own description in *Apologia*, 151-226.

ular extravagance in the Roman church. In 1837 he had written
Bishop Bagot, "We have too much to do, to keep sound doctrine and
the privileges of the Church, to be able to afford to go into the question about dresses." By 1841, however, many seemed to find Rome
as attractive for her vestments and rituals as for her particular brand
of doctrine. Earlier, as the Oxford party grew in strength and numbers, Newman had decried the "manneristic" emphasis that he had
observed in Anglo-Catholicism.[100] Yet there were deeper issues than
the fact, as Newman had once put it, that "the Via Media is crowded
with young enthusiasts," and all the Tractarian leaders recognized
the correctness of his statement.[101]

In 1840 in an article entitled "The Catholicity of the Anglican
Church," Newman had focused on the absence of unity in the
church. Epigrammatically, he contended "that the Church is one, is
the point of *doctrine*, that we are estranged from the body of the
Church, is the point of *fact*, and that we still have the means of grace
among us, is our point of *controversy*." If this latter point was the focus of difficulties, the Anglican church, Newman concluded, still retained the essential note of sanctity. In a letter to Keble in 1843,
Pusey invoked this same theme, arguing that holiness rather than
any external authority would decide the issue of unity. Replying, Keble took issue with the heart of Pusey's suggestion. If simple holiness
were adequate, he wrote, who was to judge, for was not sanctity the
very standard of the evangelicals? It was better, Keble insisted, to reaffirm primitive tradition as the best guide.[102]

Pusey's recourse to holiness reflected how deeply the tremors of
possible defection were felt, how much the concept of the via media
was buckling under pressure. Robert Wilberforce was dismayed
when he learned of the latest developments. In January 1842 on the
eve of Newman's removal to Littlemore, Wilberforce saw the warning signals of that event and told Newman, "I cannot give up the

---

[100]Pusey to Emily Pusey, 1 May 1841; Pusey to Bishop Bagot, 26 September
1837, Pusey Papers; Newman to Frederic Rogers, 5 July 1837, Newman Papers.

[101]Newman, *Apologia*, 105.

[102]Newman, "The Catholicity of the Anglican Church," *Essays and Sketches*, 2:57;
Pusey to Keble, 23 September 1843; Keble to Pusey, 3 October 1843, Pusey Papers.

hope that God will in his mercy keep you from what I do not but regard as so regretful an error."[103] Newman saw the circumstances in a different light. Smarting from the censure of Tract 90 and despairing of the church's future, Newman informed Henry Manning that, "in proportion as I think the English Church is showing herself intrinsically and radically alien from Catholic principles, so do I feel difficulties in defending her claims to be a branch of the Catholic Church." By the spring of 1845, Newman's doubts had increased; he believed that the English Church was indeed in schism. He hoped to wait until at least 1846 before making a decision, he informed a friend, but his misgivings might not allow him to hold off that long. Newman's apprehensions finally surmounted his forbearance, and he was received into the Roman Catholic Church on 9 October 1845.[104]

AFTERMATH

In the wake of 1845 the Oxford party was in shambles. It was left to Keble, Pusey, and Wilberforce to make their peace with Newman's decision and to follow the path that their own consciences dictated. Outsiders viewed the party's disarray with predictable mixtures of approval or sadness. Richard Whately, the former colleague from Oriel, spoke of the situation in 1846 with amusement. "I myself think that it would not be difficult to make out that the Tractite party has *no existence*," he told Edward Hawkins. "*This* man had nothing to do with forming it; and *another* wrote some Tracts, but disapproved of their general principles; and *another* approved of some but thought others went too far; and *another* adopted their principles but disapproved some of the conclusions, etc."[105] The commotion Whately found humorous, Pusey found deeply distressing. Even as late as February 1845, Pusey told Gladstone that he considered Newman as "God's special instrument towards us." Later

---

[103]Robert Wilberforce to Newman, 29 January 1842, Newman Papers.

[104]Newman to Henry Manning, 10 October 1843; Newman to R. F. Wilson, 11 April 1845, Newman Papers.

[105]Whately to Hawkins, 11 February 1846, as quoted by Brendon, *Hurrell Froude*, 42.

that year Pusey confided to Keble that should Newman leave, "the rent in our poor Church will be terrible; I cannot conceive where it will end, or how many we may not lose." Pusey predicted that those remaining in the Anglican church "will have to think how the fragments may be gathered up; for I fear we shall lose much of what is devotional and deepest."[106]

Pusey counted himself squarely among those who would remain; John Keble felt the same. Accordingly, Pusey requested that Keble write a short piece to reassure the doubtful still in the church. Keble to some extent fulfilled this task with a preface—entitled "On the Present Position of English Churchmen"—to a collection of his sermons published in 1847. Keble began by invoking in familiar fashion the counsel of Bishop Butler. The Anglican church where one is baptized and raised, he said, is like a nurturing mother: the faltering should put away their doubts; they should submit, they should trust. Quoting Butler's adage that "probability is the very guide of life," Keble wrote that moral questions must be decided by moral evidence; faith thus would be allowed full scope. In this way, Keble demonstrated his own unhesitant faith, his own steadfast commitment to the church. Indeed, as he began another line of thought, Keble reiterated that "a trusting resolute faith" rather than "a searching, comprehensive, historical intellect" would be most likely to assuage doubt and fortify commitment. Continuing, he toted up the marks of unity, sanctity, and universality and found the Anglican church on a par with Rome.[107]

So the situation stood until 1850, when with the delivery of the Gorham judgment, this tottering band of Anglo-Catholics again was knocked to its knees. The Gorham case, with its vindication of evangelical doctrine as interpreted by a secular court, directly repudiated the Oxford movement. It also greatly affected Robert Isaac Wilberforce. Wilberforce, of course, had been a close friend of Newman's and had been unhappy with Newman's conversion to Catholicism. When, in 1846, he heard news of the parliamentary

---

[106]Pusey to W. Gladstone, 18 February 1845; Pusey to Keble, 28 March 1845, Pusey Papers.

[107]Keble, *Sermons*, iii-iv, viii, xi-xii, xxi-xxii, xxxv-xxxviii.

debates and Peel's latest political crisis, Robert wrote his brother, Samuel, "So Peel has taken the same course with the Conservatives, as Newman took with the Tractarians. . . . As he made, so he destroys them. . . . The one has a crucifix from Rome, the other a testimonial from Manchester. The one speaks about the laws of food, the other about the laws of development." Both, he said, were "the creatures of circumstances."[108]

Wilberforce delivered a charge the following year, taking up "the great question, of the day, whether the Church of Christ has any real existence, distinct from the establishment, as it is invidiously termed by its enemies." Dismissing the view of the church as a "voluntary combination of men, being formed by arbitrary association," that "may be dissolved or reanimated by mutual consent," he contended that the essence of the church is an "actual union with the renewed humanity of Christ incarnate."[109]

This theme provided the basis for Wilberforce's study on the incarnation, which appeared in 1848. Here was the accumulated result of Wilberforce's linguistic training, patristic study, and theological investigation. As he discussed the significance of the incarnation for a doctrine of the church, Wilberforce concluded:

> It may be said in general, that our union with the manhood of Christ, or our participation in His Presence, is brought about in our union with the Church, which is His body mystical. It is not that one of these is a means or channel through which we approach the other, but that since the two processes are identical, it is impossible to divide them. For that which joins men to Christ's mystical body, the Church, is their union with His man's nature; and their means of union with His man's nature is bestowed in His Church or body mystical.[110]

This point led Wilberforce to others. First, he criticized theologians, such as Friedrich Schleiermacher, for viewing the church as primarily a human institution and thereby denigrating its sacred foundation. Wilberforce then ascribed such views as Schleiermacher's to an

---

[108]Robert Wilberforce to Samuel Wilberforce, 6 July 1842, Wilberforce Papers, Bodleian Library.

[109]Wilberforce, "A Charge to the Clergy of East Riding" (n.p., 1847) 12.

[110]Wilberforce, *The Doctrine of the Incarnation* (Philadelphia, 1849) 243.

inadequate understanding of the sacraments. For the sacraments, in Wilberforce's opinion, grew naturally out of the incarnation and were the means of grace provided from the objective reality of the church.[111] Thus, Wilberforce's arguments preserved the Tractarian emphasis upon the church as a sacramental medium of grace. They also contributed to the shift of focus from the doctrine of the Atonement to that of the Incarnation, a change symptomatic of the divergence between evangelicals and Tractarians.

The outcome of the Gorham trial was thus a crushing blow to Wilberforce and his High Church ecclesiology. Its vindication of evangelical doctrine was bad enough, but its delivery by the state authority was intolerable. Together with Keble and Pusey, Wilberforce attended a meeting in which High Churchmen plotted their response, but the counselors were divided and vacillating. Keble, for instance, first said that no matter what the cost, the ecclesiastical establishment ought to be abolished and another system, perhaps like the Scottish, substituted. Shortly thereafter, he changed his mind. Confessing his uncertainty, he wrote to Wilberforce, "I myself feel more deeply every day that it would be a deadly sin to separate from the Church of England, but how to support her and serve her best is hard to judge."[112] Robert's brother, Samuel, was equally distressed by the specter of state interference in ecclesiastical affairs and turned his attention to the revival of the convocation at Canterbury.

For his part, Robert returned to his books, hoping that he could still rescue Anglo-Catholic principles. Out of his research came a discussion of Anglican church history, published in 1851 as *A Sketch of the History of Erastianism*. Wilberforce defined the Erastian position as "that system of opinion and that course of action, which deprives the Church of Christ of independent existence, and resolves it into a function of civil government." His reference to the Gorham episode was transparent, and as he traced the contours of this policy

---

[111]Illuminating discussion of Wilberforce's theological reflections is provided in Newsome, *Parting of Friends*, 370-85; Härdelin, *Tractarian Understanding of the Eucharist*, 84-87, 141-47, 160-67.

[112]Keble to Robert Wilberforce, 16 July 1850, Keble Papers; Newsome, *Parting of Friends*, 351-52.

Wilberforce repeatedly ran up against the old Tractarian nemesis: rationalism. "Erastianism and Rationalism are in reality two forms of the self-same error," Wilberforce contended, "a denial of the existence of any divine rule in the interpretation of religious truth."[113] The same had been said in the earliest Tracts, and, before them, at the reading parties at John Keble's house in the 1820s. Tagged as rationalism or stylized as private judgment, this concept of individual authority stood foursquare against all that the Tractarians represented. The Tractarians' next decision, of course, was whether to continue struggling within the Anglican church—whether to take the path of John Keble, or of John Newman.

Robert Wilberforce's decision became clear in 1854. In September, he renounced his subscription to the Royal Supremacy and published a small pamphlet defending his position. Repudiating the sovereignty of a secular ruler in spiritual matters, Wilberforce turned his attention to the debate over private judgment versus church authority. He spelled out how an emphasis on private judgment would affect the doctrine of the church,

> according as it was supposed to be merely a combination of individuals, or an *organic* institution, endowed with a divine life. In the first case it would have no other powers than those which it derived from its members; in the second, its members would be only the materials, which it would fashion and combine through its own inherent life. In one case it would stand on human authority; in the other, on Divine appointment. On one side would be reason, enlightened it may be, but still the reason of individuals; on the other, supernatural grace.[114]

While Wilberforce's statements might be considered a flourishing defense of the divine nature of the church, to Pusey and Keble they were genuine distress signals. Pusey pointed out the ambivalent interpretations of the meaning of royal supremacy and lamented the current tendency "to make this or that a test of the validity of the Church." Keble took up the same point. Where earlier he had attempted to assuage Wilberforce's doubts, he now reprimanded him for "taking up with the very slightest evidence when its

---

[113]Wilberforce, *A Sketch of the History of Erastianism* (London, 1851) preface, 86.

[114]Wilberforce, *An Inquiry into the Principles of Church Authority, or reasons for recalling my subscription to the royal supremacy* (London, 1854) 1-2.

tells in favour of Rome, while in a hard and almost supercilious way you make much of every blemish on the other side."[115]

Amid anxiety from family members and hard counsel from friends, Wilberforce acted on a previous decision and moved to Paris. In a friendlier mood, Keble had once written to Robert that he was surprised Robert could "have so given up . . . [his] old faith in Antiquity for a philosophical dream about development—and so suddenly at that."[116] To Wilberforce the decision had been agonizingly long. One is reminded of his distress at Newman's conversion.

Consequently, whether responding to one or all of the theological, political, and social factors that affected the Oxford movement, Robert Isaac Wilberforce, son of English evangelicalism's patriarch, wrote from Paris to John Henry Newman, the former evangelical, saying: "After my own family, I must announce what has befallen me—that by God's mercy I have been received into the Catholic Church. May my few remaining years be more worthy of so high a privilege. I owe this, of course, under God to you, more than to any man."[117] Wilberforce's hopes of service were cut short by his death in 1857; Newman went on to become a cardinal of the Roman Catholic Church. Keble and Pusey continued to agitate for support of Anglo-Catholic principles. Both of them vigorously opposed the authors of *Essays and Reviews* in 1860. Both were distantly sympathetic to the Ritualists and regarded governmental involvement in the controversy concerning them as another example of Erastian interference. And quite by happenstance, a reunion of Keble, Pusey, and Newman took place at Keble's cottage in 1865. However, the following year John Keble died. Pusey followed him in 1882.

---

[115]Pusey to Wilberforce, 11 September 1834, quoted by Newsome, *Parting of Friends*, 392; Keble to Wilberforce, 8-9 July 1851; Keble to Wilberforce, 25 September 1854, Keble Papers.

[116]Keble to Wilberforce, 3 September 1854, Keble Papers.

[117]Wilberforce to Newman, Eve of All Saints, 1854, Newman Papers.

PART FOUR

AMERICA

CHAPTER SIX

A NEW DIVINITY
AND A NEW WORLD

One autumn morning in 1821 a young lawyer walked out of his office and turning away from the courthouse, proceeded toward the town church. As he was walking, he passed the client whose case he was to argue that day. When the man asked him why he was not going to the courthouse, the lawyer replied, "I have a retainer from the Lord Jesus Christ to plead his cause and I cannot plead yours." The lawyer was Charles Grandison Finney, and within a few years he would be widely acknowledged as the foremost revivalist in America.[1]

Foreign visitors to America during the early 1800s sometimes saw revival meetings with their rambunctious behavior, frenzied appeals, and mass audiences as apt symbols of America's democratic temper. Open to all comers, permeated with its participants' earnest desire to liberate individuals from the thralldom of sin, the revival meeting's popular egalitarianism and coarse informality seemed to illustrate the best and worst of the new republic.

Yet, if the revivals in Kentucky or New York struck these observers as somehow especially American, so too did the legal separation of church and state, or more broadly, the preeminence within American society of the principle of voluntaryism. The separation

---

[1]*Memoirs of Charles Grandison Finney* (New York, 1876) 24.

of the civil authority from the religious institutions was not the only example of this principle. The development of nonsectarian public education, the many moral-reform and benevolent associations, and the various denominational unions, such as the union between the Presbyterians and Congregationalists—all attested to the extensive operation of voluntaryism. The twin themes of voluntaryism and revivalism defined and pervaded American Protestantism during the first two-thirds of the nineteenth century.

NO LAW RESPECTING AN ESTABLISHMENT OF RELIGION

In his study, *Religion in America*, the American churchman Robert Baird celebrated the success of voluntaryism, or the "great alternative," as he called it. "Upon what then, must Religion rely?" Baird asked as he described its fortune in the New World. "Only, under God, upon the efforts of its friends, acting from their own free will, influenced by that variety of considerations which is ordinarily comprehended under the title of a desire to do good. This, in America, is the grand and only alternative." Yet Baird, first writing in 1844, knew that religious liberty had not always triumphed in America and that the road leading from religious uniformity, through toleration, and on to religious equality under the law, had been a hard one.[2]

During the 1770s, as Americans struggled for their political independence, many of them hoped that freedom from established religion might be involved as well. For some time in the colonies, religious toleration had been begrudgingly granted or nervously maneuvered for; perhaps victory over the sceptre might bring victory over the mitre of religious establishments too. Triumph over the British, however, did not entail complete disestablishment—not even in 1791 when the First Amendment to the Constitution, with its prohibition of an establishment of religion, was passed. For the provisions of the federal Constitution applied only to the federal government unless otherwise specified. In the matter of religion, the architects of the Constitution had left much latitude to the individual states. Most of the new states abolished many of the old re-

---

[2]Robert Baird, *Religion in America* (1856; reprint, New York, 1970) 122.

strictions, though Massachusetts maintained its Congregational establishment until 1833. Virginia and Rhode Island were first to allow, without legal qualifications, full rights of conscience. Recognition of this situation in America nicely symbolizes the two major intellectual forces favoring disestablishment—enlightened rationalism and evangelical pietism.[3]

The contributions of Thomas Jefferson and James Madison to the debates in Virginia on religious freedom articulated the position of the enlightened rationalists. Central to this position was the assumption that each individual should be left to follow the dictates of his or her own conscience. As Jefferson put it in 1776, "Compulsion in religion is distinguished peculiarly from compulsion in every other thing. . . . I may recover health by medicines I am compelled to take against my own judgment, but I cannot be saved by a worship I disbelieve and abhor." Truth, aided by unimpaired reason will prevail, the rationalists argued, and it will not use force to do so. James Madison echoed Jefferson's thoughts on how inappropriate coercion was in religious matters, and concluded that religion "must be left to the conviction and conscience of every man; and it is the right of every man to exercise it as these may dictate." The culmination of the Virginian attack on religious establishments came with Jefferson's "Bill for Establishing Religious Freedom," first introduced in 1779 and finally adopted in 1786. Attacking those who wished to use public money for religious leaders and teachers, Jefferson demonstrated his own identification of religion with ethical conduct. Should anyone be forced to pay such taxes, Jefferson stated, that person would be denied "the comfortable liberty of giving his contribution to the particular pastor whose morals he would make his pattern, and whose powers he feels most persuasive to

---

[3]On the colonial and prerevolutionary situation, see Sidney Mead, "From Coercion to Persuasion: Another Look at the Rise of Religious Liberty and the Emergence of Denominationalism" in *The Lively Experiment* (New York, 1963) 16-37; James H. Smylie, "Protestant Clergy, the First Amendment, and Beginnings of a Constitutional Debate, 1781-1791" in *The Religion of the Republic*, ed. Elwyn A. Smith (Philadelphia, 1971) 116-53; Sanford H. Cobb, *The Rise of Religious Liberty in America* (New York, 1902). For a summary of the postrevolutionary situation, see Anson Phelps Stokes, *Church and State in the United States*, 3 vols. (New York, 1950) 1:358-446.

righteousness."[4] In this way Jefferson demanded that church and state be completely separated in order that each institution might prosper on its own and avoid any collusion between king and bishop which Jefferson believed tainted so much of the European experience.

The names of Jefferson and Madison in Virginia as exponents of religious freedom and separation of church and state were matched by those of Roger Williams and Isaac Backus in New England. Williams was famous in the seventeenth century and his "lively experiment" with Rhode Island rather infamous for his espousal of separation of religious and governmental institutions. By the eighteenth century, Williams's denominational leadership of New England Baptists and his support of disestablishment had passed to Isaac Backus. Backus initially acknowledged the right of the state (as in Massachusetts) to command tax monies for religious purposes from its subjects, if allowances were made for conscientious objection to such requirements. But by 1773, Backus had rejected the "sweet harmony" of cooperation for the option of resistance. "As God is the only worthy object of all religious worship, and nothing can be true religion but a voluntary obedience unto his revealed will," Backus wrote in 1799, "every person has an inalienable right to act in all religious affairs according to the full persuasion of his own mind, where others are not injured thereby."[5]

That the pietistic Backus could match so evenly the Lockean rationalist Jefferson underscores the complex symmetry between evangelical and enlightened views on the issue of church and state separation. It also provided the American counterpart to the func-

---

[4]Thomas Jefferson, "Notes on Religion," in *The Writings of Thomas Jefferson*, ed. Paul L. Ford, 10 vols. (New York, 1892-1899) 2:102; James Madison, "Memorial and Remonstrance against Religious Assessments," in *The Writings of James Madison*, ed. Galliard Hunt, 9 vols. (New York, 1900-1910) 2:184; Thomas Jefferson, "Bill for Establishing Religious Freedom," *Writings*, 2:238; Sidney Mead, "Thomas Jefferson's 'Fair Experiment'—Religious Freedom," in *The Lively Experiment*, 55-71; H. J. Eckenrode, *Separation of Church and State in Virginia* (Richmond, 1910).

[5]Backus is quoted by William McLoughlin, *New England Dissent, 1630-1833*, 2 vols. (Cambridge, 1971) 1:600-601. For a discussion of Backus, see McLoughlin, *New England Dissent*, 1:614, and William McLoughlin, *Isaac Backus and the American Pietistic Tradition* (Boston, 1970).

tional union of evangelicals and liberals seen in Germany and England. Although the pluralistic relationship of federalist governmental and multivalent religious institutions might approximate more closely James Madison's image of "a line of separation," both Roger Williams, an evangelical, and Thomas Jefferson, a rationalist, pictured the church-state divide as a "wall of separation." Furthermore, the existence of a fundamental moral order in the universe, depicted either as divine higher law or rationalist inalienable rights, was an idea shared by both evangelicals and enlightenment thinkers. An emphasis on fellowship, in terms of a collective humanity or children of the Lord, was a common thread in pietist and rationalist thought. Finally, a belief in progress, either as the result of the millennium or of the advances of science, as well as a tendency (especially in religious affairs) to emphasize morality, experience, and action over creeds, dispositions, and beliefs, further characterized evangelicals and rationalists in the late-eighteenth and early-nineteenth centuries.[6]

Intellectual forces were not the only influences contributing to the downfall of religious establishments in America. There were social and cultural forces as well. First, there was the constantly available land to which the dissenting could move. Such vast land resources produced a multiplicity of religions. By the 1780s, with the many contending power groups of post-Revolution American society, it became clear that no one church or sect would be able to dominate the national scene. The only way for the various religious groups to obtain religious liberty for themselves, those groups saw, was to allow all faiths to have it equally. Other centrifugal forces, such as the separatist impulses of the First Great Awakening, helped weaken the possibilities of religious establishment in America. Starting new sects, splintering old churches, and gathering new members, the First Great Awakening, like its successor in 1790-1835, called believers to a revitalized faith. In doing so, it questioned old sources of religious authority in the name of its "new light" vision

[6]Mark DeWolfe Howe, *The Garden and the Wilderness* (Chicago, 1965); McLoughlin, *New England Dissent*, 1:330-32; Perry Miller, "From the Covenant to the Revival," in *Shaping of American Religion*, ed. Smith and Jamison, 1:322-68.

and in the name of its emphasis upon experience over creeds. The First Great Awakening added a widespread cultural dimension to the other forces for disestablishment.[7]

The dynamics of separatism and space contributed to the attainment of religious liberty. But to the defenders of ecclesiastical establishment at the dawn of the nineteenth century, the issue of separation of church and state did not pertain to rights of conscience, but rather, to preservation of society. As their clerical predecessors had done for so many years, these nineteenth-century theocrats argued that religion was essential to the security and health of the state. To many of their fellow Americans this premise was unquestionable. However, could this means of state health be more easily reached with coercive or voluntary means? Of course, religious liberty in the early national period did not mean license for atheists, nor did it mean civil rights for non-Christians, which the German Frankfurt Parliament had sought in 1848. The real object of the constitutional prohibition on religious establishment, Justice Joseph Story said, "was, not to countenance, much less to advance Mahometanism, or Judaism, or infidelity, by prostrating Christianity; but to exclude all rivalry among Christian sects." What some have seen as a de facto religious establishment in the United States, a cultural recognition and acceptance of particular religious values, assumptions, and attitudes, has its roots in the early nineteenth century and the recognition then of the social function religion plays.[8]

By 1800 and Jefferson's election, most of the states had moved toward the separation of church and state in their own constitutions. Nevertheless, because of its deferral of disestablishment, its close connections to the New England phase of the Second Great Awakening, and the prominence of its clerical leaders in the rise of the voluntary religious associations, the disestablishment controversy in Connecticut was important. The controversy in Connecti-

---

[7]See the discussion in McLoughlin, *New England Dissent*, 334-39; Edwin Gaustad, *The Great Awakening in New England*; Richard Bushman, *From Puritan to Yankee* (Cambridge, 1967); Sidney Mead, "From Coercion to Persuasion," in *The Lively Experiment*, 16-37.

[8]Joseph Story, *Commentaries on the Constitution of the United States*, 3 vols. (Boston, 1833) 3:1871; Howe, *Garden and the Wilderness*, 10-31.

cut contained advocates for all of the moderate and most of the extreme positions. John Leland, the Baptist minister, was unusual in arguing that non-Christians did indeed have rights of conscience that ought to be respected. At the other end of the ideological spectrum, there was Timothy Dwight, the staunch upholder of the Connecticut Standing Order. Dwight's fears of the French Revolution, the "Jacobin phrenzy," precipitated his defense of a traditional society in America. "Shall our sons become the disciples of Voltaire and the dragoons of Marat; our daughters the concubines of the Illuminati?" Dwight asked. No! he said, and he refused to countenance any loosening of the ties between church and state for fear it would relax the ligatures holding American society together and produce the same horrendous results as had occurred in France. Politics, however, and not theology, determined the Connecticut disestablishment controversy. In 1816, after two full decades of growing disaffection with Federalist rule, a new political party began. This party, called the Toleration party, drew on disgruntled Episcopalians and other renegade Federalists, and on Jeffersonian Republicans. By 1817 they had won the governorship; one year later they had overthrown the Congregational establishment.[9]

Amidst the attacks and counterattacks concerning disestablishment, which filled the newspapers and rang out from pulpit and town meeting, the odyssey of Lyman Beecher from staunch defender of the Standing Order to staunch defender of voluntaryism is especially illuminating. Beecher, delivering a sermon in 1814, catechized his listeners on the reasons for a religious establishment in Connecticut. Invoking the original settlers' belief in the importance of a godly life and the spiritual error and civil criminality of irreligion, he praised the founders' requirement of public support for the Gospel. Surveying the contemporary situation, Beecher saw many attempts to pull down the Standing Order and to subvert "that religious order which our fathers established." Prominent

[9]See Lyman Butterfield, "Elder John Leland, Jeffersonian Itinerant," *Proceedings of the American Antiquarian Society* 62 (1952): 155-60; Timothy Dwight, *The Duty of Americans at the Present Crisis* (New Haven, 1798) 21; M. Louise Greene, *The Development of Religious Liberty in Connecticut* (Boston, 1905); McLoughlin, *New England Dissent*, 2:915-1062.

among these disruptive elements, he said, were those alleged defenders of the rights of conscience who called out for disestablishment. In fact, these persons were merely fond of novelty in religion or displeased with their local minister. In this situation they "soon learned to plead a tender conscience, in order to save their money, and joined themselves to the denomination which could help them on to heaven at the least expense." The effect of their malignant influence, Beecher believed, would be to strain and perhaps destroy the ability of the religious establishment to provide cohesive moral support for the society. Spiritual desolation would result, and as Beecher sonorously concluded, "The tax of desolation is four times as expensive as the tax which is requisite to support the institutions of religion."[10]

When the Standing Order in Connecticut was overthrown in 1818, Beecher, as he recounted in his autobiography, despaired. But his gloom and apprehension slowly gave way to a reappraisal, and Beecher finally concluded that it was

> the best thing that ever happened to the State of Connecticut. It cut the churches loose from dependence on state support. It threw them wholly on their own resources and on God. They say ministers have lost their influence; the fact is, they have gained. By voluntary efforts, societies, missions, revivals, they exert a deeper influence than ever they could by queues, and shoebuckles, and cocked hats, and gold-headed canes.[11]

With all the zeal of a new convert, Beecher proclaimed the virtues of voluntaryism. In doing so, he sounded quite similar to his dissenting evangelical brethren in England and Germany. Giving a series of lectures in 1829, Beecher charged that the "unhallowed alliance" of church and state had filled the churches with members "by subscriptions to creed and conformity to ceremonies, without the evangelical qualifications of repentance towards God, and faith in our Lord Jesus Christ." This reliance on state coercion had tolerated lax morality and discipline and had crippled the true presen-

---

[10]Beecher, "The Building of Waste Places," *The Works of Lyman Beecher*, 3 vols. (Boston, 1852) 2:115-16, 120, 149.

[11]Beecher, *The Autobiography of Lyman Beecher*, ed. Barbara M. Cross, 2 vols. (Cambridge, 1961) 1:252-53.

tation of the pure Gospel message. "It has been contended that Christianity cannot exist in this world without the aid of religious establishments," Beecher observed. "But, with more truth it might be said, that, from the beginning to this day, it has existed in spite of them."[12]

Another locus of religious establishmentarianism was the field of education, and this too provided advocates of church and state separation with a challenge. Three general patterns of lower-school education existed in colonial America. In the South, education took place largely within the family circle—only the children of the wealthy were able to afford to go to academy or college. Education beyond the confines of the family usually amounted to apprenticeship. In this context the transmission of ideas, news, and viewpoints—that is, acculturation in the broadest sense—provided by parish clerics and itinerant circuit riders was especially significant. Educational opportunities for blacks, needless to say, were even more limited. In the Middle Colonies, education under parochial auspices was prevalent. Presbyterian and Episcopalian academies were numerous and assumed much of the burden of popular education. In contrast to these two patterns of education, education in New England depended on the responsibility of the local township to provide adequate basic education. The Massachusetts School Law of 1647 directed each township with a population over fifty to establish a local school, which all local children were to attend and which all members of the town were to support with taxes. The purpose of these schools, the law stated, was to thwart "the old deluder, Satan," and to insure that all children could read their Bibles and understand their religious lessons.[13]

The reasons for the destruction of these patterns of church-controlled or church-influenced education paralleled the reasons for disestablishment in general. The competition between different re-

---

[12]Beecher, "Lectures on Political Atheism," *Works*, 1:75, 320.

[13]See the studies by Lawrence Cremin, *American Education: the Colonial Experience, 1607-1783* (New York, 1970); *The American Common School* (New York, 1951); Michael Katz, *The Irony of Early School Reform: Educational Innovation in Mid-Nineteenth Century Massachusetts* (Cambridge, 1968); Donald Tewksbury, *The Founding of American Colleges and Universities before the Civil War* (New York, 1922).

ligious groups—which forced liberty for all if any were to have it—
also eroded the foundations of religious education. So too did the
perception that education could be used in the cause of nationalism
and that a message of religious persuasion would more aptly fit the
new republic than would a message of religious coercion. To be
sure, this transformation from religious education to public secular
education was a slow one. It also became the butt of arguments concerning the importance of religion as a preserver of social morality
and national union. Those who supported religious establishment
wanted religion in the public schools.

Three examples give insight into the secularization of public education. The first, and perhaps best known, is that of Massachusetts
and Horace Mann. The Massachusetts constitution of 1780, in addition to providing for an establishment of religious worship, had
provided "for the support and maintenance of public protestant
teachers of piety, religion, and morality."[14] Religious instruction thus
took place in the schools. By 1827, however, with five times as many
students in public as in private schools, the religious (though still
largely Protestant) diversity of the children attending could not be
ignored. Consequently, that year a law was passed conferring on local school committees the right to select their own textbooks so long
as no books were purchased favoring one religious sect over another. The demand for nonsectarian instruction did not exclude the
inculcation of so-called religious values. There were various disputes in the decades following the 1827 enactment, as groups such
as the American Sunday School Union attempted to have their
books approved for use in the schools. Horace Mann led the fight
against the Union's efforts and was stridently criticized for it. In
1848, in his final report on behalf of the Massachusetts Board of Education, Mann again asked for nondenominational religious instruction in the public schools. Public education in Massachusetts,
Mann wrote, "is a system which recognizes religious obligations in
their fullest extent . . . it welcomes the Bible, and therefore welcomes
all the doctrines which the Bible really contains."[15]

---

[14]*A Constitution or Form of Government for the Commonwealth of Massachusetts* (Boston, 1780) 3.

[15]Cremin, *American Education*; Horace Mann, "Report for 1848," in *Life and
Works of Horace Mann*, ed. Mary Mann, 5 vols. (Boston, 1868) 3:753-54.

What the Bible truly contained was open to dispute. Some of Mann's critics attacked his views on the basis of his personal Unitarianism. Unitarians were a growing and increasingly powerful body in the Massachusetts ecclesiastical and political scene in the 1820s and 1830s. Mann's 1848 report had stated that "our system earnestly inculcates all Christian morals; it founds its morals on the basis of religion, it welcomes the religion of the Bible, and in receiving the Bible, it allows it to do what it is allowed to do in no other system, to speak for itself." The invocation of "Bible religion" and the emphasis on "Christian morals" sounds reminiscent of evangelical religion. In view of their similar ethical emphases, as well as their common status outside the Congregational establishment, it is not surprising that Unitarians worked alongside rationalists and pietists in fighting for disestablishment in Massachusetts. That Unitarians and Trinitarians were allied was often only begrudgingly admitted, but stranger partners have been found in the annals of American religious history.

The Dedham Case of 1821 added to the growing pressures for disestablishment in Massachusetts. In this decision the court ruled that a Unitarian minister elected by the congregation might serve even if the members of the church had not voted with the majority. Second, the court ruled that church property belonged to the congregation, not to the church members proper. To many Congregationalists the Unitarian onslaught seemed invincible. Education was being torn from its moorings and set adrift without a rudder, and the church and the congregation were being ripped asunder by infidels who did not even believe in the Trinity. The portents of separation of church and state thus had been visible for some time when the Massachusetts state legislature finally formalized the division in 1833.[16]

In 1795 the state of New York first passed an act encouraging the establishment of schools. Societies designed to promote free education appeared. In 1805 a state school fund was created. DeWitt Clinton, erstwhile governor of New York and advocate of tax-supported schools, was instrumental in the development of free public

---

[16]Mann, "Report for 1848," 729-30; McLoughlin, *New England Dissent*, 2:1189-206; Donald Howe, *The Unitarian Conscience* (Cambridge, 1970).

education. Clinton was not only an advocate of education in general, he was a disciple of Joseph Lancaster. Lancaster, the British educator, had arrived in America in 1818 prepared to advertise his system of monitorial and moral (but non-Anglican) instruction. Clinton recommended Lancaster's system. "When I perceive one great assembly of a thousand children, under the eye of a single teacher, marching, with unexampled rapidity and with perfect discipline, to the goal of knowledge," Clinton told an Education Society audience, "I confess that I recognize in Lancaster the benefactor of the human race." What Clinton described might seem rather regimented to some, but above all else it represented another attempt to separate education from denominational religious instruction.[17]

The third example of educational secularization occurred in Virginia. Thomas Jefferson's "Bill for the more general diffusion of Knowledge" was a far-reaching proposal for education built on Jefferson's rationalist beliefs. His bill would mandate education for all free children at public expense for three years. The superior students from these local schools would be sent to grammar school, and the best of that lot nominated to attend William and Mary College with full scholarships. Jefferson's vision was a grand one, but his bill never passed the Virginia legislature. Instead, various less costly proposals were enacted. Jefferson's dream of a collegium of scholars, separated from the church, came closer to realization in the creation of the University of Virginia.[18]

The development of secular public education was slow in the new nation. Generally, three principles characterized American public education and were eventually made into law. First, the education provided to children under public auspices must be nonsectarian. The equation of religion, morality, and good citizenship often remained unquestioned; nevertheless, by 1835 a nonsectarian approach to instruction in public schools was prevailing. Second, the legislature had the right to tax all citizens in order to pay for this

---

[17]Clinton is quoted by William Campbell, *The Life and Writings of DeWitt Clinton* (New York, 1849) 318-19; Stokes, *Church and State*, 2:64-65.

[18]See the discussion by Robert Healey, *Jefferson on Religion in Public Education* (New Haven, 1962).

instruction, whether or not the citizens had children in a school. This law became common practice. Third, the legislature had the right to require that all parents provide their children with a basic education, either public or private. While this third principle would not be uniformly acted upon during the early nineteenth century, its roots can be seen there.[19]

The gradual secularization of education had its counterpart in higher education. Indeed, the process of secularization can be no better demonstrated than in the move from private, religiously influenced colleges in the colonial era to the public university. With their credos of amorphously nonsectarian but moral education, public universities first rose to numerical equivalence with private schools and then predominated over them, attesting to the further disestablishment of religion. In the colonial era there were nine institutions of higher learning in America (Harvard, William and Mary, Yale, Princeton, Pennsylvania, Columbia, Brown, Rutgers, and Dartmouth). All these institutions were initially private academies or colleges. America took an early step towards secularization as the states developed their own administrative systems of education. Pennsylvania, Massachusetts, Connecticut and North Carolina had followed New York's 1795 example and passed laws encouraging the establishment of public schools. The next step was the actual establishment of state universities, a move haltingly begun and fitfully accomplished. The University of North Carolina, for example, was begun in 1789; the University of Virginia (1819) and the University of Michigan (1837) followed.[20]

A turning point in American higher education occurred in 1819 with the Supreme Court's Dartmouth College decision. The implications of this decision were far-reaching, providing for the security of charters on one hand, while indirectly spurring educational development on the other. The result of the Court's findings was that states could not transform private institutions into public ones. Private contracts were inviolable, the Court argued, and could not be

[19]See the discussion by R. Freeman Butts and Lawrence Cremin, *A History of Education in American Culture* (New York, 1953).

[20]Tewksbury, *Founding of American Colleges and Universities*, 32-41.

abrogated by state legislatures. Hence, private denominational schools were encouraged to expand, safe in the knowledge that their institutions could not be tampered with. Meanwhile, state legislatures had no alternative but to develop their own institutions, as appropriation of private ones was out of the question. Supporters of both public and private education found an inviting area for their efforts in the new western territories. The Northwest Ordinance of 1787 set aside land for public schools, thereby giving an incentive for developing primary and secondary public education. The West also provided a fertile area for private education; new denominational colleges sprang up, many of which remain to the present day.[21]

THE SECOND GREAT AWAKENING

The West also figured importantly in that characteristic of American religious life: revivalism. The Second Great Awakening, lasting from 1795 to 1835, perhaps was even more significant for America than its German and English evangelical counterparts were for England and Germany. Arriving in the wake of political independence this forty-year period witnessed not only territorial expansion, but more significantly the consolidation of a new cultural consensus. This consensus was multifaceted. In theological terms, for example, it represented the collapse of an older Calvinist orthodoxy and the rise of a new emphasis upon human ability and accountability in the process of salvation. In social terms, the Awakening spawned scores of voluntary associations, many of which were modeled upon English evangelical examples or directly associated with them. These organizations helped to alleviate the social tensions confronting the citizens of the fledgling nation by locating them within a social network of common purposes and familiar faces. Broadly, the combination of newly achieved political independence, expansive geographical boundaries, and growing moral self-assurance provided the conceptual symbols and the space fueling those ideals of millennial optimism, manifest destiny, and the effi-

---

[21]Ibid., 64-66.

cacy of individual effort so characteristic of nineteenth-century America.[22]

If the Awakening held cultural significance and social importance, it was nevertheless first and foremost a religious experience. Paralleling the English evangelical movement and the German *Erweckungsbewegung*, the Awakening represented a revitalization of religious life and an attempt to bring sinners to a new belief in Jesus. Reverend William Sprague called it a renewal of "the conformity of heart and life to the will of God," sentiments with which both Gottfried Thomasius and William Wilberforce could have heartily agreed.[23] Furthermore, much like the European experience, the Second Great Awakening contained regional variations. The Awakening was made up of three approximate phases: 1)the camp meetings of the trans-Appalachian sections of Kentucky and Tennessee, 1795-1805; 2)the conservative formulations in New England, 1800-1825; 3)the new-measures revivalism of Charles Grandison Finney, 1823-1835.

The picture of revivals as wild gatherings in which sinners collapsed in convulsive convictions of personal sin, only to rise again in tearful assurance of new-found grace is the legacy of the camp meetings of Kentucky. Under the leadership of men such as Presbyterians James McGready and Barton W. Stone, and Methodists William McKendree and Peter Cartwright, the "Great Revival," as it was called, took place. Methodist circuit riders had preached throughout the Cumberland region of Kentucky during the early 1790s. Periodically, they gathered for quarterly meetings and sacramental occasions—one such meeting took place at the Gaspar River in July 1797—and it was from these quarterly meetings that camp meetings arose. Gaspar River was the site of several such as-

---

[22]See the important studies of the Second Great Awakening by T. Scott Miyakawa, *Protestants and Pioneers: Individualism and Conformity on the American Frontier* (Chicago, 1964) 213-15; Perry Miller, *The Life of the Mind in America from the Revolution to the Civil War* (New York, 1965) 6, 34; Donald G. Mathews, "The Second Great Awakening as an organizing process, 1780-1830: an hypothesis," *American Quarterly* 21 (1969): 23-43; William G. McLoughlin, *Revivals, Awakenings, and Reform* (Chicago, 1978) 98-106.

[23]William Sprague, *Lectures on Revivals of Religion* (Albany, 1832) 6.

semblages, but it was the Cane Ridge meeting in 1801 that gave the image of the camp meeting experience its stereotype. The Cane Ridge meeting lasted for several days; it is estimated that anywhere from 8,000-25,000 persons attended. Several smaller gatherings had preceded the Cane Ridge meeting, and accounts of persons being "struck down by the Word" contributed to the anticipation of those at Cane Ridge.[24]

To many observers, camp meetings such as Cane Ridge, with their vast crowds, their parade of preachers simultaneously exhorting the audience, and their displays of ecstatic and tumultuous conversion experiences, seemed just short of a religious riot. The style of camp meeting ministers, whether Baptist, Methodist, or Presbyterian, was direct—unadorned with theological subtlety. On the frontier, where death and violence were a familiar part of life, the preachers confronted their listeners with a choice of eternal salvation or eternal damnation. As their pictures of Heaven were beatific, so were their pictures of Hell vividly realistic. In a favorite sermon, James McGready described a sinner's death and his descent encircled by "the black flaming vultures" into the "liquid, boiling waves of hell," from where he fell lower "to the deepest cavern in the flaming abyss." As he plummets downward the sinner gazes above where "through the blazing flames he sees that heaven he has lost," and where his family and friends now sit in grace. "They are far beyond the impassable gulf; they shine brighter than the sun . . . and walk the golden streets of the New Jerusalem," McGready intoned, while the sinner "is lost and damned forever."[25]

Reeking of rhetorical brimstone, the message of the camp meeting revivalist preacher was a simple one emphasizing repentance. The preacher's manner was straightforward and his theology individualistic and nondenominational. "In that awful day, when the universe, assembled, must appear before the quick and the dead," McGready expostulated, "the question, brethren, will not be, were you a Presbyterian—a Seceder—a Covenanter—a Baptist—or a Methodist; but did you experience a new birth? Did you accept of

[24]Catherine Cleveland, *The Great Revival in the West, 1797-1805* (1916; reprint, Gloucester MA, 1959) 41-44, 52-55, 72-82.

[25]Ibid., 45-46.

Christ and his salvation as set forth in the Gospel?" The audience might number in the hundreds or thousands, but the appeal of the revivalist was always to the individual. The results of these exhortations ranged from quiet inward scrutiny to the furious "jerks" and paroxysms that Peter Cartwright described so graphically. In all cases, the goal was the spiritual rebirth of conversion, and as news of the numbers claiming such experiences spread throughout the countryside, the role of the minister took a more evangelical shape.[26]

Most of those who attended camp meetings, rather than being atheists who came to mock and stayed to pray, were familiar with Christianity. They were probably among those scores of nominal Christians so often derided by revivalists in America and Europe. Consequently, the Awakening in America represented a movement of renewal within American Christianity, a movement revitalizing older adherents and enlisting them with first-time converts in settling the West, building churches, and carrying out the projects of the voluntary benevolent associations. In this way the Awakening contributed, especially in the more sparsely settled western regions of the nation, to the establishment of organizational ties within the region and to the Eastern cities. The establishment of these ties promoted the economic and social organization of the trans-Appalachian West, and did so within a framework of religious experience and imagery familiar to Westerner and Easterner alike. Thus, the camp meeting provided in an often lonely frontier existence an occasion for social intercourse; at the same time it helped to build more lasting social organizations. As one English observer said, "Where the camp-meeting is really wanted and really useful, it interests a careless people in their own moral and religious wants; and is the natural and general forerunner, as the population thickens, of the school-house, the church, and all the appliances of civil life."[27]

---

[26]McGready is quoted by John Boles, *The Great Revival, 1797-1805* (Lexington, 1972) 40. Peter Cartwright, *Autobiography of Peter Cartwright* (Cincinnati, 1890) 48-51. Sidney Mead, "The Rise of the Evangelical Conception of the Ministry in America, 1607-1850," in *The Ministry in Historical Perspective*, ed. H. R. Niebuhr and Daniel D. Williams (New York, 1956) 207-49.

[27]Andrew Reed and James Matheson, *A Narrative of the Visit to the American Churches by the Deputation from the Congregational Union of England and Wales* (New York, 1835) 643.

The conversions both of nominal Christians and novitiates were part of a formalized and surprisingly uniform ritual process. Although foreign and domestic observers alike often saw only tumult in the meetings, both the conversion experience itself and the daily activities of the camp meeting tended to follow clear patterns. From his first sermon describing the disparity between ceaseless life and everlasting death, the revivalist challenged individuals to review their worldly and sinful life. Convinced of their need for righteousness and touched by divine grace, sinners wrestled with their anxieties and determined to leave the old path, to separate themselves from vice and degradation, and to travel the new avenue of joy and Christian virtue. The symmetry of the tripartite pattern—preconversion experience, conviction of sin and assurance of grace, and postconversion life—was matched by the plan of the camp meeting itself. Situated ideally beneath a cathedral-like canopy of trees, the campground was usually divided into sections for men and women with a speaker's platform at the head and the celebrated mourner's bench or anxious seat directly below the platform. The camp meeting normally lasted for four days with regularly scheduled morning, afternoon, and evening religious services interspersed with individual or family prayers. Just as the preacher's message was intended to confront individuals with the need for repentance, so the very structure and plan of the camp meeting itself was designed to enhance and reinforce that message.[28]

After traveling through Kentucky, Reverend George Baxter reported to Archibald Alexander of Princeton Seminary that "the character of Kentucky travelers was entirely changed, and that they were as remarkable for sobriety as they had formerly been for dissoluteness and immorality." Baxter believed that the revival had caused the transformation, for "it has confounded infidelity and brought numbers beyond calculation under serious impression."[29]

---

[28]See Dickson D. Bruce, Jr., *And They All Sang Hallelujah: Plain-Folk Camp Meeting Religion, 1800-1845* (Knoxville, 1974) 62-87; Charles A. Johnson, *The Frontier Camp Meeting* (Dallas, 1955) 122-44, 208-28.

[29]Baxter is quoted in Leonard Bacon, *A History of American Christianity* (New York, 1901) 237.

Despite Baxter's belief, not all observers of camp meetings were convinced that their followers were appropriately serious about their faith. To the religious leaders of New England, men such as Timothy Dwight, Lyman Beecher, Nathaniel Taylor, and Asahel Nettleton, these outbursts in Kentucky were demonic extravagances, closer to the fantastic excesses of James Davenport in the 1740s than to the proper achievements of the venerated Jonathan Edwards. New England too could have a revival, and these Connecticut Congregationalists held up the revival at Yale College in 1802 as a fine example of a proper one. With Timothy Dwight, president of the college, exerting steady leadership, no emotional outbursts took place. Instead, students met in small prayer groups to study Scripture and ponder Dwight's sermons. "The salvation of the soul was the great subject of thought, of conversation, of absorbing interests," one participant reported. "The convictions of many were pungent and overwhelming; and the 'peace in believing' which succeeded, was not less strongly marked."[30]

Here was the model of moderation that the New England conservatives embraced—a settled ministry without itinerancy, calm and patient counsel with the penitent sinner, and above all, no special devices by which to focus attention on the would-be convert. In refusing to visit another parish or church uninvited, for example, Asahel Nettleton demonstrated his antipathy for the disrupting of regular church order that had occurred in the West. The contrast between the frenzy of Kentucky revivals and the calm of New England ones was further captured in Nathaniel Taylor's account of the revival in New Haven in 1820.

> These meetings were usually opened with a short address, after which all knelt and united in a short prayer. The ministers present then proceeded to converse with every individual, in a low tone of voice, so as not to interrupt each other, or break the solemn stillness of the scene. The meeting was then closed with suitable exhortations and a prayer. It is impossible to convey to those who have not witnessed such an assembly, an adequate idea of its impressive solemnity. There was evidently much emotion, although no noise—

[30]Chauncey Goodrich, "Narrative of Revivals of Religion in Yale College," *American Quarterly Register* 10 (1838): 295.

there were many tears, although no outbreaking of the agony of their mind, save in the expressive look and the half-stifled sigh.[31]

Taylor was not alone in subscribing to the style of the New Haven revival. Lyman Beecher supported New England composure in his typically outspoken fashion when he derided those fanatical outbursts of experimental religion "superseding discretion and enlisting the animal susceptibilities. . . . It is owing to such excesses, that lasting associations of odium are attached to revivals, even where no such exhibitions are witnessed, and where the effects are pure and undefiled religion."[32]

If Taylor and Beecher were dissatisfied with the style and impropriety of the Western revivals, if they did not wish to be smeared with the stain of fanaticism, it was only because they were fundamentally committed to the Awakening. Beecher and Taylor together were responsible for the development of the New Divinity theology, a doctrinal modification that lay at the very center of the Awakening's success. This modification developed principally out of Taylor's reworking of the doctrine of free will, and his famous adage of the "certainty of sin with power to the contrary." Building on the heritage of Scottish Common Sense philosophy, Taylor repudiated the older interpretations of Calvinist doctrine with their allegations of imputed sinfulness. Instead, as Taylor phrased it in his address, *Concio ad Clerum*, delivered in 1828, sin "is man's own act, consisting in a free choice of some object rather than God, as his chief good; or a free preference of the world and of worldly good, to the will and glory of God." It was certain that man would sin, but it was not necessary. With this alteration, a more Arminianized Calvinism became characteristic of New England theology and areas farther west as well.[33]

---

[31]Quoted in Charles Keller, *The Second Great Awakening in Connecticut* (New Haven, 1942) 47.

[32]Lyman Beecher, "Lectures on Political Atheism and Kindred Subjects," *Works*, 1:78-79.

[33]Nathaniel Taylor, *Concio ad Clerum* (New Haven, 1828) 8. On Taylor see Sidney Mead, *Nathaniel William Taylor* (Chicago, 1942); Sidney Ahlstrom, "Theology in America," in *The Shaping of American Religion*, ed. James W. Smith and A. Leland Jamison, 4 vols. (Princeton, 1969) 1:257-58.

For his part, Lyman Beecher recognized his close agreement with Nathaniel Taylor and always regarded him as a dear friend. A vigorous religious activist, Beecher was a champion of revivals. Imbued with that postmillennialist hope typical of many antebellum revivalists, Beecher saw his life "harnessed to the Chariot of Christ, whose wheels of fire have rolled onward, high and dreadful to his foes, and glorious to his friends." By stressing human accountability, which by its nature implied that actions were important, Beecher and Taylor did much more for the Awakening than rebuke Western emotionalism. The New Divinity theology provided a theological legitimacy that outlasted the significance of particular revival experiences and instead undergirded the rest of the Awakening itself.[34]

By 1826, revivalism appeared well under control to the patriarchs of New England. In that year Beecher announced that the churches looked to revivals "for their members and pastors, and for that power upon public opinion, which retards declension, gives energy to law, and voluntary support to religious institutions."[35] Yet before long, news from the West would again unsettle the Easterners, and storm clouds blacken their sunny expectations for moderate evangelicism. The third phase of the Awakening was underway in the "Burned-Over District" of upstate New York, and it threatened to advance on the very citadels of Boston and New Haven.

The tempest that threatened to blow through New England was Charles Grandison Finney. First licensed to preach in 1824, Finney itinerated for several years throughout the upper Mohawk valley of New York.[36] As crowds increased and invitations and opportunities to preach multiplied, Finney's reputation as a revivalist spread. His use of so-called new measures and his self-conscious style of "worked-up" revivals set him on an inevitable collision course with men like Dwight and Beecher. Many of the items generically classified by Finney's supporters and critics as new measures first had ap-

---

[34]Lyman Beecher, *Autobiography*, 1:46; Beecher, "The Government of God Desirable," *Works*, 2:28; "Faith Once Delivered to the Saints," *Works*, 2:243.

[35]Quoted in Keller, *Second Great Awakening in Connecticut*, 222.

[36]William G. McLoughlin, *Modern Revivalism* (New York, 1959) 27-30. Whitney Cross, *The Burned-Over District* (New York, 1950) 153.

peared in camp meetings. A vigorous, exhorting style of preaching, protracted meetings lasting for several days, the prominence of women in the revivals, the use of the anxious bench—all these had been first seen in the Appalachian phase of the Awakening. Finney's audience, however, was generally middle class and urban, especially after 1830. Hence, Finney's revivals differed significantly from the Western experiences. If the preaching style was energetic, now the revivalist called on individual sinners by name to repent; if there were protracted meetings, now they took place in cities and villages, not in the countryside; if women were included, they participated more and their role was more visible; and if the anxious seat was used, its effects on middle-class, urban Americans made it all the more controversial.

Reports of the large numbers converted through Finney's methods convinced the New Divinity men that he was a force to be reckoned with. Accordingly in 1827, with all the drama of a battlefield truce, the two sides met on the neutral ground of New Lebanon, New York, to discuss their differences. As Beecher recalled, he had pointedly told Finney, "I know your plan, and you know I do; you mean to come into Connecticut and carry a streak of fire to Boston. But if you attempt it, as the Lord liveth, I'll meet you at the state line, and call out all the artillerymen, and fight every inch of the way to Boston, and then I'll fight you there." Beecher's blustering words little affected Finney, and both camps retreated. Interestingly, Finney led more revivals over the next three years in Wilmington, Philadelphia, New York City, and Rochester; and the notoriety his accomplishments achieved finally won him an invitation to Boston, an invitation cosigned by a more malleable Lyman Beecher.[37]

In 1832 Finney accepted a pastorate in New York City only to give it up three years later for the presidency of Oberlin College. In 1835 Finney published his *Lectures on the Revivals of Religion*, a book Perry Miller called "the key exposition of the movement, and so a major work in the history of the mind in America."[38] As a theory of

---

[37]Beecher, *Autobiography*, 2:75; McLoughlin, *Modern Revivalism*, 40-63.

[38]Miller, *Life of the Mind*, 9.

the cause and promotion of revivals, as an affirmation of an Armi-nianized doctrine of free will, and as an analysis of the basis for Christian social reform, these *Lectures* provide a summary of Fin-ney's thought and as such an index of the Awakening as a whole. Many of the rudiments of the ideas could be found in the works of other revivalists. In this volume, however, Finney synthesized those ideas, developing them into a coherent explanation and defense of his new-measures revivalism. Where previous revivalists such as Jonathan Edwards had insisted that every revival was a divine dis-pensation, Finney countered that a revival "is not a miracle, or de-pendent on a miracle, in any sense. It is a purely philosophical result of the right use of the constituted means—as much so as any other effect produced by the application of means." Here then was the kernel of Finney's theory of revivalism—a frank avowal of the abil-ity, legitimacy, and necessity of self-consciously produced revivals. Revivals were as amenable to the laws of cause and effect as any other natural phenomena. They were no longer to be "prayed down," no longer simply to be petitioned and then awaited in God's good time. Instead, revivals could be "worked up," and preachers should be doing so.[39]

Upon this basis Finney developed a number of stock evangelical themes. The point of all revival efforts was to "make men believe they are going to be sent to hell if they are not wholly transformed in heart and life." This call to conversion was individualistic and ran like a never-ending litany throughout the whole of the Awakening. Finney further insisted that in "the history of the church we shall find that there never has been an extensive reformation, except by new measures."[40] In saying this Finney hoped by appealing to church history to deflect some of the critics of the new measures. Furthermore, Finney stood squarely on the side of the New School in their ongoing dispute with the Old School Presbyterians.

The New School was a group sympathetic to the Awakening and its revivalistic techniques. The Old School opposed them, regarding

---

[39]Charles Grandison Finney, *Lectures on Revivals of Religion*, ed. William G. McLoughlin (Cambridge, 1960) 13.

[40]Ibid., 147, 269.

the revivals as hyperemotional extravagances. Their battle raged throughout the Awakening and was in fact a recapitulation of the First Great Awakening (1730-1760) and its division between New Lights and Old Lights. With Jonathan Edwards as their theological leader, the New Light coalition, made up largely of Presbyterian and Congregationalist clergy and laity, had sought to revitalize the reigning Calvinism of their own day. Finney and his pietistic brethren were now doing the same. The New Lights of the eighteenth century, moreover, also had had their own radical element—the Separate Baptists—paralleling the nineteenth-century Awakening and its "come-outers." Consequently, Finney's reference to the new measures of previous ecclesiastical experience was an undisguised reminder to the friends of the revival and a clear provocation to its opponents.[41]

If history demonstrated that new measures helped to combat formalism, punctilious habit, and dead tradition, it also demonstrated, Finney suggested, two other important effects: first, that the great truths of salvation were available in the Bible, and the Bible alone, to everyone. Creedal statements, such as the Westminster Confession of Faith, were superfluous. Similarly, closely examining converts upon doctrinal knowledge and disputable points of faith was counterproductive and needless. "The object is, not to find out how much they know," Finney declared regarding the nature of the tests for converts. "It is to find out whether they have a *change of heart*, to learn whether they have experienced the great truths of religion by their power in their souls." Finney never doubted the availability of the Bible to simple common sense, nor did he question the sufficiency of the Scriptures to lead a person to salvation. Indeed, Finney would have agreed completely with Robert Baird, whose very definition of evangelical religion consisted of "churches whose religion is the Bible, the whole Bible, and nothing but the Bible."[42]

---

[41]On the First Great Awakening, see C. C. Goen, *Revivalism and Separatism in New England* (New Haven, 1962); Edwin S. Gaustad, *The Great Awakening in New England* (New York, 1957); Alan Heimert, *Religion and the American Mind* (Cambridge, 1966).

[42]Finney, *Lectures*, 83, 393; Robert Baird, *Religion in America* (1856; reprint, New York, 1970) 258.

Finney's methods contained another prominent characteristic of American evangelicalism—a nondenominational approach to church life. With his pietistic emphasis upon a change of heart and his belief in a set of readily accessible fundamental religious truths, Finney had little use for what he saw as the poison of sectarianism. In discussing measures to promote revivals, Finney stated simply that "all sectarianism should be carefully avoided." Like his evangelical brethren in England and parts of Germany, Finney hoped to leave behind the denominational consciousness he believed had spawned so much division within Christendom. Hence, the pietistic emphasis upon an awakened heart and a changed life in dutiful obedience to the Lord as instructed by Biblical injunction—this was the message Finney proclaimed.

The capstone of Finney's theory of new-measures revivalism was its pragmatic justification. Taking the text "He that winneth souls is wise" (Prov. 11:30), Finney charged that the entire purpose of the Christian ministry was to win souls for God. Of course, in Finney's evangelical terms, there were no real distinctions between ordained and laypersons; when it came to saving souls, all Christians were accountable for discharging this duty. Throughout his career, Finney claimed that the numbers of persons converted in his meetings amply testified to the correctness of the new measures and justified his theory of emotional revivalism. Finney's critics, such as the moderate revivalist William Sprague, were unconvinced and argued that "it is no certain evidence of a genuine revival that *great numbers profess to be converted*. . . . There is scarcely a more uncertain test than this." Yet as revivals spread and church membership quintupled from 1800-1835, Finney's argument carried the day. The evangelical concept of the ministry, which had its beginning in the Kentucky revivals, had now hatched and roosted itself comfortably in the middle of American Protestantism.[43]

Adhering to the modifications of Calvinist orthodoxy initiated by Nathaniel Taylor and Lyman Beecher, Finney insisted that sin-

---

[43]Finney, *Lectures*, 174; William Sprague, *Lectures*, 14; see Charles Cole, *The Social Ideas of the Northern Evangelists* (New York, 1954) 13, for figures on the five-fold increase in church membership that even outstripped the three-fold increase in the national population.

ners could be active in the process of their own regeneration. To
Finney, the old-line Calvinist argument that sinners must wait for
the Holy Spirit to infuse their hearts had as little relevance as the
argument that one must wait for the Spirit to commence a revival.
In the eighteenth century, Jonathan Edwards, for example, had
maintained that humans had the natural ability to act correctly but
were morally unable to do so unless God, through the agency of the
Holy Spirit, transformed an individual's soul with supernatural
grace. Many had considered Edwards's revisions heretical, but by
the 1830s, his theology was accepted as orthodoxy in New England.
As he had argued that revivals could be produced, so Finney replied
by emphasizing the efficacy of a sinner's personal decision to repent. Too often, Finney exclaimed, sinners were not unable to repent, merely unwilling. Finney took Taylor's "power to the
contrary" one step further by aligning it with his own new measures, revealing its powers, and challenging sinner and Christian
alike with responsibility for using it.

Finney's view of free will was not his only departure from Calvinism. If free will was radically emphasized, traditional doctrines
of election became theological fictions; if the agency of the revivalist
was underscored, the sovereignty of God was undercut. Repudiating divine sovereignty, however, was hardly Finney's intention. As a
believer in postmillennialism, that is, that a thousand-year reign of
peace would be followed by the Second Coming of Christ, Finney
was as convinced as Edwards of the Lord's custody over the world.
Indeed, Finney's millennial optimism ran so high that he suggested
"if the church will do her duty the millennium may come in this
country in three years."[44] Finney thus departed radically from traditional Calvinism. When critics assailed the implications of his
theological pronouncements, Finney again fell back on his pragmatic justification of them. Repeatedly, he derided the "cannotism"
of his ministerial brethren, acidly observing that "more than five
thousand millions have gone down to hell, while the church has
been dreaming and waiting for God to save them without the use of

---

[44]See the discussion in Joseph Haroutunian, *Piety Versus Moralism* (New York,
1932); McLoughlin, *Modern Revivalism*, 65-73; Finney, *Lectures*, 302.

means. It has been the devil's most successful means of destroying souls."[45]

In addition to his theory of revivals and his doctrine of free will, Finney highlighted a third important theme when he wrote,

> God found it necessary to take advantage of the excitability there is in mankind, to produce powerful excitement among them, before he can lead them to obey. Men are so sluggish . . . that it is necessary to raise an excitement among them, till the tide rises so high as to sweep away the opposing obstacles. They must be so excited that they will break over the counteracting influences, before they will obey God.[46]

Just as Finney had earlier argued that the Bible could be perfectly understood by the common sense of an unaided individual, so now he contended for religious means directed toward the heart rather than toward the head. Based on the "excitability" of humans, Finney's approach to the emotions, to the feelings, to the sensibilities rather than to the intellect or rational foundation was significant. Just as his appeal to common sense revealed his egalitarian, democratic, and in many ways, Jacksonian temperament, so did his appeal to the heart over the head align him with other more broadly romantic impulses of the day. The influence of romanticism in Finney was muted, closer to the English example of Wilberforce than to the German Thomasius. But early nineteenth-century American evangelicalism with its attack on rationalistic formalism, and its awareness, however subdued, of mystical and mysterious divine operation betrayed a romantic influence. Likewise, what Perry Miller called "a rhetoric of romantic communication"—an evocation of spontaneity and realistic imagery turned to practical conversion—attests to the play of romantic forces. Accordingly, while the concept of a transforming and saving faith appeared throughout German, English, and American evangelicalism, the closest affinities were shared by Wilberforce of Clapham and Finney of New York.[47]

Wilberforce and Finney shared more than the concept of saving faith; they were similar in their social activism, as well. In Finney's

---

[45]Finney, *Lectures*, 107, 14.

[46]Ibid., 9-10.

[47]McLoughlin, *Modern Revivalism*, 67; Miller, *Life of the Mind*, 61.

opinion, when individuals converted to Christianity, they "renounced the ownership of all their possessions, and of themselves
. . . they made a free surrender of all to him, to be ruled and disposed
of at his pleasure . . . for the very idea of being a Christian is to renounce self and become entirely consecrated to God." In this act of
consecration they became enlisted in "the great objects of Christian
benevolence," such as the tract, missionary, temperance, and reform
societies. Predictably, Finney believed that more people needed to
participate in the work of these societies. More significantly, Finney
bluntly declared that slavery was a sin against God and a degradation of humanity, one that all true Christians must oppose. Yet Finney did not support the idea of social equality for blacks, and his
limitation attests to his circumscribed view of the relation between
politics and religion.[48] For Finney's social ethic always remained an
individualistic one. Whether exhorting sinners to repent or urging
the converted to do their part in the Lord's work, his focus was always individual and never collective. Indeed, even when he called
on the repentant to "aim at being holy," to strive for that sanctification that he later developed into the notion of perfectionism, Finney never moved outside of an additive social ethic, one
emphasizing the accumulation of individual converted souls as the
way to a regenerated social order.[49]

By 1850, Finney's *Lectures on Revivals of Religion* had gone
through several editions in America and had sold eighty thousand
copies in Great Britain. Finney himself had made the first of his two
trips to England. Built on a common language and faith, nurtured
in the shared desire to save souls, and strengthened by reciprocal
reports and visitors, transatlantic revivalism was a reality. Yet new-
measures revivalism was never as successful in England as it had
been in America. As one scholar said, "revivalism never held as religiously prominent or socially acceptable a place in Britain as in
North America. . . . Revivalism was at the center of American social

---

[48]Finney, *Lectures*, 301-303, 305, 400; McLoughlin, *Modern Revivalism*, 116-18.

[49]Finney, *Lectures*, 403, 419-20.

and religious life during that period but stood at the periphery of the British."[50]

Many of the problems facing this transatlantic connection were clearly exemplified in the meeting of the Evangelical Alliance in 1845. Gathered at the invitation of several British evangelical bodies, some eight hundred persons assembled in London. Convened in the hope that sufficient unity of doctrine, experience, and purpose existed among them, these evangelical Protestants pledged to pursue their mutual goals in good will and brotherly love. Lyman Beecher and Robert Baird were among those attending from America. Baird, whose book *Religion in America* attempted to explain American religious conditions to Europeans, was a frequent overseas visitor. Indeed, Baird's book with its simple division of all American churches into evangelical and nonevangelical sounded faintly reminiscent of Joseph Milner's earlier separation of real and nominal Christians. Yet, if this was a gathering of the evangelical elect, it was clearly taking place in the world of earthly politics. Within days of the convention's opening, the slavery issue was brought up, a motion was made to exclude slaveholders from the meeting, and the convention collapsed. Returning home soon after, Lyman Beecher recounted how his ship was struck by a hurricane in mid-Atlantic and nearly lost. To many, the stormy slavery issue seemed sure to do the same to America, but in 1846 the outcome of the slavery issue was much less certain.

By the 1840s a cultural pattern built on the separation of church and state and furthered by the Second Great Awakening had emerged. By mid-decade though, increased problems within this blend were becoming evident. The dream of public education, for example, was but one aspect of the larger controversy over the proper relationship of church and state. Yet it was an aspect that was especially susceptible to cultural influences. Just as denominational public education gave way to nonsectarian religious education, so in the 1830s and 1840s was nonsectarian education coming under at-

---

[50]See the discussion by Richard Carwardine, *Trans-atlantic Revivalism: Popular Evangelism in Britain and America, 1790-1865* (Westport, 1978) xiv, pass. On German pietism's early influence in America, see F. Ernst Stoeffler, ed., *Continental Pietism and Early American Christianity* (Grand Rapids, 1976).

tack. The source of this assault was the increasingly large and vocal Catholic population centered in the Eastern cities. With their numbers multiplied by emigration, these Catholics found that nonsectarian education all too often meant Protestant religious instruction. Their ensuing protest spelled the eventual doom of the easy equation of religion and morality that Horace Mann had so clearly espoused. If Catholic parents could not erase what they considered the teaching of overt Protestant doctrine from their neighborhood schools, they could establish private schools of their own. This they did, and by the 1830s parochial schools had become a familiar fixture in the urban East.[51]

In the mid-1840s the immigration of many Roman Catholics from Ireland and Germany to America produced other church-state tensions. The "trustee controversy" and the subsequent Protestant reaction with its development of the American party and the Know-Nothings, epitomize the strains American Catholicism experienced as it faced the challenges of adjusting to a new setting and ministering to an assorted immigrant population. The trustee issue surfaced as early as 1785 and lasted into the 1850s. In response to the assertion that the laity controlled parish appointments, the Catholic hierarchy from Father John Carroll in 1785 through the First Provincial Council in 1829 upheld the authority of the bishops. Furthermore, the Catholic hierarchy, backed by secular courts, retained control over all church properties, beating back attempts by Catholic laymen to acquire the properties themselves.[52] This battle over ecclesiastical property, although initially confined to the Catholic community, took on larger cultural proportions. Soon enough, claims that hierarchies opposed democracy turned the trustee issue into an American *Kulturkampf*, and fueled a residual Protestant and nativist sentiment in Jacksonian America. The burning of the Charlestown convent and the lurid tales of Maria Monk were only

---

[51]See the studies by J. A. Burns, *The Catholic School System in the United States* (New York, 1908) and *The Growth and the Development of the Catholic School System in the United States* (New York, 1912).

[52]R. F. McNamara, "Trusteeism in the Atlantic States, 1785-1863," *Catholic Historical Review* 30 (1944): 135-54; Thomas T. McAvoy, "The Formation of the American Catholic Minority, 1820-1860," *The Review of Politics* 10 (January 1948): 13-34.

the tip of the iceberg with regard to nativist reactions. However, the American version of this anti-Catholic episode, unlike the European versions, would be continued by voluntary associations. In this struggle, both sides could muster their forces and unite in protective associations without the state directly intervening.[53]

VOLUNTARY ASSOCIATIONS OF CHRISTIANS

With the downfall of the religious establishments of Connecticut in 1818 and of Massachusetts in 1833, a pattern of denominationalism fully emerged in America. Denominationalism was the embodiment of voluntaryism. Thomas Jefferson, for example, in his *Notes on Religion* merely improvised on Locke when he outlined his own ecclesiological views:

> A church is "a voluntary society of men, joining themselves together of their own accord, in order to the public worshipping of God in such a manner as they judge acceptable to him and effectual to the salvation of their soul." It is *voluntary* bec. no man is *by* nature bound to any church. The hope of salvation is the cause of his entering into it. If he finds anything wrong in it, he should be as free to go out as he was to come in.[54]

Associative in form and individualistic in substance, the denomination was a perfect example of a purposive voluntary society. And to the extent that its purpose was to save souls, such a society could as easily appeal to evangelicals with their emphasis upon experimental religion as it could to enlightened Jeffersonians of the Lockean mold.

The inauguration of complete voluntaryism seemed to please many. Robert Baird spoke for American evangelicals when he said that all churches now "depend, under God, for their support on the willing hearts and active hands of their friends." Voluntaryism also answered Alexis de Tocqueville's question as to how the authority of

---

[53]See the studies by Ray Billington, *The Protestant Crusade, 1800-1860* (New York, 1938); Clifford Griffin, "Converting the Catholics: American Benevolent Societies and the Ante-Bellum Crusade against the Church," *Catholic Historical Review* 47 (1961): 325-41.

[54]Jefferson, "Notes on Religion," *Writings of Thomas Jefferson* 2:101; Sidney Mead, "Denominationalism: The Shape of Protestantism in America," in *The Lively Experiment*, 103-33.

religion could survive and increase without state support. For as other observers have noticed, it was the recruitment and organization of these "willing hearts and active hands" that generated the extensive influence of religion in nineteenth-century America.[55]

As shown, Lyman Beecher, in seeing the work of voluntary societies, had been influenced to change his views about disestablishment and to support it. As one of the early organizers of voluntary associations in Connecticut, Beecher described the situation after disestablishment. "At the very time when the civil law had become impotent for the support of religion and the prevention of immorality," Beecher wrote, "God began to pour out his Spirit upon the churches; and voluntary associations of Christians were raised up, to apply and extend that influence which the law could no longer apply."[56] New England clerics gave up their "cocked hats and gold-headed canes," but they did not give up their influence. The New Divinity theology of Beecher and Nathaniel Taylor, like the New England phase of the Awakening itself, expanded Jonathan Edwards's definition of free will and stressed the moral supervision of the Lord, but always cast these themes in a conservative mold. One scholar, calling these New Englanders, "republican theocrats," summed up their stance towards religion, politics, and society at large. Opposed to those "Sabbath-breakers, rum-selling tippling folk, infidels, and ruff' scuff generally" that he associated with democracy, Beecher took heart in the stability of a written constitution and a mixed republican government. As for the new societies, Beecher had great hopes for those "local voluntary associations of the wise and the good." His description of the participants of those societies again illustrates Beecher's conservative and paternalistic perspective on social and political affairs. Beecher, however, did not support the formation of a distinct Christian political party whose purpose was to carry out his evangelical program. In keeping with his traditional and paternalistic perspective, Beecher attacked that

---

[55]Baird, *Religion in America*, 110; Alexis de Tocqueville, *Democracy in America*, ed. Phillips Bradley, 2 vols. (New York, 1945) 1:320; Philip Schaff, *America*, ed. Perry Miller (Cambridge, 1961) 76, 79.

[56]Beecher, "Lectures on Political Atheism," *Works*, 1:325.

"party spirit" and party zeal that all too often produced only naive "political experiments."[57]

As he discussed social ethics, Beecher discouraged participation in politics, preferring that Christians confine their efforts to developing channels of moral influence. Only when "great questions of national morality," were involved, such as war or, as in the case of England, the abolition of the slave trade, should Christians unite and lobby directly. Otherwise, they should avoid political parties and only assert "the silent exertions of evangelical influence" through example, selective voting, and the work of the various voluntary associations to convert individuals. In this manner, said Beecher, quoting William Wilberforce, evangelicals could fulfill their task of "restoring the influences of religion and of raising the standard of morality."[58] Reiterated was that reforming "desire to do good," that Robert Baird had noted, harnessed to the causes of righteousness. In the forty years following the organization of the Missionary Society of Connecticut (1798), hundreds of voluntary associations were begun. The quintet of the American Board of Commissioners of Foreign Missions, the American Bible Society, the American Sunday School Union, the American Tract Society, and the American Home Missionary Society were probably the best known of the explicitly religious groups. Yet for every one of these, there was a legion of other humanitarian and reform societies in which the desire to do good works played a large role.[59]

Beecher's invoking of William Wilberforce was significant. For in many ways this network of reform organizations, this "benevolent empire," had its roots in England. Indeed, voluntary associations dedicated to such causes as distributing Bibles, tracts, and other devotional literature, and to promoting home and foreign missionary

[57]Elwyn A. Smith, "The Voluntary Establishment of Religion," in *The Religion of the Republic*, ed. Elwyn A. Smith, 154-82; Beecher, *Autobiography*, 1:251, 112-13.

[58]Beecher, "The Faith Once Delivered to the Saints," *Works*, 2:276, 281, 283.

[59]See the discussion by O. W. Elsbree, *The Rise of the Missionary Spirit in America, 1790-1815* (Williamsport, 1928); C. B. Goodykoontz, *Home Missions on the American Frontier* (Caldwell, 1939); Arthur M. Schlesinger, "Biography of a Nation of Joiners," *Paths to the Present* (1949; reprint, Boston, 1964) 24-50.

work were well known in Anglo-American and Continental evangelical circles. America as a foreign mission field for Europeans and
as a field for her own missionary activity received a double dose of
action. Americans went to Europe too. Fraternal associations and
speakers, informal tourists, official delegations of inspectors—con-
voys of concerned Protestants shuttled back and forth between
America and Europe seeking information, providing assistance,
and preserving ties between coreligionists in the New and Old
Worlds. Sometimes, as with the temperance campaign, American
organization was a model for the Europeans. More often, the transit
of organizational ideas and prototypes moved from east to west, especially as the religious societies in America grew from local into national and interdenominational enterprises. Whatever the region,
the desire to restore "the standard of morality" was a language all
could understand.[60]

This summons to renewal, particularly as it figured in the example of Lyman Beecher, gives further insight into American evangelicalism in the early nineteenth century. Beecher's dissatisfaction
with democracy, like that of his fellow New Englander Timothy
Dwight, his desire to see leadership by respectable citizens, and his
wish to see moral rather than political activities, all indicate the complex nature of his adjustment to the life of the new republic. Indeed,
it was the success of the voluntary associations in conjunction with
revivalists in filling churches, reforming drunkards, and spreading
the Gospel that convinced Beecher of the wisdom of disestablishment. In this, he was much like his western colleague, Charles Grandison Finney. Both were heartened by the results of the benevolent
empire and both supported the various religious societies' efforts.
Both believed with millennial fervor that converting individuals was
the means of producing social change and both feared that if Christians affiliated with political parties, piety would be replaced by
party spirit. Yet where Beecher was a republican theocrat, Finney

---

[60]See the discussion by Frank Thistlethwaite, *The Anglo-American Connection in
the Early Nineteenth Century* (Philadelphia, 1959); Charles I. Foster, *An Errand of
Mercy* (Chapel Hill, 1960); Cole, *Social Ideas of the Northern Evangelists*; Lefferts A.
Loetscher, "The Problem of Christian Unity in Early Nineteenth-Century America," *Church History* 32, no. 1 (March 1963): 3-16.

was an egalitarian democrat more fearful of the Eastern seaboard than the Western frontier, more concerned with reaching the Jacksonian common people than organizing the Federalist good and wise. Beecher and Finney resolved their differences with one another in much the same manner that they adapted to American society. Together they recruited scores of persons into the ranks of the benevolent empire, never realizing that some social issues are more than the sum of their individual parts and that many moral questions are by their very nature political. The unfortunate legacy of this perspective was that just as the slavery issue split the transatlantic Evangelical Alliance in 1848, so would it and the subsequent Civil War split the ranks of evangelicalism in America.

THOUGHTS ON UNITY

One of the most significant aspects of the benevolent empire, especially during its heyday in the 1820s and 1830s, was its interdenominational appeal. This appeal was symbolized by the annual spring meeting of the tract, Bible, and education societies; when those societies' interlocking directorates of leaders and overlapping scores of members would scurry from one hotel and meeting room to another. The visible success of these nondenominational enterprises raised another question. If so many Protestants could work together, could they not pray and worship together too? Could not some sort of harmonious union of churches be formed that would bring together these like-minded Christians just as the voluntary societies did?

Attempts at different types of theological or denominational unions dated back to the colonial era. There were the efforts made within the denominations to strengthen and centralize their internal organizations and judicatories. The Presbyterian Union of 1758 epitomized the work taking place within the other denominations to deepen their roots in America and to coordinate their individual labors. As common purposes were identified by communions, synods, ministeriums, and councils of the same faith, denominations tightened their mutual associations and acknowledged a common leadership. Beyond such internal developments there was a raft of proposals and overtures for unions between denominations. Facing similar problems such as a lack of ministers, or (as in the case of

Dutch and German congregations) finding clergy that spoke the same language as its congregation, many groups investigated possible ways to alleviate their problems together. In 1743 an attempt was made to unite the Dutch Reformed, German Reformed, and Presbyterian churches. Continuation of this interest between Dutch Reformed and Presbyterians was seen in 1784 and 1822. In 1797 negotiations aiming at union were initiated between the Lutheran church in New York and the Protestant Episcopal church in New York. Similarly, in 1791 Thomas Coke of the Protestant Episcopal church proposed a series of conditions upon which the American Methodist Church might reunite with the Episcopalians. The following year, Bishop James Madison introduced a bill in the House of Deputies commending union between the Episcopalians and other Protestant denominations in America. As with the other overtures by the Reformed and Lutherans, the Protestant Episcopal initiatives fizzled out.[61]

In contrast to these attempts, other efforts at unions between denominations did materialize in both short-term and long-term successes. Barton Stone and Alexander and Thomas Campbell supported cooperative religious ventures. Sharing of common space for religious purposes, as by the Reformed and Lutherans of Arch Street, Philadelphia, occurred frequently, usually because of an insufficient number of ministers. This Philadelphia congregation was one of those visited by Count Nicholas Zinzendorf during his visit to America in 1741. When Zinzendorf arrived in Pennsylvania, he was welcomed by Henry Antes. Antes had the idea of establishing a federative union of all German churches, and he enlisted Zinzendorf in his project. The group was to be named the "Congregation of God in the Spirit" and drew on both Reformed and Lutheran congregations and ministers. Zinzendorf, however, left for Europe

---

[61]Robert E. Thompson, *A History of the Presbyterian Churches in the United States* (New York, 1895) 43-44, 49-50; Armin G. Weng, "The Language Problem in the Lutheran Church in Pennsylvania, 1740-1820," *Church History* 5, no. 4 (December 1936): 359-75; E. T. Corwin, *A History of the Reformed Church, Dutch* (New York, 1894) 209-10; Henry Jacobs, *A History of the Evangelical Lutheran Church in the United States* (New York, 1893) 318-19; James T. Addison, *The Episcopal Church in the United States* (New York, 1951) 85-86.

in 1743. His departure and the loss of his charismatic leadership caused this alliance to separate into its original parts. Another interesting but short-lived example of union between Reformed and Lutheran pastors took place in South Carolina. There, in 1788, five Lutheran and two Reformed ministers formed the "Unio Ecclesiastica of the German Protestant Church." Again the alliance was a federative one in which denominational confessions were recognized, and as in the Pennsylvania experience the parties divided, this time after six years.[62]

There were important union attempts that achieved longer periods of success. One of the better known was the Plan of Union adopted by the Presbyterian and Congregational churches in 1801. Designed to meet the needs of new missionary fields in New York and the Western Reserve, the Plan of Union drew on similarities of church polity and decades of mutual cooperation between the two denominations. In its operation the Plan of Union cut down on the need for ministers and aided missionary endeavors. Its clerics were prominent in the work of the interdenominational benevolent empire and generally sympathetic to the New Divinity theology and new-measures revivalism of the Awakening. These tendencies contributed to the tumult and ultimate schism within the Presbyterian church, as the Old School Presbyterians first abrogated the Plan in 1837, and then excluded the New School Presbyterians the following year.[63]

Within American Lutheranism two sets of influence exemplified the desire for interdenominational union. The first concerned the American Lutheran response to the Augsburg Tercentenary and the Prussian Union of 1817. The New York Synod in 1815 invited the Pennsylvania Ministerium and the North Carolina Synod

---

[62]J. H. Dubbs, *A History of the Reformed Church, German* (New York, 1894) 372-75; Jacobs, *The Evangelical Lutheran Church*, 320.

[63]E. H. Gillett, *History of the Presbyterian Church in the United States of America*, 2 vols. (Philadelphia, 1864) 1:437-41; Robert H. Nichols, "The Plan of Union in New York," *Church History* 5, no. 1 (March 1936): 29-51; Charles Zorbaugh, "The Plan of Union in Ohio," *Church History* 6, no. 2 (June 1937): 145-64; George Marsden, *The Evangelical Mind and the New School Presbyterian Experience* (New Haven, 1970) 59-87.

to help organize a celebration in America. The result was a variety of worship services praising the Reformation and attended by Reformed and Lutheran clergy and laity alike. In New York City, services were held in English and German with Episcopal clergymen concelebrating. Similarly, in Pennsylvania, Reformed and Lutheran groups joined together. While no formal plan was consummated, several concrete steps were taken. Informal affiliation accompanied by the sharing of ministers and buildings continued. The *Gemeinschaftliches Gesangbuch* was first published in 1817 and remained a standard hymnal through twenty-one editions. The *Evangelisches Magazin* grew in circulation following the tercentenary celebration and remained a union periodical. Finally, official committees were appointed by Lutheran and Reformed associations in Pennsylvania and continued their negotiations for a possible fusion until 1836.[64]

The desire for unity, however, had not died within Lutheranism. In 1838 Samuel Schmucker published his *Appeal to the American Churches with a Plan for Catholic Union*. Born in 1799, Schmucker was the son of a Lutheran clergyman. He was educated at Princeton Seminary, where he roomed with Robert Baird, and was awarded his license to preach in 1820. From 1826 to 1864 he was attached to Gettysburg Lutheran Seminary. Schmucker's personality reflected his pietistic bent and his broad intellectual interests. These features were also visible in his *Appeal to the American Church*. Out of the need to "arrest the intestine strife of christian brethren, and unite all their energies in effective efforts to extend the triumph of the cross to every nation upon earth," Schmucker fashioned his fraternal appeal for unity. Invoking a picture of the apostolic church in which all members were called Christians and geographic designations rather than sectarian names were the only emblems of particularity, Schmucker attacked several misconceptions about church history and unity. First, "it is admitted by all Protestants," Schmucker claimed, "that the pope is a creature as utterly unknown to the Bible as is the Grand Lama of the Tartars." The charge that Peter pos-

---

[64]Abdel R. Wentz, *A Basic History of Lutheranism in America* (Philadelphia, 1955) 95-97; Don Yoder, "Christian Unity in Nineteenth-Century America," in *A History of the Ecumenical Movement*, ed. Ruth Rouse and Stephen Neill (Philadelphia, 1967) 242-43.

sessed no distinct powers over the other apostles was standard anti-Roman fare in nineteenth-century Protestant (and especially evangelical) thought. A second theme, likewise familiar within evangelical circles, was the assertion of a set of fundamental truths that simple study of the Scriptures could display and prove. Third, in line with his antipapal strictures, Schmucker argued for a federative plan of organization. Under this plan no denomination would lose control to a centralizing hierarchy, but rather would retain its own ecclesiastical organization, government, discipline, and mode of worship.[65]

Built on the faith that everyone could agree on the fundamentals of belief, and tempered with the federated vision that sought to preserve local autonomy, Schmucker's *Appeal* presented an imaginative basis of church unity. Yet Schmucker's plan was opposed; for the Lutherans, like the Reformed and the Protestant Episcopalians, found the 1840s and 1850s to be an era of renewed confessionalism within their traditions. Although it looked for a time as if the New Divinity theologians and new-measures revivalists had swept the field, the troops of a theological counterattack were preparing themselves and would not be long in coming.

As had happened in both Germany and England, a broad combination of cultural developments had brought about a conservative reaction. The conservative movement reflected the voluntaryism of the American situation in that its spokesmen represented the three major Protestant traditions—Lutheran, Reformed, and Protestant Episcopal—that existed in America. These conservatives also demonstrated the derivative nature of much of American theology. There was no one in America who could match the philosophical and theological insights of Hegel, Schleiermacher, or Strauss. Admittedly the standards set by these Germans were high. If the course of American theology was less profound and original, if it drew on this richer (and not exclusively German) European tradition for its sources, it was a reflection as much of the pressures of

---

[65]Samuel Schmucker, *An Appeal to the American Churches with a Plan for Catholic Union* (New York, 1838) 1, 15, 26, 36, 66. For the details of Schmucker's life, see P. Anstadt, *Life and Times of Rev. S. S. Schmucker* (New York, 1896).

immediate events as it was the reflection of peculiarities of intellectual development. Still, as will become clear, these American confessional theologians, these theological and social conservatives, did attempt to construct a systematic theological response to the events of their day, a response recognizing the significance of historical continuity and opposing the rampant emotionalism of contemporary revivalism. In an era claiming to have no past but only a future; in an era championing individualism over any corporative concepts; the contributions of these conservatives are all the more deserving of attention.

CHAPTER SEVEN

CONFESSIONALISM IN AMERICA

In 1837 the General Assembly of the Presbyterian Church convened at Philadelphia for its annual meeting. These yearly sessions of Presbyterian ministers and laity were often the scene of acrimonious debate and mutual recrimination between the Old and New School parties within the denomination. The convocation in 1837 was no different, except that perhaps for the first time the Old School party held a clear majority. What followed was not unprecedented in American church history, but it was nonetheless unexpected by many who attended the meeting. In a dramatic series of actions, the Old School majority first abrogated the Plan of Union with the Congregationalists, and then retroactively eliminated from the General Assembly those synods formed under that plan, thereby excising some 28 presbyteries, 509 ministers, and 60,000 lay members. The Old School Presbyterians, waving the banner of firmer adherence to doctrinal orthodoxy and tighter ecclesiastical discipline, had excluded the New School from the church in one fell swoop. Several years later one of the leaders of the Old School, Charles Hodge, still summarized the controversy as "one party is in favor of a stricter adherence to the standards of the church, as to doctrine and order, than the other."[1]

---

[1]Charles Hodge, *The Constitutional History of the Presbyterian Church in the United States of America* (Philadelphia, 1851) 9. For a discussion of the 1837 Assembly see George Marsden, *The Evangelical Mind and the New School Presbyterian Experience* (New Haven, 1970) 63.

A new denominational self-consciousness had emerged. It was not unique to Presbyterians, however. Beginning in the 1830s and continuing through the 1860s, several movements built on adherence to historic standards of faith and practice developed within American Protestantism. Influenced by European ecclesiastical controversies and reacting to the American religious situation, advocates of a renewed confessionalism appeared within the Lutheran, Reformed, and Protestant Episcopal traditions. Nor were these confessionalists confined to any one geographical section of the country. Their disputes involved ministers on the Eastern seaboard and the Western frontier, and blazed in the hinterlands of Pennsylvania as well as at the seminary at Princeton.

Four themes characterized the beliefs of these American confessional theologians, themes similar to those of their theological counterparts in England and Germany but reflecting the peculiarities of the American situation. First, confessional theologians argued that although they strongly opposed the revivalism associated with Charles Grandison Finney and his new measures, they still supported true religion. In stating their case, these Lutheran, Reformed, and Episcopal theologians demonstrated that their religious beliefs were indebted to contemporary romantic influences and distant from eighteenth-century theological rationalism. Second, the hostility of these thinkers to the fundamental subjectivism that they perceived in American revivalism resulted in a characteristic affirmation of historic statements of faith. Creeds, such as the Augsburg Confession or the Westminster Confession of Faith, were a more adequate and less individualistic means of interpreting religious experience than was revivalism's appeal to emotion. Confessions functioned as time-tested and collectively affirmed anchors, steadying their respective theological traditions during a turbulent human history. Third, this confessional movement within American Protestantism, like those in Germany and England, displayed a social and political conservatism. Fearful of democratizing tendencies within church and society, these theologians often condemned what they believed to be the excesses of Jacksonian America, and they condemned the dangers these excesses appeared to pose for internal church affairs. Finally, drawing on these theological and secular concerns, confessional theologians contributed to a fresh rethinking of the nature of the church.

CONFESSIONAL VERSUS AMERICAN LUTHERANISM

One of the sources within the Lutheran tradition for a resurgent confessional awareness was the many emigrants that left Germany for America during the second third of the nineteenth century. Some were refugees from the battles within the German Lutheran church over the Prussian Union. Led by J. A. Grabau, a group of approximately one thousand of these refugees immigrated to America in 1839 and settled near Buffalo, New York. There they formed the Buffalo Synod or "Synod of Exiles from the Lutheran Church of Prussia." A larger and ultimately more influential group of German Lutherans also arrived in America in 1839. These Lutherans were from Saxony and were led, first by Martin Stephan, and later by C. F. W. Walther, who founded the Missouri Synod within the Lutheran Church. Although different in other respects, both the Prussian and Saxon Lutherans were deeply antipathetic to the Prussian Union and the compromise of confessional standards they believed it represented.[2]

A third contribution to confessional renewal was made by the Bavarian pastor, Wilhelm Löhe. In 1841, responding to a plea from a German Lutheran missionary in America for additional support, Löhe published a small essay in Germany, "The Lutheran Emigrants in America." In this piece he focused on the plight of recent Lutheran immigrants as they tried to cope with the immense spiritual and physical challenges of the New World. Citing the chronic lack of properly trained Lutheran ministers, Löhe reminded his readers of the desperate situation of their fellow German brothers and sisters of the faith who were confronting the twin perils of Ro-

---

[2]See the discussion in Henry E. Jacobs, *A History of the Evangelical Lutheran Church in the United States* (New York, 1893) 395-400; Walter Forster, *Zion on the Mississippi* (St. Louis, 1953) passim; Wilhelm Iwan, *Die altlutherische Auswanderung um die Mitte des 19. Jahrhunderts*, 2 vols. (Ludwigsburg, 1943) passim. For a treatment of confessionalism among Scandinavian Lutheran immigrants, see Abdel R. Wentz, *A Basic History of Lutheranism in America* (Philadelphia, 1955) 122-23.

man Catholicism and sectarianism.[3] Löhe's pamphlet initially appealed as much to nationalistic as to confessional sentiments among its readers; it bore its first fruits the following year when Löhe sent his first two missionaries to America.

In September 1842, when Löhe's men first arrived in New York City and then proceeded to Columbus, Ohio, the second phase of Löhe's relationship with America began. The association between Löhe and the Ohio Synod lasted until 1845 and illustrated many of the problems facing the immigrant Lutheran church. The Ohio Synod had been founded in 1812 and reorganized as the Joint Synod of Ohio in 1818. Its one seminary was located at Columbus and its faculty tried to shepherd the diverse and sometimes antagonistic English and German elements within the synod. The division between the English and German parties and the debate over whether to continue to use German or to adopt English symbolized the complex issue of accommodation to American culture. While the language issue often reflected disaffection between these two national groups, it also represented competing attitudes towards confessional standards and the use of new measures. Could historic Lutheran confessions be revised in order to adapt to the situation in America; did revivalistic techniques so successful in enlarging other denominations have a legitimate place in the Lutheran church— these were some of the questions hidden beneath the debate over language. By the early 1840s, with the arrival of large numbers of strictly confessional German immigrants, the language issue had flared into a major controversy in more synods than just that of Ohio.

In a pastoral letter written to the American Lutheran church in 1845 and sent by way of his men in Ohio, Löhe focused on the need for strict adherence to high confessional standards. He warned against adopting new measures and recommended traditional methods of instruction. He also insisted that German continue to be used exclusively in the churches. His insistence did not so much indicate linguistic chauvinism as it did Löhe's belief that the German

---

[3]Wilhelm Löhe, "Die lutherische Auswanderer in Nordamerika," in *Gesammelte Werke*, ed. Klaus Ganzert, 7 vols. (Neuendettelsau, 1955-) 4:16-19.

language correctly expressed the essentials of traditional Lutheranism and that alternatives were unavailable. In 1845, however, the English-speaking party in the Ohio Synod gained a majority and passed a proposal making English the official language of the synod. Shortly thereafter, Löhe's missionary left the Ohio Synod.[4]

Given his distance from the source, Wilhelm Löhe was well informed about developments within American Lutheranism. He knew of the writings of Samuel Schmucker of the Gettysburg Seminary and of those of the German Reformed theologian, Philip Schaff. Löhe was also familiar with C. F. W. Walther and his outpost of Lutherans at St. Louis and with J. Grabau at Buffalo. Yet in 1846 after his men had left the Ohio Synod and were searching for a new base of operations, two questions seemed uppermost in Löhe's mind. First, he questioned the appropriateness of an alliance with Walther's forces at St. Louis, and second, he spoke of the need for a new theological seminary to inculcate correct confessional theology, now that the seminary at Columbus had been lost. Writing to Johann Höfling in the spring of 1846, Löhe asserted,

> One can learn the Lutheran faith only from German institutions. German seminaries are thoroughly necessary unless through a progressive Anglicization Germans are to receive the Lutheran church in the English tongue. There never has been an English translation of the Symbolical Books—it is the calling of the German seminaries to preserve the Lutheran church in spite of the Yankees.[5]

Both of Löhe's concerns were resolved in 1846. In May 1846 a group of his men met with C. F. W. Walther at St. Louis and formulated a preliminary draft of a constitution for a new synodical body. Based on the Lutheran confessions and dedicated to preserving the purity of Lutheran doctrine, this statement represented the

---

[4]See Löhe, "Zuruf aus der Heimat an die deutsch-lutherische Kirche in Nordamerika," ibid., 4:84, and chapter 3 above, for a discussion of Löhe's pastoral letter. On the relations with the Ohio Synod, see James Schaaf, "Wilhelm Löhe's Relation to the American Church: a study in the history of the Lutheran mission." Ph.D. dissertation, Heidelberg, 1961, 98-102.

[5]See Löhe to A. Ernst, 28 October 1843; 4 August 1845, Wilhelm Löhe Papers, Löhe Archiv, Neuendettelsau, Bavaria, for mention of Schmucker and Schaff. For the remarks to Höfling, see Löhe to Höfling, 18 March 1846, Löhe Papers.

harmony of view existing between the Saxons of St. Louis and the Bavarians. This group met again in Fort Wayne, Indiana, in July and began formal proceedings to establish the synod of "Missouri, Ohio, and Other States." Fort Wayne was also the location of a new seminary that opened in October. Under the direction of Wilhelm Sihler, one of Löhe's most promising and best-trained missionaries, the Fort Wayne seminary became a center for German-educated students to conclude their studies for a ministry in America. Thus, along with the seminary at St. Louis, the Fort Wayne institution became a standard-bearer of confessionalism within American Lutheranism.[6]

The affiliation of Löhe's missionary enterprise with the Missouri Synod signaled a coming of age and a new organizational power for the forces of Lutheran confessionalism in America. An emphasis on confessions, however, could mask radically different interpretations of the meaning of these documents, just as support for revivals could hide the differences between two preachers like Asahel Nettleton and Charles Finney. The years from 1847 through 1853 represented a third phase in Löhe's relationship with American Lutheranism. His missionaries cooperated with those of the Missouri Synod and through teaching, preaching, and publications they promoted the development of the fledgling synod.

Yet this initial harmony soon gave way to rifts within the synodical organization. Disputes arose concerning Walther's views of the ministerial office and his emphasis upon its congregational basis. The Missouri Synod's insistence that there were no open questions in theology proved to be a further point of contention. The confessional statements of Lutheranism, Walther maintained, were identical to the spirit and content of Scripture and inaccessible to change or development. A similar set of controversies had occurred in the early 1840s between the Buffalo Synod led by Grabau and the Missourians. Grabau had argued that the ministry was a distinct class set apart from the congregation by ordination through the

---

[6]Schaaf, "Löhe's Relation," 107-109; J. L. Neve, *A Brief History of the Lutheran Church in America* (Burlington, 1916) 270-71; August R. Suelflow, "The Beginnings of 'Missouri, Ohio, and Other States' in America," in *Moving Frontiers*, ed. Carl Meyer (St. Louis, 1964) 90-141.

Word of God and placed in a seat of judgment by divine right. Grabau believed that lay persons owed unquestioning obedience to their ministers in all matters of faith. In contrast, Walther claimed that the congregation contained the promises of God and that the ministry derived from the priesthood of all believers, which the congregation represented. Hoping to avoid another such rupture, the Missouri Synod sent Walther to Germany in 1851 to consult with leading Lutheran theologians and to visit Wilhelm Löhe in Bavaria. Walther's meeting with Löhe was cordial and appeared to heal the breach. Pastor Grabau of Buffalo also visited Löhe and soon the Bavarian found himself enmeshed in the American conflict.[7]

The resolution of the dispute came in 1854, when Löhe's missionaries, with his consent, left the Missouri Synod and founded the Iowa Synod. Löhe's theology was too elastic and too much influenced by romanticism to insist that all theological questions were inarguably answered. Furthermore, Löhe distrusted Walther's congregational views, which lacked an ordering of ecclesiastical powers. Consequently, the Iowa Synod became known for an ecclesiastical position midway between that of the hierarchical organization of Buffalo and the congregationalism of Missouri. Although the Iowa Synod insisted on the importance of Lutheran confessional statements, it admitted that certain open questions still remained.[8] The formation of the Iowa Synod thus represented the final stage in Löhe's association with American Lutheranism. By 1854 his control over his missionaries had weakened as they developed their own organizations. Within a year, after a severe illness, Löhe turned to concentrating his efforts solely on Bavaria.

If the establishment of the Iowa Synod in 1854 marked the end of Löhe's active involvement in America, it did not signify the end of the battle over confessionalism. To the east, in Pennsylvania, the controversy between Charles Philip Krauth and Samuel Schmucker over "American Lutheranism" had not yet even peaked. The dispute over "American Lutheranism" again concerned the question

---

[7]Jacobs, *History of the Lutheran Church*, 407-408; Wentz, *Basic History*, 120-21.

[8]Conrad Bergendorff, *The Doctrine of the Church in American Lutheranism* (Philadelphia, 1956) 14-15; Neve, *Brief History*, 279-96, and chapter 3 above.

of whether Lutherans needed to make theological concessions for the new American environment and if so, what those concessions were to be. Must historic Lutheranism divest itself of its distinctive truths and become identical with other Protestant denominations in America? Should English, in order to accommodate the culture and the native-born Lutherans, replace German as the language of preaching, teaching, and synodical administration? Ought new measures be adopted throughout all the synods? Could subscription to confessional statements be demanded of all candidates for the ministry, and if so, could the unaltered Augsburg Confession be the basis for that subscription? These were the questions perplexing and dividing Lutherans, and these were the questions that prompted Krauth to champion the confessional status.

"I have three times defended my position and at each time offended both extremes," Krauth wrote late in his life.

> Some call me a rigid Symbolist, others an extreme New Measure man. I am neither. If I say so again I draw down upon me the extremists of both sides. I acknowledge no standard of Lutheranism but the Augsburg Confession. If an American Lutheran is a Lutheran in the United States who regards that Symbol as the only authoritative one, I am an American Lutheran. So I have said again and again.[9]

Tolerant in spirit and gracious in his personal style, Krauth nonetheless consistently advocated firm adherence to the Lutheran confessions. Krauth was born in 1797 at New Goshenhoppen, Pennsylvania. He first studied medicine and then later decided on the ministry.[10] He was licensed to preach in 1818 by the Synod of Pennsylvania and soon took charge of two small churches in Virginia. In 1827 he moved to Philadelphia, six years later beginning his duties at Gettysburg Theological Seminary. In 1834, Krauth was chosen president of the neighboring Pennsylvania College and thus divided his time between the college and his professorship of Biblical and

---

[9]C. P. Krauth to H. Schmid, 2 October 1862, quoted in Adolph Spaeth, *Charles Porterfield Krauth*, 2 vols. (New York, 1898) 1:19.

[10]For biographical details, see the unpublished manuscript by O. F. Waage, Charles Philip Krauth Papers, Lutheran Archives Center, Philadelphia; Spaeth, *Krauth*, 1:1-26; Abdel R. Wentz, *History of the Gettysburg Theological Seminary* (Philadelphia, 1927) 308-10.

Oriental Literature at the seminary. Although he was awarded an honorary doctor of divinity degree by the University of Pennsylvania in 1837, it was the year 1850 that marked a turning point in Krauth's life. In that year he relinquished his college presidency and devoted himself full time to the seminary. Additionally, although he was not a prolific writer, Krauth simultaneously assumed the editorship of the *Evangelical Review*, and contributed for the next eleven years his most important theological reflections. On 30 March 1867, Krauth died.

In two pieces appearing in the *Evangelical Review* in 1849, Krauth raised a series of issues that were determinative for his understanding of Lutheran confessionalism. In reviewing Heinrich Schmid's *Dogmatik of the Lutheran Church*, Krauth lamented the prevalent theological ignorance that characterized the clergy and laity in America. "As things are, we have no standards, no guide," Krauth said.

> Everyone is left to fix his own views; and whilst we presume there is general agreement in our own church on the fundamental doctrines of the Bible, our ministers display, in the opinions they entertain, sometimes a decided Calvinistic influence, sometimes an extreme Arminian, sometimes a Pelagian.

Such a combination of indifference and laxity was a disgrace, Krauth contended, and the best antidote would be to study a book such as Schmid's with its satisfying faithfulness to the historic Lutheran confessions. "We would have all our ministers acquainted with the Symbolical books," Krauth argued, "We would have them all versed in the distinctive theology of the church. We would have introduced into our theological schools the study of the symbols, and didactic and polemic theology so administered as to bring before the view, pure, unadulterated Lutheranism."[11]

Despite the challenge of theological instruction facing educators like himself, Krauth was guardedly optimistic about the chances for success. Increased demands by laity and clergy alike for books about the Lutheran confessions were auspicious. Such signals indicated a

---

[11]Charles Krauth, "Review of Schmid's Dogmatik of the Lutheran Church," *Evangelical Review* 1 (July 1849): 128-29.

shift away from the reigning unionism and denominational indifference of the preceding era. "The time has passed away in which we are to assume every phase which may be presented to us," Krauth wrote, "to glory that we are like every other body, and consequently, are nothing in ourselves, living only by the breath of others." The call for "unadulterated Lutheranism" and for a renewed awareness of distinctively Lutheran theological opinions were the battleflags of Krauth's attack on his opponents.[12]

As he examined the challenges to the resources of confessional Lutherans, Krauth recognized certain features specific to the American situation. Foremost among those features was sectarianism, for Krauth opposed any attempts to separate the Lutheran church in America from its European ancestors. Continually, Krauth would argue that the church in America was truly part of the Lutheran church and that if any appellation should characterize it, it should be that of doctrinal purity.[13] As he expanded on the nature of the American church, Krauth referred to the split between German and English Lutherans. Alluding to the travails of the church since her founding in America, Krauth contended that "the salt which preserves her is Germanic." Krauth's admission reflected his belief in the importance of the German language within the church. Indeed, writing to his son in 1845, Krauth advised him to study German diligently, for "so much of the best theological literature is contained in it . . . it seems almost indispensable to the learned theologian and the intelligent Lutheran." Furthermore, Krauth had delivered an address in 1832 entitled an "Oration on the Advantages of the German Language," in which he again said that fluency in German was necessary for proper theological understanding.[14]

Despite his admiration for the German language, Krauth's justification for its use stressed its applicability. Speaking of its importance, he suggested that there never "was any connexion between

---

[12]Ibid., 130.

[13]Charles Krauth, "The Relation of our Confessions to the Reformation, and the Importance of Their Study," *Evangelical Review* 1 (October 1849): 240.

[14]Ibid., 241; Krauth to his son is quoted by Spaeth, *Krauth*, 1:106.

Lutheranism and that language *as such*—some mysterious coherence between its sounds and inflections, and the truth of our church; so that in the very nature of the case, and by an essential necessity, the English language and Lutheranism could not harmonize together." Fluent in several languages himself, Krauth regarded the language issue *per se* as of secondary importance. Not the language in which it was preached, but the content of what was preached—this was the crucial issue. Recognition of this fact drove Krauth back to examining the nature of Lutheran confessional statements.[15]

In 1849 Krauth had written that through the Apostles', Nicene, and Athanasian creeds—all of which the Lutheran church recognized as authoritative—the church "vindicates her true catholicity and antiquity, and declares that the name Lutheran does not define her essence, but simply refers to one grand fact in her history." The full meaning of this statement for Krauth's doctrine of the church surfaced the following year when he published his article, "The Lutheran Church in the United States." Krauth's manifesto had been first delivered before the General Synod at its meeting in Charleston, South Carolina; it was published in the *Evangelical Review* his first year as coeditor. Speaking to his Lutheran audience, Krauth said that the Lutheran church in America was part of the wider Lutheran communion and, as such, was established on the doctrinal system provided in the Augsburg Confession, its Apology, the Smalcald Articles, the Catechism of Luther, and the Formulas of Concord. Krauth's list of confessional statements demonstrated that he saw Lutheran theology and polity as embodied in a full system of major confessional statements, not simply in the Augsburg creed. Krauth thus reemphasized that the Lutheran church, because of its catholicity and antiquity, was part of the wider Christian church, of which the Lutheran church in America participated.[16]

---

[15]Krauth, "Relation of our Confessions," *Evangelical Review* 1 (October 1849): 242.

[16]Charles Krauth, "The Lutheran Church in the United States," *Evangelical Review* 2 (July 1850): 1-3.

Having invoked the authority of the Lutheran symbolical books, Krauth proceeded to oppose the Finneyite revivals. Repudiating "an extreme leaning to the emotional in religion," Krauth stated that recently the Lutheran church had been subject to "surges of animal feeling." At present, however, Krauth happily observed, the church was moving away from these "crude views and objectionable measures" so prevalent elsewhere on the American religious scene. As he had claimed in 1849, Krauth saw the growing interest and desire for the classic Lutheran symbols as evidence of "a remarkable state of things in our Lutheran Zion."[17]

Krauth moved farther from evangelical Protestantism when he placed the Lutheran church within a tradition reaching further in the past than the Reformation. Calling upon an orthodoxy "derived from the primitive ages," Krauth traced a line of tradition that was, as he said in 1849, truly catholic and ancient. As did many other churchly Protestants, Krauth took pains here, and later in his career as well, to distinguish between "catholic" and "Roman Catholic," but there was no hiding his sense of a comprehensive historical Christian tradition and his desire to center the Lutheran church within it.[18]

Directing his attention once more to the Lutheran church's internal situation, Krauth declared that all parties within the church should try to reconcile their differences. However, he believed that it was necessary to find some means of counteracting doctrinal latitudinarianism and lax church discipline. A recognized standard with a normative authority was needed, particularly with regard to the examination of prospective ministers. Subscription to such a norm would help properly and uniformly to educate ministerial candidates and would "induct them into a deep acquaintance with the doctrines of the church, as set forth in the Symbolical books." Krauth suggested the Augsburg Confession as a suitable doctrinal basis for such required subscription. While conceding that some leeway could be given for personal interpretation and dissent, he maintained that the doctrine of sin, the necessity of regeneration,

[17]Ibid., 9-10.

[18]Ibid., 2.

and the doctrine of the two natures of Christ were essential and unquestionable.[19]

Should any pastoral candidate be unable to subscribe to these fundamentals, then the Lutheran church was not his communion. Krauth regretted the divisions within Christendom but regarded adherence to the truth as more important. Thus, he said that the Presbyterian schism of 1837 was "conducive to the glory of God," and insisted that all Lutherans must "exclude every form of Arianism, high and low, Socinianism and rationalism, and anti-trinitarianism of all kinds." Krauth concluded by lauding Lutheranism's "true position" as an influence of conservatism. Attacking Finneyite revivalism, Krauth alleged that Lutheranism "neither makes man independent of means or of God," but that it strives to uphold "a moderate orthodoxy in doctrine, ecclesiastical government and ceremonies."[20]

In his address of 1850 Krauth maintained that Lutheranism walked a middle line "between prelatical episcopacy and *jure divino congregationalism*." Krauth never wrote a systematic treatise on the nature of the church, but in a series of unpublished theses, he sketched out his ecclesiological thoughts. Central to his doctrine of the church was the belief that "the power of the congregation is derived from the power conferred on the whole Church, not the power of the whole Church from the power of the congregation." In denying the local congregation as the seat of ministerial power, Krauth aligned himself with those theologians in England and Germany who regarded the church as a divinely established institution. The authority of the ministry derived from this divine institution. It originated and evolved from its relation to the church as a whole rather than originating from a special set of persons. As he had done previously, Krauth argued that the Roman church enjoyed no special favor, for, with regard to ministerial authority, there had been no primacy among the apostles. Thus, Roman claims to a superior ministerial commission based on the experience of Peter were, in Krauth's eyes, illegitimate. Krauth joined high church

---

[19]Ibid., 12, 14.

[20]Ibid., 13-14.

views on ministerial authority and ecclesiological origins to an equally firm commitment to the symbolical books; he thus formulated one side in the mid-nineteenth century debate over American Lutheranism.[21]

Krauth's major opponent in this debate was his seminary colleague, Samuel Schmucker. Schmucker was the first professor appointed in Gettysburg Seminary and had constructed the seminary's constitution and professorial oath, both of which emphasized personal piety. A belief in the reconstructive power of like-minded pious Christians formed the basis for Schmucker's *Fraternal Appeal* in 1838. It also led him to attend the meetings of the Evangelical Alliance in London in 1846. That convocation broke up over the topic of slavery, with Schmucker vigorously opposing any mention of the slavery issue because he regarded it as a political and not religious matter. After the Alliance adjourned, Schmucker toured the Continent. Upon returning to the States, he addressed a letter to the Prussian church applauding the Union and describing the points of similarity between the General Synod in America and the Prussian Union in Germany. These alleged similarities, of course, were the very areas of doctrinal laxity that so incensed Charles Krauth.[22]

Deeper differences than these existed between Krauth and Schmucker. They surfaced in 1851 and again in 1855. In 1851, Schmucker published an essay entitled the "Vocation of the American Lutheran Church." His pamphlet demonstrated the stark contrast between the confessionalists, like Krauth, and the proponents of "American Lutheranism," like Schmucker. "One grand part of the vocation of the American church," Schmucker charged, "is to throw off the shackles of traditionary, patristic, and symbolic servitude." Coming upon the heels of Krauth's 1850 Charleston address, Schmucker's observations could not be misinterpreted by anyone.[23]

---

[21]Ibid., 14; "Theses on the Ministry of the Gospel," Krauth papers.

[22]Wentz, *Gettysburg*, 110-12, 118, 161.

[23]*Evangelical Review* 2 (April 1851): 491.

Later that year Schmucker expanded on his concept of "American Lutheranism." Schmucker believed it unnecessary to search for the truth in the symbolic books. Rather, the Augsburg Confession presented a "substantially" correct interpretation of the Bible and the doctrinal positions, thus providing a sufficient theological basis for the church. Indeed, further confessional positions were not only superfluous, they were "wedges of dissension" needlessly splintering the church. "Ecclesiastical obligations are voluntary and personal," Schmucker suggested, "not hereditary"; therefore, periodic revision of the confessional statements was legitimate.[24] Hence, Schmucker demanded that all traditional Lutheran statements of faith, except the Augsburg Confession, be abolished. Even the Augsburg Confession, which was only "substantially correct," could be thoroughly altered, and Schmucker thought several specific passages ought to be deleted.[25] In a declaration resounding throughout English, German, and American evangelicalism, Schmucker stated that the Bible was "the only infallible rule of faith and practice." No stronger repudiation of a full-bodied confessionalism would be heard within mid-nineteenth-century American Lutheran circles.

Further evidence of the disparity between Krauth and Schmucker could be seen in Schmucker's position on the nature of the church. Characterizing as "Puseyite" any corporate conception of the church, Schmucker flatly stated that every church is but a "collection" of professed believers. The controversy between Schmucker and Krauth recapitulated, admittedly at a less sophisticated level, the debate between Friedrich Schleiermacher and Friedrich Julius Stahl. Once again, views of the church as a voluntary association competed with those of the church as a divine institution. As far as Schmucker was concerned, however, the very fact that Schleiermacher and Stahl's debate dealt with the German church suggested its inappropriateness as a theoretical template for the American situation. "We claim that the American Lutheran Church is a *free, integral, independent* part of the church of Christ," Schmucker said. Referring to ideas contained in his *Fraternal Appeal*

---

[24]Schmucker, *The American Lutheran Church* (Springfield, 1851) 67-69, 158.

[25]Ibid., 237-44.

of 1838, he suggested that geographic distinctions were the only legitimate ones within the communion of faith. Just as there existed a Danish or German Lutheran church, why could there not be an American one?[26]

One of the distinctive aspects of the American church, Schmucker said, was the prevalence of revivals and "gracious showers of divine influence . . . refreshing one or another parts of the vineyards of the Lord." Schmucker's contention that revivals were unique to America was erroneous; but he was astute in sensing their importance for mid-century American Lutheranism. Benjamin Kurtz, an ardent supporter of "American Lutheranism," wrote in 1843 that the anxious bench was "the archimedian lever which with the help of God can raise our German church to that position of authority in the religious world which is its rightful due." Krauth, however, never accepted the instrumental view of conversion accompanying new-measures revivalism nor did he accept its pragmatic justification. Here, too, the two parties confronted each other over an ever-widening chasm of theological interpretation and homiletic predisposition. The controversy became so heated that when Kurtz attacked the *Evangelical Review*'s editorial policy, one of its supporters retorted that unfortunately there existed a large group within the Lutheran church

> who have no knowledge of her history, no sympathy with her doctrines, no idea of her true character, and whose whole conception of the church is that of a kind of mongrel Methodistic Presbyterianism, and of this party Drs S.S. Schmucker and Kurtz are the coryphae.[27]

This increasingly hostile factionalism was resolved in 1855. In that year an anonymous pamphlet entitled, "The Definite Synodical Platform" appeared, its authors recommending that it be studied and adopted. Despite its anonymity, the pamphlet's demand that the Augsburg Confession be revised and other confessional statements eliminated marked it as Schmucker's work. He soon acknowl-

---

[26]Ibid., 192, 233.

[27]Ibid., 235; Kurtz, *The Lutheran Observer*, 17 November 1843; Wentz, *Gettysburg*, 165; for the supporters of Schmucker's position see Vergilius Ferm, *The Crisis in American Lutheran Theology* (New York, 1927) 151-62.

edged his authorship. As a tactic for garnering support for "American Lutheranism," the "Platform" was a fiasco: it was repudiated in nearly all synods. Krauth told his son, "The American Recension of the Augsburg Confession doesn't seem to go down well. A more stupid thing could hardly have been originated, taking the standpoint of its projectors. *Quem Deus vult perdere prius dementat.* How will it end?" In February 1856 Krauth published a review of the "Platform" in the *Lutheran Observer.* He found it shallow in its theological perspective, confused in its claims, and sectarian in its spirit.[28]

Given the differences between himself and Schmucker, Krauth's review was evenhanded and fair. This same spirit of moderation was demonstrated in 1856 when a group of approximately thirty ministers, with Schmucker's consent and led by Krauth, composed the "Pacific Overture." This document was the object of some further wrangling but its publication represented a truce between the two sides, one in which the advocates of "American Lutheranism" had suffered almost total defeat. In 1857 Schmucker was almost impeached, and his influence was severely diminished. Kurtz, for his part, bolted from the Maryland Synod and organized the new Melanchthon Synod, which then lasted another eleven years. For the moment, it appeared that historical confessionalism ruled within the General Synod of the Lutheran church. Soon, however, Lutheranism, like the nation itself, would be rent by the slavery issue and the seminary at Gettysburg barraged by mortar shells and infantrymen instead of manifestos and divines.[29]

MERCERSBURG AND PRINCETON

In 1851 Charles Krauth reviewed a book by Philip Schaff. Schaff was a professor of church history in the seminary of the sister denomination of the German Reformed church located at nearby Mercersburg, Pennsylvania. Krauth praised the church historian, claiming that Schaff's volume of historical studies "will reflect last-

[28]Wentz, *Basic History,* 142; Krauth's letter and article are quoted in Spaeth, *Krauth,* 1:372-73.

[29]Wentz, *Gettysburg,* 170; Wentz, *Basic History,* 143.

ing credit on the author, and exert beneficial influences on the Church of Jesus Christ."[30] Schaff, along with his colleague, John Nevin, produced one of the most original and sophisticated nine-teenth-century American presentations of the "church question."

Yet the Reformed tradition in America had always maintained some degree of confessional consciousness. The tradition of a learned ministry based on English and Continental confessions of faith distinguished Presbyterian, German, and Dutch Calvinists alike. Moreover, the strength of this commitment had been attested to during the First Great Awakening when the demand for an emphasis on a heartfelt religion had split the Presbyterian church apart. After the split, first Princeton College under John Witherspoon and later Princeton Seminary under Archibald Alexander became bastions of Presbyterian orthodoxy. Consequently, when the Second Great Awakening arose and in 1837, the Presbyterian church again divided into Old and New School parties, the Presbyterian confessionalists were quite willing to let their errant brethren go in peace.[31]

If America was seen as the land of emotionalism and revivalism, there were still intellectual and cultural resources confessionalists could draw upon. Such resources were not only available, they were rich in nature and diverse in origin. For where the theologians of Mercersburg acknowledged their debt to German and Continental theological scholarship, the faculty at Princeton Seminary were guided by the scholastic orthodoxy of François Turretin and the pronouncements of the Scottish common sense philosophers. These two seminaries and these two intellectual heritages richly infused early nineteenth-century American theology with theological erudition.

Schaff arrived at Mercersburg in 1844. For the next ten years he actively collaborated with Nevin. Their association together lasted even longer. The significance of their work for the present study

---

[30]Charles Krauth, "Review of Schaff's *Geschichte der Apostolischen Kirche*," *Evangelical Review* 3 (July 1851): 107-108.

[31]See the discussion by Leonard Trinterud, *The Forming of an American Tradition* (Philadelphia, 1949).

rests on their ecclesiological thought; however, the Mercersburg theologians contributed to debates on eucharistic and liturgical questions as well.[32]

The blend of ecumenical theology that came out of Mercersburg drew upon Anglo-American as well as German sources and reflected a sophisticated appraisal of pietist and confessional themes. The comprehensive nature of this perspective was a result of the varied backgrounds Nevin and Schaff brought to their work.

John Williamson Nevin was born at Herron's Branch, near Shippensburg, Pennsylvania, on 20 February 1803. His family was Presbyterian Scotch-Irish. After a quiet childhood, Nevin, in 1817, attended Union College in Schenectady, New York. There he experienced a religious conversion during one of Asahel Nettleton's revival sessions. In 1823, two years after he had graduated from Union, Nevin enrolled for ministerial preparation at Princeton Seminary. Nevin remembered his days at Princeton as "the most pleasant part of my life." He studied under Archibald Alexander, Samuel Miller, and Charles Hodge; in 1826 he replaced Charles Hodge for two years as an instructor in Eastern languages, while Hodge was in Europe.[33]

When Hodge returned in 1828 Nevin was out of a job. His prospects were not entirely bleak, however. He had been taken under the care of Carlisle Presbytery and had also come to the attention of the directors of the soon-to-open Western Theological Seminary at Pittsburgh. In October 1828, Nevin passed the necessary examina-

[32]For a discussion of the Mercersburg theology as a whole, see James H. Nichols, *Romanticism in American Theology* (Chicago, 1961); George Richards, "The Mercersburg Theology Historically Considered," *Papers of the American Society on Church History* (1911): 119-49; "The Mercersburg Theology—Its Purpose and Principles," *Church History* 20, no. 3 (September 1931): 42-55; Luther Binkley, *The Mercersburg Theology* (Lancaster, 1953); Robert Clemmer, "Historical Transcendentalism in Pennsylvania," *Journal of the History of Ideas* 30, no. 4 (October-December 1969): 579-92; Sydney E. Ahlstrom, *A Religious History of the American People* (New Haven, 1972) 615-21; Kenneth M. Plummer, "The Theology of John Williamson Nevin in the Mercersburg Period, 1840-1852" (Ph.D. diss., University of Chicago, 1958); Verlyn Barker, "John W. Nevin: His Place in American Intellectual Thought" (Ph.D. diss., St. Louis University, 1970).

[33]Nevin, *My Own Life: The Earlier Years* (Lancaster, 1964) 2, 7, 9, 20.

tions and was licensed to preach. That same year he was notified that Western Seminary wanted him to assume its chair in Biblical literature. Financial difficulties prevented the seminary from operating for more than a year; thus it was not until 1830 that Nevin began his work.[34] Nevin spent ten years at Western Theological Seminary before moving to Mercersburg. During those ten years, he would discover German theology and philosophy and would plant the seeds that so fruitfully would sprout at Mercersburg. During Nevin's decade at Western, however, he was known as much for his outspoken positions on moral reform causes as he was for those on theology. In 1833 and 1834 he edited *The Friend*, a literary and moral weekly journal, which was intended "to be a Christian agency set openly and boldly for the defence of all Christian virtues, on the outside of all religious denominationalism strictly so called." Stating that "patriotism and piety" shared a common foundation, Nevin duplicated the efforts of scores of other American and European evangelicals. Confident that converted Christians had the power to make the world over in their image, Nevin, adhering to his concept of piety, led crusades for temperance and against "infidelity, fashionable amusements, ladies' fairs, theatrical entertainments, and other such objects."[35]

Nevin's stance and his paper were unpopular in Pittsburgh. The most disliked of his unpopular moral views was his belief that slavery should be abolished. At first, Nevin had agreed with the proponents of colonization, but by 1834 he had decided that only total abolition of slavery would eradicate this moral evil. Nevin's abolitionism was the kind that intuitively viewed slavery as a sin and, however ambiguously, strove to bring about its end. Nevin disapproved of William Lloyd Garrison but praised the abolitionist students at Lane Seminary. His writings earned him a reputation as "the most dangerous man in Pittsburgh," and cost his paper its financial support. In casting the slavery issue as a moral cause and in opposing alcohol and theater on religious grounds, Nevin displayed the familiar trademark of the evangelical moral reformer. That he

[34] Ibid., 29.

[35] Ibid., 82-84.

was later able to describe American evangelical theology so accurately rests in part on his familiarity with its experiential basis and moral appeal.[36]

In 1837 one of Nevin's colleagues at Western Seminary retired, and Nevin took over his courses on church history. The added class load plus his own work in biblical exegesis persuaded Nevin to learn to read German. Symbolically at least, German was the key that opened up new vistas for Nevin and directed him away from his previous evangelical upbringing. As he dug further into ecclesiastical history, Nevin credited August Neander, "the vastly learned and profoundly pious Neander," with providing order and meaning and method to the study of history. "His magic wand served to bring up the dead past before me in the form of a living present," Nevin said. Nevin and Schaff's new historical awareness, beyond all else, would color the Mercersburg theology.[37]

In 1840 Nevin was invited to be a professor of theology in the Seminary of the German Reformed Church at Mercersburg. For the Scotch-Irish, Princeton-trained Nevin, the invitation came as a complete surprise. Archibald Alexander of Princeton supported Nevin in the move, seeing it as a transition from one section of the Reformed tradition to another. For their part, the German Reformed officials acquired in Nevin a scholar probably as well versed in current German theological developments as any other American-born candidate for the job. Nevin joined Friedrich A. Rauch, formerly of Giessen and Heidelberg, whose new book, *Psychology*, was one of the first English presentations in America of Hegelian philosophy. Rauch was impressed with Nevin, describing him some months after his arrival at Mercersburg, as one "whose talents and learning and scientific spirit are not equalled by *any one* in this country. I say this with deliberation and coolness."[38]

---

[36]Ibid., 89-95; David Brion Davis, "The Emergence of Immediatism in British and American Antislavery Thought," *Mississippi Valley Historical Review* 49 (September 1962): 209-30.

[37]Nevin, *My Own Life*, 139-41.

[38]Rauch is quoted by J. H. Dubbs, *History of the Reformed Church, German* (New York, 1894) 366. For a general discussion of Rauch and of Nevin's call to Mercersburg, see 357-67.

The envisioned collaboration between Nevin and Rauch did not
occur: Rauch unexpectedly died in March 1841. Nevin assumed
Rauch's teaching duties until 1844. In 1843 the Synod of the German Reformed Church sent a delegation to Germany seeking a replacement for Rauch. The committee hoped to attract Friedrich
Wilhelm Krummacher, the well-known Reformed preacher at Elberfeld in the lower Rhine area of Germany. Krummacher, however,
declined the offer. The committee then consulted with other German theologians, including August Neander, Julius Müller, E. W.
Hengstenberg, and Krummacher, for an alternative candidate. The
name of Philip Schaff, a young teacher and recent graduate of the
University of Berlin was suggested repeatedly. Shortly before its return to America, the delegation offered the Mercersburg position to
Schaff.[39]

Philip Schaff was born on 1 January 1819 at Chur, Switzerland.
As a youngster Schaff was sent to Germany for his primary education and attended the *gymnasium* in Stuttgart. There he drank
deeply of the pietistic strain of the Württemberg *Erweckungsbewegung*, reminiscing years later, "to Württemberg, I owe, under God,
my spiritual life and the best part of my education." Graduating
from the *gymnasium* with high marks, Schaff began his university
career in the typically circuitous style of nineteenth-century German students. "I formed an inclination to the academic career during my University course," Schaff wrote, "and was strongly
encouraged in it by my beloved professors, Drs. Schmid in Tübingen, Tholuck and Müller in Halle, Neander, Twesten, and Hengstenberg in Berlin." Schaff's list of professors reads like a *Who's Who*
of nineteenth-century German theologians; his autobiographical
reminiscences indicate further the extent of his theological
education.[40]

---

[39]Dubbs, *Reformed Church*, 371-73.

[40]The quotation is taken from Schaff's unpublished "Autobiographical Reminiscences," Philip Schaff Papers, Evangelical and Reformed Historical Society, Lancaster Theological Seminary, Lancaster, Pennsylvania. In addition to citing the
influence of F. C. Baur at Tübingen, Schaff recounted being introduced to the
widow of G. W. F. Hegel.

I visited her frequently and found her a very estimable and excellent
lady. She was at that time much disturbed by the infidel developments of the

Schaff found that of all his teachers, August Neander was the most inspiring. Like others, Schaff believed that Neander's special combination of piety, learning, and pastoral concern was what most endeared him to his students and colleagues. The beliefs of most of the theological luminaries with whom Schaff associated were inclined towards a pietistic perspective. Indeed, it was through August Tholuck that Schaff upon his arrival was first introduced to the circle of the Berlin pietist, Ernst von Kottwitz. Kottwitz's entourage included Leopold von Gerlach and Ernst Hengstenberg. Schaff quickly became a protégé of Hengstenberg, submitting articles to his journal, the *Evangelische Kirchenzeitung*. When the Americans consulted these Berlin theologians about whom to place in Mercersburg, Schaff naturally came to mind.[41]

Leaving with the blessing of his Berlin professors and mindful of the challenge facing him in America, Schaff accepted the position at Mercersburg. In May 1844 with the benediction of Krummacher still ringing in his ears, Schaff left Elberfeld for his new post. Before crossing the ocean he spent several weeks in England, ten days of which were spent at Oxford. The Tractarian controversy was burning brightly; Schaff recounted an animated interview with E. B. Pusey. "The Reformers are not his pets," Schaff commented, "he misses in them sacred reverence for the church and its commands." Although the two theologians did not resolve their differences, as they discussed ecclesiastical subjects—including apostolic succession, the doctrine of justification by faith, and the meaning of German theology—they departed amicably. Ironically, it would not be long before Philip Schaff was to discover himself indiscriminately lumped together with Pusey and charged with holding views comparable to those of the Anglican priest.[42]

---

left or radical wing of the Hegelian School, especially the *Leben Jesu* of Strauss who claimed at that time to be Hegelian in his philosophical principles. She assured me that her husband was a good Christian and would have abhorred such a work. It is true, she said, she could never prevail on him to go with her to Gosseuer's church, and he would excuse himself by the remark: "Mein liebes Kind, das Denken ist auch Gottesdienst."

[41]Ibid. See chapter 2 for a discussion of the German *Erweckungsbewegung*.

[42]David Schaff, *The Life of Philip Schaff* (New York, 1897) 86-90.

In October 1844 the newly arrived Schaff gave his inaugural lecture, *Das Princip des Protestantismus* before the synodical meeting at Reading, Pennsylvania. Schaff's address outlined a set of ecclesiological themes that were to become characteristic of the Mercersburg theology. In 1845 Schaff revised the piece, and Nevin translated it into English for publication. The first theme Schaff emphasized was the developmental nature of the church, especially as it applied to a correct understanding of Protestantism. As Schaff discussed this concept, he insisted that Christianity itself had been definitively presented in the normative writings of the New Testament. In contrast, the Christian church developed in terms of an organic assimilation and a progressive understanding of the Gospel, "an apprehension always more and more profound of the life and doctrine of Christ and his Apostles." Schaff argued, furthermore, that the Reformation grew out of the Roman Catholic Church of the Middle Ages; and that Protestantism's doctrines of justification by faith and Protestantism's assignation of authoritative status to the canonical scriptures in matters of faith showed it as progressing beyond Catholicism.[43]

Schaff expanded on his concept of historical development by insisting on the importance of tradition as an aid to scriptural interpretation. Noting that tradition appeared within Protestantism in three modes, Schaff affirmed that the status of tradition was always subservient to the Scriptures. Consequently, whether ritual (for example, ancient customs and usages pertaining to order and worship); historical (for example, testimonies of antiquity on the genuineness of the canon); or dogmatic (for example, creedal statements such as the Nicene or Athanasian) tradition, Schaff maintained, held an important hermeneutical place within Protestantism.[44]

Having discussed the historical sources and shape of Protestantism, Schaff turned, second, to the major problems confronting the Protestant church in America. A threefold challenge, he be-

---

[43]Schaff, *The Principle of Protestantism* (1845; reprint, Philadelphia, 1964) 73-76, 80, 98, quotation on page 76.

[44]Ibid., 110-15.

lieved, of political revolution, rationalism, and sectarianism faced the American church. Because revolution was a topic outside his theological concerns Schaff focused on the other two challenges, insisting that they were intimately linked. Their common bond resided in their equally subjective emphasis; where rationalism was "one-sided theoretic subjectivism," sectarianism was "one-sided practical subjectivism." In either case there was a misunderstanding of tradition and Christian history and a lack of proper respect for doctrinal and ecclesiastical authority. Schaff located one of the sources for German rationalism in the pietist tradition of Spener with its "religion of sickly sentiments and sighs, aversions to clear definite conceptions, and to a regularly digested system of theology." Although rationalism later developed away from such pietist influences, in Schaff's view, it never lost that privatist tendency to isolate individual will and reason and to maintain that these provided a sufficient basis for salvation. Sectarianism was but the application of this individualistic emphasis within a context of political and religious liberty. The value of a historically continuous and organically developed perspective was overlooked in the name of a new religious ensemble. For Schaff, this situation was deplorable. He could only conclude, "The sect system, like rationalism, is a prostitution and caricature of true Protestantism, and nothing else."[45]

The third theme Schaff articulated dealt with the remedy for this subjective malady. In developing his answer Schaff remarked that he "looked upon Puseyism as *an entirely legitimate and necessary reaction against rationalistic and sectaristic pseudo-Protestantism.*" The Oxford movement, with its respect for the past, Schaff believed, strove for a realization of the universal church as Schaff did. But the Oxford movement had its faults: the most damaging was its failure to appreciate the value of the Reformation and to incorporate its ideas into the Tractarian historical theology. In contrast to the Tractarians, Schaff called for a "Protestant Catholicism," which would be truly catholic, truly historical, and truly progressive. Asserting that "every single religious truth belongs to a great organically constituted whole," Schaff envisioned a reconciliation of sectarian and

[45]Ibid., 129-31, 136, 140, 153.

church supporters and hoped that they would cooperate in creating a new state of church life.[46]

While discussing his proposed development in the spiritual life of Protestantism, Schaff provided an intriguing analysis of the Prussian Union. Connected with Hengstenberg's circle in Berlin, Schaff was familiar with the various disputes over the Union and the liturgy. When speaking to this American audience, he characterized the Prussian Union as "a great step gained toward the catholicity and unity necessarily involved in the idea of the church itself." He did not totally approve, however, and followed up his admiring remarks by observing:

> The stiff, absolute Old-Lutheranism of Prussia and Bavaria may be considered indeed a salutary reaction against the indifference of many of the friends of the union to doctrines; and in this view we are glad to find its representatives in this country also. But apart from this particular advantage, it is certainly a crying, stubborn misapprehension of the wants of our time, which reach far beyond its narrow horizon.[47]

At once sympathetic to unionist endeavors and critical of indifference to essential theological doctrine, Schaff had a complex and synthetic ecumenical vision. Indeed, Schaff's life work, even beyond his tenure at Mercersburg, would be to articulate fully the meaning and shape of his wide-ranging vision.

Concluding his essay, Schaff wrote that he hoped "to see our Protestant Zion conducted safely out of the Babylonish captivity of sectarianism and faction, without being carried to old Rome or young Oxford." Almost immediately after he finished his address though, Schaff discovered that some members of the synod feared that he was actually an agent of the enemy and not an apostle of the true faith. In October 1845, both Schaff and Nevin were subjected to an investigation of their theological orthodoxy. Nevin had done more than translate Schaff's piece; he had added an introduction and an appendix of his own. Thus he insisted upon standing with Schaff in any inquiry. Although the investigation was not formally an ecclesiastical trial for heresy, opponents of the Mercersburg theo-

---

[46]Ibid., 158-60, 172, 185.

[47]Ibid., 194.

logians, led by Joseph Berg, argued that Schaff's address showed "Romanizing tendencies." Berg and his fellow critics believed that Schaff and Nevin's linking of the Reformation to the medieval church and their appreciation of certain Tractarian contributions were erroneous. The outcome of the four-day session, however, was that Schaff and Nevin were completely vindicated. With this episode behind them they returned to Mercersburg.[48]

"I think I could not have a better colleague than Dr. Nevin," Schaff wrote in his journal shortly after his arrival. "I feared I might not find any sympathy in him for my views of the church; but I discovered that he occupies essentially the same ground that I do and confirms me in my position. He is filled with the ideas of German theology."[49] That Schaff and Nevin met was indeed fortunate. Their synchronism was no better demonstrated than in a series of essays, sermons, and books Nevin wrote between 1843 and 1848. One of Nevin's best-known pieces was his attack on new-measures revivalism entitled, *The Anxious Bench*. First published in 1843 and expanded in 1844 for a second edition, *The Anxious Bench* was a thorough critique of the psychological assumptions and theological pretensions of popular American revivalism. Nevin took the anxious bench as a symbol of the whole system of new-measures revivalism, remarking that his purpose was to depict the deleterious effects of such devices and thus discourage the German Reformed churches from using them. Nevin refused to concede that popularity or apparent success were legitimate criteria for evaluation. He countered:

> One thing is most certain. Spurious revivals are common, and as the fruit of them false conversions lamentably abound. An Anxious Bench may be crowded where no divine influence whatever is felt. A whole Congregation may be moved with excitement, and yet be losing at the very time more than is gained in a religious point of view. Hundreds may be carried *through* the process of anxious bench conversion, and yet their last state may be worse than the first. It will not do to point us to immediate visible effects, to ap-

[48]See Schaff, *Life of Philip Schaff*, 118-20 for a description of the proceedings.
[49]Ibid., 103.

pearances on the spot or to glowing reports struck off from some heated imagination immediately after.[50]

The problem, as many other critics of new-measures revivalism insisted, was that such revivalist techniques tended to foster a false sense of assurance and thus to foster invalid conversions. Individual believers, rather than focusing upon true repentance and examining their lives, were accepting the surrogate journey to the anxious bench; at least so claimed their critics. Nevin thought these sinners were being duped, and Christianity cheapened. He believed there would be additional damage if sober preaching and earnest catechistic instruction was replaced with the flashy theatrics of revivalism. Hence, the final section of Nevin's tract gave a short presentation of the "system of catechism" versus the "system of the bench." In contrasting the two, Nevin again highlighted the latter's inadequacies.

In *The Anxious Bench* Nevin had criticized the subjectivity of American revivalism in a manner sympathetic to Schaff's criticism of rationalism and sectarianism. In 1845, Nevin further demonstrated his theological compatibility with Schaff by appending one of his (Nevin's) sermons to the translation of *Princip des Protestantismus*. The sermon was entitled, "Catholic Unity," and had been delivered in 1844, shortly after Schaff's arrival. In it, Nevin spoke of "the holy Catholic Church." As he expanded upon this topic, it was clear he had independently arrived at points of analysis similar to those of Schaff. Nevin's discussion of unity displayed a twofold nature. On one hand, it represented a comprehension of different confessional positions within the church. On the other hand, it represented a mystical union between individual believers and the person of Jesus as the bond of a new spiritual life sanctified in faith. In both cases, external and internal features could be observed, yet it was this incarnate aspect that was the essence of the various relationships.[51]

---

[50]Nevin, *The Anxious Bench* (Chambersburg, 1843) 13; Theodore Appel, *The Life of John Williamson Nevin* (Philadelphia, 1889) 158-62.

[51]Nevin, "Catholic Unity," originally published as an appendix to *The Principal of Protestantism*, now reprinted in *The Mercersburg Theology*, ed. James H. Nichols (New York, 1966) 36-39.

Nevin next insisted that the church represented the eternal organic unity of Christians. Nevin's explanation of this claim further resonated with Schaff and with those German theologians who viewed the church as an *anstalt*. "The Church is not a mere aggregation or collection of different individuals, drawn together by similarity of interests and wants," Nevin argued,

> and not an abstraction simply, by which the common in the midst of such multifarious distinction is separated and put together under a single general term. It is not merely the *all* that covers the actual extent of its membership, but the *whole*, rather; in which this membership is comprehended and determined from the beginning. The Church does not rest upon its members, but the members rest upon the Church.

As he developed these organic themes, Nevin charged that an individualistic understanding of faith or of Christianity (which in this case would mean sectarianism) amounted to a "moral solecism that necessarily destroys itself."[52]

Here was an analysis of the malady of subjectivity, in terms similar to Schaff's though not identical. Interestingly, Nevin did speak harshly of sectarianism and rationalism though these movements did not figure prominently in his analysis. Of greater importance was Nevin's examination of the nature and possibility of catholic unity. He first excoriated the "pretensions" of Roman Catholicism and the "dreams" of unity High-Church Episcopalians had. Similarly, he disapproved of mere outward reform movement—an external "no-sect party," for instance—that would renounce allegiance to all confessional resources and guides. Confessional adherence should not be diminished. "The union of the Church," this seer of ecumenism proclaimed, "is not to be established by stratagem or force." Indeed, there was at present no easy lead to follow, no simple solution to adopt. Instead, Christians were "to consider and lay to heart the end state of the Church . . . for an immense object would be gained, if simply the conviction of deep and radical defect here were made to fasten itself upon the general consciousness of the Church." Even an understanding that the Church had shortcomings, Nevin believed, would be an advance for the cause. Nevin's

---

[52]Ibid., 40-41.

perspective on the church with its network of subsidiary points concerning revivalism, the dispensation of grace, and the nature of the mystical presence of Christ, represented a clear break with his evangelical past. Likewise, the similarity between his programmatic analysis of church unity and his earlier abolitionism was striking. In each case, he demonstrated an intuitive awareness of evil; in each case, he believed that publicly confronting this evil was the best action to take.[53]

A third essay, written by Nevin in 1848 and entitled *Antichrist: or the Spirit of Sect and Schism*, proved further Nevin's allegiance to Schaff's historical and theological program. Nevin began by assessing his debt to German theology. Basically, he was answering criticisms by his former teacher, Charles Hodge, that he had introduced the "cast-off clothes" of German mystics and theologians—above all, of Friedrich Schleiermacher—into American theology in an erroneous and unintelligible fashion. Nevin responded to these charges by saying that although he highly esteemed Schleiermacher, he maintained a critical distance from him. "I am a debtor then, with lasting gratitude," Nevin wrote, "both to the English and Germans, both to Princeton and Berlin." If those statements were true, it was still evident that the German influence was growing. As Nevin discussed the organic nature of Christianity, reiterated that sectarianism was a threat, and suggested a proper remedy to sectarianism, he evidenced the lengthening distance between his beliefs and the scholasticism of Princeton.[54]

Nevin also wrote of his view concerning the organic—experiential as opposed to ritual—union between the individual and Jesus. It was a view he had first articulated in his sermon on "Catholic Unity" and later expanded in his treatise on the Eucharist, *The Mystical Presence*. Now he discussed it in even greater detail. Arguing that Christianity was neither a set of doctrines nor a code of laws,

---

[53]Ibid., 45, 47; Plummer, "The Theology of Nevin," 97, 147.

[54]Hodge, *Princeton Review* 20 (April 1848): 278; Nevin, *The Antichrist* (New York, 1848) 3. See Nevin to J. Harbaugh, 28 July 1847, Nevin Papers, Evangelical and Reformed Historical Society, Lancaster Theological Seminary, Lancaster, Pennsylvania, for his further views on the tract.

Nevin maintained that Christianity's essence lay in the mystical union represented in the real presence of Christ in the Eucharist. This interpretation was significant with regard to a doctrine of the church because it emphasized the experiential nature of the church. This contention echoed earlier statements by both Schaff and Nevin and posed no new themes. What was new in this essay was Nevin's equation of Antichrist (which Nevin had heretofore identified as the papacy) and sectarianism. Consistent with earlier Mercersburg manifestos, Nevin attacked the sectarian spirit for failing to understand the church as *anstalt*—a church complete and eternal. Significantly, Nevin accepted the temporary existence of denominationalism. Both Nevin and Schaff argued that confessionally based denominations such as Lutheran, Reformed, and Protestant Episcopal traditions were legitimate, particularly in contrast to the ahistorical and charismatically based sectarian groups. Dividing those groups may have been bad sociology, but both men regarded it as theologically correct. For these confessional traditions provided a stable historical base from which their ecumenical vision might be actualized.[55]

After discussing his concepts, Nevin again surveyed the current attempts at church union and found them flawed. Where previously Nevin had discussed the "pretensions" of Roman Catholicism, here he confined his remarks to three mistaken Protestant views of church union. The first of these views, exemplified by Alexander Campbell, proposed to scrap all outward denominational structures and return to the New Testament in its alleged pure simplicity. The second, or "liberal," view proposed to form a union based on indifference to confessional traditions. The third view, which Samuel Schmucker supported, proposed a new consensual church, federative in organization and broadly derivative in doctrine. This approach, like that which simply overlooked creedal differences, was inadequate, Nevin believed. Nevin, instead of supporting these concepts, invoked the language of the ancient creeds and called for that catholic church that, if visionary, was based on the "faith in the mystery of one universal historical Church."[56]

---

[55]Nevin, *Antichrist*, 25, 69, 70.

[56]Ibid., 81-90, 92.

By 1848 it was clear that Nevin and Schaff thought alike; their unanimity on several issues was firm. If the Mercersburg theologians were unified, it was due primarily to their mutual indebtedness to romanticism. The three romantic themes that characterized the beliefs of both the neo-Lutherans and the Tractarians—an antipathy to rationalism, a sense of the mysterious in human life, and an organic perspective on historical reality—pertained to the Mercersburg movement. Of course, these aspects also applied to the beliefs of Charles Philip Krauth, but in the Mercersburg movement these romantic features were heightened.

In 1846, for example, Schaff had published as a sequel to his *Principle of Protestantism* a small volume entitled, *What is Church History.* In it Schaff charged that "the great central theme of the Present, around which all religious and theological movements revolve is the *Church Question.*" In America one of the largest obstacles to a proper understanding of the "church question," in Schaff's opinion, was the lack of historically developed thought about the church. After surveying the devastation that earlier rationalist and pietist historians had wrought, Schaff examined modern church history, or "the stand-point of organic development." He lauded the accomplishments of Herder, Schelling, and Hegel—without advocating the theological implications of those accomplishments—and used a series of organic metaphors to describe the process of ecclesiastical and secular history. He pictured the historian's task as one of providing a scientific, comprehensive, and dialectical analysis of the course of church history.

Consequently, Schaff argued for a specifically Hegelian construction of the historical process and invoked the concept of *aufheben* as the key to understanding the nature of organic development.[57] More than anything else, this characteristic emphasis on organicism stamped the Mercersburg theologians as romantic. As the series of theological reflections that they produced from 1844-1846 amply demonstrated, their replacement of a rationalist concept of the church with a visionary, indeed ineffable, concept of

[57]Schaff, *What is Church History* (Philadelphia, 1846) 9-10, 74-75, 85, 89-90.

Protestant Catholicity was grounded on this view of historical development.

The Mercersburg position on ecclesiology was well developed by 1848. For Nevin and Schaff, the years from 1848-1854 marked a time of events rather than a time of intellectual change. In 1848 Schaff began the publication of *Der Deutsche Kirchenfreund*. In 1849 Nevin inaugurated the *Mercersburg Review*. Both of these journals were designed to represent the Mercersburg position. They also allowed their editors more flexibility in commenting on the theological, political, and social issues of the day.

In 1849, for example, Nevin published an article entitled, "The Year 1848; or the American Epoch." Reviewing the last twelve months, Nevin wrote that the world had passed "the Rubicon of a revolution that is destined to turn all its fortunes into a new channel for centuries to come."[58] Although his remarks could be taken as plaudits for the actions of the revolutionaries in France, Germany, and Austria, this was not Nevin's intention. For as he expanded on his theme he betrayed a political philosophy reminiscent of conservative Hegelianism. Characteristically, Nevin reiterated that world history was an organic process, one progressing unevenly but inevitably towards its goal. The tumult of 1848 was caused by the clash between old institutions and new visions—a clash grown from the very nature of historical reality. This conflict signaled the development of a new historical period, a new epoch struggling to be born. Consequently, Nevin accorded no importance to the revolutionary forces, whose spirit "is from beneath rather than from above," except as they figured in the transition to this new historical era. Nevin similarly disapproved of monarchical tyranny.[59]

Nevin believed that this new age or "metempsychosis in the flow of universal history," was already taking shape in America. He scoffed at "the sophomorical style of self-glorification" that had characterized the jingoistic rhetoric of America during the 1840s. Instead, Nevin said, the historical process was working "through the

---

[58]Nevin, "The Year 1848; or the American Epoch," *Mercersburg Review* (January 1849): 5.

[59]Ibid., 39, 19, 20.

medium of American influence," to embody this new development, for

> the historical significance of America thus far, lies mainly in this, that the substance of its life, as it is to be hereafter, is *not* yet fixed, but in the process only of general formation. . . . the nation is ruled indeed by its own independent genius, and carries in itself a certain inward law or type, that may be expected to determine permanently the leading form of its history.[60]

History is neither radical nor traditional but synthetic—that was Nevin's message. As the fervor of the revolutionary experience of 1848 died down, the man who had once been called an "incendiary" for his views on abolition evinced a more public conservatism. Nevin had stopped publicly discussing abolition ever since he had moved to Mercersburg. Similarly, giving a speech in 1850, which was later published, Nevin denounced "Radicalism and Red Republicanism" as disrespectful of authority and seeking of immediate political change. In an article on "The Moral Order of Sex," Nevin lashed out at those "modern Fourierites and Socialists" who sought "what is sometimes styled the *emancipation of women.*" Such attempts, he said, disrupted the natural balance of human life and its spheres of social existence. Not so much forgetful of his historical emphasis as convinced of the error of such social innovations, Nevin charged that these changes severely threatened the bulwark of society, the family. In his declamations, Nevin was echoing those other voices in American culture who were defining the role of women in exclusively domestic terms.[61]

Philip Schaff, unlike Nevin, confined his topical commentary largely to ecclesiastical subjects. Perhaps he did so because he was self-conscious about his immigrant status, especially after the furor his inaugural address had caused. In 1851, for example, in an address entitled *Systematic Benevolence*, Schaff reflected on the particular nature of religious charity and missionary societies in America. Schaff applauded the separation of church and state existing in America and cautioned his audience not to "lust after the flesh-pots

---

[60]Ibid., 17, 21, 22.

[61]Nevin, *Faith, Reverence, and Freedom* (Mercersburg: n.p., 1850); "The Moral Order of Sex," *Mercersburg Review* (November 1850): 554, 559, 560, 569.

of a wealthy State-church." State support too easily degenerated into state control; Schaff's sentiments duplicated those of other confessional adherents in both America and Europe. In addition, Schaff's remarks contained a noticeable, if quiet, plea for a proper confessional basis for such benevolent work as giving charity and missionizing. "We are not only members of a single congregation, but of a confession or denomination," Schaff said, "and through these at the same time members of the whole christian church." Basing his discussion on the premise that the welfare of the individual depends on the welfare of the whole, Schaff said, "individual or personal piety must necessarily enlarge itself into congregational; congregational into denominational, or confessional; denominational, that it may not degenerate into sectarianism or party spirit, into churchly, or in a good sense, catholic piety."[62]

Schaff thus directed a confessional orientation to benevolent activity, yet it was one that fit into the Mercersburg concern for the church as a whole. Indicative of Schaff's ability to accommodate contrasting beliefs was a series of related remarks he made in 1846 concerning the use of German. Arguing that German emigrants must accommodate themselves to the reality of the American situation, Schaff called for the blending of German and English elements in America. In a footnote commentary he took notice of the efforts of Bavarian missionaries in America "under the direction of the Rev. Mr. Loehe." Schaff asserted that although Löhe's belief that German should be used exclusively "deserves every consideration on account of its well-meant object, it rests, however, upon ignorance or wrong apprehension of the state of affairs in this country, and must have directly the opposite effect from that intended." Schaff thus showed himself reconciled with his new homeland, as in later years he was to criticize its chauvinistic and utilitarian ethos.[63]

Mercersburg theologians were concerned with more than the question of language. In 1851 and 1852 John Nevin found himself

---

[62]Schaff, *Systematic Benevolence* (Mercersburg, 1851) 14, 22.

[63]Schaff, *Anglo-Germanism* (Chambersburg, 1846) 16-17. For Schaff's later political and social commentary, see *American Nationality* (Chambersburg, 1856); *Slavery and the Bible* (Chambersburg, 1861).

acutely perplexed. This personal crisis had many sources, some near at hand, others far away. Nevin, like Schaff, had always closely observed European theological and ecclesiastical events. Both, for example, had followed the story of the Oxford movement. They had watched what they regarded as its participants' well-meant but misdirected efforts suffer censure, succession, and ridicule. Nevin believed that the Gorham decision of 1850 had delivered a final and crushing blow to the movement. A series of articles written by Nevin in 1851 appeared to indicate that he too would follow John Newman into the Roman Catholic Church. As Nevin saw it, the present crisis in the Anglican church clearly posed the "heart and core of the Church Question." Sacramental versus private-judgment Protestantism—these were the possibilities. Later that year and into the next Nevin explored the nature of early Christianity. His conclusions seemed to bode an imminent change. Charging that the beliefs of private-judgment Protestants had no relation to Christianity in the second century and were in fact ahistorical, abstract, and subjective, Nevin announced that the anti-Roman strictures of the Anglican Church were groundless.[64]

Nevin's private worries kept pace with his public doubts. In the spring of 1851 he tendered his resignation from the seminary. In October the synod met to consider the matter and refused to accept his resignation. Nevin was touched, but his uncertainties remained. He wrote to a friend that his sympathies toward Roman Catholicism had grown, but he neither felt inwardly certain nor convinced by the current situation within Catholicism that her apostolic claims were true. Once again he tried to resign his professorship: this time, in 1852, it was accepted. Nevin's retirement lasted nine years—until 1861—when he was appointed to the faculty at Franklin and Marshall College. In 1866 he was named president of that institution, a position he retained until his final retirement in 1876. On 6 June 1886, he died.[65]

---

[64]Nevin, "Anglican Crisis," *Mercersburg Review* (July 1851): 362-97; "Early Christianity," *Mercersburg Review* (November 1851): 537-58; "Early Christianity," *Mercersburg Review* (January 1852): 55.

[65]See Nichols, *Romanticism in American Theology*, 207-208; Nevin to J. A. McMaster, 8 June 1852, Brownson Archives, Notre Dame University Library, Notre Dame, Indiana.

With Nevin gone, it fell to Schaff to take over the remaining teaching duties; from late 1851 through the spring of 1853, he was the principal instructor at the seminary. In late 1853, the synod voted him a year's leave of absence, and Schaff returned to Europe. Ever since he had left Germany—ten years before—Schaff had nurtured a fondness for Scotland and England. It was thus to the British Isles that he first went. While in England Schaff met with Robert Isaac Wilberforce and his brother, the bishop of Oxford. He also renewed his acquaintanceship with Pusey and met Baron Christian Bunsen. By February 1854 he was in Germany enjoying reunions with many of his former theology professors and journeying to Berlin to deliver a series of lectures and to receive an honorary doctorate from the university.[66]

Schaff gave three separate lectures while he was in Germany. In 1855, after he had returned to Mercersburg, these lectures were translated and published together under the title *America: a sketch of the political, social, and religious character of the United States of North America*. Although he discussed the whole of the American experience, Schaff's reflections on the implications of America's state of religious affairs are of most interest in the present context. His tone and presentation were pacific and moderate, but his conclusions must have shocked his German listeners. Instead of telling the customary tales of fanatic excess which inevitably arose out of the practices of popular American evangelicalism, Schaff contended that the very future of Christianity lay in America. Employing the same vision of promise, though now shorn of its explicit Hegelian structure, that Nevin had had in 1848, Schaff emphatically told his listeners that America was a land of the future. As Nevin had done, Schaff repudiated the pretensions of advocates of American expansionism. But he concluded: "America seems destined to be the Phenix grave not only of all European nationalities, but also of all European churches and sects, of Protestantism and Romanism."[67]

---

[66]Schaff, *Life of Philip Schaff*, 171-81.

[67]Schaff, *America: a sketch of its political, social, and religious character*, ed. Perry Miller (1855; reprint, Cambridge, 1961) 16, 32, 80-81.

In order to defend his claim, Schaff discussed the two features Europeans typically found most questionable about American religion—voluntaryism and sectarianism. Although Schaff politely refrained from recommending the American model of separation of church and state for Germany, he clearly approved of its operation in the United States. The natural corollary to this legal separation was voluntaryism for the churches. Again, Schaff did not insist that the American situation was problem-free, but he believed that church-state separation was a model that boded well for the future. When he turned to analyzing sectarianism, Schaff reiterated many themes characteristic of the Mercersburg perspective. Sectarianism was still subjectivism and individualism par excellence. As he spoke in Germany—the land of his theological education and spiritual upbringing—on the meaning of sectarianism, Schaff wondered aloud whether "Protestantism constitutionally involves a tendency towards denominationalism and sectarianism, wherever it is not hindered by the secular power." Schaff, in his lectures, could give his audience no definitive answers. He was convinced, however, that the present divisions within Protestantism were temporary and that a transition to a "true Evangelical Catholic Church" was underway. Whether the location of that church was to be in America or in Europe Schaff could not say, but he was certain of the correctness of his synthetic, organic vision. Moderate in tone and comprehensive in scope, this theme of ecumenical catholicity infused the entirety of Mercersburg theology and could be seen in works as early as Schaff's inaugural address.[68]

Schaff returned to Mercersburg in 1855 and resumed teaching. He remained there until 1863, when he moved to New York City. In 1869 he became professor of church history at Union Theological Seminary. He died on 20 October 1893. Throughout their decade of collaboration the Mercersburg theologians had engaged in an active and sometimes acrimonious debate with their fellow American Protestant theologians. Two reviews, which appeared in 1854 while Schaff was in Europe, of the English translation of Schaff's *History of the Apostolic Church* demonstrated the criticism the Mercersburg

---

[68]Ibid., 75-76, 78, 96-100, 101.

theologians often received. "Dr. Schaff's theory of historical Christianity is thoroughly Papal in all its essential features and tendencies," wrote the Dutch Reformed minister, John Proudfit. Proudfit was one of the bitterest critics of the Mercersburg movement and his vitriolic assessment of Schaff's work was typical.[69]

Equally distressed though more moderate in tone was the review by Charles Hodge of Princeton Seminary. The relationship between Princeton and Mercersburg was an intriguing one, built on personal acquaintance, equal devotion to scholarship, and mutual distance from new-measures revivalism. It was Hodge's decision to go to Europe in 1826 that provided John Nevin with the opportunity to teach at Princeton. Archibald Alexander wrote glowing reports to Hodge, assuring him that "Mr. Nevin fills his place with dignity and propriety, and is very acceptable to the students." Hodge must have found that news pleasant for he found Germany very disconcerting. He had befriended August Tholuck, and through him met many distinguished theologians such as Neander, Hengstenberg, and Otto von Gerlach. Yet as he confided to his mentor, Alexander, "philosophy is utterly beyond the grasp of common english understanding, that *esse*, and, *non esse*, are identical, altho' rather a startling proposition, is here so evident that it forms the first sentence of Hegel's *Logic*."[70]

Hodge soon returned to the familiar surroundings of Princeton. The gulf he described that lay between his own intellectual background and the radically different perspective he found in Germany was indeed a wide one. It was because of this difference in perspective that the first major difference between Hodge and the Mercersburg theologians arose. In his review of Schaff's *Principle of Protestantism*, Hodge's final sentence blessed the author for his "evangelical character" and "seriousness and warmth of feeling." Before he did so, however, Hodge complained of the volume's ob-

---

[69]Proudfit, *New Brunswick Review* (May 1854): 8.

[70]See the manuscript journal of Hodge's European trip, Hodge Papers, Princeton Theological Seminary, Princeton, New Jersey; Archibald Alexander to Charles Hodge, 25 December 1826, Hodge Papers, Princeton University Library, Princeton, New Jersey; Charles Hodge to A. Alexander, 19 September 1827, Hodge Papers, Princeton University Library.

scurity. "The book is thoroughly German, the mode of thinking, and the forms of expression are so unenglish, that it is not easy for an American to enter into the views of the author." The chasm separating Princeton and Mercersburg was not simply a linguistic one but a deeper philosophical one. As heavily indebted to organic and romantic philosophical concepts as Mercersburg was, so too was Princeton dependent upon scholastic and Scottish common-sense traditions.[71]

This dispute could be seen in the differing theories of the church espoused at Princeton and Mercersburg and in Hodge's review of 1854. Hodge, like Nevin, Schaff, and Charles Philip Krauth, insisted that confessional standards must be adhered to; he was thus in some sense a distinctly confessional theologian. In 1836 he had written, "No such thing exists on the face of the earth as Christianity in the abstract . . . . Every man you see is either an Episcopalian or a Methodist, a Presbyterian or an Independent, an Arminian or a Calvinist; no one is a Christian in general." Hodge thus stood with those who favored a clear denominational basis for any foreign or domestic missionary work. He also supported the split within the Presbyterian church in 1837 as a move toward strengthening and reaffirming the Westminster Confession as the true basis of the Presbyterian church. Hodge's fundamental departure from the Mercersburg style of confessionalism arose over the issue of historical development. Hodge believed, as he had shown in his 1854 review and elsewhere, that Christian doctrine has been revealed definitively in the Bible. All major controversies had been settled by the fifth century and had received their authoritative interpretation in the scholastic formularies of François Turretin. To Hodge, organic categories of development had stopped at the Reformation. Moreover, the bond holding the visible church together was the elec-

---

[71]Hodge, *Princeton Review* 17 (October 1845): 636. For a general discussion of Scottish common-sense philosophy, see Torgny Segerstedt, *The Problem of Knowledge in Scottish Philosophy* (Lund, 1935); Wilson Smith, *Professors and Public Ethics* (New York, 1956); D. H. Meyer, *The Instrumental Conscience* (Philadelphia, 1972); Theodore D. Bozeman, *Protestants in an Age of Science* (Chapel Hill, 1977); Sydney E. Ahlstrom, "The Scottish Philosophy and American Theology," *Church History* 25, no.3 (September 1955): 257-72.

tion of its constituent saints. The true church was thus an aggregate of individuals, and the Mercersburg construction mediated the individual through the church rather than emphasizing the availability of direct access to Jesus. This was an interpretation overtly papist in Hodge's view, and he was quick to denounce it.[72]

HIGH CHURCH EPISCOPALIANISM

Charges of popery and deviation from Protestant truth were also levied against the Protestant Episcopal church in America. A revived High Church movement had developed first under the auspices of Bishops John Henry Hobart, Theodore Dehon, and John Stark Ravenscroft, and later in response to the Oxford movement in England. This American High Church perspective within the Protestant Episcopal Church contained both indigenous roots and imported graftings. Because it was hybrid, it responded more moderately than its English counterpart did to the criticism that it supported Anglo-Catholic beliefs and might secede to Rome.

John Henry Hobart was born in Philadelphia on 14 September 1775. He attended a local academy in Philadelphia and later studied at the University of Pennsylvania, from which he was graduated in 1793. From there he moved to New Jersey and took up further studies at Princeton under the aegis of John Witherspoon and Stanhope Smith. Although he tutored at Princeton, Hobart declined further advancement within the Presbyterian-dominated school and instead took up work in an Episcopal parish in nearby New Brunswick. He soon left for a church at Hempstead, Long Island. In 1801, he was finally ordained and appointed assistant minister at Trinity

---

[72]Hodge, *Princeton Review* 8 (July 1836): 430; Hodge, *Constitutional History*, 9; Hodge, *Princeton Review* 26 (January 1854): 148-92. For further discussion of Hodge's theology, and especially his ecclesiology, see Leonard Trinterud, "Charles Hodge," in *Sons of the Prophets*, ed. Hugh Kerr (Princeton, 1963) 22-38; James Nichols, "John Williamson Nevin," in *Sons of the Prophets*, 76-77; Ernest Sandeen, "The Princeton Theology," *Church History* 31, no. 2 (September 1962): 307-21; A. A. Hodge, *The Life of Charles Hodge* (New York, 1880); John J. Deifell, Jr., "The Ecclesiology of Charles Hodge" (Ph.D. diss., University of Edinburgh, 1969); John O. Nelson, "The Rise of the Princeton Theology" (Ph.D. diss., Yale University, 1935).

Church in New York City.[73] Hobart prospered at Trinity and was elected as assistant bishop of the diocese in 1811. His consecration in May 1811 was particularly auspicious, for Alexander Griswold was consecrated as Bishop of the Eastern Diocese alongside him. Griswold was a committed evangelical. The administrations of the high churchman Hobart and the evangelical Griswold were to cause the Episcopal church to recover from the confusion and lethargy of its post-Revolution existence.

The basis for Hobart's High Church theology, which emphasized apostolic authority and the divine foundation of the church, can be found in his youth and ministerial apprenticeship. The diocese of Pennsylvania reflected the low doctrinal standards of the day in its decision to accept a revised Book of Common Prayer in 1785. This revised edition expunged the Athanasian and Nicene Creeds, rewrote the Apostles' Creed, and reduced various aspects of the liturgy. From Pennsylvania, Hobart journeyed to Presbyterian Princeton; there he was frequently called upon to defend the correctness of episcopacy. Defending himself from these influences, Hobart developed a theology more aligned with the High Church views of Samuel Seabury and Thomas Chandler.[74] Hobart took as his motto, "Evangelical Truth and Apostolic Order," and his theology was steeped in the tradition of the nonjuring bishops with their claim to apostolic authority. He emphasized the external commission of the church as well as its inward vitality; and insisted that the three ministerial orders of deacons, priests, and bishops were warranted by Scripture, apostolic appointment, and historic tradition. Significantly, Hobart applauded the Reformation legacy, venerating the martyrdom of Latimer, Ridley, and Cranmer and calling the Church of England, "the glory of the reformed Churches."[75]

---

[73]For biographical information on Hobart, see J. F. Schroeder, *Memorial of Bishop Hobart* (New York, 1831); J. McVicker, *Early Years of the Late Bishop Hobart* (New York, 1834), *Professional Years of Bishop Hobart* (New York, 1836); and the biographical sketch in *The Correspondence of John Henry Hobart*, in *Archives of the General Convention*, ed. Arthur Lowndes, 6 vols. (New York, 1911-1912) 1:xcix-cxix.

[74]George DeMille, *The Catholic Movement in the American Episcopal Church* (Philadelphia, 1950) 6, 17-18.

[75]Hobart, *Apology for Apostolic Order* (New York, 1807) 272; *The Origins, the General Character, and the Present Situation of the Protestant Episcopal Church in the United States of America* (Philadelphia, 1814) 27, 12.

In "The Churchmen," an essay published in 1819, Hobart further demonstrated his views. He castigated the contemporary doctrinal laxity that emphasized sincerity of intention as the standard of truth and caused an "age of liberality" to become an "age of indifference." Fighting this perceived laxity, Hobart called upon all true churchmen to vindicate the "distinctive principles of their Church." The Episcopal church in America, by adhering to confessional and apostolic standards, could avoid both the errors of Roman Catholicism and the errors of Protestantism. Because Hobart believed that auricular confessions and private absolutions were "an encroachment on the rights of conscience, an invasion of the prerogative of the Searcher of Hearts," he found no attraction in Roman Catholic practices. Similarly, where earlier he had acknowledged that the evangelical testimony of a real message of salvation was important, Hobart reiterated that the church was a divinely constituted society whose rites should be observed and whose authority should be scrupulously obeyed. Neither the impulse toward enthusiastic fervor nor toward private judgment should be succumbed to: only liturgy and apostolically grounded canonical decisions provided a true path for the righteous.[76]

Theodore Dehon of South Carolina and John Ravenscroft of North Carolina also provided active leadership and strong voices on behalf of High Church principles. Although Theodore Dehon's name is closely associated with the church in the South, he was actually born in Boston in 1776 of French immigrant parents. Dehon graduated from Harvard in 1795. Two years later Bishop Edward Bass ordained him deacon, and Trinity Church in Newport, Rhode Island, elected him rector. In 1800 Bass ordained Dehon as priest, and in 1812 Dehon was elected the second bishop of South Carolina.[77]

In his annual address to the diocesan convention in 1815, Dehon happily reported that doctrinal purity, liturgical correctness, and unity in faith could be found in South Carolina. Dehon was an accomplished preacher, and these three attributes figured often in his

---

[76]Hobart, *The Churchman* (New York, 1819) 4-5, 7, 14, 26-28.

[77]For biographical information on Dehon see C. E. Gadsen, *An Essay on the Life of the Right Reverend Theodore Dehon* (Charleston, 1833).

pastoral charges and sermons. Conversely, he rarely hesitated to chastise those who failed to uphold these standards. Invoking the primitive origins of the Episcopalian liturgy, Dehon denounced proponents of liturgical revision as persons too much influenced by "the whims, and errors, and dangerous speculations of innovating ages and restless men." He characteristically noted that the safeguards of the episcopacy structure discouraged the possibility for liturgical change. "Where, indeed, would be the unity and integrity, the soundness and beauty of our service," Dehon wrote, "if every individual could alter it to suit his fancy, or the fancies of others."[78]

Like Hobart and Dehon, John Ravenscroft was a champion of institutional episcopal authority. But Ravenscroft arrived at his beliefs slowly. Meanwhile, his life had the kind of drama biographers love. Born in 1772 in Prince George County, Virginia, Ravenscroft was the eldest son of a well-to-do Southern family. The Ravenscrofts moved to Scotland when John was less than a year old, and he spent his first seventeen years living in the Highlands. Upon his return to Virginia, Ravenscroft entered William and Mary College to study law. Not only his choice of profession but his life-style made the future first bishop of North Carolina an unlikely candidate for the ministry. As Ravenscroft admitted, "from the year 1792 to the year 1810, I was not present at any place of public worship more than six or seven times, and then not from choice, but from some accidental accommodation to propriety, in surrendering to the opinion of others." He also admitted to a fierce temper and a salty vocabulary, and many of his classmates knew him by his nickname, "Mad Jack."[79]

In 1810, after a conversion experience, Ravenscroft's life abruptly changed, and he joined first the Republican Methodists and later the Episcopal church. The issue of ministerial authority was the basis for his dissatisfaction with the Republican Methodists. He became convinced that the Gospel would "never be thrown out into the world to be scrambled for, and picked up by whosoever

[78]Ibid., 146, 326-27; Dehon, *Sermons on the Public Means of Grace*, 2 vols. (Charleston, 1821) 1:209.

[79]John S. Ravenscroft, *Works*, 2 vols. (New York, 1830) 1:13-14; Marshal D. Haywood, *Lives of the Bishops of North Carolina* (Raleigh, 1910) 44.

pleased to take hold of it . . . something more was needed which could only be found in the *outward* delegation of authority, from that source to which it was originally committed."[80] Ravenscroft found this source in the Episcopal claims to apostolic succession. In 1817 at the age of forty-five he was ordained a priest; five years later he joined that succession with his consecration as bishop.

Much of the new bishop's energies were taken up in visitations and tours through his diocese. He recorded in his journal that in 1825-1826 he traveled 2,218 exhausting miles on horseback and coach preaching daily to scattered congregations. Ravenscroft's message was distinctly High Church. In an early manuscript sermon of 1819 he coupled the progress of the Church with "the excellency of its Doctrine" and the rectitude of its life. In his later episcopal charges, he likewise spoke of the "one Catholic and Apostolic Church," an institution divine in origin and thus "beyond the reach of any human appointment, addition, or alteration." Furthermore, like Hobart and Dehon, Ravenscroft emphasized the external commission as well as the internal calling that formed the basis for ministerial authority. A divine right in the ministry, he stated "can be derived only from the apostles of our Lord Jesus Christ by succession in the Church, through the line of Bishops, as distinct from Presbyters." That he considered this interpretation the only permissible one within the Episcopal church Ravenscroft demonstrated by concluding: "It is either divine right, or no right at all. I therefore know nothing of any barometrical measurement into high or low Church; higher than its source I attempt not to carry it— lower than its origin I will not degrade it, and only by its proper proof will I acknowledge it."[81]

Three issues afforded these church leaders the opportunity to put their principles into practice. The first was the organization of a variety of religious societies founded on a confessional basis. As

---

[80]Ravenscroft, *Works*, 1:18.

[81]John S. Ravenscroft journal, Ravenscroft Papers, Church Historical Society, Austin, Texas; Ravenscroft, mss. sermon, "The End and Design of Religion," Ravenscroft Papers, Southern Historical Collection, University of North Carolina, Chapel Hill, North Carolina; Ravenscroft, *Works*, 1:76, 97, 308.

with other parts of American Christianity, the Episcopal church formed moral, education, and literary societies on confessional bases or joined in interdenominational ventures. Hobart consistently advocated a strong and distinctive confessional foundation. In an address to an Episcopal Sunday School Society he insisted that both the Bible and prayer book should be taught. His demand for the two pieces effectively excluded him from any interdenominational enterprises, while it likewise distinguished him from those evangelical organizations in the Episcopal church that held the Scriptures alone as sufficient. While Hobart could agree with his evangelical colleagues that religious and moral improvement were appropriate goals, he still maintained that "indifference to forms of faith is indifference to truth or falsehood."[82]

Theodore Dehon, in 1810, had been instrumental in establishing an interdenominational Bible Society in Charleston. Three years later, he resigned from its Board of Managers when it became clear that his attachment to the Episcopal church conflicted with the board's approach. Correspondingly, Dehon's involvement with the Protestant Episcopal Society For the Advancement of Christianity in South Carolina grew during this time. This organization operated exclusively within denominational auspices, and, like Hobart's group, distributed both the Scriptures and the prayer book.[83] Ravenscroft also opposed nondenominational Bible societies. In 1824, he spoke to the nondenominational Bible Society of North Carolina. Conceding that his remarks were not what the society was accustomed to hearing, he condemned as specious the society's distribution of Bibles without proper interpretive commentaries and stated that the work of such interdenominational societies was "unfounded, dangerous, and ultimately subversive of all revealed religion."[84]

The second issue, which concerned proper educational facilities, surfaced in the deliberations over the establishment of a theo-

---

[82]Hobart, *The Beneficial Effects of Sunday Schools* (New York, 1818) 14, 20, 22; William Manross, *A History of the American Episcopal Church* (New York, 1959) 227.

[83]Gadsen, *Life,* 216-18; Dehon, *Sermons,* 2:252-58.

[84]Ravenscroft, *Works,* 1:168-70.

logical seminary. A proposal for a seminary was first made in 1814: however, it was defeated. Although Hobart favored a new seminary, he opposed this motion, preferring the older plan of a diocesan seminary. In this action could be seen Hobart's belief in tighter doctrinal control. Nevertheless, in 1819 a seminary under the auspices of the General Convention was established in New York City. Hobart still opposed it, and when the decision was made to move the institution to New Haven in 1820, he set up a diocesan seminary. The following year, the original seminary's odyssey came to an end when it returned to New York City and merged with Hobart's diocesan institution. Hobart became professor of pastoral theology and assumed many administrative duties, thereby insuring that the character of General Theological Seminary would be in keeping with his views.[85]

The third and final issue concerned new-measures revivalism. With his aversion to enthusiasm and his veneration for liturgy, Hobart was a sure opponent of the new-measures experience. Reiterating that the church was a divinely established institution, Hobart cited scriptural warrant for liturgical modes of worship and further claimed that they provided for dignified devotion. Expanding on this theme of dignity he criticized a series of changes currently being advocated: "the encouragement of men not ordained to lead the devotions, and to expound the Scriptures in what are called *prayer meetings*—to overthrow our unrivaled Liturgy, by the introduction of extemporaneous prayers into the public services of the Church—to establish and to cherish insubordination to Episcopal authority." It was the responsibility of the bishop to warn against these errors, Hobart said, and especially against those "got-up revivals" that "excite the passions [and] catch the false fires of enthusiasm."[86] Dehon, meanwhile, called for home missionaries with "sound theological attainments" who could be sent to minister to the unchurched population of the interior hinterlands and to com-

[85]P. Mills Dawley, *The Story of the General Theological Seminary* (New York, 1969) 27-82.

[86]Hobart, *The High Churchman Vindicated* (New York, 1826) 3; *Address* (New York, 1827) 18; *The Christian Bishop* (New York, 1827) 28.

bat the "wild fanaticism" of the camp meetings. And Ravenscroft's repeated attacks on "the spurious liberality of opinion" that down-played confessional attachments in favor of an emotional or latitu-dinarian approach to religion left little doubt concerning his opposition to the new-measures revivalism.[87]

In 1823 Hobart left for Europe to recuperate from an illness. He stayed for two years, during which time he traveled in France and Italy, but he enjoyed his stay in England the most. In 1807 Hobart had written a tract on episcopacy; now in March 1824 Hobart met at Oxford with the future author of another series of tracts. This meeting between the established Hobart and the young Newman was a pleasant encounter for them both, and in 1839 Newman at-tested to it with a commendatory article in the *British Critic*, "The American Church." By 1825 Hobart was back in America. Five years later the ranks of High Church Episcopalianism were depleted when both he and Ravenscroft died.[88]

If Newman's influence on Hobart was minimal, the English-man's influence in America during the late 1830s was much greater. The repercussions in America from the Oxford movement were complex. In certain respects the movement clearly continued High Church themes, but in other ways it did not. Given the existence of High Church theology in Hobart's style—which emphasized the church, the sacraments, and the ministry, and which was far re-moved from anything like the pretentiousness of the "High and Dry" English Anglicans—Tractarian theology could find a com-fortable footing. Similarly, the anti-Erastian fusillades of the En-glish Tractarians lost much of their force in the context of voluntaryism and were simply accepted. Finally, the strong anti-Ro-man pronouncements of Hobart were compatible with that quest for an Anglo-Catholic theology.

Tractarian writings therefore did not initially cause much of a stir in American Episcopal circles. Bishop George W. Doane of New Jersey had published an edition of John Keble's *Christian Year* in

---

[87]Dehon, *Sermons*, 2:276; Ravenscroft, *Works*, 1:81.

[88]See the discussion in C. K. L. Clarke, *Bishop Hobart and the Oxford Movement* (Milwaukee, 1933).

1834, and in 1841 he had journeyed to England to visit Keble and Pusey. In 1839 an American edition of the *Tracts* themselves was begun. Predictably, evangelicals such as Alexander Griswold worried about "the introduction of Popish corruptions," while High Churchmen such as Benjamin Onderdonk called for a "patient and unbiased hearing of the Oxford theology which was endeavoring to distinguish popery from scriptural and primitive catholicity." Developments of a more controversial nature took place in 1841. In that year a group of three young men, influenced by the devotional themes in the Tractarian writings, established the first monastery in the American church. Located at Nashotah, Wisconsin, it was founded on principles of celibacy, asceticism, and rigorous discipline. When Newman published Tract 90, Samuel Seabury, grandson of the patriarch and editor of the journal *The Churchman*, gave Newman's essay a measure of support. "We do not deny," Seabury wrote,

> there are some views advanced in the Tract, both doctrinal and historical, which are not in accordance with our own; but we mean to say, that the principles of interpretation adopted in the Tract, are, in our opinion, neither evasive, nor slippery, but honest, manly, and straightforward.[89]

The first full counterattack against the defenders of the Tractarians came from Bishop McIlvaine of Ohio. In his book, *Oxford Divinity*, McIlvaine charged the English Tractarians and their American followers with deserting Protestantism. The Tractarian writings were unscriptural and led naturally to a secession to Rome. In another essay McIlvaine expanded these charges in a manner reminiscent of Thomas Arnold and others. "The whole system," he wrote, "is one of church instead of Christ; priest instead of Gospel; concealment of truth instead of 'manifestation of truth'; ignorant superstition instead of enlightened faith; bondage where we are promised liberty." Bishop Eastham made much the same point in

---

[89]E. Clowes Chorley, *Men and Movements in the American Episcopal Church* (New York, 1946) 198-201; William C. Doane, *Life and Writings of George Washington Doane*, 4 vols. (New York, 1860-1861) 1:255-64, 271-72, 283; DeMille, *Catholic Movement*, 45-46, Seabury is quoted on page 42.

his terse statement that the Tractarians were "advocates of the Dark Ages and followers of the Scarlet Woman."[90]

The main engagement between the defenders and critics of the Tractarians occurred in a series of episodes between 1843 and 1853. The first concerned the ordination of Arthur Carey, a student at General Theological Seminary. Daring in thinking, ascetic in lifestyle, and committed to Newman, Carey appeared destined to play the role of the American Froude. The two were similar in more than outlook. Carey, like Froude, died in the Carribean of tuberculosis. Before he died, however, Carey was examined for heresy. In 1843 Carey's bid for ordination was challenged by Low Church forces. An examination took place, Carey's views were determined to be sufficiently orthodox, and he was ordained by Bishop Benjamin Onderdonk. Not all parties were satisfied, however, and critics of the Tractarians mounted a campaign to investigate the General Theological Seminary for soundness. A committee of the House of Bishops conducted the inquiry, in which professors were questioned about their views, but in the end the committee found no evidence of papal practices. There had been a similar event in the General Convention itself. Attempts to condemn Tractarianism were beaten back by the still powerful High Church party, and instead a substitute motion reaffirming "the Liturgy, Offices, and Articles of the Church" was passed.[91]

If the Tractarian opponents failed to gain a decisive victory, they did make the most of three episcopal inquiries taking place between 1844 and 1853. In 1844, Henry U. Onderdonk, Bishop of Pennsylvania and a strong supporter of the Oxford movement, was brought before the House of Bishops on charges of intemperance. Alleging that the habit initially had been gained through the use of medicinal spirits, Onderdonk confessed his guilt and was relieved of his office. His brother, Benjamin, was also brought to ecclesiastical trial. Ben-

---

[90]DeMille, *Catholic Movement*, 48; Raymond Albright, *A History of the Protestant Episcopal Church* (New York, 1964) 232-33; James Addison, *The Episcopal Church in the United States* (New York, 1851) 158.

[91]On this set of conflicts see DeMille, *Catholic Movement*, 55-62; Chorley, *Men and Movements*, 207-17; Dawley, *Story of the General Theological Seminary*, 145-79.

jamin Onderdonk had succeeded Hobart as Bishop of New York and was one of the foremost champions of the Tractarians in America. Onderdonk's hearing provided an opportunity for an ecclesiastical vendetta, and his many opponents in the church pressed their case with sufficient strength to win Onderdonk's suspension from ministerial office. A final trial in 1852-1853 brought Bishop George Washington Doane under scrutiny. Charged with financial incompetence Doane persuasively convinced the examining bishops that he was an honest man if not an able administrator. In the end Doane was fully acquitted.[92]

The proceedings against the Onderdonks had come on the heels of the news that Edward Pusey had been suspended as a university preacher at Oxford. Evangelicals in the American church clearly had hoped to achieve the same results their English brethren had and perhaps to root out Tractarianism altogether. Yet the battles over the Carey ordination and the trial of Benjamin Onderdonk, especially, demonstrated the persistence, if not resurgence, in the 1840s and 1850s of a High Church tradition. William Whittingham, bishop of Maryland, and George Doane, bishop of New Jersey, were two of the most prominent leaders in this phase of confessional Episcopalianism. Both had supported Benjamin Onderdonk during his trial: Whittingham had approved Carey's ordination and Doane had abstained.[93]

Onderdonk, Whittingham, and Doane were all Episcopalians in the Hobartian fashion. They all knew him personally, had received sacerdotal orders from him, and had come to treasure his theological perspective. All three publicly admired the Tractarian quest and, like Keble and Pusey, were unswervingly loyal to the Episcopal faith. Yet with Onderdonk suspended and Doane's credibility undermined, it fell to Whittingham to lead the High Church forces during the 1850s and 1860s. William Whittingham had been

---

[92]Albright, *History of the Protestant Episcopal Church*, 240-41; E. Clowes Chorley, "Benjamin Tredwell Onderdonk," *Historical Magazine of the Protestant Episcopal Church* 9, no. 1 (March 1940): 1-51.

[93]Richard Salomon, "The Episcopate on the Carey Case, New Sources from the Chase Collection at Kenyon College," *Historical Magazine of the Protestant Episcopal Church* 18, no. 3 (September 1949): 240-81.

elected bishop in 1840 after serving as a faculty member for several years at the General Seminary. He aggressively defended the prerogatives of the "Church Catholic and Apostolic" and insisted on the Apostles', Nicene, and Athanasian creeds as the basis of doctrinal teaching. Chastising those who regarded "the Church as a secondary police, or the Gospel as a Sunday philosophy," he depicted the Episcopal faith as the true deposit of the apostles and the Episcopal churches as a branch of the tree of divine salvation. Towards Roman Catholicism he was unrelentingly hostile. "The real ends of the papal system," he wrote, "I suppose to be its setting the letter above and instead of the spirit; authority above and instead of conscience; dogmatic formula above and instead of evangelical faith." In later decades, in fact, it was Whittingham's animosity towards the Roman church that fueled his crusade against ritualism in the American church.[94]

By the time Doane was acquitted in 1853 there was a relative truce within the Episcopal church in America. Critics such as McIlvaine could point out that secessions to Rome had taken place: most noticeable were those made by a handful of students at General Seminary and Nashotah monastery. Levi S. Ives, Bishop of North Carolina, also transferred to Rome, as did John Murray Forbes. Yet defenders of Anglo-Catholicism, such as Bishop Whittingham, were quick to reassert their case. Whittingham wrote Pusey shortly after Newman's secession, that "if schism be sin, we must treat schismatics as sinners, or be ourselves partakers of their guilt." For Whittingham, as for Keble and Pusey, the secessions may have caused confusion, but they never challenged the legitimacy of the Anglican church. Here the particular American traditions of High Church theology, which contained the Tractarian argument, were significant. For it was this theological setting that gave meaning to the Tractarian appeal and that cushioned the attack when it came. The challenge for High Church Episcopalianism at mid-century was not to articulate its confessional theology, but to reaffirm

---

[94]William F. Brand, *Life of William Rolinson Whittingham*, 2 vols. (New York, 1883) 2:319; William R. Whittingham, *The Doctrine of the Church* (Baltimore, 1849) 10-13; William R. Whittingham, *The Work of Christ By His Ministry* (Baltimore, 1856) 12-14.

its Protestantism as it faced the social challenge of the Eastern urban centers where it was located.[95]

Confessionalism in America thus suffered a mixed fate. Clearly it appealed to particular groups, such as German immigrants or High Church Anglicans, groups either dissatisfied with the superficiality of revivalism or else closely tied to Europe. Likewise, because of church-state separation in America, the American confessionalists did not need to fight the issue of Erastianism and thus were spared the official condemnation that was directed toward the Tractarians and that threatened the neo-Lutherans. Finally, because of the fluid nature of antebellum society, the confessionalists could invoke an older corporative ethic, one that was still meaningful and attractive to some Americans in the early nineteenth century.

Yet the very dynamics of American society contributed to the confessionalists' undoing. Revivalism gained a position within American culture far more secure and accepted than either pietism in Germany or evangelicalism in England. When the American confessionalists were not being ignored, they were being reduced to the rank of an inconsiderable minority within their denominations. For all its intellectual prowess, Mercersburg remained isolated—intellectually even more than physically—from the mainstream of American life. To an even greater extent, the theological forces of Princeton and of Löhe's followers in Iowa were relegated to an increasingly marginal position, as American religious life in the years following the Civil War became embroiled in the issues of evolution, urban reform, and racial tension. Even the Anglo-Catholics within Episcopalianism drew back into a few congregations, distinct as much for the peculiarity of their rituals as for the content of their theology. By 1866 these confessionalists found themselves left behind as the attention of the nation turned to a new cultural agenda.

---

[95]DeMille, *Catholic Movement*, 65-69, 106-107.

PART FIVE

EPILOGUE

CHAPTER EIGHT

THE DECLINE OF CONSERVATIVE CONFESSIONALISM

By 1866 the confessional theologians had experienced one setback after another. Ecclesiastical councils had rebuked them for demanding high confessional standards; popular misunderstanding had mired confessional interpretations in renewed anti-Catholic prejudices; the religious innovations they had opposed were established and the social and cultural changes they had tried to stop were advancing.

Several overlapping sets of events and influences account for the reverses conservative confessionalism suffered. Biographical circumstances played a role. John Newman's conversion to Roman Catholicism ruptured the Anglo-Catholic movement in England and America, throwing its Anglo-American advocates into disarray and diminishing its power. Age and illness claimed Wilhelm Löhe, August Vilmar, John Keble, and John Nevin, causing them to retire from active involvement in their former ecclesiastical causes. So too changes of locale—as in Philip Schaff's case—and the assumption of additional responsibilities—as in Theodor Kliefoth's, redirected confessionalist energies.

More importantly, Germany, England, and America were becoming modern capitalist states, and the confessionalists were on the losing side of the struggle to determine the future direction of those countries. By the 1860s, a new dynamic unity had finally co-alesced in Germany, England, and the United States—one high-lighted by a reaffirmation of national purpose, an increased popular participation in government, and an entry into the world economic order. Technological developments heralded the birth of a new industrial age that was to be associated with names like Car-negie, Krupp, and Whitworth. Political change was just as evident. In Germany in 1866, the Seven Weeks' War with Austria ended; the subsequent formation of the North German Confederation under Bismarck anticipated the eventual unification of the Empire. In En-gland, agitation for electoral reform continued; by 1867 another significant reform bill had passed. In America, the Civil War had fi-nally ended—reaffirming the Union in principle though nearly de-stroying it in fact—and promising, in what were to be the Fourteenth and Fifteenth Amendments to the federal Constitution, greater legal equality and political participation for its citizens.

The changes in world view that accompanied these political, economic, and social changes were just as revolutionary in their im-plications for the Western world. The orientation of the new entre-preneurs and liberal social thinkers, who emphasized the individual as an abstract entity, broke new ground. Persons as well as goods were now weighed, measured, and rationally analyzed as to how they could best be utilized.[1] The factual calculus of Dickens's Thomas Gradgrind epitomized the cultural meaning of the new bourgeois modernity, even if it did not quickly or easily replace the older familiar affability and presumption of a Squire Allworthy or Barchester's Warden Harding. Nor did it go unobserved that this rationalist perspective was an assault on time-honored patterns of religious belief and action with their ineffable mysteries and elabo-rate rituals.

Many welcomed this uprooting of the old ways. They saw in this Promethean call to liberation freedom from the trammels of hered-itary privilege and a future of increased opportunity and individual growth. But if some cheered the liberals' new world of autonomy

---

[1]See the discussion of this point in Karl Mannheim, *From Karl Mannheim*, ed. Kurt Wolff (New York, 1971) 142-52.

and economic and political innovation, others resisted it in the name of an older social vision. The cast of these nineteenth-century opponents of liberalism included Ultramontane Catholics and Protestant confessionalists, Silesian weavers and English Luddites, American Federalists, English back-benchers, and retired Prussian generals. These critics of modernity represented a cultural Old Guard temporarily thrown together by their anger, discontent, and sense of injury rather than by any tight programmatic agreement or common solutions.

THE WORLD VIEW OF CONFESSIONALISM

During this era of cultural change, the confessionalists figured as exponents of a conservative vision. They believed in that older *Weltanschauung* of paternalism—an ideology, explanation, and social vision that by the mid-nineteenth century was finally breaking up. This confessional world view was built on a corporate rather than an individualistic approach to the social world. As Wilhelm Löhe had said, humanity needed a community in order to be fully human, for "as long as a man is alone, he cannot even be blessed."[2] Confessional social philosophy recognized the existence and importance of the individual, but placed that individual within a framework of duties, expectations, specific times, places, and persons.

Like other nineteenth-century conservatives, the confessionalists were caught in a complex yearning for an idealized and distant past. Using such nostalgic appeal as a rhetorical foil, conservatives deplored the unleashing of the individual, the dissolving of familiar and reciprocal duties and rights that emphasis on individual autonomy and natural rights represented. August Vilmar captured the confessionalists' disenchantment when he lamented, "Our age is in many ways an age of atomism. Each wants to be for himself, no one can stand to be with or under anyone else."[3] The confessionalists,

---

[2]Wilhelm Löhe, *Three Books About the Church*, trans. and ed. James Schaaf (Philadelphia, 1969) 47.

[3]August Vilmar, *Kirchen und Welt oder die Aufgaben des geistlichen Amts in unserer Welt*, 2 vols. (Gütersloh, 1872) 1:40-42.

like conservatives throughout the West, wished to return to a more traditional social order. The essence of social and political paternalism was a set of clearly defined social relationships built on centuries-old expectations, relationships that would not depend on actual acquaintance so much as on mutually understood expectations.

Corresponding to their criticism of the concept of the self-reliant individual, the confessionalists supported a local or regional orientation in national politics. Löhe, Vilmar, and Kliefoth opposed the unification of Germany under Prussian domination. Keble, Pusey, and Newman viewed the growth of parliamentary power and the growth of industrial urban centers with foreboding. Even in America, where democratic aspirations dictated political language and goals, the confessionalists continued to defend ethnic contributions and regional bonds in the face of demands for acculturation and national bureaucracies.

With regard to religion the confessionalists' interpretation of creedal statements and doctrine of the church mirrored the critique of individualism so prominent in their social philosophy. In contrast to evangelicals like Zinzendorf, Wilberforce, and Finney—who believed that the Bible sufficiently fulfilled doctrinal needs—confessional theologians insisted on the necessity of extra-scriptural statements. But although confessional theology was a distinct alternative to evangelical theology, its own dealings with the relation of scriptural and confessional statements demonstrated important interpretive cleavage.

Differing points of view were demonstrated in the writings of the Tractarians and German neo-Lutherans. For the Tractarians, the Scriptures contained all that was sufficient and necessary for salvation. The Scriptures were, as Newman phrased it, "the documents of ultimate appeal in controversy, and the touchstone of all doctrine." But the Scriptures were not clear in meaning and intent; readers who sought to follow Scripture needed an authoritative guide. Such a guide was subordinate to the Scriptures but crucial for proper interpretation. Hence, the Tractarians invoked the value of a primitive tradition. "Scripture is verified by Tradition, Tradition is verified by Scripture," Newman wrote. "Tradition gives form to the doctrine, Scripture gives life; Tradition teaches, Scripture proves." Tractarians often insisted that it was not always obvious that the Scriptures needed exegesis. Sometimes the meaning of Scripture was literal, sometimes figurative. Because of this complexity, the Tractarians argued, the simple biblical religion that the evangelicals appealed to did not exist.[4]

What did exist was a mysterious revelation of infinite depth made manifest through the Scriptures. In this portrayal the influence of Joseph Butler and the Alexandrian Platonists can be clearly discerned. The Tractarians appropriated the particular ensemble of sacramental views that posited an ineffable bond between the natural and supernatural worlds—a bond that could be perceived analogically and symbolically but always contained multiple levels of meaning. Adherence to the beliefs of Butler and the Alexandrians set off the Tractarians from their continental brethren. For not only the tradition of the nonjuring bishops, but the particular views of Butler and, more broadly, of the Caroline divines had no counterpart in Germany.

If tradition was necessary as a guide to the Scriptures, it also served to mediate between the mystery of divine revelation—as it appeared in the Word—and the mundane experience of the individual. Tradition was not only an extra-biblical referent for scriptural interpretation, but a means of comprehending and reconciling biblical texts with daily life. In announcing that tradition teaches, Newman demonstrated the Tractarian belief in a divine pedagogy that interweaves the human and the sacred and thereby provides a means for understanding.

To argue that the Scriptures were obscure, even though a method for their comprehension had been provided, raised an important question: why were they not made clear in the beginning? Edward Pusey argued that this inscrutability was not a sign of divine weakness but was designed "to excite our diligence in the research after those truths, to influence the heart by the occupation of the understanding, and to increase our interest by the very effort of collecting them." Later in life Pusey suggested that two systems, Ultra-Protestant and Anglo-Catholic, existed within the church. The dif-

---

[4]John Newman, "Lectures on the Prophetical Office of the Church," in *The Via Media of the Anglican Church*, 2 vols. (London, 1895) 1:309, 274.

ference between the two, especially regarding attitudes towards Scripture, Pusey argued, was fundamentally a moral one: where Catholic attitudes produced reverence towards the Scriptures, Protestant principles produced presumption and conceit. The Tractarian belief that there was much hidden in Scripture was so integral to Tractarian theology that its acceptance or rejection, rather than constituting an open question, amounted to a primary indication of personal moral rectitude.[5]

The Tractarians built upon the premise of the necessity of tradition a trio of subsidiary points. First, they recognized the legitimacy of an unwritten element within the canon of tradition. As John Keble put it, "The full tradition of Christianity existed before the Christian Scriptures." He in this way acknowledged that an oral tradition existed among the apostles and early church prior to the writing and establishment of the canonical scriptures. Such a point was a historical contention and more. For the Tractarians held tradition in such high esteem that while they subordinated it to Scripture they nevertheless believed that it too was of special origin. This belief led to a third point, that any proper understanding of doctrinal authority in religion must recognize that other channels in addition to the Scriptures and tradition had been established by the Lord, and that these channels were again broadly sacramental in nature. This third point led to a consideration of the church as one of the divinely established vehicles for the transmission of grace and the message of salvation. It also reaffirmed that venerable understanding of the sacraments, in Newman's words, as "a Mystery, or (what was anciently called) a Truth Sacramental; that is a high invisible grace lodged in an outward form, a precious possession to be piously and thankfully guarded for the sake of the heavenly reality contained in it."[6]

---

[5]E. B. Pusey, *An Historical Enquiry into the Probable Causes of the Rationalist Character Lately Predominant in the Theology of Germany* (London, 1828) 38; Pusey to A. Tholuck, 18 November 1839, Pusey Papers, Pusey House, Oxford.

[6]John Keble, *Sermons, Academical and Occasional* (Oxford, 1847) 347; Alf Härdelin, *The Tractarian Understanding of the Eucharist* (Uppsala, 1965) 39. Newman is quoted on page 32.

The neo-Lutheran construction of the status of Scripture and confession was different from that of the Tractarians. For example, while the Oxford theologians argued that tradition provided a kind of conceptual unity for the church over time, Wilhelm Löhe replied that the real unity of the church was established by the apostolic word and adherence to its doctrines. More significantly, Löhe insisted that this resource of the Word was not only sufficient for salvation, it could be understood by all persons. In Löhe's opinion, to argue that the Scriptures were sufficient but not immediately understandable was to impute weakness, malevolence, and worse, to the author of the divine plan.[7]

Consequently, Löhe interpreted the meaning of tradition differently from the Tractarians. Since the Scriptures provided all the necessary information for the gospel of salvation, tradition—both written and unwritten—was no substitute for Scripture and in many cases was superfluous. Löhe, countering Roman Catholic arguments, maintained that both papal pronouncements and council decisions, such as those at Trent, were unsatisfactory. He did concede that a unanimous consensus of the Church Fathers would be helpful because it would corroborate the Scriptures. His concession in this regard paralleled the intent of the Tractarians, who also sought a position of supplemental assistance for apostolic pronouncements. But unlike the Tractarians, Löhe believed it would be extraordinarily difficult to establish such a consensus, and he asserted the efficacy of the apostolic word. Where the Oxford theologians emphasized that true antiquity and catholicity were internally consistent and could never contradict one another, Löhe saw problems in establishing the unity of each author's writings and in establishing the unity of the corpus as a whole. Perhaps in a thousand years, Löhe contended, scholars would be able to demonstrate this alleged unanimity, but for the present it was best to stay with the apostolic word.[8]

While Löhe was skeptical regarding the use of an apostolic tradition, he was confident regarding the applications to which the

---

[7]Löhe, *Three Books About the Church*, 62-65.

[8]Ibid., 75-78.

confessional statements of the Lutheran church could be put. As he developed this theme, he touched on three points further illustrating the extent of agreement between the confessional theologians of Germany and England. First, Löhe insisted that these extra-biblical statements of faith were written by humans. Though the authors were probably aided by the Holy Spirit, Löhe said, one could not claim in any technical sense that they were inspired. If this contention distinguished the Tractarians and neo-Lutherans, Löhe's second point affirmed other areas of agreement. Löhe, considering the usefulness of confessional statements as an aid to scriptural interpretation, argued that confessional statements mediated between experience and the apostolic word in ways comparable to what the Tractarians believed. For Löhe and the neo-Lutherans, confessional statements mediated between the subjective aspects of faith—encountered in the religious dimensions of human experience—and the objective side of faith—exemplified by the Word and the administration of the sacraments. They believed that the recognition of this mediational role distinguished them from the pietists, who tended to overplay the subjective, and from the Roman Catholics, who tended to underplay the subjective. Reconciliation of the subjective and objective aspects of experience and sacrament produced correct doctrine. This belief led to the third point: the neo-Lutherans believed that such confessional statements safeguarded proper doctrine by setting the boundaries of the correct view of the administration of the sacraments and the interpretation of the Word. In short, the confessional statements distinguished truth from falsehood. By strict adherence to such statements, the Lutheran communion was insured of following the proper path.[9]

Building on this analysis of confessional statements Löhe made a final point, one the American confessionalist, Charles Philip Krauth, also emphasized. While the symbolical books of the Lutheran faith determined the understanding of that faith, Löhe re-

---

[9]Ibid., 99-115; Löhe, *Gesammelte Werke*, ed. Klaus Ganzert, 7 vols. (Neuendettelsau, 1951-) 3:230; Holstein Fagerberg, *Bekenntnis, Kirche, und Amt in der deutschen konfessionellen Theologie des 19. Jahrhunderts* (Uppsala, 1952) 137-49; Max Keller-Huschemenger, *Die Lehre der Kirche in der Oxford Bewegung: Struktur und Function* (Gütersloh, 1974) 53-59.

iterated that they had left some questions open for further discussion, clarification, and resolution. This statement did not mean that an essential doctrinal foundation had been left unestablished. In Löhe's view it was available in the Apostles' Creed. Charles Krauth also maintained that the symbolical books, added to the Apostles' Creed, summarized the fundamental doctrines of Christianity. By adhering to the primitive creeds, Krauth maintained, the Lutheran church demonstrates its "true catholicity and antiquity, and declares that the name Lutheran does not define her essence, but simply refers to one grand fact in her history."[10] Löhe would have agreed.

The confessionalists matched their preference for the mediational role of creedal statements with a high regard for the church as a medium for the dispensation of divine grace. Although the romantic religion of the confessionalists found common ground with the heart religion of the pietists—in that they both opposed rationalist theology and recognized such central Christian concepts as human sinfulness and the need for spiritual rebirth—that common ground could not mask the disparity of their views concerning the availability of unmediated grace. The evangelicals' hermeneutical principle of "the Bible and nothing more," and their call for sinners to be "saved and washed in the blood of the Lamb," were deemed too shallow by theologians whose guidepost was Protestant catholicity.

The confessional theologians insisted that the church was the vehicle through which the gospel message of salvation was transmitted. The church had been entrusted with the message that salvation must be attained. Thus, one should turn to the church for instruction on how to attain salvation. The church had existed before the formation of any given congregation; it therefore had an ecclesiological perspective superior to that of an individual congregation. This belief paralleled the confessional belief that tradition was more valuable than private judgment and rationalism. If any theme ran consistently through confessional ecclesiological

---

[10]Löhe, *Werke*, 5/1:389-94; Krauth, *Evangelical Review* 1 (October 1849): 244; *Evangelical Review* 11 (July 1859): 12, 15-16.

thought, it was that the church was a divinely established institution, an organic being that was more than the sum of its individual parts—certainly more than an alliance of like-minded individuals. That claim was akin to a broader conservative philosophy within Europe and America, as is clear from these confessional theologians' attitudes towards political upheavals in their countries. For confessional theologians, society was a parallel to the church—if indeed society and the church could be separated—in that as an institution, society too was as little the product of whatever voluntary associations might exist as the church was a product of its own voluntary ecclesiastical organizations.

On this foundation these confessional theologians addressed a series of subsidiary ecclesiastical concerns. For example, confessional theologians of all three countries agreed that the church should be spiritually independent. Whether they based their arguments on apostolic succession and the privileges due thereto or on the sanctity of creedal obligations, confessional theologians supported the separation of church and state. That this separation had already been achieved in the United States fueled the American confessionalists to press for further reform, while their ties to Europe strengthened the Europeans' resolve. These theologians also were united in their insistence upon a strict confessional basis for all foreign and domestic missionary work. Again, whether Lutheran, Reformed, or Anglican, these confessional spokesmen believed that adherence to the proper doctrine was crucial. Finally, these clerics argued that the authority and independence of the ministerial office must be recognized. As Emanuel Hirsch has noted, the teaching on the ministerial office that emerged from neo-Lutheranism (and that was equally applicable to Tractarianism and American confessionalism) emphasized that special powers were transmitted by the ordaining of apostolically descended and apostolically empowered ministers. The efficacy of the sacraments was tied to the proper ordination of the minister. Ordination and the powers associated with it were thus extremely important. Confessional theologians in all three countries demonstrated that the prerogatives of the ministerial office were significant and that the clergy could expect to be called to responsibilities equal in size to its powers.[11]

The confessionalists lent their support to many of those conservative causes that had moral order and social cohesion as their stated goals. Such goals were broad enough to contain a host of humanitarian reformers. Religious reforms across a wide ideological spectrum sought to deflect the anarchic potential of individual liberation by channeling it into moral reform organizations—organizations that functioned indirectly to reintegrate the individual back into the social whole.

There is an intriguing ambivalence in the confessionalist attitude toward reform associations. As Karl Mannheim once pointed out with reference to Germany, conservative thought in the early nineteenth century often contained progressive elements.[12] His observations applied to more than Germany. Support for the separation of church and state most clearly exemplifies this blend within the confessional viewpoint of progressive and conservative elements. Context was important, but along with insisting on the spiritual independence of the church as a divine institution, all three sets of confessional theologians were prepared to accept an administrative and even a financial separation of church and state.

The confessionalists' debt to romanticism distinguished them during the early nineteenth century as much as did their mediational social and religious philosophies. The concepts of confessionalism and romanticism both conflicted with the concepts of rationalism and utilitarianism. Where the latter measured, weighed, and analyzed; romanticism and confessionalism emphasized intuition, envisioned invisible wholes, and spurned the analytical thrust of bourgeois liberalism. Where the liberal contemplated the future, the romantic invoked the past; where the liberal spoke of urban growth and civic pride, the romantic recalled the pastoral landscape of the village and *Dorf*.

---

[11] Emanuel Hirsch, *Geschichte des neuern evangelischen Theologie im Zusammenhang mit den allgemeinen Bewegungen des europäischen Denkens*, 2d ed., 5 vols. (Gütersloh, 1960) 5:194.

[12] Mannheim, "Conservative Thought," in *From Karl Mannheim*, 152-77.

The confessionalist emphasis on the meaning of development as it applied to religious life and doctrine testified to the influence of romanticism in confessional theology and stamped the confessionalists as part of the larger nineteenth-century intellectual movement. Whether calling upon a tradition of primitive apostolicity or upon creedal statements, confessionalists realized that it was necessary to establish a link with the past—a comprehensive past reaching back to the first days of the church. They saw the development of tradition as the development of human understanding—as an unfolding and clarification of human consciousness—not as the revelation or development of a new message of salvation.[13] To their claim that any correct portrayal of religious life should include its earlier historical roots, the confessionalists added a moral dimension. Not only was such a developmental picture accurate, they believed, it was morally correct and true as well; duration throughout the ages and continuity of content were safeguards of veracity and bulwarks against innovation. Thus the confessionalists consciously wove a net of descriptive and normative lines of argument in which they hoped to capture their living quarry: Christian experience.

Within the Protestantism of that day, the confessional emphasis upon development represented a distinctive choice. Evangelicals were content in large part to begin the history of the church at the Reformation. Little better from the standpoint of confessionalism was the interpretation, advanced by Charles Hodge, that aborted previous doctrinal developments at the Reformation and preserved the results in an airtight jar of scholastic orthodoxy. Yet if the confessionalists stood out from such stationary ideas, theirs was not a monolithic consensus but rather a range of graduated and subtly shaded differences regarding the nature of the dynamic process.

At one end of the spectrum was the Oxford movement. Although John Newman's *Essay on Development* represented one of the more sustained studies in nineteenth-century Christian theology on

---

[13]A series of similar investigations was taking place in Roman Catholicism under Johann Adam Möhler at Tübingen and in the Russian Orthodox church by Alexis Khomiakov. While discussion of these movements is beyond the range of this study, a complete examination of the "church question" in the early nineteenth century would include these theologians.

the doctrine of development, it properly belonged to Newman's Roman Catholic career. But even while he was an Anglican priest, Newman's thought on the concept of development was the most fully elaborated among the Oxford theologians. In Newman's understanding there was a tension between static and dynamic elements within tradition. In part, his understanding betrayed his early evangelical background. In his youth Newman had admitted to certainty regarding only his own existence and that of his creator, and as late as 1843, he would similarly insist that there are "but two beings in the whole world, God and ourselves."[14]

Such a polarization might admit little movement, but in Tract 41, written in 1834, and in the "Lectures on the Prophetical Office of the Church" published in 1837, Newman coupled a dynamic concept to this static one. In Tract 41 Newman argued for a progressive unfolding of doctrine to meet the demands of circumstances. Such doctrines, Newman maintained, had been the possession of the church throughout its history, and thus did not constitute anything like a new creation. In his "Lectures" Newman identified two types of tradition, episcopal and prophetic. Both of these types were equally apostolic—that is, both were attested to as universal, ancient, and catholic. Episcopal tradition for Newman represented a set of definite and correct beliefs as was embodied in the Apostles' Creed, which had been handed down through the ages from one bishop to the next as a *depositum fidei*. Newman balanced this static set of doctrines with a prophetic tradition,

> a vast system, not to be comprised in a few sentences, not to be embodied in one code or treatise, but consisting of a certain body of Truth, pervading the Church like an atmosphere, irregular in its shape from its very profusion and exuberance . . . partly written, partly unwritten, partly the interpretation, partly the supplement of Scripture, partly preserved in intellectual expressions, partly latent in the spirit and temper of Christians; poured to and fro in closets and upon the housetops, in liturgies, in controversial

---

[14]Quoted by David Newsome, "The Evangelical Sources of Newman's Power," in *The Rediscovery of Newman: An Oxford Symposium*, ed. John Coulson and A. M. Allchin (London, 1967) 21. In addition, see the discussion by Härdelin, *Tractarian Understanding of the Eucharist*, 42-47, and those by Günter Biemer, *Newman on Tradition* (New York, 1967) and Nicholas Lash, *Newman on Development* (Sheperdstown, 1975).

works, in obscure fragments, in sermons, in popular prejudices, in local customs. This I call Prophetical Tradition.[15]

Ranging to and fro, bounding like some vital spirit over and through forms, this latter tradition provided Newman's system with its principle of development. It was this prophetic tradition that leavened the otherwise static deposit of faith contained in the episcopal tradition—a tradition whose very transmission and guardianship appeared to be designed to prevent any change. Bishop John Henry Hobart's theology fit into Newman's blend of stasis and dynamism. Hobart also recognized the reality of growth within the church and the transmission by episcopacy of the deposit of faith. While Newman deplored some aspects of the condition of the Protestant Episcopal Church, he demonstrated his respect for Hobart's theology as he expounded on the American bishop's dictum of "Evangelical Truth and Apostolical Order."[16]

If Newman's schema occupied one end of the developing spectrum, a belief held by the German neo-Lutherans and the American, John Nevin, occupied the middle. Central to this belief was a depiction of organic growth, of smooth continuity, of renewal. Wilhelm Löhe, for example, likened the development of the church to a plant whose blossoms unfold in due course and whose stem grows in uninterrupted majesty. In this model, contradictions between different stages of growth could not properly exist. Instead, deep roots sunk into the soil of past ages provided a firm foundation for a persevering maturity. Löhe emphasized that the history of doctrinal development was the history of the conflict between truth and falsity. The existence of such deceit was unfortunate—perhaps some day it would desist—but not until the distant future.[17]

John Nevin also invoked a series of organic images to describe his view of development. In analyzing the Apostles' Creed, for example, Nevin excoriated the view that saw life as the sum of arithmetical parts, rather than as a true spiritual unity that was always

---

[15]Newman, "Lectures," 1:247-50; quotation is on page 250.

[16]Newman, "The Anglo-American Church," in *Essays: Critical and Historical*, 2 vols. (London, 1910) 1:364-66.

[17]Löhe, *Three Books*, 56, 118, 150; *Werke*, 5/1:393.

deeper and more comprehensive than such a sum could be. In this regard the creed was "the free spontaneous externalization of the Christian consciousness, the substance of living Christianity as a whole, in its primary form of faith." Within this gradual progress and growth the creed as a document and the corpus of Christian doctrine as a whole both came into being.[18]

In the works of August Vilmar and Theodor Kliefoth a conception of growth was evident too. Vilmar constructed a periodization of Christian history with each new point incorporating the previous epochs and growing beyond to the next. Growth, if periodized, was still continuous and smooth. Furthermore, in Vilmar's view, these several stages culminated in the present age of the church, which would in turn give way to the millennium. An emphasis upon periodicity also characterized the beliefs of Theodor Kliefoth. For him, development of doctrine took place successively from the apostolic age through to the present. Each individual era represented a doctrinal position that in turn gave rise to its opposite. In contrast to Löhe's view, Kliefoth allowed for contradiction and confrontation within his organically developmental framework. But Kliefoth's dialectic was additive rather than synthetic, one in which consecutively generated oppositions finally were incorporated in the apocalyptic age of the church.[19]

On the other end of the spectrum from the Oxford movement was the belief held by the Mercersburg theologian, Philip Schaff. The theme of development ran throughout his work at Mercersburg, and in his essay *What is Church History*, he gave it particular prominence. There Schaff constructed a dialectical presentation, but one that was synthetic. A dialectical form in this context could still exist easily within an overall organic framework. While all confessional theology contained a developmental component, that ranging from Nevin to Schaff presented this development within an

---

[18]Nevin, "The Apostles' Creed," *Mercersburg Review* 1 (May 1849): 215.

[19]For Vilmar's views see his address, "On The Future Of The Church," quoted by Wilhelm Hopf, *August Vilmar*, 2 vols. (Marburg, 1913) 1:421-26. For Kliefoth see his *Einleitung in die Dogmengeschichte* (Parchim und Ludwigslust, 1839) 133, 291; *Acht Bücher von der Kirche* (Schwerin, 1854) 351-52.

essentially organic schema. Schaff divided the whole of church history into several eras embodying opposing principles. Unlike Kliefoth, he foresaw a new synthesis forming within history. That synthesis might realize the potential for ecumenical unity latent in Protestant Christianity.[20] The confessional theologians of Germany, England, and America contributed to a rich and varied understanding in nineteenth-century Christian theology of the concept of development. Indeed, in combination with their emphasis upon confessional statements, this notion of development more than any other feature characterized their technical theology.

Confessional theology presented a religious and cultural alternative within Germany, England, and America during the early nineteenth century. In an age of innovation and change, it yearned for restoration and conservatism; in an era of growing liberalism, it invoked a more traditional social vision; in a time of diminished doctrinal concern, it demanded stronger standards of belief and practice. In their struggle to preserve the remnants of an older ideal of the meaning of church and society, the confessional theologians confronted the rising forces of liberalism, revivalism, social reform, and capitalism. They lost this battle; but if their corporate vision was overwhelmed by that of bourgeois individualism, the confessional perspective was still intellectually powerful and historically significant.

Moreover, while the confessional theologians were indeed conservative, their conservatism was never so blind, never so atavistic, as to be unable to recognize the reality of contemporary social problems and the need for their resolution. They were convinced that the answers of their liberal opponents to these problems were misguided, shortsighted, and wrong. Whether their opponents were called liberals, rationalists, or simply "men of the present era," the confessionalists' battles with them could be seen taking place in all three national settings. If the confessionalist struggle was a defensive one, still confessionalist theologians realized the inherent dangers of unbridled individualism—which both pietism and liberalism

---

[20]Schaff, *What is Church History* (Philadelphia, 1846) 83-91; Fagerberg, *Bekenntnis, Kirche, und Amt*, 155-59.

represented—and they were aware of the potential for personal confusion in social liberation.

Sensitive to what a later generation reaping the fruits of emancipation and autonomy would call anomie, anxiety, and existential crisis, confessional theologians championed a religious and social vision corporate in outlook. If their vision was anachronistic, they nevertheless understood a message that the twentieth century has been at pains to recover—that human development consists of a balance of intellect and emotions, and that such a balance can only be found in community.

BIBLIOGRAPHY

I. MANUSCRIPTS

Froude, R. Hurrell. Papers. Birmingham Oratory, Birmingham, England.

Hodge, Charles. Papers. Princeton Theological Seminary, Princeton, New Jersey.

——————. Papers. Princeton University Library, Princeton, New Jersey.

Keble, John. Papers. Keble College, Oxford, England.

Kliefoth, Theodor. Papers. Staatsarchiv Schwerin, Schwerin, German Democratic Republic.

Krauth, Charles Philip. Papers. Lutheran Archives Center at Philadelphia, Philadelphia, Pennsylvania.

Löhe, Wilhelm. Papers. Löhe Archiv, Neuendettelsau, Bavaria, Federal Republic of Germany.

Nevin, John. Papers. Evangelical and Reformed Historical Society, Lancaster Theological Seminary, Lancaster, Pennsylvania.

Newman, John. Papers. Birmingham Oratory, Birmingham, England.

Pusey, Edward B. Papers. Pusey House, Oxford, England.

Ravenscroft, John Stark. Papers. Southern Historical Collection, University of North Carolina, Chapel Hill, North Carolina.

——————. Papers. Church Historical Society, Austin, Texas.

Schaff, Philip. Papers. Evangelical and Reformed Historical Society, Lancaster Theological Seminary, Lancaster, Pennsylvania.

Vilmar, August. Papers. Hessisches Staatsarchiv Marburg, Marburg, Federal Republic of Germany.

332   Church and Confession

332   Church and Confession

_____. Papers. Universitätsbibliothek Marburg, Marburg, Federal Republic of Germany.

Wilberforce Family. Papers. Bodleian Library, Oxford, England.

II. PRINTED SOURCES

A. Germany

Adam, Alfred. *Nationalkirche und Volkskirche im deutschen Protestantismus.* Göttingen: Vandenhoeck & Ruprecht, 1938.

Amelung, Eberhard. "Die demokratischen Bewegungen des Jahres 1848 im Urteil der protestantischen Theologie." Ph.D. diss., Marburg University, 1954.

Bachmann, J. *Ernst Wilhelm Hengstenberg.* 3 vols. Gütersloh: C. Bertelsmann, 1876-1892.

Barczay, G. *Ecclesia semper reformanda. Eine Untersuchung zum Kirchenbegriff des 19. Jahrhunderts.* Zurich: Evangelische Verlag, 1961.

Barth, Karl. *Protestant Theology in the Nineteenth Century.* London: Sheed and Ward, 1972.

Bauer, Johannes. *Schleiermacher als politischer Prediger.* Gießen: Töpelmann, 1908.

Beckmann, Klaus-Martin. *Unitas ecclesiae. Eine systematische Studie zur Theologie-geschichte des 19. Jahrhunderts.* Gütersloh: Gerd Mohn, 1967.

_____. *Der Begriff der Häresie bei Schleiermacher.* Munich: Kaiser, 1959.

Bernard, F. M. *Herder's Social and Political Thought.* Oxford: Oxford University Press, 1965.

Beyreuther, Erich. *Die Erweckungsbewegung.* Göttingen: Vandenhoeck & Ruprecht, 1963).

Birkner, Hans-Joachin. *Schleiermachers christliche Sittenlehre im Zusammenhang seines philosophische-theologischen System.* Berlin: Töpelmann, 1964.

Blum, Jerome. *End of the Old Order in Rural Europe.* Princeton: Princeton University Press, 1977.

Bouman, W. R. "The Unity of the Church in Nineteenth Century Confessional Lutheranism." Ph.D. diss., Heidelberg University, 1962.

Cassirer, Ernst. *The Problem of Knowledge.* New Haven: Yale University Press, 1950.

Coker, F. W. *Organismic Theories of the State.* New York: Columbia University Press, 1910.

Dawson, Jerry. *Friedrich Schleiermacher, the Evolution of a Nationalist.* Austin: University of Texas Press, 1966.

Deinzer, J. *Wilhelm Löhes Leben.* 3 vols. Gütersloh: C. Bertelsmann, 1880-1901.

Delius, Walter. *Die evangelische Kirche und die Revolution 1848*. Berlin: Evangelische Verlagsanstalt, 1948.

Dilthey, Wilhelm, and L. Jonas, eds. *Aus Schleiermachers Leben: in Briefen*. 4 vols. Berlin: G. Reimer, 1860-1863.

Drucker, P. *Friedrich Julius Stahl: konservative Staatslehre und geschichtliche Entwicklung*. Tübingen: Mohr, 1933.

Epstein, Klaus. *The Genesis of German Conservatism*. Princeton: Princeton University Press, 1966.

Fagerberg, Holstein. *Bekenntnis, Kirche, und Amt in der deutschen konfessionellen Theologie des 19. Jahrhunderts*. Uppsala: Almquist, 1952.

Foerster, Erich. *Die Entstehung der Preußischen Landeskirche unter der Regierung König Friedrich Wilhelm III*. 2 vols. Tübingen: J. C. B. Mohr, 1905-1907.

Friedberg, Emil. *Die Grundlagen der Preußichen Kirchenpolitik unter König Friedrich Wilhelm IV*. Leipzig: Grunow, 1882.

Geiger, Max. "Das Problem der Erweckungstheologie." *Theologische Zeitung* 14 (1958): 430-50.

Haack, E. D. *Theodor Kliefoth, ein Charakterbild aus der Zeit der Erneuerung des christlichen Glaubensleben und der lutherische Kirche im 19. Jahrhundert*. Schwerin: F. Bahn, 1910.

Hafter, Herbert. *Der Freiherr vom Stein in seinem Verhältnis zu Religion und Kirche*. Berlin: Rothschild, 1932.

Hamerow, Theodore. *Restoration, Revolution, Reaction: Economics and Politics in Germany, 1815-1871*. Princeton: Princeton University Press, 1966.

Harnack, Adolf. *History of Dogma*. Translated by Neil Buchanan, 7 vols. London: Williams, 1894.

Hebart, S. *Wilhelm Löhes Lehre von der Kirche, ihrem Amt und Regiment*. Neuendettelsau: Freimund Verlag, 1939.

Hedderich, H. F. *Die Gedanken der Romantik über Kirche und Staat*. Gütersloh: Gerd Mohn, 1941.

Henderson, W. O. *The Rise of German Industrial Power, 1834-1914*. Berkeley: University of California Press, 1975.

Henke, E. L. *Schleiermacher und die Union*. Marburg: N. G. Elwert, 1868.

Hermelink, Heinrich. *Das Christentum in der Menschenheitsgeschichte*. 3 vols. Stuttgart: J. B. Metzlersche Verlagsbuchhandlung, 1951-1955.

Hirsch, Emanuel. *Geschichte der neuern evangelischen Theologie im Zusammenhang mit den allgemeinen Bewegungen des europäischen Denkens*. 2d ed. 5 vols. Gütersloh: C. Bertelsmann, 1960.

Holstein, Günter. *Die Staatsphilosophie Schleiermachers*. Bonn: Schroeder, 1923.

——————. *Die Grundlage des evangelischen Kirchenrecht.* Tübingen: Mohr, 1928.

Hopf, Wilhelm. *August Vilmar.* 2 vols. Marburg: N. G. Elwert, 1913.

Hundeshagen, K. B. *Beitrage zur Kirchenverfassungsgeschichte und Kirchenpolitik.* Wiesbaden: Niedner, 1864.

Jensen, Gwendolyn E. "A Comparative Study of Prussian and Anglican Church-State Reform in the Nineteenth Century." *Journal of Church and State* 23, no. 3 (Autumn 1981): 445-63.

Kähler, Martin. *Geschichte der protestantischen Dogmatik im 19. Jahrhundert.* Berlin: Evangelische Verlagsanstalt, 1962.

Kaiser, Gerhard. *Pietismus und Patriotismus im literarischen Deutschland.* Wiesbaden: Steiner, 1961.

Kantzenbach, Friedrich W. *Die Erweckungsbewegung.* Neuendettelsau: Freimund Verlag, 1957.

——————. *Die Erlanger Theologie.* Munich: Evang. Pressverband, 1966.

——————. *Gestalten und Typen des Neuluthertum.* Gütersloh: Gütersloher Verlaghaus G. Mohn, 1968.

Kehnscherper, G. "Das Wesen der Kirche nach Kliefoth." Ph.D. diss., Leipzig University, 1955.

Kißling, Johannes. *Der deutschen Protestantismus.* 2 vols. Münster: Aschendorf, 1917-1918.

Kliefoth, Theodor. *Einleitung in die Dogmengeschichte.* Parchim and Ludwigslust: Hofbuchhandlung, 1839.

——————. *An die Gesitlichkeit und den Lehrstand des Superintendent Schwerin.* Hamburg: privately printed, 1844.

——————. "Unsere Aufgabe." *Zeitblatt für die evangelische-lutherische Kirche Mecklenburgs* (1848).

——————. *Denkschrift.* Schwerin: Stiller, 1849.

——————. *Beluechtung . . . des historische Bericht.* Schwerin: Stiller, 1851.

——————. *Acht Bücher von der Kirche.* Schwerin: Stiller, 1854.

——————. "An die hochwürdige theologische Facultät der Georg Augustus Universität zu Göttingen." *Kirchliche Zeitschrift* (1854).

——————. "Die Erklarung der theologischen Fakultät zu Göttingen in Veranlassung ihrer Denkschrift . . . über die gegenwärtige Krisis des kirchliche Lebens." *Kirchliche Zeitschrift* (1855).

Kressel, Hans. *Wilhelm Löhe: ein Lebensbild.* Erlangen: Martin Luther Verlag, 1954.

_____. *Wilhelm Löhe, der lutherische Christenmensch*. Berlin: Lutherisches Verlagshaus, 1960.

Kupisch, Karl. *Die deutschen Landeskirchen im 19. und 20. Jahrhundert*. Göttingen: Vandenhoeck & Ruprecht, 1966.

Lill, R. *Die Beilegung der Kölner Wirren, 1840-1842*. Düsseldorf: Schwann, 1962.

Löhe, Wilhelm. *Gesammelte Werke*. Edited by Klaus Ganzert. 7 vols. Neuendettelsau: Freimund Verlag, 1951-.

_____. *Three Books About the Church*. Translated and edited by James Schaaf. Philadelphia: Fortress Press, 1969.

Lütge, Friedrich. *Deutsche Sozial-und Wirtschaftsgeschichte*. Berlin: Springer, 1960.

Lütgert, W. *Die Religion des deutschen Idealismus und ihr Ende*. 2d ed. 3 vols. Gütersloh: C. Bertelsmann, 1923.

Mandelbaum, Maurice. *History, Man, and Reason*. Baltimore: Johns Hopkins University Press, 1974.

Marsson, R. *Die preußiche Union. Eine kirchenrechtliche Untersuchung*. Berlin: Riemer, 1923.

Masur, G. *Friedrich Julius Stahl*. Berlin: Mittler, 1930.

Maurer, W. *Aufklärung, Idealismus, und Restoration*. 2 vols. Gießen: Topelmann, 1930.

Milward, Alan, and S. B. Saul. *The Economic Development of Continental Europe, 1780-1870*. Totowa NJ: Allen and Unwin, 1973.

Müller, J. *Die evangelische Union ihr Wesen und gottliche Recht*. Berlin: Reimer, 1854.

Müller, K. *Die religiöse Erweckung in Württemberg am Anfang des 19. Jahrhunderts*. Tübingen: Mohr, 1925.

Niebuhr, Richard R. *Schleiermacher on Christ and Religion*. New York: Scribners, 1964.

Nigg, Walter. *Kirchliche Reaktion*. Leipzig: Beck, 1939.

Nipperdey, Thomas. "Verein als soziale Struktur in Deutschland im spaten 18. und fruhen 19. Jahrhunderts." In *Geschichtswissen und Vereinwesen im 19. Jahrhundert*, edited by H. Boockman. Göttingen: Vandenhoeck & Ruprecht, 1972.

Noyes, P. H. *Organization and Revolution: Working-class Associations in the German Revolution of 1848-1849*. Princeton: Princeton University Press, 1966.

Ranke, Leopold, ed. *Aus dem Briefwechsel Freidrich Wilhelms IV mit Bunsen*. Leipzig: Duncker, 1874.

Reiss, H. S. *The Political Thought of the German Romantics, 1793-1815*. Oxford: Oxford University Press, 1955.

Rendtorff, T. *Kirche und Theologie*. Gütersloh: Gütersloher Verlagshaus, 1966.

Rohr, Donald G. *The Origins of Social Liberalism in Germany*. Chicago: University of Chicago Press, 1963.

Ruhbach, Gerhard, ed. *Kirchenunion im 19. Jahrhundert*. Gütersloh: Gütersloher Verlagshaus, 1967.

Samson, Holgar. *Die Kirche als Grundbegriff der theologischen Ethik Schleiermachers*. Zollikon: Evang. Verlag, 1958.

Schaaf, James L. "Wilhelm Löhe's Relation to the American Church." Ph.D. diss., Heidelberg University, 1961.

Schaper, Ewald. *Die geistespolitischen Voraussetzungen der Kirchenpolitik Friedrich Wilhelm IV von Preußen*. Stuttgart: Kohlhammer, 1938.

Scheider, Theodor. *Vom Deutschen Bund zum Deutschen Reich, 1815-1871*. Stuttgart: Ullstein, 1970.

Schleiermacher, Friedrich. *Sämmtliche Werke*. Edited by G. Reimer. 31 vols. Berlin: Riemer, 1834-1864.

——————. *The Christian Faith*. New York: Harper and Row, 1963.

——————. *On Religion*. New York: Harper and Row, 1958.

Schmaltz, Karl. *Kirchengeschichte Mecklenburgs*. 3 vols. Schwerin and Berlin: Evangelische Verlagsanstalt, 1935-1952.

Schmidt, J., ed. *Claus Harms: ein Kirchenvater des 19. Jahrhunderts*. Gütersloh: Gerd Mohn, 1976.

Schmidt, Martin. "Die innere Einheit der Erweckungsfrömmigkeit im Uebergangsstadium zum lutherischen Konfessionalismus." *Theologische Literaturzeitung* 74 (1949): 17-28.

——————. *Pietismus*. Stuttgart: W. Kohlhammer, 1972.

Schmidt-Clausen, K. *Vorweggenommene Einheit: Die Grundung des Bistums Jerusalem in Jahre 1841*. Berlin: Lutherisches Verlaghaus, 1965.

Schnabel, Franz. *Deutsche Geschichte im Neuenzehnten Jahrhundert*. 2d ed. 4 vols. Frieburg: Herder, 1951.

Schnoor, W. "Kliefoths Lehre von der Kirche." *Evangelische-lutherische Kirchenzeitung* (15 June 1951): 165-68.

Schoeps, Hans-Joachim. *Das andere Preußen*. Stuttgart: F. Vorwerk, 1952.

Schrörs, H. *Die Kölner Wirren*. Berlin: F. Dummler, 1927.

Shanahan, William O. *German Protestants Face the Social Question*. Notre Dame: University of Notre Dame Press, 1954.

Sheehan, James. *German Liberalism in the Nineteenth Century*. Chicago: University of Chicago Press, 1978.

Simon, Matthias. *Evangelische Kirchengeschichte Bayerns.* 2 vols. Munich: Müller, 1942.

—————————. *Die Evangelische-Lutherische Kirche in Bayern im 19. und 20. Jahrhundert.* Munich: Claudius Verlag, 1961.

Spiegel, Yorick. *Theologie der bürgerlichen Gesellschaft. Sozialphilosophie und Glaubenslehre bei Friedrich Schleiermacher.* Munich: Kaiser, 1968.

Srocka, Werner. "Der Kirchenbegriff Friedrich Julius Stahl." Ph.D. diss., Erlangen University, 1927.

Stahl, Friedrich Julius. *Die Kirchenverfassung nach Lehre und Recht des Protestantismus.* Erlangen: Bläsing, 1840.

—————————. *Was ist Revolution?* Berlin: Evang. Verein, 1852.

—————————. *Der Protestantismus als politischen Princip.* Berlin: Schultze, 1853.

—————————. *Die lutherische Kirche und die Union.* Berlin: Hertz, 1859.

—————————. *Die gegenwärtige Parteien in Staat und Kirche.* Berlin: Hertz, 1863.

Steitz, Heinrich. *Geschichte der Evangelischen Kirche in Hessen und Nassau.* 4 vols. Marburg: Verlag Trautvetter und Fischer, 1961-1977.

Stephan, Horst and Martin Schmidt. *Geschichte der deutschen evangelischen Theologie seit dem deutschen Idealismus.* 3d ed. Berlin: Walter de Gruyter, 1973.

Stiewe, Martin. *Das Unionverständnis Friedrich Schleiermachers.* Witten: Luther Verlag, 1969.

Stoeffler, F. Ernst. *German Pietism During the Eighteenth Century.* Leiden: Brill, 1973.

Stoll, H. *Theodor Kliefoth als Kirchenführer.* Göttingen: Vandenhoeck & Ruprecht, 1936.

Strunk, Reiner. *Politische Ekklesiologie im Zeitalter der Revolution.* Munich: Kaiser, 1971.

Thomasius, Gottfried. *Die Wiedererwachen des evangelischen Lebens in der lutherische Kirche Bayerns. Ein süddeutscher Kirchengeschichte, 1800-1840.* Erlangen: Deichert, 1867.

Tiesmeyer, L. *Die Erweckungsbewegung in Deutschland während des 19. Jahrhunderts.* 4 vols. Kassel: Rottiger, 1901-1912.

Troeltsch, Ernst. *The Social Teachings of the Christian Churches.* 2 vols. New York: Harper and Row, 1931.

Vilmar, August. *Die Theologie der Tatsachen wider die Theologie der Rhetorik.* Marburg: Bertelsmann, 1857. Reprint. 1938.

—————————. *Kirche und Welt.* 2 vols. Gütersloh: Bertelsmann, 1872.

—————————. *Schulreden über Fragen der Zeit.* 3d ed. Gütersloh: Bertelsmann, 1886.

Wallman, Johannes. *Kirchengeschichte Deutschlands II*. Frankfurt: Ullstein, 1973.

Wangemann, Theodor. *Sieben Bücher preußicher Kirchengeschichte*. 3 vols. Berlin: Schultze, 1859-1860.

Wellek, Rene. *Concepts of Criticism*. Edited by Stephen Nichols, Jr. New Haven: Yale University Press, 1963.

——————. *Confrontations*. Princeton: Princeton University Press, 1965.

Wendland, W. *Studien zur Erweckungsbewegung in Berlin, 1810-1830*. Berlin: Riemer, 1924.

——————. *Die Religiosität und die kirchenpolitischen Grundsätze Friedrich Wilhelms des Dritten*. Gießen: Töpelmann, 1909.

Wolff, Kurt, ed. *From Karl Mannheim*. New York: Oxford University Press, 1971.

Zechlin, Egmont. *Die deutsche Einheitsbewegung*. Frankfurt: Ullstein, 1967.

B. England

Abbey, Charles and John Overton. *The English Church in the Eighteenth Century*. London: Longmans and Co., 1887.

Abrams, M. H. *The Mirror and the Lamp*. New York: Oxford University Press, 1953.

Adamson, John. *English Education, 1789-1902*. Cambridge: Cambridge University Press, 1930.

Akenson, Donald H. *The Church of Ireland: Ecclesiastical Reform and Revolution, 1800-1835*. New Haven: Yale University Press, 1971.

Arnold, Thomas. *The Life and Correspondence of Thomas Arnold*. Edited by A. P. Stanley. 2 vols. Boston: Scribners, 1860.

——————. *The Miscellaneous Works of Thomas Arnold: first American edition with nine additional essays*. New York: Appleton, 1845.

Baker, William J. "Hurrell Froude and the Reformers." *Journal of Ecclesiastical History* 21, no. 3 (July 1970): 243-59.

Balleine, G. R. *A History of the Evangelical Party in the Church of England*. London: Longmans, 1908.

Battiscombe, G. *John Keble: A Study in Limitations*. London: Constable, 1963.

Beck, G. A., ed. *The English Catholics, 1850-1950*. London: Burns, 1950.

Beck, W. J. A. *John Keble's Literary and Religious Contribution to the Oxford Movement*. Nijmegen: Stockum, 1959.

Becker, Werner. "Newman in Deutschland." In *Newman-Studien*, edited by H. Fries and W. Becker. 6 vols. 2:281-306. Nürnberg: Glock und Lutz, 1948-1964.

Bentham, Jeremy. *Church of Englandism and its Catechism Examined*. London: Wilson, 1818.

_____. *Analysis of the Influence of Natural Religion on the Temporal Happiness of Mankind*. London: Truelove, 1822.

Best, G. F. A. *Temporal Pillars*. Cambridge: Cambridge University Press, 1964.

_____. "The Protestant Constitution and its Supporters, 1800-1829." *Transactions of the Royal Historical Society* 8, ser. 5 (1958): 105-27.

_____. "Popular Protestantism in Victorian Britain." In *Ideas and Institutions of Victorian Britain*. Edited by Robert Robson, 115-42. London: G. Bell, 1967.

_____. "Establishment in the Age of Grey and Holland." *History* 95, no. 154 (June 1960): 103-18.

_____. "The Evangelicals and the Established Church in the Early Nineteenth Century." *Journal of Theological Studies* 10, part 1 (April 1959): 63-78.

_____. "The Religious Difficulties of National Education in England, 1800-1870." *Cambridge Historical Journal* 12, no. 2 (1956): 155-73.

Biemer, Günter. *Newman on Tradition*. London: Herder, 1967.

Bouyer, Louis. *Newman: His Life and Spirituality*. London: Kenedy, 1958.

Bowen, Desmond. *The Idea of the Victorian Church*. Montreal: McGill University Press, 1968.

Brendon, Piers. *Hurrell Froude and the Oxford Movement*. London: Paul Elek, 1974.

_____. "Newman, Keble, and Froude's *Remains*." *English Historical Review* 87, no. 345 (October 1972): 697-716.

Bricknell, W. Simcox, ed. *The Judgment of the Bishops upon Tractarian Theology*. Oxford: J. Vincent, 1854.

Brilioth, Yngve. *The Anglican Revival*. London: Longmans, 1933.

_____. *Three Lectures on Evangelicalism and the Oxford Movement*. London: Oxford University Press, 1934.

Brock, Michael. *The Great Reform Act*. London: Hutchinson, 1973.

Brose, Olive. *Church and Parliament: The Reshaping of the Church of England, 1828-1860*. Stanford: Stanford University Press, 1959.

_____. "The Irish Precedent for English Church Reform: The Church Temporalities Act of 1833." *Journal of Ecclesiastical History* 7, no. 2 (October 1956): 204-25.

Brown, Ford K. *Fathers of the Victorians: The Age of Wilberforce*. Cambridge: Cambridge University Press, 1961.

Cardwell, Edward and Lord Mahon, eds. *Memoirs by the Right Honourable Sir Robert Peel*. 2 vols. London: Kraus, 1856-1857.

Chadwick, Owen. *The Victorian Church*. 2 vols. London: Adam and Charles Black, 1966-1970.

——————————, ed. *The Mind of the Oxford Movement*. Stanford: Stanford University Press, 1960.

Chambers, J. D. and G. E. Mingay. *The Agricultural Revolution, 1750-1850*. London: Batsford: 1966.

Church, Richard W. *The Oxford Movement*. London: Macmillan, 1892.

Clark, G. Kitson. *Churchmen and the Condition of England, 1832-1885*. London: Macmillan, 1973.

Coleridge, J. T. *A Memoir of the Rev. John Keble*. 2 vols. New York: J. Parker, 1869.

Cornish, F. W. *The English Church in the Nineteenth Century*. 2 vols. London: Macmillan, 1910.

Coulson, John, and A. M. Allchin, eds. *The Rediscovery of Newman: An Oxford Symposium*. London: Sheed & Ward, 1967.

Cowherd, Raymond. *The Politics of English Dissent*. New York: New York University Press, 1956.

Davis, R. W. "The Strategy of 'Dissent' in the Repeal Campaign, 1820-1828." *Journal of Modern History* 38, no. 4 (December 1966): 374-93.

Dawson, Christopher. *The Spirit of the Oxford Movement*. London: Sheed and Ward, 1933.

Deane, Phyllis. *The First Industrial Revolution*. London: Cambridge University Press, 1967.

Dessain, C., et al., eds. *Letters and Diaries of John Henry Newman*. 33 vols. Oxford: T. Nelson, 1961-.

Dick, Klaus. "Das Analogieprinzip bei John Henry Newman und seine Quelle in Joseph Butler's 'Analogy.' " In *Newman-Studien*, edited by H. Fries and W. Becker. 6 vols. 5:9-228. Nürnberg: Glock und Lutz, 1948-1964.

Dunn, Waldo H. *James Anthony Froude*. 2 vols. Oxford: Clarendon Press, 1961-1963.

Edwards, Maldwyn. *Methodism and England: A Study of Methodism in Its Social and Political Aspects During the Period, 1850-1932*. London: Epworth, 1944.

Elliott-Binns, L. E. *Religion in the Victorian Era*. London: Lutterworth Press, 1936.

——————————. *The Early Evangelicals*. London: Lutterworth Press, 1953.

Every, George. *The High Church Party, 1688-1718*. London: Church Historical Society, 1956.

Finlayson, G. B. "The Politics of Municipal Reform, 1835." *English Historical Review* 81 (1966): 673-92.

Fries, H., and W. Becker, eds., *Newman-Studien*. 6 vols. Nürnberg: Glock und Lutz, 1948-1964.

Froude, Richard Hurrell. *See* John Keble.

Gash, Norman. *Reaction and Reconstruction in English Politics, 1832-1852*. Oxford: Clarendon Press, 1965.

―――――――. *Aristocracy and People, Britain 1815-1865*. Cambridge: Harvard University Press, 1979.

―――――――. *Politics in the Age of Peel*. London: Longmans, 1953.

―――――――. *Mr. Secretary Peel*. London: Longmans, 1961.

―――――――. *Sir Robert Peel*. London: Longmans, 1972.

Gloyn, Cyril. *The Church in the Social Order*. Forest Grove OR: Pacific University, 1942.

Greaves, R. W. "Golightly and Newman, 1824-1845." *Journal of Ecclesiastical History* 9, no. 2 (1958): 209-28.

―――――――. "The Jerusalem Bishopric, 1841." *English Historical Review* 64, no. 252 (July 1949): 328-53.

Griffin, John R. *The Oxford Movement: A Revision*. Front Royal VA: Christendom Press, 1980.

Härdelin, Alf. *The Tractarian Understanding of the Eucharist*. Uppsala: Lund, 1965.

Halevy, Elie. *The Growth of Philosophic Radicalism*. Boston: Beacon, 1955.

Hampden, R. D. *The Scholastic Philosophy considered in its relation to Christian Theology*. Oxford: J. H. Parker, 1833.

Harrold, Charles F. "Newman and the Alexandrian Platonists." *Modern Philology* 37, no. 3 (February 1940): 279-91.

Hechler, W. H. *The Jerusalem Bishopric*. London: Trübner, 1883.

Henriques, Ursula. *Religious Toleration in England, 1787-1833*. Toronto: Routledge, 1961.

Hexter, J. H. "The Protestant Revival and the Catholic Question in England, 1778-1829." *Journal of Modern History* 8, no. 3 (September 1936): 297-319.

Hook, Walter. *A Letter to the Lord Bishop of St. David's*. London: J. Rivington, 1846.

Houghton, Esther Rhoads. "The British Critic and the Oxford Movement." *Studies in Bibliography* 16 (1963): 119-37.

Howse, Ernest M. *Saints in Politics: The 'Clapham Sect' and the Growth of Freedom*. London: Allen and Unwin, 1953.

Jennings, Louis, ed. *The Correspondence and Diaries of John Wilson Croker*. 3 vols. London: Longmans, 1884.

Keble, John. *Sermons, Academical and Occasional*. Oxford: John Henry Parker, 1847.

——————and John Newman, eds. *Remains of the late Reverend Richard Hurrell Froude*. 4 vols. London: J. G. and F. Rivington, 1838-1839.

Keller-Huschemenger, Max. *Die Lehre der Kirche in der Oxford Bewegung: Strucktur und Function*. Gütersloh: Gerd Mohn, 1974.

Kenny, Terence. *The Political Thought of John Henry Newman*. London: Longmans, 1957.

Knox, E. A. *The Tractarian Movement, 1833-1845*. London: Putnam, 1933.

Landes, David. *The Unbound Prometheus*. London: Cambridge University Press, 1969.

Lash, Nicolas. *Newman on Development*. Sheperdstown WV: Patmos Press, 1975.

Liddon, H. P. *Life of E. B. Pusey*. Edited by J. O. Johnston and R. J. Wilson. 4 vols. London: Longmans, 1893-1897.

Linker, Robert. "The English Roman Catholics and Emancipation: The Politics of Persuasion." *Journal of Ecclesiastical History* 27, no. 2 (April 1976): 151-80.

Lock, W. *John Keble, a biography*. London: Houghton, 1893.

Locke, John. *A Letter Concerning Toleration*. Edited by Mario Montuori. The Hague, Netherlands: M. Nijhoff, 1963.

Machin, G. I. T. *The Catholic Question in English Politics, 1820-1830*. Oxford: Clarendon Press, 1964.

——————. *Politics and the Churches in Great Britain, 1832-1868*. Oxford: Oxford University Press, 1977.

——————. "The Duke of Wellington and Catholic Emancipation." *Journal of Ecclesiastical History* 14, no. 2 (October 1963): 190-208.

——————. "The Maynooth Grant, the Dissenters and Disestablishment, 1845-1847." *English Historical Review* 82 (1967): 61-85.

——————. "Lord John Russell and the Prelude to the Ecclesiastical Titles Bill, 1846-1851." *Journal of Ecclesiastical History* 25, no. 3 (July 1974): 277-95.

Manning, Bernard. *The Protestant Dissenting Deputies*. Cambridge: Cambridge University Press, 1952.

Manning, Henry. *The Principles of the Ecclesiastical Commission Examined*. London: Rivington, 1838.

Mathieson, W. *English Church Reform, 1815-1840*. London: Longmans, 1923.

May, Lewis. *The Oxford Movement*. London: Longmans, 1933.

Middleton, R. D. *Newman at Oxford: His Religious Development*. London: Oxford University Press, 1950.

—————————. "Tract Ninety." *Journal of Ecclesiastical History* 2, no. 1 (1951): 81-100.

Moore, David. *The Politics of Deference*. New York: Barnes and Noble, 1976.

Mozley, Anne. *Letters and Correspondence of John Henry Newman*. 2 vols. London: Longmans, 1897.

Mozley, Thomas. *Reminiscences: chiefly of Oriel College and the Oxford Movement*. 2 vols. Boston: Houghton, 1882.

Munson, J. E. B. "The Oxford Movement by the End of the Nineteenth Century: The Anglo-Catholic Clergy." *Church History* 44, no. 3 (September 1975): 382-95.

Newman, John Henry. *The Via Media of the Anglican Church*. 2 vols. London: Longmans, 1895-1896.

—————————. *Essays: Critical and Historical*. 2 vols. London: Longmans, 1910.

—————————. *Correspondence of John Henry Newman with John Keble and others, 1839-1845*. Edited at the Birmingham Oratory. London: Longmans, 1917.

—————————. *Essays and Sketches*. Edited by Charles F. Harrold. 2 vols. London: Longmans, 1948.

—————————. *Apologia pro vita sua*. Edited by A. Dwight Cutler. Boston: Houghton, 1956.

Newsome, David. *The Parting of Friends*. London, Murray, 1966.

—————————. "Justification and Sanctification: Newman and the Evangelicals." *Journal of Theological Studies* 15 (April 1964): 32-53.

—————————. "The Evangelical Sources of Newman's Power." In *The Rediscovery of Newman: An Oxford Symposium*, edited by John Coulson and A. M. Allchin, 11-30. London: Sheed and Ward, 1967.

O'Connell, Marvin. *The Oxford Conspirators*. New York: Macmillan, 1969.

Orr, Edwin J. *The Second Evangelical Awakening in Britain*. London: Marshall, 1953.

Overton, John and Frederic Relton. *The English Church from the Accession of George I to the End of the Eighteenth Century*. London: Longmans, 1906.

—————————. *The English Church in the Nineteenth Century, 1800-1833*. London: Longmans, 1894.

Palmer, William. *A Narrative of the Events Connected with the Publication of the Tracts for the Times*. New York: Sparks, 1843.

Parker, Charles, ed. *Sir Robert Peel: from his private papers*. 3 vols. London: J. Murray, 1891-1899.

—————————, ed. *Life and Letters of Sir James Graham*. 2 vols. London: J. Murray, 1907.

344   Church and Confession

Perceval, A. P. *A Collection of Papers Connected with the Theological Movement of 1833*. London: J. G. F. Rivington, 1842.

Prickett, Stephen. *Romanticism and Religion*. Cambridge: Cambridge University Press, 1976.

Pusey, E. B. *An Historical Enquiry into the Probable Causes of the Rationalist Character lately Predominant in the Theology of Germany*. London: J. Rivington, 1828.

Reynolds, J. S. *The Evangelicals at Oxford, 1735-1871*. Oxford: Packer, 1953.

Reynolds, James. *The Catholic Emancipation Crisis in Ireland, 1823-1829*. New Haven: Yale University Press, 1954.

Roberts, David. *Paternalism in Early Victorian England*. New Brunswick: Rutgers University Press, 1979.

Roe, W. G. *Lamennais and England*. London: Oxford University Press, 1966.

Russell, George. *A Short History of the Evangelical Movement*. London: Macmillan, 1915.

Semmel, Bernard. *The Methodist Revolution*. New York: Basic Books, 1973.

Seynaeve, Jaak. *Cardinal Newman's Doctrine on Holy Scripture*. Louvain, Belgium: University of Louvain, 1953.

Shaw, P. E. *The Early Tractarians and the Eastern Church*. London: Longmans, 1930.

Smyth, Charles. *Simeon and Church Order*. Cambridge: Cambridge University Press, 1940.

──────────────. "R. D. Hampden." *Theology* 18 (1929): 259-65, 312-22.

Soloway, R. A. *Prelates and People: Ecclesiastical Social Thought in England, 1783-1853*. Toronto: University of Toronto Press, 1969.

Southey, Robert. *Sir Thomas More: or Colloquies of the Progress and Prospects of Society*. 2 vols. London: J. Murray, 1829.

Stansky, Peter, ed. *The Victorian Revolution*. New York: Holt, 1973.

Stephen, James. *Essays in Ecclesiastical Biography*. London: Longmans, 1875.

Storr, Vernon. *The Development of English Theology in the Nineteenth Century*. London: Longmans, 1913.

Stunt, T. C. F. "John Henry Newman and the Evangelicals." *Journal of Ecclesiastical History* 21, no. 1 (January 1970): 65-74.

Tracts for the Times, by Members of the University of Oxford, 6 vols. London and Oxford: J. G. and F. Rivington, 1833-1845.

Tulloch, John. *Movements of Religious Thought in Britain During the Nineteenth Century*. New York: Longmans, 1893.

Vaughan, Michalina and Margaret Archer. *Social Conflict and Educational Change in England and France, 1789-1848*. Cambridge: Cambridge University Press, 1971.

Venn, Henry. *The Complete Duty of Man*. New York: North American Tract Society, 1836.

Walsh, John. "Origins of the Evangelical Revival." In *Essays in Modern Church History*, edited by G. V. Bennett and J. D. Walsh, 132-62. New York: Oxford University Press, 1966.

——————. "Joseph Milner's Evangelical Church History." *Journal of Ecclesiastical History* 10, no. 2 (October 1959): 174-87.

Ward, B. *The Sequel to Catholic Emancipation, 1840-1850*. 2 vols. London: Longmans, 1915.

Ward, J. T., and J. H. Treble. "Religion and Education in 1843: Reactions to the Factory Education Bill." *Journal of Ecclesiastical History* 20, no. 1 (April 1969): 79-110.

Ward, W. R. *Religion and Society in England, 1790-1850*. New York: Schocken, 1973.

——————. "The Tithe Question in England in the Early Nineteenth Century." *Journal of Ecclesiastical History* 14, no. 1 (April 1965): 67-81.

Wardle, David. *English Popular Education, 1780-1970*. Cambridge: Cambridge University Press, 1970.

Wearmouth, Robert. *Methodism and the Working-Class Movements of England, 1800-1850*. London: Epworth Press, 1937.

Welch, P. J. "Blomfield and Peel: A Study in Cooperation between Church and State, 1841-1846." *Journal of Ecclesiastical History* 12, no. 1 (April 1961): 71-84.

——————. "Contemporary Views on the Proposals for the Alienation of Capitular Property in England, 1832-1840." *Journal of Ecclesiastical History* 5, no. 2 (October 1954): 184-95.

——————. "The Revival of an Active Convocation at Canterbury (1825-1855)." *Journal of Ecclesiastical History* 10, no. 2 (October 1959): 188-97.

——————. "Anglican Churchmen and the Establishment of the Jerusalem Bishopric." *Journal of Ecclesiastical History* 8, no. 2 (October 1957): 193-204.

Whately, E. Jane. *Life and Correspondence of Richard Whately, D. D.* 2d ed. London: Longmans, 1868.

Whately, Richard. *Essays on Some of the Peculiarities of the Christian Religion*. London: Fellowes, 1831.

——————. *The Use and Abuse of Party Feeling in Matters of Religion*. London: Parker, 1833.

——————. *Essays on Some of the Difficulties in the Writings of St. Paul*. London: Fellowes, 1833.

——————. *Charges and Other Tracts*. London: Fellowes, 1836.

Wilberforce, Robert I. *A Charge to the Clergy of East Riding*. N.p., 1847.

_____. *The Doctrine of the Incarnation*. Philadelphia: Hooker, 1849.

_____. *A Sketch of the History of Erastianism*. London: John Murray, 1851.

_____. *An Inquiry into the Principles of Church Authority, or reasons for re-calling my subscription to the Royal Supremacy*. London: Longmans, 1854.

Wilberforce, William. *A Practical View of the Prevailing Religious System of Professed Christians in the Higher and Middle Classes Contrasted with Real Christianity*. London: 1797. Reprint. New York: American Tract Society, n.d.

Willey, Basil. *Nineteenth Century Studies*. New York: Columbia University Press, 1949.

Williamson, Eugene L., Jr. *The Liberalism of Thomas Arnold*. University AL: University of Alabama Press, 1964.

Willoughby, L. A. "On Some German Affinities with the Oxford Movement." *Modern Language Review* 29, no. 1 (1934): 115-25.

Young, G. M. *Victorian England: A Portrait of an Age*. New York: Oxford University Press, 1937.

C. America

Addison, James. *The Episcopal Church in the United States*. New York: Scribners, 1951.

Ahlstrom, Sydney E. "Theology in America." In *The Shaping of American Religion*, edited by James Smith and A. Leland Jamison, 4 vols. 1:232-321. Princeton: Princeton University Press, 1961.

_____. "The Scottish Philosophy and American Theology." *Church History* 25, no. 3 (September 1955): 257-72.

_____. *A Religious History of the American People*. New Haven: Yale University Press, 1972.

Albright, Raymond. *A History of the Protestant Episcopal Church*. New York: Macmillan, 1964.

Anstadt, P. *Life and Times of Rev. S.S. Schmucker*. York PA: P. Anstadt & Sons, 1896.

Appel, Theodore. *The Life of John Williamson Nevin*. Philadelphia: Reformed Church Publication House, 1889).

Bacon, Leonard. *A History of American Christianity*. New York: Scribners, 1901.

Baird, Robert. *Religion in America*. 1856. Reprint. New York: Harper & Row, 1970.

Barker, Verlyn. "John W. Nevin: His Place in American Intellectual Thought." Ph.D. diss., St. Louis University, 1970.

Beecher, Lyman. *The Works of Lyman Beecher*. 3 vols. Boston: Jewett, 1852.

_____. *The Autobiography of Lyman Beecher*. Edited by Barbara M. Cross. 2 vols. Cambridge: Harvard University Press, 1961.

Bergendorff, Conrad. *The Doctrine of the Church in American Lutheranism*. Philadelphia: United Lutheran Publication House, 1956.

Billington, Ray Allen. *The Protestant Crusade, 1800-1860*. New York: Macmillan, 1938.

Binkley, Luther. *The Mercersburg Theology*. Lancaster: Franklin and Marshall College, 1953.

Boles, John. *The Great Revival, 1799-1805*. Lexington: University Press of Kentucky, 1972.

Bozeman, Theodore D. *Protestants in an Age of Science*. Chapel Hill: University of North Carolina Press, 1977.

Brand, William F. *Life of William Rolinson Whittingham*. 2 vols. New York: Young & Co., 1883.

Bruce, Dickson D., Jr. *And They All Sang Hallelujah: Plain-Folk Camp Meeting Religion, 1800-1845*. Knoxville: University of Tennessee Press, 1974.

Bruchey, Stuart. *The Roots of American Economic Growth, 1607-1861*. New York: Harper & Row, 1965.

Burns, J. A. *The Catholic School System in the United States*. New York: Benziger Bros., 1908.

———————. *The Growth and Development of the Catholic School System in the United States*. New York: Benziger Bros., 1912.

Bushman, Richard. *From Puritan to Yankee*. Cambridge: Harvard University Press, 1967.

Butterfield, Lyman. "Elder Joseph Leland, Jeffersonian Itinerant." *Proceedings of the American Antiquarian Society* 62 (1952): 155-60.

Campbell, William. *The Life and Writings of DeWitt Clinton*. New York: Scribners, 1849.

Cartwright, Peter. *Autobiography of Peter Cartwright*. Cincinnati: Strickland, 1890.

Carwardine, Richard. *Transatlantic Revivalism: Popular Evangelicalism in Britain and America, 1790-1865*. Westport: Greenwood, 1978.

Chorley, E. Clowes. *Men and Movements in the American Episcopal Church*. New York: Scribners, 1946.

Clarke, C. K. L. *Bishop Hobart and the Oxford Movement*. Milwaukee: Bowden Press, 1933.

Clemmer, Robert. "Historical Transcendentalism in Pennsylvania." *Journal of the History of Ideas* 30, no. 4 (October-December 1969): 579-92.

Cleveland, Catherine. *The Great Revival in the West, 1797-1805*. 1716. Reprint. Gloucester: Peter Smith, 1959.

Cobb, Sanford. *The Rise of Religious Liberty in America*. New York: Macmillan, 1902.

Cole, Charles. *The Social Ideas of the Northern Evangelists, 1826-1860*. New York: Columbia University Press, 1954.

Corwin, E. T. *A History of the Reformed Church, Dutch*. New York: Christian Literature Co., 1894.

Cremin, Lawrence. *The American Common School*. New York: Columbia University Press, 1951.

_____. *American Education: The Colonial Experience, 1607-1783*. New York: Harper and Row, 1970.

_____and R. Freeman Butts. *A History of Education in American Culture*. New York: Holt, 1953.

Cross, Whitney. *The Burned-Over District*. New York: Harper and Row, 1950.

Davis, David Brion. "The Emergence of Immediatism in British and American Antislavery Thought." *Mississippi Valley Historical Review* 49 (September 1962): 209-30.

Dawley, P. Mills. *The Story of the General Theological Seminary*. New York: Oxford University Press, 1969.

Dehon, Theodore. *Sermon on the Public Means of Grace*. 2 vols. Charleston: Thayer, 1821.

Deifell, John J. "The Ecclesiology of Charles Hodge." Ph.D. diss., University of Edinburgh, 1969.

DeMille, George. *The Catholic Movement in the American Episcopal Church*. Philadelphia: Church Historical Society, 1950.

Doane, William C. *Life and Writings of George Washington Doane*. 4 vols. New York: Appleton, 1860-1861.

Dubbs, J. H. *A History of the Reformed Church, Germany*. New York: Christian Literature Co., 1894.

Dwight, Timothy. *The Duty of Americans at the Present Crisis*. New Haven: Thomas Green, 1798.

Eckenrode, H. J. *Separation of Church and State in Virginia*. Richmond: Bottom, 1910.

Elsbree, O. W. *The Rise of the Missionary Spirit in America, 1790-1815*. Williamsport: Williamsport Printing Co., 1928.

Ferm, Vergilius. *The Crisis in American Lutheran Theology*. New York: Century Co., 1927.

Finney, Charles Grandison. *Memoirs of Charles Grandison Finney*. New York: Barnes, 1876.

_____. *Lectures on the Revivals of Religion*. Edited by W. G. McLoughlin. Cambridge: Harvard University Press, 1960.

Forster, Walter. *Zion on the Mississippi*. St. Louis: Concordia Press, 1953.

Foster, Charles I. *An Errand of Mercy*. Chapel Hill: University of North Carolina Press, 1960.

Gadsen, C. E. *An Essay on the Life of the Right Reverend Theodore Dehon*. Charleston: Miller, 1833.

Gaustad, Edwin S. *The Great Awakening in New England*. New York: Harper and Row, 1957.

Gillett, E. H. *History of the Presbyterian Church in the United States of America*. 2 vols. Philadelphia: Presbyterian Board, 1864.

Goen, C. C. *Revivalism and Separatism in New England*. New Haven: Yale University Press, 1962.

Goodrich, Chauncey. "Narrative of Revivals of Religion in Yale College." *American Quarterly Register* 10 (1838): 289-310.

Goodykoontz, C. B. *Home Missions on the American Frontier*. Caldwell: Caxton, 1939.

Greene, M. Louise. *The Development of Religious Liberty in Connecticut*. Boston: Houghton, 1905.

Griffin, Clifford. "Converting the Catholics: American Benevolent Societies and the Ante-Bellum Crusade Against the Church." *Catholic Historical Review* 47 (1961): 325-41.

Haroutunian, Joseph. *Piety versus Moralism*. New York: Henry Holt, 1932.

Haywood, Marshall D. *Lives of the Bishops of North Carolina*. Raleigh: Williams, 1910.

Healey, Robert. *Jefferson on Religion in Public Education*. New Haven: Yale University Press, 1962.

Heimert, Alan. *Religion and the American Mind*. Cambridge: Harvard University Press, 1966.

Hobart, John Henry. *Apology for Apostolic Order*. New York: T. Swords, 1807.

_____. *The Origins, the General Character, and the Present Situation of the Protestant Episcopal Church in the United States of America*. Philadelphia: T. Swords, 1814.

_____. *The Beneficial Effects of Sunday Schools*. New York: T. Swords, 1818.

_____. *The Churchman*. New York: T. Swords, 1819.

_____. *The High Churchman Vindicated*. New York: T. Swords, 1826.

_____. *Address*. New York: T. Swords, 1827.

_____. *The Christian Bishop*. New York: T. Swords, 1827.

Hodge, Alexander A. *The Life of Charles Hodge*. New York: T. Nelson, 1880.

Hodge, Charles. "The General Assembly of 1836." *Princeton Review* (July 1836): 415-76.

——————. "Schaff's Protestantism." *Princeton Review* (October 1845): 626-36.

——————. "Nevin's *Mystical Presence.*" *Princeton Review* (April 1848): 227-77.

——————. *The Constitutional History of the Presbyterian Church in the United States of America*. Philadelphia: W. S. Martien, 1851.

——————. "Schaff's Apostolic Church." *Princeton Review* (January 1854): 148-92.

Howe, Daniel. *The Unitarian Conscience*. Cambridge: Harvard University Press, 1970.

Howe, Mark DeWolfe. *The Garden and the Wilderness*. Chicago: University of Chicago Press, 1965.

Iwan, Wilhelm. *Die altlutherische Auswanderung um die Mitte des 19. Jahrhunderts*. 2 vols. Ludwigsburg: Kallenberg, 1943.

Jacobs, Henry E. *A History of the Evangelical Lutheran Church in the United States*. New York: Christian Literature Co., 1893.

Jefferson, Thomas. *The Writings of Thomas Jefferson*. Edited by Paul Ford. 10 vols. New York: Putnam, 1892-1899.

Johnson, Charles. *The Frontier Camp Meeting*. Dallas: Southern Methodist University Press, 1955.

Katz, Michael. *The Irony of Early School Reform: Educational Innovation in Mid-Nineteenth-Century Massachusetts*. Cambridge: Harvard University Press, 1968.

Keller, Charles R. *The Second Great Awakening in Connecticut*. New Haven: Yale University Press, 1942.

Kerr, Hugh, ed. *Sons of the Prophets*. Princeton: Princeton University Press, 1963.

Loetscher, Lefferts. "The Problem of Christian Unity in Early Nineteenth-Century America." *Church History* 32 (March 1963): 3-16.

Lowndes, Arthur. *Correspondence of John Henry Hobart*. In *Archives of the General Convention*. 6 vols. New York: Scribner, 1911-1912.

McAvoy, Thomas T. "The Formation of the American Catholic Minority, 1820-1860." *The Review of Politics* 10 (January 1948): 13-34.

McLoughlin, William G. *Modern Revivalism*. New York: Ronald, 1959.

——————. *New England Dissent*. 2 vols. Cambridge: Harvard University Press, 1971.

——————. *Isaac Backus and the American Pietistic Tradition*. Boston: Little, Brown, 1970.

_____. *Revivals, Awakenings, and Reforms*. Chicago: University of Chicago Press, 1978.

McNamara, R. F. "Trusteeism in the Atlantic States, 1785-1863." *Catholic Historical Review* 30 (1944): 135-54.

McVicker, J. *Early Years of the Late Bishop Hobart*. New York: Protestant Episcopal Press, 1834.

_____. *Professional Years of Bishop Hobart*. New York: Protestant Episcopal Press, 1836.

Madison, James. *The Writings of James Madison*. Edited by Galliard Hunt. 9 vols. New York: Putnam, 1900-1910.

Mann, Horace. *Life and Works of Horace Mann*. Edited by Mary Mann. 5 vols. Boston: Dillingham, 1868.

Manross, William. *A History of the American Episcopal Church*. New York: Morehouse, 1959.

Marsden, George. *The Evangelical Mind and the New School Presbyterian Experience*. New Haven: Yale University Press, 1970.

Mathews, Donald G. "The Second Great Awakening As an Organizing Process, 1780-1830: An Hypothesis." *American Quarterly* 21 (1969): 23-43.

Mead, Sidney. *Nathaniel William Taylor*. Chicago: University of Chicago Press, 1942.

_____. *The Lively Experiment*. New York: Harper and Row, 1963.

Meyer, Carl. "Lutheran Immigrant Churches Face the Problems of the Frontier." *Church History* 29, no. 4 (December 1960): 440-62.

_____, ed. *Moving Frontiers*. St. Louis: Concordia Publishing House, 1964.

Meyer, D. H. *The Instructed Conscience*. Philadelphia: University of Pennsylvania Press, 1972.

Meyers, Marvin. *The Jacksonian Persuasion*. Stanford: Stanford University Press, 1957.

Miller, Perry. *The Life of the Mind in America*. London: Gallancz, 1966.

_____. *Nature's Nation*. Cambridge: Harvard University Press, 1967.

_____. "From the Covenant to the Revival." In *The Shaping of American Religion*, edited by James Smith and A. Leland Jamison. 4 vols. 1:322-68. Princeton: Princeton University Press, 1961.

Miyakawa, T. Scott. *Protestants and Pioneers: Individualism and Conformity on the American Frontier*. Chicago: University of Chicago Press, 1964.

Nelson, John O. "The Rise of the Princeton Theology." Ph.D. diss., Yale University, 1935.

Neve, J. L. *A Brief History of the Lutheran Church in America*. Burlington: German Board, 1916.

Nevin, John W. *The Anxious Bench*. Chambersburg: German Reformed Church Publication House, 1843.

——————. *The Antichrist*. New York: Taylor, 1848.

——————. "The Year 1848; or the American Epoch." *Mercersburg Review* (January 1849).

——————. *Faith, Reverence, and Freedom*. Mercersburg: Rice, 1850.

——————. "Anglican Crisis." *Mercersburg Review* (July 1851).

——————. "Early Christianity." *Mercersburg Review*. (November 1851).

——————. "Early Christianity." *Mercersburg Review* (January 1852).

——————. *My Own Life: the earlier life*. Lancaster: Historical Society of the Evangelical and Reformed Church, 1964.

——————. "Catholic Unity." In *The Mercersburg Theology*, edited by James H. Nichols. New York: Oxford University Press, 1966.

Nichols, James H. *Romanticism in American Theology*. Chicago: University of Chicago Press, 1961.

——————. "John Williamson Nevin." In *Sons of the Prophets*, edited by Hugh Kerr, 69-81. Princeton: Princeton University Press, 1963.

——————, ed. *The Mercersburg Theology*. New York: Oxford University Press, 1966.

Nichols, Robert H. "The Plan of Union in New York." *Church History* 5, no. 1 (March 1936): 29-51.

Niebuhr, H. R. and Daniel D. Williams, eds. *The Ministry in Historical Perspective*. New York: Harper and Row, 1956.

North, Douglass C. *The Economic Growth of the United States, 1790-1860*. New York: Norton, 1961.

Persons, Stow. *American Minds*. New York: Holt, 1958.

Plummer, Kenneth M. "The Theology of John Williamson Nevin in the Mercersburg Period, 1840-1852." Ph.D. diss., University of Chicago, 1958.

Ravenscroft, John S. *Works*. 2 vols. New York: Protestant Episcopal Press, 1830.

Reed, Andrew and James Matheson. *A Narrative of the Visit to the American Churches by the Deputation from the Congregational Union of England and Wales*. New York: Harper, 1835.

Richards, George. "The Mercersburg Theology Historically Considered." *Papers of the American Society of Church History* (1911): 119-49.

_____. "The Mercersburg Theology—Its Purpose and Principles." *Church History* 20, no. 3 (September 1931): 42-55.

Rouse, Ruth and Stephen C. Neill, eds. *A History of the Ecumenical Movement, 1517-1948*. Philadelphia: Westminster Press, 1967.

Salomon, Richard. "The Episcopate on the Carey Case, New Sources from the Chase Collection at Kenyon College." *Historical Magazine of the Protestant Episcopal Church* 18, no. 3 (September 1949): 240-81.

Sandeen, Ernest. "The Princeton Theology." *Church History* 31, no. 2 (September 1962): 307-21.

_____. "The Distinctiveness of American Denominationalism: A Case Study of the 1846 Evangelical Alliance." *Church History* 45, no. 2 (June 1976): 222-34.

Schaff, David. *The Life of Philip Schaff*. New York: Scribners, 1897.

Schaff, Philip. *What is Church History*. Philadelphia: Lippencott, 1846.

_____. *Anglo-Germanism*. Chambersburg: Kieffer, 1846.

_____. *Systematic Benevolence*. Mercersburg: Kieffer, 1851.

_____. *American Nationality*. Chambersburg: Kieffer, 1856.

_____. *Slavery and the Bible*. Chambersburg: Kieffer, 1861.

_____. *America: a sketch of its political, social, and religious character*. Edited by Perry Miller. 1855. Reprint. Cambridge: Harvard University Press, 1961.

_____. *The Principle of Protestantism*. Reprint. Philadelphia: German Reformed Church Publication House, 1964.

Schlesinger, Arthur M. "Biography of a Nation of Joiners." *Paths to the Present*. 1949. Reprint. New York: Macmillan, 1964.

Schmucker, Samuel. *An Appeal to the American Churches with a Plan for Catholic Union*. New York: Gould and Newman, 1838.

_____. *The American Lutheran Church*. Springfield: Harbaugh, 1851.

Schroeder, J. F. *Memorial of Bishop Hobart*. New York: T. Swords, 1831.

Segerstedt, Torgny. *The Problem of Knowledge in Scottish Philosophy*. Lund: Gleerup, 1935.

Smith, Elwyn, ed. *The Religion of the Republic*. Philadelphia: Fortress Press, 1971.

_____. "The Voluntary Establishment of Religion." In *The Religion of the Republic*, edited by Elwyn Smith, 154-82. Philadelphia: Fortress Press, 1971.

Smith, James and A. Leland Jamison, eds. *The Shaping of American Religion*. 4 vols. Princeton: Princeton University Press, 1961.

Smith, Wilson. *Professors and Public Ethics*. Ithaca: Cornell University Press, 1956.

Smylie, James H. "Protestant Clergy, the First Amendment, and Beginnings of a Constitutional Debate, 1781-1791." In *The Religion of the Republic*, edited by Elwyn Smith, 116-53. Philadelphia: Fortress Press, 1971.

Spaeth, Adolph. *Charles Porterfield Krauth*. 2 vols. New York: Christian Literature Company, 1898.

Sprague, William. *Lectures on the Revivals of Religion*. Albany: Webster, 1832.

Stoeffler, F. Ernst, ed. *Continental Pietism and Early American Christianity*. Grand Rapids: Eerdmans, 1976.

Stokes, Anson Phelps. *Church and State in the United States*. 3 vols. New York: Harper, 1950.

Story, Joseph. *Commentaries on the Constitution of the United States*. 3 vols. Boston: Little, Brown, 1833.

Suelflow, August R. "The Beginnings of 'Missouri, Ohio, and Other States,' in America." In *Moving Frontiers*, edited by Carl Meyer. 90-141. St. Louis: Concordia Publishing House, 1964.

Taylor, George R. *The Transportation Revolution, 1815-1860*. New York: Harper and Row, 1951.

Taylor, Nathaniel W. *Concio ad Clerum*. New Haven: Howe, 1828.

Tewksbury, Donald. *The Founding of American Colleges and Universities Before the Civil War*. New York: Columbia University Press, 1922.

Thistlewaite, Frank. *The Anglo-American Connection in the Early Nineteenth Century*. Philadelphia: University of Pennsylvania Press, 1959.

Thompson, Robert E. *A History of the Presbyterian Church in the United States*. New York: Christian Literature Co., 1895.

Tocqueville, de, Alexis. *Democracy in America*. Edited by Phillips Bradley. 2 vols. New York: Vintage, 1945.

Trinterud, Leonard. "Charles Hodge." In *Sons of the Prophets*, edited by Hugh Kerr, 22-38. Princeton: Princeton University Press, 1963.

Ward, John William. *Andrew Jackson—Symbol for an Age*. New York: Oxford University Press, 1962.

Welter, Rush. *The Mind of America, 1820-1860*. New York: Columbia University Press, 1975.

Weng, Armin. "The Language Problem in the Lutheran Church in Pennsylvania, 1740-1820." *Church History* 5, no. 4 (December 1936): 359-75.

Wentz, Abdel. *A Basic History of Lutheranism in America*. Philadelphia: Muhlenberg Press, 1955.

————. *History of the Gettysburg Seminary*. Philadelphia: United Lutheran Publication House, 1927.

Wilson, John F., ed. *Church and State in American History*. Boston: Heath, 1965.

Yoder, Don. "Christian Unity in Nineteenth-Century America." In *A History of the Ecumenical Movement*, edited by Ruth Rouse and Stephen C. Neill. 221-62. Philadelphia: Westminster Press, 1967.

Zorbaugh, Charles. "The Plan of Union in Ohio." *Church History* 6, no. 2 (June 1937): 145-64.

INDEX